www.wadsworth.com

www.wadsworth.com is the World Wide Web site for Wadsworth and is your direct source to dozens of online resources.

At *www.wadsworth.com* you can find out about supplements, demonstration software, and student resources. You can also send email to many of our authors and preview new publications and exciting new technologies.

www.wadsworth.com
Changing the way the world learns®

Group Leadership Skills

INTERPERSONAL PROCESS IN GROUP COUNSELING AND THERAPY

MEI-WHEI CHEN
Northeastern Illinois University

CHRISTOPHER J. RYBAK
Bradley University

THOMSON

BROOKS/COLE

*Australia • Canada • Mexico • Singapore • Spain
United Kingdom • United States*

THOMSON

BROOKS/COLE

Executive Editor: *Lisa Gebo*
Aquisitions Editors: *Julie Martinez,*
  Marquita Flenning
Assistant Editor: *Shelley Gesicki*
Editorial Assistant: *Amy Lam*
Technology Project Manager: *Barry Connolly*
Marketing Manager: *Caroline Concilla*
Marketing Assistant: *Mary Ho*
Advertising Project Manager: *Tami Strang*
Signing Representative: *Marc Hatfield*

Project Manager, Editorial Production:
  Katy German
Print/Media Buyer: *Doreen Suruki*
Permissions Editor: *Kiely Sexton*
Production Service: *Mary E. Deeg, Buuji, Inc.*
Copy Editor: *Linda J. Ireland, Buuji, Inc.*
Cover Designer: *Ross Carron*
Cover Image: *Getty Images*
Printer: *Webcom*

Printed in Canada
1 2 3 4 5 6 7 07 06 05 04 03

For more information about our products,
contact us at:
Thomson Learning Academic Resource Center
1-800-423-0563

For permission to use material from this text,
contact us by:
Phone: 1-800-730-2214   Fax: 1-800-730-2215
Web: http://www.thomsonrights.com

Library of Congress Control Number:
2003104295

ISBN 0-534-25267-2

Brooks/Cole—Thomson Learning
10 Davis Drive
Belmont, CA 94002
USA

Asia
Thomson Learning
5 Shenton Way #01-01
UIC Building
Singapore 068808

Australia/New Zealand
Thomson Learning
102 Dodds Street
Southbank, Victoria 3006
Australia

Canada
Nelson
1120 Birchmount Road
Toronto, Ontario M1K 5G4
Canada

Europe/Middle East/Africa
Thomson Learning
High Holborn House
50/51 Bedford Row
London WC1R 4LR
United Kingdom

Latin America
Thomson Learning
Seneca, 53
Colonia Polanco
11560 Mexico D.F.
Mexico

Spain/Portugal
Paraninfo
Calle/Magallanes, 25
28015 Madrid, Spain

Contents

Chapter 2

On Becoming a Group Leader   30

Part Two

BASIC LEADERSHIP SKILLS: GETTING THE GROUP TO WORK 51

Chapter 3

Creating a Group from Scratch: Program Planning and Member Preparation 52

Chapter 4

Leading the First Session   82

Chapter 5

Facilitating, Opening, and Closing: The Foundation of Group Skills   104

Chapter 6
Working on Agendas: Basic Framework of a Group Session   136

Chapter 7
Working with Tension and Conflict   *185*

Part Three

ADVANCED LEADERSHIP SKILLS: GETTING THE GROUP TO UNCHARTED WATERS   219

Chapter 8

Taking Risks in Communication: Toward Greater Group Closeness   220

Chapter 9
The Hot-Seat Method: A Knee-Jerk Experience   257

Chapter 10

Method of Stirring the Pot: Stimulating Group Affect   292

Chapter 11
Skills of Termination: Completing the Cycle   318

Preface

The power of group ever fascinates its witnesses, even those who are most seasoned. No matter how many times you sit in a group, you cannot help but be captured by the ever surprising richness, complexity, and forces at work within each group. Each group and each session seem to have a life or personality of their own that commands unfaltering respect and appreciation. To work within a group, one must enter it with utter openness, curiosity, willingness, humility, and a sense of awe—with an attitude that can be called a Zen mind, or a beginner's mind. It is with this attitude that this book has been written.

This book is designed to serve as a practical tool to help readers get right into the heart and the action of group practice, without being put off by overly long discussions in the realm of abstraction. Group counseling and therapy has emerged as the treatment of choice by many practitioners across the spectrum of mental health services. Under the managed-care demands of cost containment, various forms of short-term therapy have proliferated. So has the field of group practice. In this economically minded time, most groups are held as some form of brief therapy. Short-term group counseling and therapy can be a cost-sensitive treatment option. If well run, the group can be a powerful way of bringing about therapeutic change for clients. To be effective, however, short-term groups must operate within a framework or an approach that provides focused interventions for setting client change into motion. This need for focused interventions leads us right to the heart of any type of group work—*the interpersonal process.*

Many therapists are inexperienced in group work and feel like they lack the skills and competency to run a group. Even when they have been trained, many of them still feel ill-equipped for direct group practice. This anxiety and sense of inadequacy stem from the fact that, from the one or two group training courses that they had taken, their preparation has often been too general to provide an in-depth understanding of how to tackle the intricacies inherent in each group session, much less how to help clients change. The mere thought of leading a group is often overwhelming to new group facilitators. Their sense of inadequacy and anxiety is realistic, given the complex, fast-moving, and elusive dynamics that are part of the nature of any group. Understandably, many beginning therapists thirst for practical instruction that will provide specific guidelines to help them meet the challenge of clinical practice in group settings.

This book has been written to meet this thirst for practical instruction. It provides an organizing framework to help therapists bring about client change in the real life of group settings within a relatively brief period of time. This framework is a well-developed one that utilizes interpersonal process, a central force in groups, as an active change agent. The methods are practical and will help to orient group therapists regarding where they are going in various group sessions and why they proceed in certain sessions with certain intervention strategies. These methods can be easily applied to group therapists' treatment plans and intervention strategies. The text contains a wealth of examples, case histories, techniques, and creative ways of conducting groups—information that can be a rare find.

This book is an outgrowth of our years of teaching group leaders in training how to use focused interventions in group work. The approach outlined in this book is active, experiential, and integrative. When we teach, we encourage trainees to get in the "driver's seat" and experience what running actual group therapy sessions feels like. Over an extended period of time (approximately three months), trainees personally experience the whole spectrum of group dynamics in each developmental stage. Each skill in this book is based on actual observations of what group therapists need in live sessions in order to tackle the ever fluid, ever intricate group dynamics. Many skills were created on the spot in live group sessions, as well as during postsession supervision meetings.

If you are a clinical trainee preparing yourself for future practice in group counseling and therapy, this book is for you because it has been written for the beginning group therapist who wants to feel competent and to effectively perform her tasks. If you are a professional therapist who has not gone through group training but are facing the prospect of doing group work, you will find this text a valuable road map toward competency. If you are a paraprofessional who has been given the responsibility of running groups without prior training, your runaway sense of self-doubt and uncertainty is understandable—and this text might be just the guide you need to jump-start your skills.

The methods suggested in this text also may be used as material for in-service training and staff development for anyone running groups: agencies and organizations, including mental health centers; hospital-based programs; adolescent treatment facilities; group homes; rehabitualization or addiction treatment agencies; private practice; and so on. The skills and intervention techniques suggested within this framework are meant to be guideposts. Users will find it easy to wed this framework to their own values, personalities, and settings, and refine it when necessary to shape it to their own leadership styles.

This book is intended as a guide to group practice; it is not meant to provide definitive answers to each and every situation that a group leader will encounter. It does, however, provide guidelines that will be helpful to any group counselors and therapists who wish to improve their competency in group leadership.

Additional materials are available on this book's Web site at http://helpingprofs.wadsworth.com.

ACKNOWLEDGMENTS

From Mei

I feel privileged to be given the honor of creating this book. The precise honor, however, must go to the numerous trainees and group participants who have given me insights into group dynamics and the change process that no amount of study in literature and theories can achieve. It is through seeing groups at work that the ideas and concepts in this text literally come alive. Without the trainees and group participants, my understanding and appreciation of group work would have remained abstract. It is with the deepest gratefulness that I thank them, especially those who have given me permission to use their personal cases and journals, though anonymously, to demonstrate points in the text. I thank them for their generosity and the trust they have placed in me.

My profound thanks go to my coauthor, Chris, for being so kind as to join me in this creative process. It was through his excellent research skills and significant contributions to various parts of the text that the completion of this writing project became possible. I am forever indebted to him for his openness to and his unfaltering support of my vision.

Special thanks to Dr. Rex Stockton of Indiana University, Bloomington, for ushering me into the fascinating world of group work; to Dr. Allen Bell for discovering the gift of the healer within me that I did not know existed; and to Dr. Tom Froehle for cultivating the confidence of the thinker in me. My gratitude also goes to the larger community of group counseling and therapy through which the heritage of group work is maintained and precious knowledge is handed on to the generations of therapists to come.

As for my parents, family, and friends, words are inadequate to express my gratitude for their ongoing love, support, and acceptance of me. This book is my way of saying thank-you to them all, and a way of sharing their love for me with the greater world.

From Chris

I offer my most profound thanks to Mei for inviting me to cowrite this book. I cannot express enough appreciation for her exceptional clarity of vision and for her conceptualizing skills in putting such complex material together. I also want to express my love and deep appreciation for my wife, Nancy, who provided support for this writing project and put up with stacks of reference material in our dining room. My dogs were there, too, heartbeats at my feet as I wrote.

I also thank my mentor and group class instructor, Dr. Beverly Brown, for first unraveling some of the mysteries of group work for me, and then offering instruction and support as I navigated my way through the beginning stages of group leadership.

Joint Acknowledgments

Mei and Chris both acknowledge the helpful comments of the following reviewers:

Paula Helen Stanley, Radford University
Dick Rundall, Rock Valley College
Michelle Muratori, University of Iowa
Diane McDermott, University of Kansas
Shirley Haulotte, University of Texas, Austin
Jane Fried, Central Connecticut State University
Claire Calohan, Florida State University
David Westhuis, University of Southern Indiana
James Borling, Radford University

In addition, both authors thank Linda J. Ireland, whose work as the copy editor was beyond excellent. Finally, the authors thank Caroline Concilla, Lisa Gebo, Julie Martinez, and other staff members at Wadsworth for their passionate enthusiasm for this book. Their professionalism made the undertaking of this project clear and focused; their supportive approach added an extra measure of positive energy to the entire authoring process.

INTRODUCTION AND OVERVIEW

THEORIES AND ASSUMPTIONS

Interpersonal dynamics affect the essence of who we are. It is through interpersonal dynamics that we come to discover and understand the various facets of ourselves and to unlock psychological blocks that may hinder our growth. In most therapeutic modalities, including family therapy as well as individual counseling, this interpersonal aspect is at the center of the work. In group counseling and therapy, the centrality of interpersonal dynamics is even more pronounced.

At the heart of group work lies the interpersonal process, which is ever complex, fertile, and elusive. The interpersonal dynamics of groups challenge even the most seasoned therapist, yet it is the interpersonal process itself that fascinates us and rewards us with a deep sense of satisfaction. As a powerful force, the interpersonal process provides, as Bohart (1999) puts it, an organizing mechanism that gives meaning to our human experiences. Members' experiences of a group revolve around this mechanism to a large degree. The outcome of group therapy is literally at the mercy of the group's interpersonal process, especially now when the length of group life is being cut shorter and shorter.

In our era, as cost containment has become a major thrust in health care, the length of group therapy has been cut ever shorter. Group counseling and therapy have been increasingly called upon to be conducted in the fashion of brief therapy. In the wake of this trend, group leaders are searching for therapeutic methods with an immense focusing capacity. This focusing capacity can be found only when group therapists zero in on the eye of the storm—the interpersonal process—of the group.

Focused intervention enables a group therapist to meet her clients on issues that matter. Research with clients who have experienced the most successful therapy outcomes showed that those clients who have a knack for focusing are more likely to find satisfaction in therapy

(Gendlin, 1996). To be effective, group counseling and therapy must do just that—get clients to focus on the heart of their issues. The heart of clients' issues is primarily interpersonal. The ears of the therapist, therefore, must be able to sharply tune in to the interpersonal process, inside and outside the group, that is so central to the meaning-making and healing in clients' lives. This book is written to provide a well-developed framework in which therapists use a focused interpersonal approach to facilitate client change.

In this first chapter, it is fitting to lay out a brief description of the theories, assumptions, and therapeutic factors that are the foundation upon which the intervention techniques of this focused interpersonal approach are built. This chapter covers:

- Theoretical foundation
- Underlying assumptions
- Tasks of the process-focused group
- Therapeutic factors in group

THEORETICAL FOUNDATION

To sharply tune in to group members' interpersonal processes so as to formulate focused interventions, therapists must have a basic grip of the theoretical underpinning of this approach. This section introduces a collection of theories that are central to the focused interpersonal approach to group counseling and therapy. These theories include Sullivan's interpersonal theory, object relations theory, family systems theory, experiential therapy, and brief therapy. Among them, the domains of the first three theories are quite distinctive, yet these theories share an emphasis on interpersonal relation and process, which we consider, is the heart of group work. Experiential therapy offers us a powerful way of helping clients change within the immediacy of interpersonal relationships. And brief therapy gives us a mind-set and attitude for working with clients that is effective within the increased demands of time-limited practice.

This section aims to briefly introduce the guiding concepts of these theories; it is not meant for elaborated discussion in the realm of abstraction. These theories are immensely complex; any attempt to specify them will be far beyond the scope of this section. We can only highlight ideas that are relevant to the theme of our framework. When suitable, we will also identify how each of these theories informs and shapes the way we conduct groups as illustrated throughout the book.

Sullivan's Interpersonal Theory

Harry Stack Sullivan (1953, 1964) was the first to present a systemic theory of interpersonal relationships in psychotherapy. His work has since spawned a lineage of interpersonal theory and study (Kiesler, 1982a; Strupp & Binder, 1984; Teyber, 1997). Rather than focus on intrapsychic processes, which was the emphasis that prevailed in psychotherapy theory in his time, Sullivan accentuated interpersonal processes. The major interpersonal concepts developed by Sullivan include:

1. Human personality is "the relatively enduring pattern of recurrent interpersonal situations which characterize a human life" (1953, pp. 110–111).
2. It is the need for control, affiliations, and inclusion—the three interpersonal forces—rather than the sexual drive that influences human motivations, actions, and experience.
3. Anxiety in interpersonal relations is the central force that organizes human behavior. Most people have a pervasive anxiety that is rooted in the fear of being discounted, rejected, or disapproved of by others, especially significant others.
4. Clients' problems are primarily embedded in disturbed interpersonal relations and often manifest themselves in handicapped interpersonal communication.
5. Recurrent interpersonal patterns and communication styles create a reciprocal loop in the client's environment. They create a type of feedback loop wherein the effect and the cause become circular, that is, the client not only affects but also is affected by his or her interpersonal environment.

Sullivan's theory has contributed enormously to many therapists' understanding of their clients' underlying struggles. Through Sullivan's theory, we come to see that our clients live in a reciprocal dynamic of interpersonal relationships; their maladaptive behaviors are often the mechanisms they use to cope with their anxiety of interpersonal rejection and disapproval.

Rejection and disapproval by others often breeds derogation by the self. On the other hand, others' esteem often leads to self-esteem. The dread of painful rejection is often the force that drives people to develop all sorts of strategies, early in life, to cope with anxiety in interpersonal arenas. These coping strategies then become well established or patterned later in life. According to Sullivan, these patterned coping strategies are interpersonal defenses originally devised with the best intentions to ward off anxiety and protect the self. Unfortunately, many interpersonal defenses become overarching, sprawling into other areas of the adult's life, thus generating the difficulties that bring the clients to therapy.

Kiesler (1982a) gives an example of the reciprocal loop created by people with obsessive features that may well demonstrate this point: To avoid rejection and disapproval, people with obsessive features often take pains to present themselves as rational, logical, and self-controlled persons. They communicate in a careful and cautious style, often shown in their use of words, and they frequently qualify their opinions and feelings, use a monotonous voice tone, and demonstrate rigid nonverbal behaviors. This communication style in turn makes the people interacting with them feel bored and impatient. The listeners feel they are being evaluated by the obsessive person, and thus become cautious themselves in their own expressions. Often the ultimate consequence is that other people begin to withdraw from the obsessive person, making the obsessive person feel increasingly isolated, lonely, depressed, and more anxious. Most importantly, the obsessive person often has no clue as to how he has constructed this miserable fate for himself. We can guess that to avoid their feared misery, people with obsessive features would interact with others in an ever self-controlled manner. And thus, the cycle goes on.

Though not phenomenally new for today's clinicians, Sullivan's emphasis on interpersonal processes represented a radical, or at least astonishing, shift from Freud's biologically based drive theory. Since intrapsychic process, presented by Freud's libido theory, was the prevailing paradigm in Sullivan's time regarding human behaviors, experiences, motivation and accompanying clinical applications, his interpersonally oriented theory and practice represented a rather prophetic vision.

What is most valuable about Sullivan's theory is that there is much more respect for human dignity as compared to Freud's libido theory. Sullivan's understanding of the interpersonal nature of human anxiety continues to influence contemporary theorists, including the influential figure in group psychotherapy, Irvin D. Yalom. Many of Yalom's (1995) concepts and his practice of group psychotherapy can be traced back in some form to Sullivan's original concepts.

Sullivan's interpersonal theory greatly informs the way we conceptualize group members' problems and the way we formulate leadership interventions. Starting from Chapter 6 in this text, we provide ways to explore the interpersonal coping patterns and strategies that group members manifest in their lives. The coping patterns of group members will inevitably show up in their interactions with one another and/or with the group leader in the immediacy of the group context. Interpersonal patterns are often reenacted in close relationships within the group. Chapters 9 and 10 discuss how to address the difficult dynamics, making them the grist for the mill of group work. When clients reenact interpersonal patterns in the immediacy of the group, they are presented with an opportunity to gain intense personal awareness and insight if their group experiences are appropriately processed.

Object Relations Theory

Object relations theory helps therapists appreciate the many layers of clients' issues. A client's issue is like an onion; at the center of the inner-most layer is often the most sensitive and reactive substance. The name of the theory, "object relations," may seem dubious, but readers need not be turned off by it. Simply put, "object" means people, including our inter-nalized perception of people. "Relations" means relationships. Stripped to its core, object relations theory is about interpersonal relationships. Although object relations theory is historically written in obscure and impersonal terms that are difficult for readers to digest, it is a powerful theory. If understood well, it can help therapists comprehend the core of their clients' predicaments.

According to object relations theory, all of us internalize the ways in which our early significant others interacted with us. If our early signifi-cant others are empathic and responsive to our needs, a sense of self-worth and trust will become the basic constituents of our psychic devel-opment. On the contrary, when our significant others and early home atmosphere deprive us of empathy and nurturance, this environmental deficiency can lead to an enfeebled, fragmented, or disordered self. Object relations theory believes that as humans, we are originally motivat-ed, not to seek anxiety reduction (as Sullivan's theory postulated), but to seek relatedness, attachment, and connection to others. However, if a severe injury is inflicted to the self and its relations early in life, then our search for that connectedness will deteriorate into self-preoccupation or defensive rage. The injurious and conflicted ways of interaction are then deeply internalized within us. These internalized perceptions and impres-sions are rather enduring. They serve as a kind of cognitive schema or a subjective landscape that shapes our relationships with others later in life (Greenberg & Mitchell, 1983; Kohut, 1977; Sandler, 1981; Strupp & Binder, 1984; Teyber, 1997).

Using object relations theory, therapists can help their clients see how their recurrent problematic relational patterns are a by-product of their unresolved issues rooted in their history, and how these patterns are reen-acted in their present relationships with others, with significant others, and, even more likely, with their therapists. Therapists can help clients see that their relationship patterns are often interpersonal strategies used early in life to manage their *pain* stemming from relational problems (as compared to the management of anxiety in Sullivan's theory). These interpersonal strategies are used recurrently, though not so consciously, throughout various stages of life.

An example may help to clarify this concept. People who come from a background where emotional nurturance was lacking—such as families in which parents were emotionally unavailable, unresponsive, neglectful, depressed, disengaged, or abusive—often felt pained and hurt greatly in their tender age. The more their self and relations were injured, the more they felt disquieted and insecure, and the more urgently they sought affirmation and reassurance. In their search for affirmation, they compulsively induced others to play desirable roles. When affirmation and reassurance were still unavailable, however, the unbearable pain may have driven them to apply coping strategies that were symptomatic or were in disguised forms. These coping strategies differ with each individual. Examples of coping strategies include, but are not limited to, intellectualization, rationalization, deflecting, caretaking, people-pleasing, dramatization, externalization, and impersonalization.

These coping patterns, though useful initially, become problematic later in life. To live productively, people need to develop new sets of responses to effectively manage the unique demands and tasks of each life transition. Entrenched in their coping patterns, however, these people continue to use their old strategies and find themselves stuck in a rut. The first step toward client change is bringing these unrecognized relational patterns to clients' awareness level through therapeutic help.

In our focused interpersonal approach to group work, we often use insights drawn from object relations theory to help us fathom many of our group members' problems. Through such understanding and insight, we gain great respect and compassion for the dilemma with which our clients live day to day. At the same time, our intervention strategies strive to target the heart of group members' issues, that is, their recurrent relational patterns. In Chapter 6, we offer intervention strategies that describe how to peel, with sensitivity and empathy, the outer layers of problems that group members initially present. In Chapters 7, 8, 9, and 10, we suggest methods for slowly moving the group to touch on one another's more reactive inner layers. These methods are used only when the timing is right and the trust level is adequate. This peeling of the "onion", if successful, often leads members to great insight, self-compassion, and motivation to change.

Family Systems Theory

Working with groups requires therapists to be acquainted with the forces of family systems, especially those of the family of origin, which have a tremendous impact on the individual clients who make up the group. Family systems theory provides therapists with a rich understanding of how the roles and rules in family systems shape who our clients are and how early learning has perpetuated their problems in their adult lives. Theorists in family systems, such as Gregory Bateson, Murray Bowen, Salvador Minuchin, Virginia Satir, and Carl Whitaker, have observed various *communication and interaction patterns* in families and the *fixed roles* people play in their family of origin (Becvar & Becvar, 2000; Goldenberg & Goldenberg, 1996; Nichols & Schwartz, 1998). They observe that in a family, all members tend to abide by family rules and act consistently within certain roles. All members seem to develop intricate overt and covert communication patterns in order for the family to maintain its homeostasis. The relationship between members of this organized system is multilayered and is based largely on shared history and shared internalized perceptions. The patterns of communication and perception, often unstated, are not always within the conscious awareness of the family members themselves.

These roles and communication patterns, once learned, can be hard to change. Actually it is not that the roles themselves are hard to change, but that they are reciprocal and complementary. Roles reinforce each other, making all behaviors recursive. A brother's domineering role reinforces his sister's submissive role, and the sister's submissive role reinforces her brother's domineering role. A mother's critical role reinforces her son's passive role, and vice versa. So it is not that the roles themselves are hard to change, but that the reciprocal, recursive patterns make it hard to change the system.

Family systems theory consistently indicates that our family of origin remains within us. Wherever we go, we carry with us unresolved emotional reactivity to our parents. Our vulnerability is disguised by our reactivity, and we repeat the same old pattern in new relationships. The ways we relate to the people in our family of origin have an elemental quality that touches the deepest layers of our inner life, stirring our most primitive emotional responses. Any close interaction later in life, including in group therapy, has the potential to recreate within us some of the same feelings of rivalry, the same separation struggle we engaged in with a parent, the same dependency needs, the same vulnerability, the same conflict, the same deficit, or the same ambivalence. Unresolved issues with our original families are the most important unfinished business of our lives.

The family systems perspective urges therapists to look for recurring patterns of interaction in clients' lives. It helps therapists take a broader view, shifting attention from outward content of conversation toward family process and group process. Family systems theory also influences therapists to focus their therapeutic effort on helping clients become aware of the roles they play in the here-and-now of the group. We believe that to change behavior, we must bring its hidden messages out into the open. It is through examining the relationship and communication patterns in the here-and-now of the group interaction that the hidden can become visible. Chapter 9 illustrates how to work with roles that are reenacted within the group.

Most importantly, family systems theory helps therapists focus on clients' self-differentiation. The best way to increase one's degree of self-differentiation is to establish person-to-person relationships with as many members within one's family as possible. This means getting in touch and speaking with them directly, instead of talking about other people or impersonal topics. In the group setting, a client's self-differentiation is increased through remaining intimately engaged with others in the group, even when the client feels anxious. It is also increased through practicing in group the skills of setting boundaries, constructive confrontation, self-validation, assertiveness, and honest feedback. Chapter 5 offers a list of skills that members can practice for increased self-differentiation. The various skills and interventions shown in this text are, at their core, a reflection of our intent toward helping our clients increase their self-differentiation.

Experiential Therapy

Another theoretical model that greatly contributes to our focused interpersonal approach to group work is experiential therapy. An emphasis on the felt experience is the philosophical foundation of experiential therapy. The experiential therapy approach is based on the idea that clients need direct experiences rather than cognitive explanations (Greenberg, Rice & Elliott, 1993). It is through direct experience that people derive a myriad of ideas and feelings that are not typically accessible through simply talking about a situation.

The prominent existential psychotherapist Rollo May once said, "The patient needs an experience, not an explanation" (May, 1983, p. 158). This statement highlights a critical element at the heart of experiential therapy. To truly know something, one must get that knowing through a personal, immediate experience rather than through mere listening, talking, or cognitive processing (Bohart, 1993). When it comes to truly recognizing and relearning one's interpersonal patterns, one must first feel those interpersonal patterns contextually. One must feel them by personally experiencing them right here, right now, in live relationships. Although the root of the problem may be in the past, its solution lies in the here-and-now, in the present.

The perspective of experiential therapy encourages group therapists to facilitate emotionally meaningful experiences in the here-and-now relationships of the group session. When group members are emotionally engaged with people in front of them, a surge of energy and life is brought to the session, inspiring them to reach deep within their psyches and interpersonal relationships to uncover long-hidden issues, wounds, and emotions.

Many self-in-relationship skills are difficult to develop in isolation without others to observe, to practice with, and to be in relationships with. The experiential approach, with its built-in emphasis on the here-and-now engagement, is probably the only valid way to delearn and relearn about interpersonal matters. Shaped by experiential therapy, our focused interpersonal approach emphasizes that the group provides opportunities for group members to develop a host of self-in-relationship skills, including the ability to become self-aware, to listen, to be empathic, to assert, to confront constructively, to resolve conflicts, and to allow others to be close to them. These self-in-relationship skills are pragmatic and empowering to clients.

Brief Therapy

At its core, brief therapy is about an attitude and mind-set of doing therapy, not just about the number of therapy sessions. In brief therapy, focused intervention is the key to success. Treatment attention must be selectively focused on a central, dynamic theme. This requires that therapists look into the past or the future for an indication of where the clients have gotten themselves "stuck" and what they need to get "unstuck." This focused endeavor does not allow time for free association but, rather, requires therapists to take an active approach. Another fundamental tenet in brief therapy is that clients have crucial responsibility for their own well-being. Therapists, for that reason, strenuously avoid taking responsibility away from their clients (Hoyt, 1995; Kreilkamp, 1989; Levenson, 1995).

Many therapists who are used to doing open-ended therapy worry that the time limit inherent in brief therapy might short-change their clients in terms of treatment quality. This worry is not warranted. In actuality, the limit of time can increase and intensify the work done in each session and help clients become more active in consolidating their learning throughout the course of therapy. A time-limited framework often spawns a sense of urgency, stimulating group members to get quickly and deeply involved. This can serve as an antidote to the passive attitudes to change and the inertia that many clients seem to harbor. Of course, in brief therapy, our mind-set must shift from idealism toward pragmatism and optimism. Capped with a time limit, therapists cannot pursue the ideal of a perfectionistic "cure" (Budman, 1994; Budman & Gurman, 1988; Hoyt, 1995), but must focus on small changes. These small changes are more important than a "cure," since it is small changes that have the power to snowball into significant changes later.

Influenced by brief therapy, our approach to group work stresses a "radically" focused direction. We strive to help each group member enter the group with an explicit goal to achieve at the end of the group. If overly general goals are presented by group members, leaders help them refine and reframe them into goals that are behaviorally concrete, specific, and achievable. The skills of goal setting suggested for the screening interview and the first session (see Chapters 3 and 4) clearly demonstrate this focusing element.

Within the brief therapy mode, we also stress the importance of quickly developing trust, empathy, and group bonding. In so doing, a safe group environment is built, within which deeper self-exploration into the inner layers of client issues becomes possible. Chapter 6 clearly demonstrates this emphasis. As trust and empathy deepen within the group, group cohesiveness (which is the equivalent of the therapeutic alliance in individual counseling) is fortified. Group cohesiveness itself can be a powerful experience for many people who have difficulty in interpersonal relationships. Chapter 8 demonstrates how to facilitate greater risk-taking behaviors within a group as group cohesiveness thickens.

The concept of brief therapy reinforces our belief that the group energy should start with members' current life situations and then move to observations of their recurrent relationship patterns. Members' recurrent relationship patterns can be observed within the here-and-now of the group. Less focus is thus spent in review of members' there-and-then history. This here-and-now orientation is consistent with the experiential therapy approach, which is the foundation for the framework of our group therapy approach. Chapters 9 and 10 specifically illustrate the pragmatic aspect of the here-and-now orientation.

Brief therapy also teaches us that most changes occur between sessions (Budman, 1994). This fact leads us to encourage our group members to write reflective journals between sessions. We believe that intense interpersonal learning does not happen only within group sessions, but also after the sessions have ended. Indeed, insight and self-awareness often start just a few days after a particular session, when members have had some time to let the messages of the feedback sink in. Throughout this text, we include members' and leaders' reflective journal entries when suitable. These journals demonstrate that change does happen between sessions. In Chapter 12, we provide more detailed rationales for encouraging members to write in journals between sessions.

Under the influence of brief therapy, our approach marks a leadership style that is active, clear, direct, and directive. To beginning group therapists, this direct and directive style might feel unfamiliar and challenging, as many of them are used to the Rogerian style of individual counseling. This highly direct style, however, is intentional. Direct leadership is required to hold members accountable for their own individual goals and tasks as well as for the group goal as a whole. The direct leadership style might trigger transference and authority issues for some members who have issues with power and authority. Leaders need to be cognizant of this possibility. When these issues do arise, leaders can tackle them with sensitivity and nondefensiveness and treat them as grist for the mill for group work, as illustrated in Chapter 7. When these issues are explored and examined using whole-group processing, they become raw materials for interpersonal learning for all involved.

UNDERLYING ASSUMPTIONS

With the previously discussed theories as the backdrop, our focused interpersonal approach to group work assumes six underlying premises about the nature and sources of people's problems, about the built-in forces within the group, and about how problems can be resolved through the relationships within the group. This section discusses these assumptions in detail.

Assumption 1: Most Problems Are Interpersonal in Nature

All humans have an inner drive to search, in one way or another, for happiness. At times that search leads them to seek answers in counseling or therapy. People use counseling or therapy for many different reasons: They may feel isolated or depressed. They may be having problems with their spouse, coworkers, or other significant others. They may have a taxing issue that holds them back from building the lives they desire. According to Yalom (1995), most clients in therapy share two common difficulties. First, they have difficulties in establishing and maintaining meaningful interpersonal relationships. Second, they have difficulties maintaining a sense of personal worth. Both of these difficulties are interpersonal in nature. Yalom points out that most clients seeking counseling carry with them certain self-defeating interpersonal patterns that hinder them from maintaining fulfilling lives. These maladaptive interpersonal patterns inadvertently create a vicious cycle, perpetuating their problems. For change to occur, clients' ineffective and rigid interpersonal patterns must be replaced with more effective and adaptive ones in their interactions with others.

Obviously, solving the problems that plague them is the main reason people come to counseling; our job as therapists, without a doubt, is to help our clients reach that goal. As logical and simple as this sounds, the road toward that end is not a direct line. The first thing we must realize is that we cannot directly solve our clients' problems. But what we can do is much more influential: We can rebuild a sense of self-worth in our clients and foster their interpersonal growth so that a new way of healthy relating can replace the old, handicapped one. We can restore our clients' ability to embrace their self and to connect to people around them. When it comes to rebuilding a person's sense of self-worth and fostering interpersonal growth, group therapy is the perfect instrument.

Assumption 2: Family Experiences Are the Primary Source of Interpersonal Process

If it is accepted that most clients' problems are interpersonal in nature, the next question to ask is: Where do these interpersonal problems come from? Sullivan's interpersonal theory, object relations theory, and family systems theory all inform us that people's interpersonal difficulties are often rooted in past interpersonal causes and conditions, especially those in their family of origin, and have manifested themselves in the clients' current relationships. Family systems theory also informs us that many maladaptive interpersonal styles stem from the hurtful interaction patterns in the family of origin (Goldenberg & Goldenberg, 1996; Nichols & Schwartz, 1998).

For example, on the enmeshment-disengagement dimension, clients from enmeshed families often find themselves still avoiding conflict and still suppressing their undesirable emotions, especially anger. They often struggle with a sense of guilt whenever attempting to assert themselves or to set boundaries. On the other hand, clients from disengaged families tend to lack a sense of introspection and are other-focused. They have difficulty containing their emotions, especially anxiety. Since a disengaged family often uses cutoff as a way to shut out rising anxiety in the relationships, clients with this background generally lack experience in regulating, containing, or working through their anxiety. They become hyperreactive in the face of life stressors. They have a poor tolerance of anxiety, and avoidance is the way they go about dealing with it. Cutting people off deprives these clients of the most-needed opportunities in learning to contain their emotions while working out their issues. People with cutoff in the background generally have difficulty having actual intimacy with the self. Lack of intimacy with the self, of course, corresponds to fear of intimacy with others.

Regardless of their family experiences, most clients suffer one of two difficulties in interpersonal process: difficulty in individuation or difficulty in interpersonal intimacy. With difficulty in individuation, these clients struggle a great deal in the areas of initiative and personal power. With difficulty in interpersonal intimacy, these clients struggle greatly in the areas of closeness, trust, and commitment. Either way, they both suffer from a low degree of self-differentiation. These clients have difficulty with remaining engaged in interpersonal interaction when they feel anxious or with remaining emotionally available and responsive when the climate of relationships heats up. They use patterned coping mechanisms (such as withdrawal, suppressing emotions, shutting down, cutting-off, and so on) to ward off anxiety and undesirable emotions once they are aroused in interpersonal interactions. These coping mechanisms, though occasionally serving them well, impede the development of the client's integrated self. The goal in group therapy is to help clients increase their self-differentiation through practicing genuine emotional engagement with others even when they are anxious.

Assumption 3: Group Reactivates People's Interpersonal Processes

Group interaction provides a rich soil where members' interpersonal problems have a chance to show. And when they do, the same soil then becomes the perfect setting for the active quest for interpersonal growth. People's direct experiences within the immediacy of the group are usually a vivid example of how their experiences are organized in their personal lives. All of us carry our families within us; in the group, we carry our patterned emotional reactivity spawned from our family of origin. Sooner or later these interpersonal patterns, mostly concocted to protect our vulnerabilities, will manifest themselves within the group for all to see.

Almost religiously, clients reenact their deeply embedded and often subconscious patterns and roles within the group. Almost without fail, the interactions within the group engage their deepest sense of vulnerability. With this "repetition compulsion," the group embodies an emotionally charged setting. Through group interactions, many dormant feelings—such as shame, guilt, pain of abandonment, rejection, and mistrust—feverishly sprout in the present encounter. Although threatening, the experience of these charged interpersonal encounters is a blessing in disguise because the emergence of these feelings urges us to work through issues within the group. Subsequently, a sense of secure attachment, mastery, acceptance, and adaptive engagement with others—qualities that make up healthy living—can be experienced (Riester, 1994).

As a given, the evoked experiences within the group become grist for the mill. They give members an opportunity to examine how and why their interpersonal experiences get organized in a certain way. Note that experiencing and studying our interpersonal patterns is very different from talking about them or getting caught up in them. In the group, instead of just talking about their experiences, clients actually witness how they coconstruct their interpersonal reality with those with whom they come in close contact in the group.

Given this premise, the group leader must give priority to interventions that help members become aware of their relational patterns. The leader must identify clients' characteristic interpersonal styles by naming how a member's patterns affect those of other members as well as the leader's own inner engagement. This requires the leader to first disengage himself from the pull of the members' styles and thereby break the reciprocal loop of responses. All these attributes work together to provide the members with a "corrective" experience (Kiesler, 1982b).

Assumption 4: Here-and-Now Relationships within Group Can Bring about Change and Healing

If it is the relationships back in time that hurt and trouble people, then it is the here-and-now relationships that heal. Within the group, the therapist and the group exert a pull on each other. Awareness of this pull can help both clients and the therapist see their own relational patterns. In addition, in interacting with the group, a genuine emotional contact among members is developed. This genuine emotional contact carries an intimacy and an authenticity that are new to the members, allowing them to transcend their old maladaptive relational patterns. Thus, the here-and-now relationships within group have enormous creative potential for helping clients to reconstruct the past and re-vision the future. For this to happen, the group therapist must strive to engage, to intervene, to participate, and to transform maladaptive patterns of relationships (Blaney, 1986; Ferencik, 1991; Greenberg & Mitchell, 1983; Perls, 1969; Yalom, 1995).

The power of the here-and-now rests in its magnetism of providing a "personal and direct" impression of interpersonal events. Healing and learning occur only when clients' attention is drawn to their direct experiencing of *present* emotions and interpersonal relations. Sometimes it is important to trace the causal origins of people's emotions and interpersonal relations back in time, yet no course of therapy can afford the luxury of endlessly dwelling on the past. When the focus is on events back in time, the vitality of therapy is lost. Therefore, the therapeutic focus must be on the client's whole constellation of emotions and interpersonal relationships at each moment of the interpersonal process.

The healing power of here-and-now relationships within a group is fourfold. First, this here-and-now focus facilitates a client's sense of responsibility. When a group seeks to deepen members' experiences of the present and to focus on what is happening in the here-and-now of the relationships, it works to facilitate resolutions of whatever emerges in the interpersonal process. This approach requires that members make moment-to-moment decisions regarding their own behaviors and feelings in relating to others. They have to learn to take responsibility for "authoring" the events within the group (Slife, 1991; Wedding, 1974).

Second, this here-and-now focus propels people to get to know their interpersonal patterns contextually. When they truly know their embedded patterns, they will have the freedom to make conscious choices—to reorganize their experiences in new ways. They can change *what* they experience with others as well as *how* they organize such experiences. A therapeutic leap then happens. They transcend old habits and past conditioning of interpersonal processes stemming from early experiences that have long trapped and controlled them.

Third, personal metamorphosis and interpersonal growth are possible only when accurate interpersonal feedback is made available. Most people, however, do not receive honest and open feedback in everyday social interactions, except in certain intimate relationships. The here-and-now relationships within the group provide clients with truthful and caring feedback, which is much needed if they are to become aware of their interpersonal patterns. For people who have been unable to express anger, the dynamics within the group provide a safe opportunity for taking risks and learning that such expression, when done appropriately, is not dangerous or destructive (Yalom, 1995). On the other hand, for overly aggressive people, the group dynamics provide an opportunity to learn some of the interpersonal consequences of their behaviors, so that they can come to appreciate the impact of their behaviors on others.

Fourth, the here-and-now relationships within group allow people to learn interpersonal skills not available elsewhere. Within groups, interpersonal dynamics unfold with rapid speed and rich complexity. The precious materials embedded within these interpersonal dynamics make group counseling distinctively different from individual counseling. If facilitated by a skilled leader, people in the group can learn to be attuned to the nonverbal and the metacommunication in each interpersonal exchange, give empathic responses that are the foundation of interpersonal intimacy, and resolve relational conflict rather than sweep it under the carpet. Conflicts, when unresolved, tend to distort our interpersonal perceptions and hinder our psychospiritual growth. Within the here-and-now relationships of the group, people learn to communicate disagreement in constructive ways that enable others to listen. They learn to be receptive, rather than defensive, to the individual differences that may initially rub them in uncomfortable ways.

Assumption 5: To Last, Interpersonal Learning Must Be Experiential

Skillfully led, group can be a top-notch laboratory for interpersonal learning. But for interpersonal learning to last, the group must be experiential. As the saying goes, "I hear and I forget, I see and I remember, I do and I understand." Most learning of significance in life comes from direct experience, not from speculation and intellectualization. A person's interpersonal pattern becomes evident when she and others have a chance to directly observe her interactions with others over time. This direct witness of how a person's interpersonal patterns play out with a group of others is only possible when the group is experiential.

In their direct interactions with others in the group, members' "entire composite behavior is open to scrutiny within the group" (Leszcz, 1992, p. 50). When members' interpersonal dynamics are in action, the group gets what it came together for—to catch the patterns in the act. The group gets a chance to study and examine the interpersonal interactions between and amongst its members in the immediately occurring moment. Clients thus learn about their interpersonal processes and themselves through a direct experience of interaction with others. This direct experiencing of one's own self is a luxury that only the group can afford.

Counseling and therapy are often referred to as a "talking cure" (Bankart, 1997). However, talking and storytelling do not warrant change. As Slife (1991) states, "Therapeutic discussions of past emotions and interpersonal relations cannot be experiential. Past experiences can perhaps be reexperienced through the presentness of our memories, but few psychotherapists would call simple remembering 'experiential'" (p. 151). This infertility is due to the fact that talking without experiencing does not always touch life's central and deep issues. To truly understand our ongoing patterns in life, we must first have a felt experience of ourselves through personally experiencing how our styles play out with others in relationships and interpersonal dynamics. This emphasis on the felt experience is what makes a group experiential.

To facilitate direct experiences, group counseling and therapy must facilitate emotionally meaningful experiences in the session for all members. Emotional experiences bring aliveness to the group sessions, inspiring members to reach deep within their intrapsychic and interpersonal processes so as to unveil unresolved issues, injuries, and emotions. For a group session to be emotionally meaningful, it must "engage members in experiential, as opposed to purely conceptual, processing" (Greenberg, Rice, & Elliott, 1993, p. 112).

Experiential learning is a robust method for people to develop emotional intelligence. Emotional intelligence involves a host of self-in-relationship skills, including the ability to become self-aware, to practice self-control, to listen, to be empathic, to resolve conflicts, and to cooperate with others (Goleman, 1995). These kinds of skills are difficult to develop in isolation without others to observe, practice with, and be in relationships with. The experiential approach is probably the only valid way to learn about interpersonal intricacies.

To achieve the type of experiential learning described here, a group has to meet the following criteria:

1. It must be able to identify the specific relational patterns that have created or maintained problems for a member.
2. It must be able to observe how these problematic patterns are played out in group interactions.
3. It must be able to track the elusive interpersonal process within the group and to counter it with a different and more nourishing and vitalizing relationship than the one the member has been experiencing.

These criteria are expounded in the next section.

Assumption 6: Sustaining Change Can Happen within a Short Time

In working with clients, it is important to assume that every group member, irrespective of her present issues, will respond to short-term group treatment unless she proves herself too fractious for it. This assumption is based on the belief that long-lasting change can happen within a short time (Hoyt, 1995; Levenson, 1995; Malan, 1976). This belief has its root in brief therapy. As mentioned, it is not a rigid timetable that defines brief therapy, but the focused innovative interventions. It is not the exact time limit that is important, but the awareness that *there is* a time limit. If leaders address members with a genuine belief and mind-set that change can happen within a short period of time instead of years, that time is not endless, and that *now* is the best time to move forward, they will give the members an opportunity to benefit from short-term treatment until they reach the limit of their potential. If this brief approach fails with certain members, they can be referred to long-term therapy.

To instill the awareness that time is limited and today is the time for change, we start each session by asking group members to respond to this question: "What interpersonal skills are you willing to practice in today's session to bring about your change?" Coded within this question are the key elements of brief therapy: *what skills, you, willing, change, today.* Our emphasis on here-and-now experience, rather than there-and-then explanation, also conveys a sense that therapy is present-centered and that change can be derived from the experiences of the pivotal moment in the present.

TASKS OF THE PROCESS-FOCUSED GROUP

With the assumptions discussed in the previous section in mind, we now turn to the essence of this text: conducting a group by using a focused interpersonal approach to facilitate client change. A group with interpersonal process as the focus is often called a process-focused group. A process-focused group is the answer to many problems encountered in today's groups, but not all groups can be called process groups. The distinction is based on whether a group can implement its central tasks on the process level.

Most Problems in Groups Are Process-Related

Therapists who have had experiences in leading groups often testify that most problems in today's groups arise from elusive interpersonal processes that are difficult to get a handle on, rather than from members' tough presenting issues. Following is a list, by S. D. Rose (1989), of the most typical problems in any group session. All of these problems are clearly process-related; they seem, on the surface, miles away from problems presented by members when they enter the group.

- The group has low cohesion caused by some member missing many sessions or by group collusion among certain members, making others feel unsafe.
- Many members step back and allow one or two members to do all the emotional work for the group.
- One or more members dominate the session, constantly speaking up to contribute and not giving quieter members their chance to contribute.
- Some members check out emotionally from the session.
- Some members don't self-disclose, making it difficult for other members to help them, support them, give them feedback, or challenge them.
- Some members are angry all the time and tend to criticize others in a negative way.
- Some members simply refuse to participate in the process at all and state this refusal early on.
- Some members form subgroups, such as pairs, triads, or cliques, excluding others in communication.
- Put-downs, defensiveness, or passive-aggressiveness become the norm among members, without their recognizing it.
- The group becomes dependent on the leader; interaction occurs primarily between the leader and members.

If we truly believe that group reactivates people's interpersonal processes originating from their families of origin, it should come as no surprise when these interpersonal problems happen within group. It would invalidate our assumption and theories if these problems didn't occur. Since all these problems are interpersonal in nature, it takes a process-focused group to address the heart of these problems.

Tasks of a Process-Focused Group

Not all groups work to address the interpersonal processes among their members. Some groups may actually work to skirt around these very processes. The following tasks must be performed for a group to be called process-focused: (1) establishing a safe environment; (2) responding to members' emotions and inner needs; and (3) translating problems into patterns, recognizing the coping mechanisms that have maintained those patterns.

A process-focused group places high priority on establishing a safe environment where group cohesiveness can be developed and where members will gradually drop their guard as they become willing to peel off defenses and delve into the deeper layers of their issues. This safe environment proves to be especially important during periods of members' intense resistance, ambivalence, and negative interpersonal enactment.

A process-focused group responds to members' emotions and inner needs. Intimate sharing takes place in sessions as group members make contact with one another in personal ways. Many therapists assume that most members know how to be personal, but in reality many group members wobble on this skill. Perhaps it is because the socialization process in our society steers people away from dealing with and expressing strong feelings. A process-focused group leader facilitates group members to share in personal ways an array of feelings that they have not been able to express effectively on their own.

A process-focused group translates members' problems into underlying interpersonal patterns and central conflicts, as well as recognizes the maladaptive coping mechanisms that have served to maintain the patterns and problems. By recognizing these patterns and coping mechanisms, clients can make conscious choices to change them.

Process-Focused Leadership: A Tall Order

A process-focused group requires a leader who has knowledge and skills at the process level, rather than merely at the content level. This process focus is both exciting and challenging to new group therapists. Particularly challenging to new leaders is the third task—translating members' problems into underlying interpersonal process and central conflicts. This task, which requires an ability to conceptualize client problems at a metacommunication level, is a task of tall order. As Zaslav (1988) points out, process focus is a most unnatural and difficult task for many therapists and clients. Yalom (1995) repeatedly observed the difficulty many therapists have in directing the group to the process level of the here-and-now. Although group therapists often display an all-out desire to do experientially focused or process-focused group work, Slife (1991) questions how many groups actually do so.

Maintaining groups effectively at the process level is the greatest challenge to many group therapists. The practice of here-and-now in therapy "continually challenges our most cherished assumptions about abnormality and interventions" (Slife, 1991, p. 164). In addition, engaging in the here-and-now involves a much higher level of exposure and intimacy than is customary in social interaction (Leszcz, 1992). Even more tricky is that a therapist needs a very high level of mastery to identify and address the often subtle, yet complex, processes underlying here-and-now dynamics. The required mastery level is much higher than that required to lead structure-oriented groups, such as psychoeducational groups and task groups. Therefore, it is not surprising that few groups among those observed by Yalom (1995) actually had the process focus that leaders wish to achieve.

THERAPEUTIC FACTORS IN GROUP

To end this introductory chapter, we will address the factors that make group therapy therapeutic. All research points to therapeutic relationships as the central force across all types of therapy. In the group, here-and-now relationships have the power to restore people's self-worth and to rebuild their personal and interpersonal competency. But what mechanisms within those relationships account for the therapeutic effect? In answering this question, we draw our insights primarily from the research studies by Yalom (1995) and Waldo (1985).

Instillation of Hope

Jerome D. Frank (in McGinnis, 1990) states, "Psychotherapists should above all be 'purveyors of hope'" (p. 37). One of the reasons group can be therapeutic is that group is a setting where all members become the "purveyors of hope." Group is where people learn to grow their roots of hope. Hope may be rooted in the actual experience of learning to manage situations in which one was previously stuck, learning to disclose "secrets" in a safe way within an appropriate context, and learning to share a fuller range of emotional responses in constructive ways that provide release and open doors to more fulfilling relationship with others. Hope may also be rooted in vicarious learning as members see improvement in others.

To instill hope, therapists must praise every step of progress, however small, that members make toward their goal. Furthermore, therapists need to believe in the process of the group. This belief in the group process will enable them to radiate a sense of optimism from within.

Universality

Most people who come to counseling and therapy experience a sense of inadequacy, doubts about their worth, a sense of interpersonal disconnection, and concern about the quality of their relationships. But many people think they are the only ones who experience this distress. They feel alone in their personal predicaments. Within the intimacy generated in a small group, however, people soon find out they are not so utterly alone in their human struggles. Everyone has experienced a range of highs and lows, joy and grief, pain and sorrow, good and bad, confusion and clarity—just like their fellow travelers in the group. Members of the group feel a sense of connectedness to their fellow humans in their basic struggle. This is another factor that makes group so therapeutic. Researchers have found that in groups composed of clients suffering from a variety of emotional and physical afflictions, the members' sense of equanimity toward their life circumstances increases substantially as their sense of connection to others increases over the course of the group meetings (Salzberg & Kabat-Zinn, 2000).

Recognizing the power of universality, group therapists work hard to cultivate a safe environment in the group where clients' struggles are validated as human conditions rather than as individual members' pathology. Not only do the therapists make a point of acknowledging clients' difficulties, but the whole group is prompted to give the sufferers due validation of their feelings.

Altruism

Life can feel rather constricted and narrow if one focuses only on oneself. Focus on the self breeds a sense of disconnection that can thwart and sap emotional energy. When one is able to extend one's gifts to others, however, one can feel as though prison gates have been suddenly flung open. We all need to feel that we have something to offer, that what we can give is important to others. When we have something important to give, we feel better, life feels broader, and living itself has greater meaning. This is the power of altruism.

To experience the power of altruism, however, there must be a real relationship with others that develops, so that living becomes more conscious. In the field of interpersonal relationships, the spirit of giving finds its home. One of the reasons group therapy works is that, in the group, people can, paradoxically, gain self-esteem and increase their sense of meaning through learning to attend to the needs and concerns of others. This enables members to transcend the narrow universe in which they previously dwelled.

To help members experience the power of altruism, the group leader must direct the group interaction in a way that makes it possible for members to give support, validation, insight, and meaningful feedback to one another. To achieve this, the leader must avoid being the expert who offers answers, but rather give group members maximum opportunity to offer responses or feedback to one another. Leaders should constantly remind themselves that group members need to feel that they are needed and that they have something to offer, and also remind themselves that through giving the members will boost their self-esteem and achieve some sense of self-actualization. This is why we emphasize the group-centered or member-centered leadership style, instead of a leader-centered leadership style. The group- or member-centered leadership style allows members to experience the maximum power of altruism.

Corrective Recapitulation of the Primary Family Group

Group provides a great possibility for people to reexperience past emotional states, but in more positive ways. Patterns of relationship established early in life tend to be fairly well "locked in." Long-standing patterns of relationship are formed, primarily, as a response of love or fear. Through fear of being unloved, overwhelmed, or annihilated, a pattern of aggression or holding back is established. On the contrary, through experiences of love, caring, and acceptance, the door to real relationship with others is opened. Group counseling and therapy can help people because joining a group is like being reborn with an opportunity to work through previously unfinished business and unlock unproductive patterns.

Group has such reworking power because the group itself is a social microcosm of real life. People in group tend to reenact fixed roles carried with them from the past. In the group, we are likely to interact with others as we have interacted with our parents and siblings. In so doing, early family conflicts are relived in the safe environment of a well-led group. Conflicts are relived correctly, not just relived. Therefore, groups can provide a safe environment for reexperiencing past emotional states in more positive ways.

To cash in on the recapitulative capacity of the group, leaders need to steer group members to mindfully challenge the fixed roles they carry with them from the past—roles that are played out within the groups. Leaders needs to relentlessly encourage members to check their perceptions of how others view them, to examine their assumptions about others, and to test new behaviors within the groups so that unfinished business from their families of origin can be worked through in the present groups.

Development of Socializing Skills

Social skill learning is possible when there is accurate interpersonal feedback. Most people do not get honest and open feedback from social interaction in general. Many clients have ineffective interpersonal styles that not only hinder them from having fulfilling interpersonal relationships but also perpetuate their problems. In some cases, clients have overlearned particular rules in order to meet the expectations of others. The result is that they are unduly anxious and rigid in their interpersonal encounters for fear of offending others. Such ineffective interpersonal styles need to be delearned and relearned. Developing effective interpersonal skills is an important therapeutic factor for clients. Group, as opposed to social interaction, is a powerful place for learning socializing skills because it provides sufficient feedback within the safe confines of the group environment.

When there is a sufficient level of acceptance and trust within a group, members can release the shackles of fear, risk dropping the masks of their personas, and relate to one another on a more authentic level. When appropriately designed, groups that offer the right mix of supportive closeness and honest feedback can help members find more effective ways of relating to others, which may include:

- Being attuned to the nonverbal and the metacommunication
- Being verbally responsive to other members, rather than keeping reactions to themselves
- Learning to resolve conflict rather than sweep it under the rug
- Communicating disagreement in constructive ways that make it easy for others to listen
- Communicating agreement before disagreement
- Expressing accurate empathy to others, as empathy skills are the foundation of interpersonal intimacy

Imitative Behavior

We all covertly learn from one another through observation. For example, when we visit a foreign country where we do not understand the language and cannot read the signs, we watch others and follow their lead, doing what they do when they do it. In interpersonal learning, imitation also plays an important role. One example has to do with interpersonal risk-taking. If some group members have not previously learned an appropriate level of risk-taking in building intimacy within relationships, then being able to observe others in the group doing it can be an eye-opener. Seeing others open up and share vulnerable parts of themselves within the group, and seeing that they are *not* ridiculed for this behavior (rather, their social status in the group *actually increases* as a result), can empower the observing members to take similar risks.

Group members have a great opportunity to grow through observing of how the group leaders and other group members interact within the group. This opportunity for intimate observation and imitation makes group a great therapeutic vehicle. To maximize the imitation factor, leaders should frequently acknowledge positive behaviors immediately when they appear to reinforce the member engaging in the desired behavior and to point out to other members the benefits of interacting in these whole-some ways.

Interpersonal Learning

When a group is both supportive and challenging, it engages its members in reality testing. Members become aware of the impact of their behaviors on both fellow group members and themselves. This motivates people to try out new and different behaviors, which constitutes interpersonal learning. The member testing out new behaviors within the group learns how others in the group respond and react to the new behaviors. Initially, a member may have little confidence in trying a new behavior (say, interpersonal risk-taking); but as she begins to use it in an appropriate way, she is likely to experience positive reactions from fellow group members. Further interpersonal learning occurs as she sees the impact of her new behavior and learns whether or not it will increase the level of interpersonal intimacy with others inside and outside the group.

Long-lasting interpersonal learning happens when there are events in the group that not only touch the heart of a client's problem but also give the client an "aha" experience before she tries out new behaviors. This critical experience is called the "corrective emotional experience" (Yalom, 1995). The term *corrective emotional experience* was first coined by Franz Alexander (in Alexander & French, 1946), the Hungarian psychotherapist, and has since been used by the therapeutic profession as a generic description of an avenue of client change (Gaylin, 2000).

A corrective emotional experience occurs in two steps. First, a group member becomes fully aware of an intense emotional reaction to the present circumstance within the group that is based almost entirely on past experiences and is thus inappropriate in some way to the current relationships in the group. Secondly, this awareness allows the member to realize that he may need to react to the precipitating event in alternative ways that are more in keeping with his personal growth and development. Research in the field of neurobiology has explained why a corrective emotional experience can initiate behavioral change. Researchers have discovered that the brain is able to grow new neural connections in the body through an "emotional meaningful experience." New cells are created in the presence of emotional and interpersonal interactions; therefore, new patterns of behavior can bring about profound change within the whole individual on the gross behavioral level (Kranzberg, 2000).

Group Cohesiveness

In individual counseling and therapy, the quality of the client-counselor relationship defines the effectiveness of therapy. In group counseling, on the other hand, group cohesion is what ultimately determines the outcome of the therapy (Yalom, 1995). Group cohesion is the overall quality of member-to-member relationships—the level of attraction and strength of relationship that the members have for one another. Higher levels of group cohesiveness contribute to the group's capacity to weather the storms of interpersonal conflicts and bring about the birthing process of personal growth. Cohesion makes interpersonal closeness within the group possible, while the level of closeness among members contributes to the experience of group cohesiveness.

Sometimes the things people dread most about group are the very things that bring cohesion to the group. For example, confronting one's own issues to a roomful of people is an often-dreaded aspect of group. It can raise a client's anxiety and increase the client's sense of vulnerability. Yet, when people start to confront their own issues, they give others an opportunity to get to know them and, thus, care about them. As a result, people can care for one another and relate to one another at a deeper-than-surface level. This kind of mutual self-disclosure tends to increase attraction within the group. This attraction helps members to remain in the group when they feel especially anxious or challenged.

Group cohesion is built, not given. To make a group cohesive, leaders need to highlight similarities among members' struggles, help the group be comfortable with members' expressions of conflict, and protect group norms. Most importantly, the leader needs to build a group spirit through which each member is accepted as who he is, regardless of his past life experiences, transgressions, or social failings (e.g., deviant lifestyle, past suicidal ideation, history of criminal offenses, or other socially undesirable behaviors). When a group is cohesive, members feel the freedom to express conflict and work through it. This kind of accepting, liberating, member-to-member relationship is therapeutic to all members.

Catharsis

To be able to talk over one's own emotions and thoughts without censure is cathartic. Group provides a safe place for members to express their emotions and thoughts that need an accepting audience. Of course, catharsis itself is not sufficient for personal change, but when the group is able to give a balanced mixture of challenge and support, members find it difficult to avoid encountering their ghosts, demons, and maladaptive behaviors within the field of interpersonal relationships. At the same time, with the existing support of the group, members find it easier to overcome the old walls of defensiveness as insight and understanding gained within the group shatter these old blocks to pieces. As barriers to personal development are dissolved, prodigious levels of energy can be released in new and more positive ways.

Imparting Information

If knowledge is power, then information certainly helps feed that power. Many group members enter groups with a relatively low sense of personal power for many reasons, including disadvantaged socioeconomic status, gender, culture, or ethnic background. Many times such members have not had access to important information that can help them more successfully navigate in the larger cultural environment. The group is a powerful therapeutic medium for such people because the leader as well as the members offer one another helpful knowledge concerning the problems members are facing. This factor is especially potent for diverse groups, especially immigrant populations whose members do not have the host cultural background from which to work through the difficulties they face (Han & Vasquez, 2000).

Existential Factors

Because of the profound interpersonal intimacy that can take root within the here-and-now of groups, many existential issues we carry with us can be raised as a part of the group experience. These existential aspects include our endless thirst to understand life, our attachment to our loved ones despite their and our eventual deaths, and our own personal limitations in articulating the profoundness of the moments when these issues touch us. We are short of words when touched by the fact that regardless of our social status, level of wealth, or access to fantastic feats of modern medicine, each of us must die and have our bodies disintegrate and return to the earth. Each of us will face this ultimate death, even though we usually try to push this fact out of our everyday thoughts. Many times, in the shared silence of interpersonal connection within the group, profound moments confront us with issues of mortality and spirituality. The silence confronts us more than does any verbal analysis of the myriad feelings and thoughts at such times. Such sharing on a nonverbal level helps people reach a fuller emotional understanding of themselves and of life.

Participating in a group affords members the possibility of sharing with one another on an intimate level that goes beyond the usual polite surface-level conversations that make up many interactions. When members are able to share the essential joy, loss, crisis, and death issues of life that they face, they come to understand one another and feel understood by one another on a deeper level. A greater level of meaning is thus brought to their lives.

SELF-REFLECTION

Heightening one's self-awareness is a key aspect of development as a group leader. You are encouraged to reflect on the following questions.

1. Which of the theories addressed in this chapter do you think most fits with your view of group work? What is it about that theory that fits best for you?
2. Of the theories identified in this chapter, which least matches your present view of group work? What areas of this theory are in conflict with your outlook?
3. Is this your first introduction to any of the theories described in this chapter? If so, which ones? Are there aspects of these theories that you need to read more about?
4. In your present view of group work, which of the therapeutic factors are the most potent in terms of promoting positive change and healthy personal growth?
5. What is your view of the role that experience should play in groups? Of what importance are the experiential aspects of a group as compared to other dimensions?
6. What is your sense of a process-focused group at this point? Have you had any prior experiences with a group that was process-focused?
7. Of the assumptions about group work discussed in this chapter, which would you personally rank as the most important for a successful group?

8. Are there any additional assumptions about groups that you think should be added to the list?
9. Recall the details of a time when you strongly experienced the therapeutic impact of a group. What therapeutic factors were involved? In what type of group did you have this experience?
10. Consider the small groups in which you have participated. In what direct and indirect ways did these groups build cohesion among the members? Did they have specific ways of encouraging the expression of interpersonal caring? Did they have ways of diminishing any anxieties and fears that participants had about the group?

ON BECOMING A GROUP LEADER

Leading a group well is an art. When done well, leading a group may appear to be seamless and effortless, but it is not. To get the group to the heart of the matter, a therapist needs to cultivate both her own person and the skills of leadership. Before we present the technical skills of leadership later in the text, we want to address the personal part of leadership, that is, the process of becoming a leader.

Leadership is not about having the answers. Leading is not as much about telling as it is about hearing at the metacommunication level. It is not as much about knowing as it is about facilitating interaction. It is not as much about being in charge as it is about enabling the group to reach its goals. These concepts should be remembered when leading a group. Leading a group is not about curing members' symptoms; no one can cure anyone's symptoms. In fact, therapists can only help clients change the underlying processes that perpetuate their symptoms and problems. Essentially, to lead a group is to inspire, mentor, challenge, and advance the members—to help them become free of whatever is blocking their personal growth.

This chapter addresses the personal part of leadership, especially the self of the group therapist—the most essential instrument of change. Topics covered in this chapter are:

- Leadership development
- Coleadership practice
- Self as the instrument
- Personal growth and group experiences

LEADERSHIP DEVELOPMENT

An effective group leader is much more than a mere technician attempting to apply a long list of rules or techniques to members' interactions. A technical and linear approach is inadequate for the complexity inherent in groups. On the other hand, an effective group leader is also more than just an intuitive, motivational helper. True knowledge and skills in group process cannot be replaced by charisma and sheer inspiration. A solid development and training in leadership is necessary. This section addresses the qualities a therapist needs to develop if she aspires to become an effective group leader.

Development of Group Leadership

Poorly trained leaders can yield harmful outcomes. Many people, however, assume that they can easily develop leadership skills by themselves. Certainly, given enough trial and error, people do pick up leadership skills on their own, but often at the clients' expense. Leadership is an art; there is no simple set of rules to follow. However, effective leadership can be taught. It does not belong to a select, talented few. All of us can be seen as leaders-in-training.

Some counselors and therapists make better group leaders than others because of their innate gifts. Every counselor and therapist, however, can become a skillful group leader. Even the most painfully shy person can be trained to lead a group at the required competence level. Actually, it is those who believe they have their leadership skills already figured out who tend to block their own development as group leaders, and who turn out to be less competent in facilitating breakthrough and growth for their group members than other leaders who are more aware of their own need for continued learning.

The development of leadership consists of two parts. The first part is practicing the related complex skills and techniques. Practicing is an indispensable first step toward mastering any complex art. Many piano players practice playing piano while they are riding on trains or in other situations without a piano. One of the greatest baseball players, Ted Williams, stated that he regularly swung the bat at imaginary pitches. The skillfulness and confidence of most disciplines increase as one practices. This also applies to skills and techniques of group leadership.

The second part of leadership development is mastering the interpersonal processes and dynamics that are always in flux at any given moment in the group. Mastering interpersonal dynamics requires a great degree of self-awareness and self-knowledge on the part of the therapist. The vision of yourself as an inspiring leader will not come overnight. The sense of yourself as a leader grows and becomes rooted through training and experience. But you can accelerate your growth by developing self-awareness of your interpersonal styles and of any existing unresolved issues of your own. Later sections of this chapter discuss this part of personal development in more depth.

Qualities of an Effective Group Leader

Developing oneself as an effective group leader involves a consistent focus back and forth between two domains: first, conceptual and technical knowledge about groups, and second, adequate self-knowledge and depth of character. The following text discusses various qualities that cover both of these domains. The last three qualities involving honesty, compassion, and relaxed attitude were identified by Kottler (2001).

Conceptual and Technical Knowledge   Conceptual and technical knowledge includes theoretical rationale of working with groups, knowledge of group dynamics, supervised group leadership experiences, knowledge of working with members of diverse backgrounds, and knowledge of what members need to know to be successful in the group as well as in their interpersonal relationships outside the group. In addition, group leaders need to have basic knowledge about what issues the members must deal with in the group. These issues include the ways in which members deal with feedback and interpersonal conflict, test out new ways of relating interpersonally, communicate effectively, and deal with diversity within the group. The conceptual and technical knowledge offers the group leader a "clear-headedness"—a sense of clarity that is needed to take the group in the desired direction (Corey & Corey, 2002; Kottler, 2001; Yalom, 1995).

Self-Knowledge and Balance   While technical knowledge plays an important role in being an effective group leader, group leaders themselves are the most important aspect of leadership. They must know themselves. Self-knowledge of group leaders involves knowing how and when to balance a moderate level of the executive or control function with a moderate amount of emotional stimulation. Lieberman, Yalom, and Miles (1973) point out that leaders who contribute to successful group outcomes are those who (1) facilitate the needed amount of emotional stimulation, such as challenging and confronting one another, and promoting self-disclosure and self-awareness within the group; (2) offer caring, such as support, encouragement, and protection to members; (3) use meaning-attribution skills, such as clarifying unspoken meanings and interpreting members' underlying patterns; and (4) provide an executive function, such as setting rules, boundaries, limits, and norms. These mechanisms can be boiled down to two key factors: support and challenge.

Many beginning leaders have no difficulty in leading group members to give support to one another but find it difficult to facilitate challenge and corrective feedback within the group. These leaders have difficulty achieving balance of leadership. Technical knowledge can assist group leaders to become wiser in their choices of intervention strategies, but it is self-knowledge that assists leaders in deciding when to direct and when to let be, when to stimulate and when to step back, and how to create the kind of meaning from group events that heals and instills hope (Corey & Corey, 2002; Lieberman, Yalom, & Miles, 1973).

Cultural Sensitivity   Most group counseling concepts are developed for majority populations. When working with diverse populations, group leaders need to have the sensitivity to make certain modifications to concepts and intervention techniques. Indeed, group therapists are expected to first understand their own attitudes and beliefs in relation to diversity, and then to gain knowledge and develop skills appropriate to working with groups of diverse individuals (Association for Specialists in Group Work [ASGW], 1997). Diversity factors may include gender, sexual orientation, ethnicity, race, religion, disability, socioeconomic status, geographic origin, and age, as well as other aspects. Effective group leaders usually place a high value on diversity and learn about the ethnocultural contexts that contribute to both the group leader's and group members' experiences. They tend to facilitate the group process in a way that helps group members internalize a more self-affirming identity than that with which they entered group.

Most importantly, group leaders work from a relational-cultural framework (Han & Vasquez, 2000). A relational-cultural framework promotes healing through validation, empowerment, and self-empathy of group members. Validation helps to counteract the disbelief and disregard that minority members frequently experience. Empowerment helps minority members overcome the internalized messages of inability and inferiority. Self-empathy allows minority members to reflect on the difficulties they have faced in dealing with oppression.

Trustworthiness and Honesty   Trustworthiness and honesty are important, since members typically enter a new group with some doubt and question how much they can trust the leaders and the other members. Building trust usually begins with the group leader. A leader who offers honest feedback and perspectives is likely to have a positive influence on group members.

Self-Compassion and Compassion for Others   Without self-acceptance, group leaders will find it difficult to accept others. They will be burdened by expectations of "letter-perfect" group work, which is an impossibility. Only when group leaders grow to accept themselves will they radiate a sense of confidence and enthusiasm from within that will help group members overcome their own excessive self-doubts and take the interpersonal risks necessary to change their behaviors in a positive way. Self-compassion is the foundation for compassion and empathy for others. Caring and compassion from the group leader can offer members the kind of boost they need to enact desired changes in their lives.

Relaxed Attitude (Humor and Flexibility)   Related to self-acceptance is a relaxed attitude about life. When relaxed, the group leader is more likely to exhibit her sense of humor and flexibility. A sense of humor is essential to helping all of us reframe dead-end perspectives and lighten the burden of life in general. Flexibility is an important characteristic in a group leader because the interactions and progress of any given group are not entirely predictable, so a group leader needs to be relaxed enough to flow with the energy of the group. A relaxed leader is more likely to be creative and spontaneous, allowing the group to evolve at its own pace according to its particular mix of members and the leader.

Intuition and Discovery-Oriented Practice

Our discussion of the qualities required of a group leader clearly indicates that leadership is not about applying a set of mechanistic methods to any group situation. While certain guidelines can be offered to promote skill development in the leader, leadership cannot be learned by using a strictly mechanical approach. Instead, group leadership is built on a flexible, creative, and intuitive discovery-oriented practice (Bohart, 1999). A group is not a predict-and-control assembly-line machine that sends emotional clones out into the world. Leadership is neither simple nor mechanical. The complex nature of groups requires leaders to possess a large repertoire of skills, available for use in the multidimensional wonders of each unfolding moment.

Even when practicing within the framework presented in this text, personal intuition and creativity must play an active role in every given moment of the group interaction that flowers directly from the rich soil of the here-and-now. A leader's intuition becomes more reliable when it is refined and tempered with a large repertoire of knowledge and skills related to group dynamics. More details on how to cultivate clinical intuition and emotional intelligence are covered in Chapter 14.

Five Phases of Process-Focused Leadership Training

Leading a group is a demanding task. Leading a process-focused group is even more so. The skills required to lead a process group are, to say the least, complex and challenging. Given this fact, you must be patient and gentle with yourself in the journey of developing yourself as a leader of process-focused groups. Mastering this art is a wonderful journey. A number of developmental stages await you. You must give yourself permission to build your leadership muscles ever so gradually at your own pace.

Generally, a new leader goes through five developmental stages, as analyzed by Zaslav (1988), in learning the skills of leading a process group. Within each phase, valuable lessons can be extracted.

Group Shock Stage   Leading a process group for the first time will probably feel very threatening to you. Unlike individual therapy, group therapy provides an overwhelming wealth of stimuli at a fast pace within each single session. Even more nerve-wracking is the fact that the process-focused group is nonstructured in principle. Within the nonstructured interpersonal environment, the comfort of predictability and a sense of control are inevitably low. Facing this, a neophyte leader may feel overwhelmed, threatened, or confused. This reaction is evident in one trainee's reflection on her first experience with leading a process group: "It's sort of like juggling nine balls at once. You have to keep your eye on every ball, and keep your attention on the one that's about to fall." This initial experience can be called *group shock*.

Often the neophyte leader attempts to cope with this reeling challenge by using his favorite individual counseling techniques, such as probing, reflection of feelings, or paraphrasing with members in the group. This coping strategy results in a series of leader-member dyads that preclude the powerful interaction a group so uniquely affords. Some neophyte leaders may be tempted to cope with their group shock by focusing on the content level and attempting to solve problems presented or to give advice to the members. These coping strategies, however, create a group atmosphere that is detached, lethargic, or intellectualized.

Reappraisal Stage   After the attempted coping strategies prove ineffective, a neophyte leader will probably retreat into a more inhibited mode of functioning. As she reappraises the process of the group and struggles to adjust to the overwhelming complexity of the group, she will continue to struggle with her feelings of confusion or frustration. Her inexperience with group dynamics may fill her with self-doubt, or she may simply complain about members' various behaviors. But eventually her effort to adjust will produce results, and she will become more ready to recognize the differences between individual and group counseling. This recognition will help her give up her infertile reliance on individual counseling skills. As she gives up on individual therapy skills, she will be more able to use basic group facilitating skills with greater awareness of their effects on the group.

One Step Behind   At this stage of leadership development, you begin to identify and follow the various threads of the interactive and often elusive process. You may begin to understand the process level of interpersonal interactions when they happen right in front of your eyes. You are able to connect what happens within the group with the theory and intervention methods you have learned from textbooks, lectures, and didactic materials. Although you might be able to recognize the process level of group interaction, you still cannot quite use the here-and-now or process-focused interventions on the spot when crucial events happen; it is only after the fact that your mind starts to recognize which ones you could have used to bring forth some new understandings for the members. You feel as though you are always one step behind, as if you are always one step too slow.

Using the Here-and-Now   At this stage of leadership development, you are able to actively formulate interventions that focus on the here-and-now and the process level. You go beyond what is said on the content level. You start to take risks in experimenting with your own unique personal style and with those skills and techniques that bring higher intensity and greater illumination to the group. Sometimes you make mistakes; sometimes your process-focused intervention is not effective because you do not present it precisely enough for the group to understand your intention. Other times your process interventions are effective and you recognize the powerful effects they have on the group. You start to carefully observe the effect of each process intervention, and you start to develop a manner of working in the here-and-now that is comfortable and theoretically consistent. At this point, you begin to internalize a sense of competence.

Polishing Skills   In this phase, you continue to experiment with and polish various here-and-now activation and process-focused intervention techniques. You also learn to become more transparent, risk sharing more here-and-now disclosures, and learn creative ways of dealing with difficult members. This stage of polishing skills is a lifelong journey for all of us.

Total Concentration: The State of Flow

Leading on the process level demands a total concentration of one's energy that is similar to the experience of being in a state of flow. One of the authors experienced this power of concentration firsthand. During Chris's training days as an intern, he led an experientially focused group that met each week for 90 minutes. One day Chris developed a severe allergic reaction, and his eyes and nose would not stop running. That night he was unsure about whether he would be able to lead the group, since he was feeling so distressed and distracted by the severity of his allergic reaction.

However, the second Chris walked into the group meeting, his nose and eyes completely stopped running, as though someone had turned off a faucet. He proceeded to conduct the entire 90-minute group session without giving another thought to his allergies. Interestingly, the second the last of the group members left the room, Chris's nose and eyes started running again, and the problem continued for several days afterward. The demand of being totally present when leading an experientially oriented group had been so great that it had given Chris some temporary relief from his physiological symptoms and suffering. He entered into the flow of the group dynamics, and his symptoms disappeared; but in absence of that demand, his symptoms quickly returned.

COLEADERSHIP PRACTICE

Coleading a group can be a valuable experience in the evolution of the beginning group therapist. Coleading provides a dual perspective and doubled energy that are not available in solo leadership. Group members benefit from the relationship modeling between the cotherapists. In a situation where one leader has to be absent, the other leader can ensure that group treatment remains uninterrupted. This treatment continuity is important (Hoyt, 1995). Given the economic pressures of managed care today, however, coleadership practice is not a realistic option. We believe that coleadership is best practiced during professional training. For this reason, we devote this section to the issues and practice of coleadership.

Three Models of Coleadership

In general, there are three models of coleadership: the alternate-leading model, the shared-leadership model, and the apprenticeship model (Jacobs, Masson, & Harvill, 2002). When the *alternate-leading model* is used, coleaders take turns planning before a particular session, and there is a rhythm by which the two leaders alternate to facilitate and intervene. In the *shared-leadership model,* the coleaders jointly share every step of the group intervention and management; therefore, the leadership flows back and forth seamlessly between the coleaders. With the *apprenticeship model,* one of the coleaders is clearly the experienced group leader, while the other is a relative novice. The experienced group leader takes the primary initiative and responsibility within the group, at least during the initial phases of the group. At some point that seems appropriate, a shift is made as the apprentice begins to take on a more active role and coleadership becomes more shared.

Advantages and Disadvantages

To a beginning group therapist, coleading provides many advantages. It offers the leaders the luxury of having someone with whom to share group planning, and the leaders obtain feedback from each other, thereby gaining different perspectives and observations. The combined effect of dual leadership is richer and more robust. Group is so inherently complex that it is difficult for a beginner to attend to all its aspects. Having a supportive partner can be invaluable because attention and care to the group are doubled (Jacobs, Masson, & Harvill, 2002; Kottler, 2001). To the group members, coleaders serve as models of communication and cooperation, especially when the group leaders are a male and female pair.

However, coleadership is not without a flip side. The planning process may actually take longer because there are two perspectives on every issue. If the approaches and perspectives of the coleaders are not well coordinated, the result may be confusing and inconsistent for the group members. In addition, group members may ally themselves closely with one leader, in opposition to the other leader, especially when they detect a note of strife between the leaders. On the other hand, two leaders may exert such a level of influence together on a group member that she feels "ganged up on," especially if both leaders unintentionally push too hard to break through her initial resistance without balancing that pressure with adequate acceptance (Jacobs, Masson, & Harvill, 2002; Kottler, 2001; Yalom, 1995).

Four Principles for Coleadership Practice

From our observation of coleadership practice, we conclude that four principles can make a difference in therapists' coleadership experience: mutual support, balancing each other, active communication both pre- and postsession, and in-session communication. Each of these is discussed further in the following text.

Mutual Support   The first thing we recommend that the leaders-in-training do is to adopt the shared-leading model and stay away from the alternate-leading model. Although dividing tasks seems to be easier and more alluring, it does not provide the group with the modeling of mutual support and communication between coleaders. Therefore, both leaders should be active in all parts of the session. Both leaders need to be engaged in every facilitation and intervention step in the group. If one leader initiates an intervention, the other leader should help to carry it through. If one leader's intervention is unclear, the other leader should step in to make clear the intention of the intervention. The two leaders are there to complement each other in every step of the group procedure. This collaboration is learned through practice and developed through negotiation. Negotiating should begin as soon as the coleaders agree to work together on a group.

An example of mutual support will help to illustrate effective coleadership. Maria and Mike were coleading a group. At one point, Maria initiated an intervention by saying to the group, "Ted has told us the problems he is having with his boss. I wonder, can the group share with Ted what emotions you sense in him in his experience?" One member, Jean, responded by mentioning anger and hurt. The other group members were touched by Jean's validation of Ted's feelings, but did not respond immediately, as they were still deep in thought. Eventually another member responded, but with remarks about a totally unrelated subject. Seeing that the group would lose the moment of connection and intensity if no one intervened, the other coleader, Mike, stepped in and redirected the group to Maria's original intervention. Mike said:

> I sense that some people are still deeply touched by Ted's story. So let's
> go back to Maria's question for a moment. Does anyone else want to
> tell what emotions you sense Ted might have in this experience with his
> boss?

With this redirection, the group was able to explore the topic further and reflect Ted's feelings of shame and humiliation that he had been unable to articulate. One member even pointed out that the way Ted reacted to his boss seemed similar to the way he reacted to his alcoholic father. This member's observation brought great insight for Ted. This precious moment of heightened insight and awareness would have been lost if Mike had not stepped in to reinforce Maria's initial intervention. You can see that through watching the teamwork between coleaders, group members can learn how to be sensitive to one another's needs and how to support one another at critical moments.

Another situation calling for mutual support is when a coleader is challenged by a group member. In this situation, the other coleader can serve as a mediator to help direct the communications. In any instance where one of the coleaders is put on the "hot seat," the other coleader should pick up the slack. Having been an observer, this other coleader can help by reframing the issues at hand, thus moving the group along. For example, Enrico and Golda were coleading a personal growth group. A group member, Sawetha, confronted Enrico, saying that, as the leader, he had allowed the group to overlook her when she related her story. This confrontation aimed at one of the leaders caused other members to fret. At this junction, Golda, the other coleader, stepped in to help the confronting member, Sawetha, clarify what she was referring to and, at the same time, to reframe why Enrico decided to focus on the subject at hand rather than on Sawetha's story. As a result of Golda's mediation, the entire group became more clear about both leaders' high level of commitment to the group, as well as about reasons for specific decisions that had been made along the way.

Balancing Each Other   The second principle of coleadership is that each coleader should balance the other during the session. One leader's challenge needs to be balanced by the other leader's support so as to avoid the situation where both leaders push too hard to get through a member's resistance, resulting in a member's feeling "ganged up on." It is almost as if one leader plays a father role and the other a mother role. The reason that coleaders need to balance each other is that there is an inner conflict involved whenever a group member is stuck in a rut. One side of the member wants to get started on the hard work of therapy, but the other side is afraid, and so the member digs in her heels. In this situation, one leader can back the courageous side of the member and press her to take on fear-provoking work, while the other leader supports the member's anxious side and states that the member may not be ready to take on such a task yet. In this way the member is given the chance to see her own dilemma played out between the two sides and so can choose more freely. Often the member chooses to undertake the difficult task.

Active Communication Pre- and Postsession   The third principle is for both leaders to engage in active communication pre- and postsession. Coleaders need time together to talk, to learn one another's views and approach to group leadership, and to build their relationship as coleaders. The pre- and postsession communication can alert the coleaders to critical incidents arising in the group and how best to address them. It is a serious mistake for coleaders to attempt to "wing it" without having a sufficient period of time to work out important issues through pre- and postgroup meetings. Without this important block of time, it is too easy for coleaders to make erroneous assumptions about what the other leader may choose to do, and create unnecessary difficulties within the group. This is not to say that group leaders cannot disagree, but serious disagreements between coleaders usually are better resolved outside the group. Although group members may learn from how the group leaders handle disagreements, usually there are plenty of other conflictual issues within a group from which the group members can learn.

In-Session Communication   The fourth principle of coleadership is for both leaders to be communicative with each other in-session. Kottler (2001) emphasized that coleaders need to communicate frequently both nonverbally and verbally during the group session. Similarly, we encourage coleaders-in-training to clarify things with each other during the session. When issues arise in the group that need clarification, the coleaders should acknowledge this need and communicate openly with each other regarding their reactions and intentions. For example, the coleader Mike, mentioned earlier, was confused in one group session when Maria turned the group's attention to Tracy, a group member who sat next to Mike. Mike thought the group should have stayed a bit longer with Elix, who had presented his agenda. To clarify his confusion, Mike communicated openly with Maria during the session by saying,

> Maria, I sense that there are other dimensions in Elix's agenda to be explored. Are we going to come back to Elix later?

To this, Maria replied,

> Oh, thank you for checking that out, Mike. Yes, we will loop back to Elix later. But I saw Tracy having intense emotions just now and thought that we should help her explore for a moment what's behind those emotions; then we can go back to Elix.

This kind of communication provides the group with a model of how to honestly communicate reactions to each other. In addition, it demystifies any unrealistic status that group members might attribute to leaders. It helps increase leaders' transparency.

Besides verbal communication, coleaders need to exchange eye contact or hand gestures with each other to increase the understanding of each other's intentions. Although nonverbal communication is encouraged, whispering is not. Whispering tends to give an impression of secrecy, hampering the leader's intention of being transparent. To enhance in session communication, coleaders have to avoid sitting next to each other. Sitting across the room from each other in the group can help both verbal and nonverbal communication. It also helps each other round out the observation of the group dynamics. In the earlier example, Mike was unable to see Tracy's eyes tearing up because he was sitting next to Tracy. Fortunately, Tracy's emotion was not missed by Maria, who was sitting across the room from Tracy and Mike.

SELF AS THE INSTRUMENT

It takes a centered and balanced leader to rise to the challenge of serving others without being encumbered by his or her own unmet needs. Duran and Duran (1995) described this in the following manner: "The client usually comes for treatment because s/he is out of balance. In the therapeutic encounter, the client should be able to come to the core of themselves. . . . [T]he therapist should, in the span of the therapeutic encounter, at least be able to be in touch with his/her own center, otherwise the therapist's imbalance will only throw the client even further out of balance" (p. 77).

When centered and balanced, leaders are more likely to respond spontaneously to group dynamics without much censoring or second-guessing of themselves. They can rely on their inner self to respond to members' needs with support, challenge, or a combination of the two. A sufficient level of mental health and emotional development of group leaders, thus, is essential. From what we have observed, the self of the group leader is the most important instrument deciding the outcome of the group. This section explores some ways through which group leaders can cultivate the self to become the most important instrument in group work.

Self-Differentiation

The key to developing the self as an instrument of therapy hinges on our ability to increase our self-differentiation. Self-differentiation is the degree to which one can differentiate feeling from thinking and, at the same time, balance both. A differentiated person is able to think things through while resisting the pull of emotional reactivity but, at the same time, is able to have strong emotions and to spontaneously express them without undue censorship. He is capable of being in intimate connection with others, but remains free in his own stand on issues. Enmeshment and disengagement are actually the two opposites of self-differentiation (Nichols & Schwartz, 1998). Self-differentiation is the index of a person's emotional, mental, and spiritual development. It is the barometer that reads the degree of our integration and individuation as a person.

The best way to increase one's self-differentiation is by learning to face one's own anxiety, and learning to face it without trying to escape. The barometer of our level of self-differentiation is most clearly shown in our way of being in our significant relationships. If we find ourselves withdrawing or shutting down whenever tense issues arise in our relationships, that is a sign we are lacking a central "inner leadership" within ourselves; we are not adequately integrated and individuated in our own core. Practicing open communication without slipping into withdrawal whenever anxiety arises in relationships gradually increases our level of integration and individuation. If we find ourselves unable to do this, then seeking personal therapy might be helpful.

Another way to increase self-differentiation is by learning to differentiate our own "stuff" from that which occurs in a group. We need to sort out our reactions in group—which parts are strictly about us, and which parts are evoked by group members. When experiencing boredom, fear, anger, or disinterest during a session, we need to listen attentively to our inner self and attend to particular sensations in our body (e.g., a queasy stomach, pain in the back, or a creepy, tingly sensation on the back of the neck). It is important to explore the possible meaning of such sensations. All these feelings contain significant information about the self, the particular members of the group, and the way in which the group operates.

Pushing Beyond Current Capacity

Another way to become a better leader is to push just a bit beyond your current capacity in each step of your training. To undertake this effort, you must first understand the concept of "flow" experience. Csikszentmihalyi (1990) first described the concept of flow. According to his theory, when our skills are just developed enough to meet a stretching and demanding challenge, we tend to immerse ourselves in that task and experience a sense of flow. Since we are skillful enough, but still challenged, we are neither bored by a repetitive action nor overwhelmed by a demand that greatly exceeds our existing abilities and training. During such flow, all our senses and thoughts are totally engaged in the activity, yet we have the confidence to meet the challenges being faced. We lose a sense of time and self-consciousness. This peak experience is often found during optimal performance. Applying this concept to the development of the self, if we are to grow to the optimum of our potential as a leader, we must open ourselves to each unprecedented group situation and allow ourselves to be immersed in each present moment. We do not merely use a checklist of approaches or possible solutions; instead, our inner capacities are called forth to comprehend group dynamics in a novel way and to respond to those demanding circumstances without fear. Being in the flow contributes to a leader's capacity to respond with creativity to any given situation.

If you are in the flow, you may find yourself acting with confidence when addressing unspoken group dynamics. Some presenting issues may seem unrelated on first glance to the goals that a member brought to the group. If you tap into the dynamics of the group, however, you are much more likely to connect the dots and see that they are, in fact, closely related, despite the lack of direct association. As a result, you may state the connection tentatively as a hunch and invite the member to explore that possibility. With practice, you can refine your inner radar so you will know when that feeling can be relied upon and when it cannot.

Cooper and Sawaf (1997) also suggest that leaders build their inner radar through immersing themselves into the experience at hand. By allowing ourselves to be challenged at our present level of capability, we stretch our skill one level up each time. Therefore, do not allow fear to block you from staying open to demands and challenges. Find ways to open that which blocks you so that you can deal with distractions, fatigue, and other blocks. Learn to set your vision a bit beyond your current capacity.

Personal Reflective Journal

Journaling is an excellent way for a leader-in-training to cultivate the inner self. Group leader trainees can use journaling to explore the varied and sometimes jumbled thoughts, feelings, and even physical reactions to all that is occurring within a group. This is especially important when significant events occur in our own lives that could have an impact on our perceptions and reactions within the group.

Journaling offers us opportunities to work with a mix of emotions and meaning in addition to the work done in class or under supervision. It helps us attend closely to the energized inner flow of emotions and meanings as well as to possible blocks that may stifle our self-awareness in certain areas.

Journaling also helps cultivate our empathic ability. As we all know, the ability to create an empathic environment in the group is of pivotal importance to group success. It is a required leadership skill. Empathy can be described as a therapist's effort to vicariously experience the inner life of members while at the same time retaining objectivity as an observer (Kohut, 1984, as cited in Kleinberg, 1991). To cultivate one's capacity for empathy is the trainee's urgent developmental task. Journal writing can assist leader trainees in their efforts to sensitize themselves to other's inner experiences while retaining an objective perspective. Chapter 12 addresses the methods of journaling in depth. Although the discussion focuses on member journaling, the same benefits and processes apply to group leaders.

One-to-One Supervision

One-to-one supervision, when used effectively, can be a great way to better ourselves as group counselors and therapists. The self-discovery that occurs in journaling can become material to be explored in one-to-one supervision. We all need some type of initiation to step into a new kind of awareness. Group leader trainees also need to be initiated into their role by more experienced group leaders. Supervision can serve to deepen, accelerate, and contribute to the overall quality of the learning.

The best way to use one-to-one supervision is to discuss key elements of your emerging intrapersonal awareness. Within the safety of the supervision meeting, intrapersonal thoughts, feelings, and impulses can be analyzed and considered for their true meanings. For example, if you come to a supervision session with some vague feelings of uneasiness, fear, anger, or other reactions triggered by the group, these responses can be discussed with the supervisor in order to identify their sources. Through exploration within supervision, the rich meanings behind these feelings may be appreciated, and your ability to lead more objectively will be enhanced. Therefore, take time to evaluate your own experiences after each group session; try to understand what goes on within yourself as well as within group members more fully. Explore these ideas with your supervisor until you can sort them out more easily on your own.

Group Supervision

When one-to-one supervision is unavailable, one may still benefit from group supervision. Group supervision has three goals. The first goal is to help trainees make the most of the multimodal learning possibilities inherent in the group of people. The second goal is to illustrate an effective means of group interaction and leadership. The third goal is to promote a healthy forum for personal and professional growth.

Within the group, supervisees can explore just about every kind of feeling and concern that they have about leading groups (Kees & Leech, 2002). Issues explored within a supervisory group may include anxieties about dealing with conflict, anger, or personal pain and tragedy and any personal barriers that inhibit supervisees from working effectively in the groups they lead. The personal insights and growth resulting from the supervision group may be linked directly to group leadership behaviors and approaches so that supervisees can overcome barriers and increase their effectiveness.

It is understandable that leader trainees might feel a great degree of anxiety in thinking about exposing personal difficulties in group supervision. This anxiety, however, can be a key element of their learning process if they do not let it shut them down but choose to open up to the deeper meanings of their experiences (Christiansen & Kline, 2001b). Generally, it is wiser to manage the anxiety by facing it rather than by suppressing the anxiety or the source of the feeling.

Research shows that the benefit of participating in group supervision is worthwhile. Group supervision offers valuable opportunities for trainees to build leadership skills, increases knowledge of group dynamics, provides a supportive environment to test out new skills, contributes to personal development, offers a forum to share a broad range of ideas on group leadership, and serves as a confidence builder (Christiansen & Kline, 2000). Other research shows that supervisees often experience an identifiable growth trajectory in their skill and professional orientation to group work (Christiansen & Kline, 2001a). Typically, leader trainees begin group supervision at a very dependent level, since they lean heavily upon the supervisor to "show them the ropes." With time and experience, trainees gradually move toward greater independence and initiative. The trainees increase their levels of self-confidence and ability to trust their peers, thus moving the experience to a higher level of interdependence and intimacy.

PERSONAL GROWTH AND GROUP EXPERIENCES

To become an effective group leader, therapists need to develop a sense of peace and balance within their own lives. From this position, they will be better able to manage, digest, and respond to the needs of the group at hand. Chris once heard an interesting story. Someone purchased a bicycle made in the Far East. Excited to get it assembled, he jumped into action only to find that the first line of the assembly instructions said, "First, have inner peace." Whether this story is true is immaterial. The point is that having "inner peace" is the exact place where any complex activity, such as assembling a bicycle, should begin. This principle applies to group leadership.

Personal group experience can bring about the growth, inner peace, and balance that therapists need. Personal group experiences can strengthen therapists' relational skills and better prepare them to connect with their future group members on the level of humanity. Through the personal growth process, group leaders can learn to embrace their own vulnerabilities, appreciate flexibility, and build relational confidence and resilience in the face of conflict or daily anxiety (Comstock, Duffey, & St. George, 2002). This section addresses the need for prospective group therapists to experience their own growth in their own personal group experience.

Resolving One's Own Unresolved Issues

A therapist may find a number of strains on himself professionally or personally when working with clients. This is especially the case in group work. The interpersonal pull or "button pushing" is multiplied within a group. Unresolved personal issues, likely to be drawn out within a group, may retard a leader's ability to identify and work with the issues that members bring with them. In the worst case, leaders with unresolved issues may damage group members.

By way of example, in a counseling group, one of the members, Alice, began describing an experience involving a recent violent attack against herself. The leader, Mike, found himself suddenly very emotionally distanced from this client and other group members to the point of feeling angry. He tried to divert attention away from Alice, but other members kept bringing the attention back to her. Mike finished the session feeling very frustrated and confused. As he was reviewing the circumstances in supervision, Mike recalled a childhood incident in which his brother was viciously mauled by a dog and Mike had been unable to stop the attack. Mike then recognized that he had been attempting to protect his old painful feelings about this incident by distancing himself instead of helping Alice and other group members. With his supervisor's help, Mike worked out a plan to better deal with Alice's pending issues within the group, and at the same time, he sought counseling for himself to work through his unresolved feelings about this incident in his own life.

A second example revolves around Bridgett, who was a group coleader with Echart. In the sixth session of the personal growth group they were leading, a member, Suthy, disclosed that she had an abortion at the age of 14, about two decades previously. In response to this disclosure, Echart noticed that a look of contempt flashed across Bridgett's face. Outwardly, Bridgett did not acknowledge Suthy's disclosure, nor did she address Suthy directly during the remainder of the group. Echart did acknowledge Suthy's disclosure and helped her draw some important connections to the work she was doing in the group. Right after the group session, Bridgett disclosed to Echart that she was a member of a very fundamentalist religious group that taught its members to condemn and disassociate from those who did not follow the precepts of their sect. She said that she was struggling to know how to respond therapeutically to Suthy because she had been taught that all abortions are wrong. In supervision, a great deal of discussion was devoted to helping Bridgett find a way to work from a position of support instead of a position of exclusion and separation. Bridgett was able to identify some immediate steps she could take to help with this group and relate more effectively with Suthy. In addition, Bridgett identified a religious individual whom she could consult in order to find a responsible resolution to the conflicts she felt between the ethical and professional standards for a counselor and the teachings of her religious sect.

Group therapists are expected to meet a high standard in terms of delivering professional services. Personal unresolved issues and preconceptions can stand in the way of providing high-quality counseling services to clients. To be responsible service providers, group therapists need to work on resolving their personal barriers through various routes of professional and personal development.

Trainees' Personal Group Experience

We believe that personal group therapy is the most important part of group leadership training. For group therapist trainees, Yalom (1995) asserts that personally participating in an experiential group is a must. Stockton and Toth (1996) also assert that personal group experience is one of the essential components of adequate group training. In leading, a therapist is constantly in tune with the swirling dynamics of members' emotional struggles. This ability to be tuned in to others' inner struggles can be acquired only through a therapist's personal experience as a client. Therapists must experience for themselves their own sense of vulnerability. They must become aware of their own dark sides, impulses, strengths, and weaknesses before they can fully appreciate their future clients' personal struggles and the courage it takes to change. This approach can be called the "Person-practice model" (Aponte, 1994), where therapists' personal issues related to interpersonal patterns are identified and exposed in a personal therapeutic relationship.

Only by being a member of a live group can a group therapist come to truly appreciate the force of group pressure, the catharsis of telling one's story, the bliss of having one's feelings validated, the influential status of the leader, and the painful but valuable process of receiving feedback about one's interpersonal patterns (Yalom, 2002). It is in a live group that trainees learn, at an emotional level, that which they previously learned cognitively through reading, lecture, and discussion. With such a personal experience, trainees get to see theory in action.

In a similar vein, Pierce and Baldwin (1990) state that therapists' sensitivities and skills can be acquired only through their own experiences with self-disclosure and personal participation in a live group, because role-playing simply fails to "model many of the genuine subtleties of group leadership" (p. 151). Research shows that group leader trainees generally report being helped by personal group experience as they gain a better awareness of personal experience, build a more clear understanding of their own behaviors within groups, and gain greater wisdom with the give and take of the feedback process (Kline, Falbaum, Pope, Hargraves, & Hundley, 1997).

Just participating in personal group therapy, however, is not enough. To really benefit from personal group experience, therapist trainees need to ensure that their goal of participating in a live group is not so much to improve their own effectiveness as a therapist/counselor as it is to explore personal issues (Aponte, 1994). Without exploring their personal issues within the context of a live group, therapist trainees are cheating themselves.

Making Group a Safe Setting for Personal Development

Many training programs offer, as part of the curriculum, an experiential training group (Yalom, 2002). When the experiential group is at the same time as a training group, relationships become easily blurred. Steps must be taken to ensure that the setting is safe for trainees to deal with personal development issues. To trim the potential threat of dual relationships, any activities related to personal disclosure during the experiential group must not be graded (Sklare, Thomas, Williams, & Powers, 1996). Rather, only academic assignments, including critical reflection on or critiques of the observed group, are graded. Trainees' critical reflections on the group process will show how well they comprehend and identify the interpersonal process in the group. Limiting grading in this way will diminish trainees' fear of being evaluated by their instructors and make it possible for trainees to become more open to exploring the personal issues that could have an impact on their ability to be an instrument for client change.

Assigning critical reflection as a homework assignment for trainees who are participating in a group is a wise choice. Cummings (2001) reported on a journaling approach that involved graduate-level trainees in group counseling and therapy. Trainees were asked to write in a reflective journal after each group session about their personal experience of the group—that is, their reactions to the group process and the group leader, their key learning experience of the session, and what they might draw from this experience to apply in future groups they lead. After the group experience was completed, almost all trainees reported that the journaling helped them understand the developmental stages of the group, their own interpersonal process, and the way group theories are lived out in group reality. Thus, critical reflection has the power to assist trainees in deepening their self-awareness and understanding essential group concepts.

SELF-REFLECTION

1. In past groups in which you have participated, what group leader behaviors contributed most to the quality of the experience? How did the leader(s) balance safety and challenge within the group? What is the optimum mix of safety and challenge that you prefer for yourself?

2. What past experiences have you had serving in a leadership capacity? Did you find yourself focusing strictly on the task(s) at hand, or did you also attend to the emotional needs and experiences of others?

3. How confident do you feel at this point in your training to use your "self" as a tool for your work with groups?

4. Think back to a time when you had a fair to high level of confidence. How do you think this happened? What experiences did you have that contributed to building your confidence in this way?

5. If you have a low level of confidence, what kinds of experiences do you think might be of the most benefit in helping you develop confidence?

6. What are some options for you to increase your level of group leadership experience? What kinds of groups would these experiences include? What opportunities would be available for you to receive supervision from a group leader who is experienced in working with the type of group in which you are interested?

7. How comfortable are you with using humor in your work with groups? What guidelines might assist you in deciding what is an appropriate use of humor as compared to what would likely detract from a group?

8. What are some ways in which you might bring some of your creativity into your work with groups? Can you identify some specific direct and indirect ways of bringing in creativity with groups?

9. For you, what would be an ideal coleadership arrangement? What are some key features that you would want in your coleadership relationship? How will you try to ensure that these factors will be part of any coleadership arrangement in which you participate?

10. What factors described in this chapter do you anticipate will be most helpful for you in developing your group leadership skills? Are there factors not addressed in this chapter that you expect will also contribute to your development of group leadership skills? If so, what are these additional factors?

11. In terms of your current developmental level and your experience in leading groups, at which stage would you put yourself based on the developmental stages described in this chapter?

BASIC LEADERSHIP SKILLS

GETTING THE GROUP TO WORK

CREATING A GROUP FROM SCRATCH

Program Planning and Member Preparation

Before starting to work with groups, it is critical that therapists know the unique parameters of group counseling and therapy. These parameters include ethical and professional guidelines, and conceptual and practical knowledge of working with the tasks unique to the various stage of group development. This chapter presents the very starting point of group work—the critical tasks of program planning and screening.

Some therapists walk into a group that is already formed. This presents a special kind of challenge because the newly arrived therapist may need to work particularly hard to fit into the group. Other times therapists start from scratch if a group does not already exist. Creating a group from scratch provides a therapist with the best chance of success because she is given an opportunity to build a solid foundation for the group.

The procedure for creating a new group includes the following steps: (1) assessing the needs of potential members; (2) writing a proposal; (3) recruiting members; (4) giving pregroup orientations; and (5) conducting screening interviews. The first through the third steps are called program planning. Steps four and five are called pregroup training or member preparation. All these preliminary labors are part of the business of group work. Group therapists who put thought and care into this preparatory homework will see it pay off in the end.

This chapter addresses these preparatory homework steps. It covers:

- Ethical and professional guidelines
- Four group specializations
- Program planning: needs assessment, proposal, and recruitment
- Member preparation (i): pregroup orientation
- Member preparation (ii): screening interview
- A case in point

ETHICAL AND PROFESSIONAL GUIDELINES

Before establishing any therapeutic relationship, including group counseling and therapy, practitioners must thoroughly familiarize themselves with the ethical codes and professional guidelines of the professional conduct. This section presents the ethical and professional expectations specifically related to group practice.

Informed Consent

Before starting a group, the therapist must know that prospective group members have the right to be informed of necessary information about a group and its leader so they can make an informed decision about whether the group will be appropriate for their needs. The professional disclosure should include information about any potential risks with respect to the particular group. Potential risks of participating in group include experiencing some level of stress, dissonance, and anxiety at times. Groups are designed to help people increase their levels of consciousness about themselves and their relationships with others. However, increased awareness is not always pleasant. Often it can lead individuals to reassess themselves and the quality of their relationships. As members reassess themselves, they may experience some degree of dissonance if they begin to let go of overly narrow restrictions from the past and open themselves to new choices and new ways of being. Whether these personal growths are small or sweeping, others around them may become ruffled about the changes and react in ways to try to "bring back the person they knew." This sets the stage for possible conflict as well as the potential for deeper levels of interpersonal understanding and intimacy. Members need to be informed of this risk before joining the group.

Group workers are ethically obligated to inform the interested public of the nature of group services before they decide to participate. The most efficient way to fulfill this requirement of informed consent is to provide a pregroup orientation (detailed in a later section of this chapter). If pregroup orientation proves to be impossible, then prospective members may be given the necessary information through phone calls or letters.

Professional Disclosure

Group leaders should offer information regarding their approach to group work in language that is clear and understandable for the population coming to the group. Additional information to be included in the professional disclosure statement should include the group leaders' professional backgrounds and experiences relevant to group work. Any special credentials that are applicable should also be included.

Voluntary Participation

Potential group members should be informed that any personal disclosure within the group setting is voluntary. They have the right to only reveal personal information at the level and pace they feel to be appropriate. They have the right to wait and watch for awhile, if they so desire, before exposing personal information to the group. Group members have a right to maintain their personal boundaries in whatever way they choose.

Of course, not all groups are voluntary groups. Sometimes therapists work with mandated groups wherein members are court-ordered or school-ordered to attend the group. In this circumstance, the members are mandated to be physically in the group, but they still have the right to determine the level and pace of their personal participation. When working with a mandated group, it is important to know how to work with resistance. Starting from the position of encouragement and respect will go a long way. Allowing the reluctant members to watch one or two sessions without personal participation is often helpful. When a sense of trust is developed with the therapist, some group work can be done with these mandated members.

Freedom to Withdraw

Prospective group members have the right to know that they have the freedom to withdraw, at any time, from the group if they find the group experience unsuitable. However, it is usually best for the remaining members if the leader invites the person who is withdrawing to come to group and share with the members his reason for withdrawal. This helps the withdrawing member handle the departure in a responsible way and obtain appropriate closure. It also offers a sense of closure for the remaining members, rather than suddenly having a member disappear from the group with no explanation.

Group leaders should invite the withdrawing member to discuss with the group her reasons for dropping out. There may be private reasons for dropping out, which a member should not be compelled to share. In this situation, she can just say that her outside personal issues require all her attention. This can be sufficient for closure, especially in the first few sessions of a new group. Of course, the scenario is quite different if the withdrawing member has come to play an integral role within the group and the withdrawal follows a major conflict in the group. If the withdrawing member is willing to come, for one last time, to explain her reasons for dropping out, chances are that the processing of the misunderstanding and the unmet needs will rectify the very reason that is compelling her to withdraw. Then she will be likely to stay in the group.

If no explanation for a member's withdrawal is provided, the remaining members in a group may feel guilty, believing the withdrawal is due to a conflict between them. And they may be right on target. In such a situation, the remaining group members must process the incident by themselves if the withdrawing person refuses to come and obtain a sense of closure.

To prevent premature dropout, leaders should prepare prospective members by letting them know that it is normal to experience some level of anxiety when people enter a new group. It can take several sessions for group members to begin to build trust and allay some of that anxiety. For this reason, group leaders sometimes ask members to commit to attending a minimum number of sessions (e.g., four sessions) without premature withdrawal in order to give the group a chance to prove itself. With a voluntary population, this is not meant to be a hard-and-fast rule. Rather, the four-session commitment primarily serves to notify potential group members that building group cohesion and a sense of comfort within group really does take time.

Screening and Member Protection

Ethically, group leaders must screen members so that only those whose needs and goals are compatible with those of others in the particular group are admitted to the group. Those who would block the work of the group or who would have their own state of well-being threatened by the group should not be chosen. The purpose of the screening procedure is to protect group members because group members have the right to be protected from physical and psychological harm from the group experience.

More details on the function of and the procedure for conducting screening interviews are provided later in this chapter.

Confidentiality within Groups

Prospective group members should be informed of their right to confidentiality. They also have to be clearly informed of the limitations on that confidentiality—it cannot be guaranteed within the group because their fellow members are not professionally bound in this regard. It is important, however, to emphasize that each member should commit himself to maintaining confidentiality for fellow group members. If this commitment is lacking, trust within the group will be hampered. Without trust, cohesion cannot develop. As a result, the members will not feel safe to risk any significant level of self-disclosure. Such a group will be dead on arrival.

Diversity

Ethically, group counselors and therapists must practice nondiscrimination. Therefore, therapists should not discriminate against members on the basis of age, color, culture, disability, ethnic group, gender, race, religion, sexual orientation, marital status, or socioeconomic status. Group leaders must respect these differences and make an active effort to comprehend the diverse backgrounds of group members.

When it comes to diversity issues within a group, mere tolerance of differences is insufficient. Instead, difference must be accepted and even welcomed within the group. While all group members have much in common, substantial differences often exist within a group. Some of these differences might be quite visible, while others might not readily be known if the members choose not to reveal them. However, the more afraid that members are of disclosing differences lest they be ostracized, the more tense and less productive the group is likely to be.

Group leaders must establish the model of acceptance of difference. When obvious characteristics cause a member to appear to be alone, the group leader should extend herself to this individual in order to help him feel welcomed and supported. For example, if there is one Muslim in a group of otherwise Christian members, the group leader will be wise to connect with that lone member. This effort to connect must be sincere and sensitive without being overdone lest it embarrass the person it is intended to help. By being obvious in reaching out, the group leader sets the tone for acceptance in the group, and hopefully the rest of the group will emulate this acceptance. Additionally, the leader sends the meta-message: "We heartily accept member differences in this group." This can set the stage for less obvious differences to emerge later.

Practicing within Competence

Professional guidelines require that group therapists practice within their own competencies. Group leadership is a highly complex process. Group counselors and therapists practice this complex art only within their areas of professional competence. Later in this chapter, we describe and discuss four types of group specializations. Although some principles are common to all groups, each specialization requires advanced specific knowledge, skills, and training for the scope of practice. Specific guidelines about how group leaders can obtain the appropriate level of training and supervised experiences are discussed in Chapter 13.

Achieving competence in group leadership requires a profound effort at learning to use wisely the various therapeutic factors in the group. One key therapeutic factor is the "self" of the group leader. To develop the self as the best instrument for group work, the leader needs to develop a considerable level of self-discipline and sustained growth through reflective practice. We elaborate on this concept of furthering one's personal and professional growth in Chapter 14.

THE FOUR GROUP SPECIALIZATIONS

Before starting a group, the therapist must ask himself, "What kind of group am I competent to lead?" Competency comes with training and personal experience. Most therapists are trained to lead a certain type of group. In general, there are four types of group specialization. These are discussed in the following text.

Task Groups

Task groups are designed to address the needs of *work groups* whose members come together to accomplish specific tasks or goals. Task groups might be called *teams* because they possess certain common elements, including goals, shared commitment, a sense of interdependence, and overall accountability within their organizations or within their shared context. The goals of these task groups usually have to do with increasing the efficiency and quality of the team or work group (Conyne, Rapin, & Rand, 1997; Kormanski, 1999). Rather than leading the team directly, group specialists assist task groups in addressing their process of working together to better achieve the common goals assigned to the team. Therefore, group specialists are sometimes referred to as "process consultants" (Kottler, 2001). Process consultants employ various strategies to assist the team with on-the-job training, in-service development, and streamlining the system within which teamwork is taking place.

Examples of task groups include elementary school parent/teacher committees, a Native American powwow committee, and *task forces* such as those formed to develop a strategic plan for an organization. In the business world, a task group might be a team assembled to test and evaluate new products for use by a company, or a group assembled to determine the impact of planned changes in the products of information technology the company uses.

Psychoeducational Groups

Psychoeducational groups serve to teach members life skills related to a specific topic. Generally, psychoeducational groups serve two types of clientele: The first type are those clients of different age groups who face special *developmental* needs and issues. Here the intent of psychoeducational groups is to provide a boost to client development with an eye on *preventing* possible difficulties in the future. The target population may include either those at some risk for encountering problems or those seeking to further their own personal development. For these clients, psychoeducational groups can provide education, offer *support*, and teach problem-solving skills.

The second type of clients that psychoeducational group serve are those who are severely disturbed, or those clients with limited ability to communicate effectively with others, limited ability to recognize and express their feelings, or limited ability to perceive others and/or self accurately. Through structured activities, psychoeducational group can address these clients' needs, identifying and building on their skills. In general, psychoeducational groups are like *support* groups. This supportive nature may be the reason why disturbed clients tend to respond better to structured psychoeducation groups than to nonstructured counseling groups and psychotherapy groups (Remocker & Storch, 1992).

In psychoeducational groups, sessions are structured around leader-designed topics or exercises in order to achieve predetermined goals in a short time. Cognitive-behavioral methods that teach coping skills and strategies to deal with various life stressors fit especially well into psychoeducational approaches. Members often experience a sense of universality that can counter the stigmatizing effects from which many in these populations suffer. In addition, such groups ease some of clinicians' tedious and repetitive maintenance work with individual clients.

Examples of psychoeducational groups include stress reduction groups, grief support groups, anger management groups, assertiveness training groups, couples communication enhancement groups, groups for new parents, caregiver training groups for adults with aged parents, phobia and panic management groups, chronic pain management groups, groups for chemical dependency early recovery, chemical dependency graduate groups, groups for persons coping with physical illness, and groups for chronically mentally ill patients.

Counseling Groups

Counseling groups, also referred to as experiential groups, are provided for individuals with difficulties in adjusting to life transitions. Such groups serve not only those who are at risk of developing personal or interpersonal difficulties but also those who seek personal growth. Whatever the goals are, the issues tend to be interpersonal in nature. Leaders of counseling groups use a variety of intervention strategies to address patterns of maladaptive cognition, emotions, actions, and systems. The aim is to help people become more aware of themselves, their own interpersonal behaviors, and their interpersonal interactions with others.

Counseling groups tend to be nonstructured, or at most semistructured. The approach used is often experiential in nature. Compared to psychotherapy groups (addressed next), counseling groups tend to be short-term. Counseling groups are supposed to be not only *preventive* and *developmental*, but also *remedial*. Budman and Gurman (1988) state that, as treatment groups, counseling groups are "interpersonally oriented rather than symptom oriented. This means that rather than emphasizing, for example, the depression or anxiety experienced by those dealing with strained relationships, it is the nature of those relationships themselves that is examined. The interpersonal environment of the group is uniquely suited to the examination of such issues" (p. 252).

Examples of counseling or experiential groups include interpersonal problem-solving groups; men's groups; women's groups; groups for couples with relationship problems; divorce groups; groups for clients who have recently left inpatient settings; groups for socially awkward men; groups for adult children of alcoholics, codependents, or adults who were molested as children; groups for at-risk students; gay men's groups; minority women's groups; and cancer groups.

Psychotherapy Groups

Some professionals consider the psychotherapy group and the counseling group to be the same thing, but by design, psychotherapy groups are more in-depth and tend to be longer-term than counseling groups. Participants in psychotherapy groups may range from those who function well but have some barriers that limit their well-being in life, to those with a high level of maladjustment that is severe and/or chronic. These groups focus on addressing the maladaptive patterns of individuals who may have significant blocks in their cognition and perceptions. Using interpretation as a tool to work with various psychological blocks (e.g., resistance, distortions, and defenses) and unconscious materials (e.g., transferences and dreams), this type of long-term group has the greatest degree of therapeutic leverage in reconstructing members' deeply ingrained personalities.

Examples of psychotherapy groups include long-term therapy groups, groups for physically or sexually abusive individuals, groups for people suffering from schizophrenia, and groups for the substance-addicted. Psychotherapy groups are *remedial* by nature and often are nonstructured.

In short, all four types of groups are important parts of a comprehensive treatment program. Working with task groups, psychoeducational groups, and counseling groups requires a knowledge of normal human development. Working with psychotherapy groups involves awareness of both normal and abnormal human development, with a focus on heightened emotional arousal.

PROGRAM PLANNING: NEEDS ASSESSMENT, PROPOSAL, AND RECRUITMENT

The importance of program planning can be illustrated with a story told by Conyne (1999). Two therapists working at a human services center decided unilaterally to develop a group program at the center because they noticed that individual therapists were becoming burdened with the demands of managed care. The two collaborated in secret, however, about their decision and sprang it on their colleagues at a clinical staff meeting without first proposing it to their director. The result was a disaster. The lack of program planning prevented it from being well received by the director and colleagues. No one accepted their ideas, and several colleagues were actually resistant and became frustrated.

Good intentions with poor planning can end up making one feel embarrassed and incompetent. If the two therapists had done their homework and developed a good program plan, the result might have been opposite of what it was. Program planning is the homework that group therapists cannot avoid. It involves those managerial tasks including needs assessment, proposal writing, and member recruitment. Group therapists need to be competent in these managerial functions, and not leave the tasks in the hands of others who have little understanding of group work.

Needs Assessment

Any program planning, regardless of the setting, starts with a careful assessment of the needs, demands, and interests of the community. Identifying what kinds of problems and unmet needs are out there, as well as what kinds of resources already exist, can help therapists determine what kind of group should be offered to fill the gaps in the service delivery system.

Surveys can be used to identify the unmet needs of the community. Formal methods of survey may include mailed questionnaires, telephone contacts, and personal interviews (Lewis, Lewis, Daniels, & D'Andrea, 1998). Less formally, therapists may check with other therapists in local agencies to determine what services they currently provide and which community needs are still unmet.

Developing a Proposal

After needs are identified, the next step in program planning is to develop a clear proposal. The functions of a proposal are twofold. First, the process of developing a proposal propels the therapist to prepare with greater clarity for many practical matters at hand. Second, a well-developed proposal increases the likelihood of convincing whomever the proposal is submitted to for review of the applicability of the service. An example of a proposal can be found in Appendix A. In the following text, we discuss areas the therapist may need to address in the proposal.

Purpose of the Group   Clarity of purpose is one of the most important factors in a successful group. Will the group be a psychoeducational group or a counseling or therapy group? The methods and emphases of psychoeducational and therapy groups are vastly different. (See the discussion of four group specializations in the previous section.) Will the group be a support group or a process group? A support group would not focus as much on feedback, immediacy, and interpersonal confrontation as would a process group. Will the group serve clients with similar problems or clients with a wide range of diverse issues? These are questions the therapist must answer in the proposal.

Voluntary or Nonvoluntary Membership   Another area to be clarified is whether the members will be voluntary or nonvoluntary participants. Group participation is basically voluntary, yet not all groups are voluntary groups. Sometimes therapists have to work with group members who are court-mandated or school-mandated. The planning for nonvoluntary groups will be different from that for voluntary groups. During preparation for the former, the therapist has to spend more time planning how to adapt to the negative attitude that members will have about being in the group (Jacobs, Masson, & Harvill, 2002; Yalom, 1995). If the resistance and resentment of such group members are well accepted and adapted to by the therapist, even the nonvoluntary group can prove to be beneficial to clients who did not want to be there in the first place.

Closed or Open Group   The therapist also needs to decide whether the group will be a closed or an open group. A closed group is one where no new members are admitted after the group starts. A brief counseling group tends to be a closed group because members need to develop trust and intimacy with each other and hold one another accountable for working on their goals within the limited life of the group. Members in a closed group also greatly benefit from going through the various stages of group life; the progression of group development often leads to a deepening of personal exploration and the working through of difficult issues.

In an open group, members come and go sporadically. This kind of group is best suited to the hospital or residential treatment setting. In these settings, group services must remain open to readily absorbing on a weekly basis, new arrivals as well as to graduating those ready to check out of the agencies. The open groups certainly present challenges for both leaders and group members. For members, the challenge rests in the fact that they do not have the benefit of progressing through various group stages before departing. For leaders, the challenge lies in the toll of having to constantly orient new members to the group and say good-bye to those who leave. Group cohesiveness is difficult to establish in an open group; however, if healthy group norms are developed and there is some continuity of membership, these groups need not pay a high price with each change of membership. The healthy norms can be perpetuated through the remaining members, who can "carry the torch" for new members and help them learn about how the group functions.

Group Size   When deciding how many members to have in a group, it is important to understand that group size greatly influences group dynamics. The size of the group will depend on the purpose of the group and the population of the members. An ideal size for a process or counseling group with an adult population is approximately eight members. A psychoeducational or support group can be slightly larger in size—approximately twelve members. For younger populations, the group size should be smaller, around three or four members for children and six to eight for adolescents (Corey & Corey, 2002).

When a group is too big, full participation from each member becomes unattainable, rendering some members' needs neglected. When a group is too small, the dynamics become strained because there is more pressure on each member to talk, and less time for members to ponder and reflect. There is also a lack of adequate perspective and stimulation when a group is too small. The power of reality testing within group is sacrificed when the group consists of only two or three members.

Length of Session and Frequency of Meeting   The length of the session should be set early during the planning stage. How many minutes should a session last? The answer depends on the composition and nature of the group. For children's groups, the length of the session should be only 30 to 45 minutes, because that is the maximum length of their attention span. For groups in a school setting, the session usually corresponds with the class period, ranging from 40 to 50 minutes (Jacobs, Masson, &

Harvill, 2002). These groups can meet twice weekly to compensate for the shortness of the sessions. Groups for adolescents outside the school setting can have a slightly longer session length and meet just once weekly.

For an adult counseling or therapy group, the session needs to be 90 minutes to two hours per week. Such length is necessary for members to get emotionally engaged in the group and with one another. If sessions are too short, members will have difficulty getting into issues of any depth and therefore will not accomplish much.

Adequacy of the Location   The location for group meetings must be taken into consideration during the planning stage. Is privacy adequate where the group meets? To make group members feel safe enough to open up, the meeting room should ideally be closed and free from intrusion or distraction. There should be flexibility in seating so chairs can be moved to form a circle. In counseling and therapy groups, no tables should be placed in the center of the circle because they create distance and erect barricades between members. In task and psychoeducational groups, tables present less of a problem.

Leaders' Qualifications   It is important to indicate in the proposal that the therapist is qualified to lead the group. Without competency, a leader can harm innocent members. Basic competencies of a group leader include: experience in working with individuals, adequate training in group theories and dynamics, personal experience in group, knowledge of the topic specific to the group under consideration, and awareness of the best practices in group counseling and therapy (see Chapter 13).

Screening Procedure   To protect group members from unnecessary emotional harm, leaders have an ethical responsibility to screen unsuitable members from the group. In the proposal, it is advisable to state the criteria that will be used for screening.

Ground Rules   Preplanning about group rules will ensure the reviewer of the proposal that the group will be carried out within agreeable boundaries and in order. Boundaries and order create a sense of safety in and evoke commitment from prospective group members. Although rules vary with different groups, typical group rules may include, but need not be limited to:

- No dual relationships are allowed among members outside group.
- Keep confidentiality for fellow members.
- Bring any outside-group conversation about the group to the group.
- Call to notify the leader of any absence.
- Be punctual.

- No food, chewing gum, or beverages are permitted during the session.
- No alcohol or substances may be used before the session.

Structures and Techniques   Whether the nature of the group will be structured, semistructured, or nonstructured, the structure must be pre-planned. The nature of structure will be closely related to the mechanisms used to make the group work. A structured group will use leader-designed activities and topics to propel the group, and leaders will use facilitating techniques and other techniques specific to the group activities. On the other hand, an unstructured group will use the group dynamics as the grist of the mill for group work. The techniques used in such groups will focus strongly on the here-and-now, feedback, risk-taking, reality testing, and process examination.

Whatever structure is chosen, it should best suit the particular group. Of prime consideration will be the cognitive and emotional developmental levels of the group members. In general, a structured group is best suited for less-developed individuals. A structured format, on the other hand, might stifle more highly developed individuals. If the group is designed for younger children, the structure might be oriented toward play. For adults the structure generally can be oriented toward more complex cognitive and emotional pursuits, although this is not to say that creativity, humor, and play should be omitted from adult groups. On the contrary, these aspects can be essential to reaching a balance in adult groups.

Possible Issues or Topics for Group   The issues and topics suitable for group exploration depend on the type of group being proposed. In the proposal, the therapist may want to list possible issues and topics that potential group members would work on. Solid in-depth background knowledge of the population from which the group is drawn is an essential starting point. A needs assessment of the group will help point the way to what concerns, issues, and areas of life members need to explore. The ability to identify issues and concerns allows group leaders to plan for the types of group interventions that will best address the members' needs.

Recruiting Members

Knowing the type of population from which the group will be drawn is essential in recruiting members. Once you know what population you are targeting, you can look for leverage to use in reaching out to potential members. When it comes to recruiting, three strategies can be used: soliciting referrals from other therapists; informing key individuals in the community; and advertising extensively.

Soliciting Referrals from Other Therapists   Do not overlook the value of peer and agency referrals. Your peers and those with whom you have contacts at other human service agencies are more likely to have confidence in group work you are planning than those who have had no prior professional contact with you. Many times the targeted population is already receiving some type of counseling or other services. In such cases, the counselors and therapists already providing services can be potential allies in attracting members to the group. Contact the agencies and specific therapists who work with the population that is appropriate for the group you are planning, and. provide them with flyers and other written descriptions of the group's purpose and goals.

Informing Key Individuals in the Community   With some populations, especially those that are traditionally underserved by counseling and therapy services (e.g., minority and immigrant populations), it can be helpful to seek out key individuals within those communities to talk with and provide them with written information about the group. These key individuals include religious, educational, and sometimes business leaders who tend to be highly respected within the community and who can influence whether an "outsider" might be given an opportunity to work with community members. These individuals are also likely to have in-depth knowledge about the special needs and issues of that population.

Advertising Extensively   All things considered, it is worthwhile to advertise extensively through traditional methods of advertising: flyers, written announcements, newspaper articles, and posters placed in key locations frequented by members of the population being considered. Depending on the population, you also might consider creating a Web page or Internet announcement, but first consider carefully whether you will be likely to reach your intended population that way. For example, if you are planning a group for low-income individuals, much of your population may not even have access to the Web.

MEMBER PREPARATION (I): PREGROUP ORIENTATION

Once you have advertised your group, interested individuals may call with questions for you. It is inappropriate to ask the secretary of your agency to answer such questions, but it is too time-consuming for you to answer them on an individual basis. Hereby comes the pregroup orientation. A preliminary group orientation is an efficient way to answer, once and for all, those important yet often redundant questions from potential members.

Pregroup orientation is not a luxury, but an ethical obligation. It fulfills the therapist's ethical obligation to provide professional disclosure, obtain informed consent, and prepare members for group (see Chapter 13).

Orientation as Pretreatment Training

Orientation serves to alert potential members to how the group may be a new experience for them. When deciding whether to join a new group, potential members often experience a high level of anxiety. Lack of familiarity with participating in a group magnifies this anxiety. The anxiety can be reduced by educating the potential members through a pregroup orientation (Sklare, Keener, & Mas, 1990). In preparing potential members for group experiences, we need to inform them about group rules, the necessity of self-disclosure, and the need to be patient. It is especially important to educate the potential members about the need to attend the group for at least four sessions before making any judgment about its effectiveness. When educated, interested individuals will be prepared to respond optimally to the challenges inherent in the new experience.

The orientation also clears up any misinformation members have about groups. Even if members are joining the group on a voluntary basis, they often will come to the group with certain fears of and myths about groups. Myths that potential members might harbor include:

- Group counseling is only for people with major issues.
- Group counseling waters down real counseling because there are more clients than counselors/therapists.
- Group counseling is less effective than other types of counseling.
- Group counseling would be entirely unnecessary if only there were more counselors/therapists available. (Carter, Mitchell, & Krautheim, 2001)

The pregroup orientation gives the group therapist an opportunity to lessen potential members' fears and eliminate misconceptions about group. For the leader, the time and energy spent in member preparation will pay off, as this preliminary education often greatly reduces subsequent dropouts.

Making the First Contact Engaging

The pregroup orientation is your first personal encounter with individuals who are interested in the group. Through this first encounter, potential members will form impressions about your interpersonal skills, communication skills, degree of likeability, and level of competence. In a sense, they are sizing you up. If you are a new leader, you will need to get prepared so that you can be as professional, knowledgeable, empathic, and enthusiastic as possible. The pregroup orientation should truly reflect who you are as a professional and your beliefs in the group process.

During this first contact, there are many tasks to be done, including providing oral and written disclosure about the purpose of the group, the expectations for group members in terms of participation, the requirements for joining and leaving the group, guidelines about the handling of and limits to confidentiality, necessary information about the time frame and cost for the group experience, and the possible results of participation in the particular group. As you can see, there are a lot of bases to cover. If you cover all of them in a lecture or a speech, the orientation may not be as interactive and interesting as you wish. One way to make your orientation alive is to cover the basic information in written disclosure and save the precious face-to-face time for more personal and dynamic interaction. This allows time for interested members to ask questions, making your orientation session interactive and engaging. It also offers you a chance to use your responses to connect with the audience of potential members.

Clarifying Mutual Expectations

One of the major tasks in pregroup orientation is to clarify mutual expectations between members and the leader. Hannah (2000) emphasized several expectations that must be addressed. These expectations include:

- Members being expected to establish a commitment to working in the group
- The leader setting the context for nonhierarchical group interaction among equals
- The leader promoting a here-and-now focus where members are encouraged to honestly share feelings and perceptions
- Members being encouraged to express member-to-member support
- Group leaders clearly describing their role within the group context
- Members being encouraged to take appropriate risks and to test out new behaviors in group

Hetzel, Barton, and Davenport (1994), also suggest that it is useful, both during the pregroup orientation and throughout the course of the group, to let members know that they may experience periods of discouragement. By doing so, you normalize difficult feelings when they do surge, which mostly likely will happen, and you may prevent premature dropout. As mentioned, some of the expectations can be conveyed in handouts to the interested audience.

In Appendix B, you will find four examples of orientation handouts:

- Rights and Responsibilities of Group Members
- Orientation to Being in Group

- How to Get the Most from Group
- Informed Consent Form

We encourage you to create your own handouts to suit your specific groups.

Connecting and Positive Reframing

When some of the important information is covered in handouts, time may be spent during the orientation in answering questions and making connections with the audience. To connect, allow yourself to convey the feelings and core message that you sense behind each question. Reflecting the audience's implicit feelings is as important as providing straightforward answers to questions. Your deep listening to and positive reframing of potential members' concerns often become the critical elements that shape their first impressions of group work and of the leader.

For example, suppose someone asks, "If someone in the group dominates the group, for example, by talking all the time, how will the group handle that?" Rather than just responding to the content of this question, you should try to sense what is behind it. What is the feeling underneath this question? If you sense apprehension, you can convey your understanding of the questioner's apprehension by saying,

> Yes, it is often frustrating and oppressing when someone dominates the floor and nobody does anything about it. [reflection of feelings] In group counseling, things like this do happen because group is just like any other interpersonal setting. But what is different in group is that the leader is here to make sure the group interaction moves in a way that those difficult things can be talked about in a safe way, so that each member becomes more aware and from there all can grow. [positive reframing]

Suppose another person asks, "Aren't people going to think that I am weak or that I have psychological problems if I decide to join the group?" The leader can again answer with empathy and positive reframing:

> It's understandable that we might be afraid of being seen as weak in seeking group experience. Judgment from others is a very powerful force in our lives. [empathic response] If we look more deeply, we will find that struggling for change is not a sign of psychological problems, but rather a sign of courage. We all have some internal blocks that we need to work on so as to expand our capacity to live a more fulfilling life and form closer ties with people we care about in our lives. Therefore, joining a group is, indeed, a wise investment for all. [positive reframing]

Membership Match

An often-asked question in orientation is: "How much should people be similar to one another in the group?" Ideally, for a group to work well together, members should be similar in terms of functioning level. Functioning level is the most important group composition factor. An adequate degree of homogeneity is crucial for active group interaction. More specifically, the functioning level may be discerned through signs of willingness to change, excitement about joining the group, awareness of reality and self, openness to feelings, willingness to tolerate anxiety, willingness to disclose, sensitivity to others, risk-taking ability, creativity, and nonaggressiveness (Riva, Lippert, & Tackett, 2000). When there is a goodness of fit in these characteristics, it is very likely that the group members will be well matched.

Gender is an important factor in groups for children. Mixing boys and girls can have a negative impact, especially when dealing with developmental issues or with issues that are specific to boys or girls. For adults, however, a group of mixed gender can provide greater interpersonal learning for each gender. Other multicultural dimensions of identity are important considerations both for the makeup of a group and for the manner in which the group members will interact.

Best Candidates

Another popular question is, "What kinds of people can benefit from group, and what kinds cannot?" Generally speaking, most people can benefit from group counseling. But the best candidates are people who are motivated to change, people who understand the benefits of group, people who feel isolated or lonely at times, and people who struggle with self-esteem and social skills problems.

On the other side, those who are not likely to benefit from group are people who are not motivated to change, those who do not believe in group, sociopathic individuals, and people with brain damage, extreme narcissism, paranoia, acute psychosis, or extreme depression (Yalom, 1995). Other types that are poor candidates for group include people with high levels of resistance to participation and change; individuals who are hostile, passive-aggressive, or actively abusing drugs or alcohol; and those with cognitive retardation, poor skills in managing anxiety, or with excessive neediness as compared to others in the group (Riva, Lippert, & Tackett, 2000). These people are likely to present serious management problems in groups. They need special attention and usually are best referred to specialized programs. At least, they need to be stabilized before entering group counseling and therapy.

Poor selection of members can significantly impede the achievement of members' goals. It can precipitate members to feel mistrustful, angry, guilty, and/or impatient, depending on the particular circumstances involved. Potential members have a right to know that group leaders will use the predetermined criteria to select appropriate members. They need to know that screening procedures will be carried out to ensure that members are appropriately matched.

Diverse Clients

The issue of whether to include diverse members has many facets to be considered. The less diverse the group is, the more homogeneous it will be. The advantage of homogeneous groups is a more rapid trust-building, which should lead to greater cohesion (Han & Vasquez, 2000). However, members of homogeneous groups are sometimes afraid to "rock the boat" and challenge one another, even when it would be in their best interests to do so. The more diverse the group is, the more heterogeneous it will be. The advantage of a diverse group is that members have the opportunity to learn to relate more fully to those who are different. However, if not properly monitored and challenged by the leaders, the heterogeneous group may run the risk of reenacting difficult power dynamics (Han & Vasquez, 2000).

When a heterogeneous group is the choice, leaders must be sensitive to nonmainstream members, such as an elderly woman, a gay man, or an individual with a disability. A vast difference in real-life experience of power dynamics does exist between mainstream individuals and nonmainstream individuals. If leaders are not careful, group norms may inadvertently develop that obscure, ignore, or invalidate the experiences of nonmainstream people. The pain caused by oppressive actions in society may be denied through various defense mechanisms by mainstream members.

Other factors to be considered in regard to group composition include rates of verbalization, status of acculturation, and gender issues (Han & Vasquez, 2000). Rate of verbalization can vary widely between ethnic groups. Certain cultures encourage respect and noninterference; people from these cultures seldom interrupt each other, and they find it difficult to aggressively take the floor in groups. Clients from these cultural backgrounds may include Mexican Americans, American Indians, and Asian individuals.

Concurrent Therapies

In the pregroup orientation, interested people may ask about whether concurrent therapies are advisable. The bright side of concurrent therapy is that issues identified in group can be explored further in individual therapy. For example, concurrent individual and group therapy is good for people with borderline and narcissistic personality disorders because these clients need both extensive intrapersonal exploration in the individual setting and external support in the group setting. However, for most people, concurrent individual and group therapy creates a problem: The client who receives attention in individual therapy may be inclined to talk more in that setting and to disclose less in the group context. The opportunity of working out interpersonal issues with the group is thus lost.

If a member needs to be placed concurrently in both group and individual counseling, it is often best if the individual counselor and the group counselor can support each other's therapeutic efforts through consultation with each other as needed. However, under the ethical guidelines of the American Counseling Association, when clients are already receiving counseling or other mental health services, client consent should be sought in order for consultation to take place between counselors (American Counseling Association, 1995).

The Challenge of Confidentiality

Another topic frequently asked about in orientation is confidentiality. As a group leader, you are ethically and legally obligated to maintain confidentiality. Group members, however, are not legally bound to maintain confidentiality. This presents a challenge for the group. You must stress how important it is to maintain confidentiality if people are to build a sense of trust for the group. You ought to discuss ethical issues of confidentiality in the pregroup orientation and in the screening interview. Additionally, the issue of confidentiality is likely to arise during group sessions, sometimes directly and sometimes indirectly. Acknowledging, during pregroup training, the impact that confidentiality can have on a group will help establish a foundation for later work with this issue. The importance of confidentiality, both during the group and afterward, cannot be stressed enough.

Frequently Asked Questions

The following are examples of other frequently asked questions in pregroup orientations. Before gaining personal experience and acquiring knowledge of group process, it is understandable that you will not be able to answer these questions. We include these questions here because questions have a way of provoking learning. After you finish group counseling training, come back and answer these questions. You will find that by that time, you will be able to answer these questions with confidence and competence. Questions frequently asked in pregroup orientation include:

- What kinds of problems are suitable to work on in the group?
- If the area of my problem is different from those of others in the group, how will the group be able to help me?

- Each member has very different problems to work on. How can the group help people with so many different areas of concerns at the same time?
- Is everyone suitable for this? What kinds of people are suitable for the group? What kinds are not?
- If my husband wants to know what's going on in the group, can I tell him what happens in the sessions?
- After the group starts, if a friend of mine wants to join the group, would she be admitted?
- What's the next step after the orientation? Are we admitted to the group now?
- What can I expect during the screening interview?
- How am I going to know whether I am making progress in the group?
- If I figure out after a few sessions that I really don't like the group, can I drop out?
- If I miss a few group sessions, will it matter?
- Will there be a lot of homework assignments for members to do between sessions?
- If someone in the group dominates the group, for example, by talking all the time, how will the group handle that?
- If I have a pressing issue to talk about in a session but someone is more aggressive and thus prevents me from having time to discuss my situation, how will this be stopped?
- I am a very quiet person; will I really get a chance to talk about my issues?
- If I don't get along with someone in the group, what will happen?
- If I have a problem with someone in the group, can I consult with the leader in individual meetings?
- I am very afraid of confrontation. I am afraid of being attacked by others. What would you say about that?
- If I find myself attracted to someone in the group, may I date that person outside the group?
- Is there anything I should be cautious about before deciding to join the group?
- How long does a session usually last? For how many sessions will the group run?
- I am in individual counseling now. Would it be possible to participate in group counseling simultaneously?

MEMBER PREPARATION (II): SCREENING INTERVIEW

A screening interview is equivalent to an intake for individual counseling. A screening procedure is conducted with each potential member. This screening interview is a time-consuming process that can add extra work into the already-tight schedule of the therapist. However, time-consuming as it is, ethically the therapist needs to go through this process. The *Best Practices Guidelines* by the Association for Specialists in Group Work (ASGW, 1998) state that group practitioners need to properly screen members. An unscreened group may be an unsuitable collection of individuals, causing psychological harm to the group members.

Two other functions are served by the screening interview. First, it serves to build a preliminary rapport between the leader and individual members. The time the leader spends with potential members in the screening interview is not wasted time. Through this screening, the leader gains the bonus of building valuable rapport with the clients, reducing their anxiety when they come face to face with the group. Second, it serves to help potential members define goals. For time-limited groups, members' work must be guided by goals. A clearly defined goal leads to a clear vision and focused task. Goals motivate us. Goals direct how our energy will be invested.

In the screening interview, each member must be probed to clarify his goal. Most people's goals need some shaping in order to become practical and achievable within a group. A clear definition of a goal is half the success of reaching it. Goals must be defined in such a way that progress toward them is measurable and achievable within the course of the group life (Barker, 1985). The major task of the screening interview is to probe the member into formulating a goal that is specific and workable within the group context. This part of the screening interview qualifies it as one form of pretreatment training.

If a potential member becomes unresponsive or defensive toward your efforts in shaping an achievable goal, this defensiveness is likely to indicate how she functions interpersonally. A decision will need to be made concerning that person's suitability for the particular group.

A screening interview may take from 30 minutes to an hour, depending on the depth you endeavor to go into. You may conduct the interview with your coleader if you have one. Following we suggest several steps for conducting the screening interview. You may tailor them to suit your specific circumstance.

Greeting

This step provides a continuity from pregroup orientation to pregroup screening. It also provides a general picture of what the procedure will involve. The therapist may say something like,

> Hi, Tom, I'm glad to see you again. It was a pleasure to see you in last week's pregroup orientation. I am glad that you are interested in joining the group. Today we have about 30 minutes together. To decide whether the group is suitable for serving you, we need to gather some information from you. If any of the questions I ask you are too personal, you can decide to what extent you want to answer. Toward the end, I would also like to know whether you have questions to ask of me.

Asking Clients about Presenting Problems

With the brevity of time, it is wise to get to the heart of business—what the client wants from the group. If a client is uncertain where to start, it may be helpful to ask about her issues of concern, that is, her presenting problems. These issues can be translated later into a personal goal. Following are some possible questions to initiate this discussion:

> Have you ever been in a group before? If so, what was the experience like?
>
> Group is a place where people help one another to improve their lives. If you were to identify a problem area in your life that you would like to change, what would it be?
>
> If you don't change this problem area, what are be the possible negative outcomes?

Remember to reflect the client's core messages after each probing so that a rapport can be built between you and the client. A reflective response may sound like:

> So you are saying that you have had difficulty controlling your temper, and your work and family relationships have suffered a great deal because of this.

Do not just fire a series of questions at the interviewee. The screening interview should not be turned into an interrogation session.

Translating Problems into Personal Goals

Influenced by brief therapy, we see setting realistic and on-target goals as an essential building block of later group work. After the therapist gets a sense of the client's presenting problem, it is important to translate the problem into a personal goal. In general, a goal means something to be achieved. This something could be a new behavior repertoire, a new competency area, a new attitude, or a new outlook on life. The goal should be concrete enough that others in the group can say whether or not the client has reached it at the end of the group. Therefore, the goal should be specific and achievable. If the goal is too broad or general, the therapist needs to probe for more concreteness to achieve clarity. Following are prompts therapists can use to translate the presenting problems into a personal goal:

> What change would you like to see happen by the end of the group?
>
> What made you decide to make this change at this specific stage of your life?
>
> So you would like to feel more at peace with yourself and with others by the end of the group. [reflective response] When you feel more at peace with yourself and with others, what will you be doing that is different from what you are doing now?
>
> Could you give me an example?

Reflective listening should be applied after each exchange.

Interviewing Clients about Their Interpersonal Backgrounds

Gathering specific information about clients' interpersonal background offers group leaders an opportunity to get a sense of where clients come from. Influenced by object relations theory and family systems theories, we often look into aspects of the clients' family of origin, such as earlier life and family experiences, by asking questions such as those that follow:

> The group is like a family, so how does or did your family of origin interact? Would you give me an example?
>
> How did your family of origin handle anger, intimate feelings, and other intense emotions?
>
> How did your family respond to differences within and outside the family?
>
> While all these things were going on in your family of origin, what did you do? How did you cope?
>
> In other words, what was the role you played in your family of origin?
>
> How do your coping strategies learned in the past influence your life today as an adult? How do you handle emotions differently now?

To avoid turning the interview into a series of questions, the therapist can constantly reflect the client's core messages after each exchange to maintain the rapport. For example,

> It sounds like, given the way things were in the household, you kids had to tiptoe around about what you did and said because you never knew what kind of mood your mom was going to be in when you walked in the door. You were exasperated by her drinking, yet you learned to fix

whatever went wrong to keep things in order. You learned to keep
everything stuffed inside.

Summarizing Clients' Goals in Behavioral Terms

It is a good idea to summarize the large amount of information obtained
from the client, especially that which relates to his personal goal.
Summarizing the goal in behavioral terms makes it clear and succinct. For
example,

> Tom, our time is running out pretty soon, so before we end, let me
> summarize what you have said so I know I heard you correctly. Your
> goal for joining the group is to learn to express yourself in a way that is
> not defensive when facing disapproval from others. You want to learn to
> express yourself in a way that demonstrates that you have heard what
> others have said, and in a way that is truthful to your inner experience,
> rather than shutting down your feelings as you have in the past. Am I
> hearing you right?

The counselor also may want to prepare the client for subsequent group
interactions and help the client understand that she will have a role in the
formation and actions of the group:

> In a group, people work together to help each other toward change.
> However, there might be situations where interaction gets a bit
> intense and disagreements pop up. How do you see yourself in this
> type of situation?

Giving Clients a Chance to Ask Questions

Before ending the screening interview, allow the interviewee a chance to
address any questions he might have. For example,

> Tom, we have about two minutes left. I would like to see if there are
> any questions about the group or about me that you would like to ask.

Closing the Interview

The therapist may close the interview by thanking the client for his sharing. The therapist should also identify future steps, so the client knows
what to expect:

> Thank you, Tom, for sharing with me this very meaningful information.
> You should expect to hear from me within a week.

After the Interview

The screening interview is not complete until the screening decision is made and the notification contact is made.

Making Screening Decisions   During the screening interview, the group therapist uses all his senses to absorb any information that might provide hints about the client. After the interview, the therapist must put all the pieces together and decide whether the interviewee is a good match for the group. Clinical judgment is called upon in this task:

- Is this person motivated to change?
- Will he benefit from the learning environment of a group?
- Can he contribute to the group?
- Is he likely to bring serious management problems to the group?
- Is there a goodness of fit between this person and other candidates in terms of functioning level?

If a serious concern surfaces in the process of clinical assessment, the group therapist will need to make the difficult decision to not accept the client. A tactical explanation must be provided for the rejection.

After-Interview Contact   After the screening decisions are made, the therapist contacts the interviewees about the results of the interviews. The method of the contact (e.g., by phone or by mail) should be defined by the interviewees. If a client is accepted, the therapist may want to remind the client to review the orientation handouts. The client also should be reminded to bring the signed consent form (see Appendix B) to the first group session. If a client is not accepted, the language of the notification should be phrased in a way to reduce the person's sense of rejection. The language should sound like the group and the therapist are to blame for not having the capacity to serve the client regarding his need. If possible, a referral should be made to a resource that is more equipped to provide for the person's care.

A CASE IN POINT

After going to a pregroup orientation for a personal growth group that was recruiting prospective members, Anne (masked name) became increasingly motivated to participate in the group. She made an appointment with the leader for a screening interview for the following week. It was a brief interview, lasting around 30 minutes. Though lean, the interview did cover the essence of issues that had badgered Anne for a long time. Together, the leader and Anne developed a goal that seemed to be realistic for the short-term nature of the group. The leader, who was a counselor-in-training, mindfully took summary notes after the interview session. These notes served as an important resource for the leader to review for landmarks during the course of the group. They offered critical information about Anne's starting point and about her original problems and struggles. They reminded the leader of the issues that had brought Anne to the group in the first place. The group's work with Anne can be found in the case example in Chapter 6. Following are the summary notes the leader made after the screening interview with Anne:

Anne is a 31-year-old single woman who works in the city as a first-grade teacher. Anne's issues surround the fact that she has difficulty in forming a long-term relationship. The longest relationship she ever had was shy of six months, and that was back in high school. Anne says she generally dates two types of men: the noncommittal, and the "nice guys." She finds the noncommittal type exciting and intriguing at first—not knowing when he will call or what he's thinking. However, she soon finds that this noncommittal type has little interest in going deeper or investing in the relationship. And it eventually ends. The second type, the nice guys, Anne interprets as being needy, so she soon grows tired of their requests to see her on a regular basis. She gets downright annoyed, and the pattern is usually to shut herself off quickly. Anne states that a nurturing and kind man turns her off but that the nurturing relationship type is what she ultimately wants.

Anne said that people perceive her as always happy and at ease in any situation. She has a confident manner and is always smiling. She admits, however, to feeling insecure inside. She covers it by being a good listener. Anne does not divulge a lot of information about herself. When this was pointed out in the intake, she was able to get to the real issue: that she doesn't want people to reject her; therefore, she doesn't open up. She is able to keep her emotions in check because she never really invests much of herself in a dating relationship. This lack of emotional investment makes it easy when the relationship is broken. Anne justifies her actions by stating that she doesn't want to hurt anyone and beat around the bush by prolonging a relationship that isn't going to go anywhere.

When we look at her family history, some of Anne's behaviors become understandable. Her parent's marriage has been troubled all along. Her mother and father argued constantly while she was growing up. She has two brothers; both are much older than she is, and both are married with children. She feels closer to the second brother and talks with him often. Anne remembers a defining moment with her mother during her teen years. Because her mother and father were constantly fighting and arguing, her mother needed someone to confide in. Anne became the person her mother chose to talk to about her problems. As a result, Anne learned to be a listener instead of a person who shares her inner self. She listened to all of her mother's problems and provided the support her mom needed. However, in the process of helping, Anne did not develop the ability to communicate her own needs and wants or to share her inner thoughts and feelings.

As I (the interviewer) sat and listened to Anne, her issue became more apparent. Because she has developed such a good listening capacity, people turn to her with their problems. She is a good sounding board and listens intently and patiently to what they have to say. With this role of being a sounding board so ingrained, Anne doesn't get the opportunity to practice revealing and opening up to others. It's very difficult to develop intimacy with others when one doesn't share intimate parts of oneself. Intimacy develops from shared and mutual conversation. As Anne is not used to disclosing personal and meaningful parts of herself, intimacy becomes difficult to develop and her dating relationships thus do not endure. In addition, she feels insecure that what she has to say might not be substantial or interesting and might be rejected.

As Anne's issue became clearer, she narrowed her goal to one she felt would be very worthwhile for her. Anne stated that her goal is to practice opening up to members of the group in a personal and intimate way. This goal will allow her to experience firsthand how people respond to her when she is doing the revealing as opposed to the listening. She hopes that as she changes her behavioral pattern and the role she plays, she might be able to carry the new part of herself into her dating relationships.

SCENARIOS FOR YOUR PRACTICE

1. As you are interviewing potential group members for a general counseling group, one person blurts out that he is open to being in the same group with people having any issue except he refuses to work with anyone who is homosexual. As a group leader who abides by the American Counseling Association's *Code of Ethics and Standards of Practice,* what are some possible ways you could handle this situation? Suppose that this person claims his religion tells him to condemn and avoid homosexuals. What are appropriate possible responses?

2. Suppose a respected colleague refers to you a potential member for a general counseling group, but that person is an unrecovered alcoholic. What are your thoughts about including this type of member in a general therapy group that very likely will be focusing on such things as personal growth, unresolved grief, lingering depression, loneliness, and social anxiety?

3. As you move into the third session of a group, a member states that she overheard another member at a local restaurant recounting to friends various personal issues shared by group members. As the group leader, how would you address this issue? Would you consider it as mere "tattling" and quickly move to the agenda the members have set for the day? Would you immediately toss out the offending member? Or would you discuss the issue among the group members, and then vote on whether to remove the offending member? Might you ask the accused member to explain, and then review the issue with the group for possible responses?

4. Just after you graduate with your master's degree in counseling, you are looking for ways to earn extra income. An acquaintance offers you a chance to work with a sexual predator group for an attractive level of remuneration. However, you are informed that there will be no experienced supervisor to guide you in your work, and you have no experience in working with this type of group. What issues should you consider in deciding whether to accept this offer?

SELF-REFLECTION

1. Visualize a prospective group member who is considering entering a new group. Imagine the kinds of feelings she might have. Can you imagine the kinds of fears she might have? Would she have any general anxiety? Might she experience doubt about how she will fit in with the other group members? What actions on the part of the group and the group leader will be most helpful for her?

2. What kinds of questions do you think people have when joining a new group? Are there specific kinds of information that might help to address these questions?

3. When a member enters a new group, what might be some of his concerns about the group leader? About the other members?

4. What kinds of feelings will be most difficult for a member to share in a new group? Are these the kinds of feelings that you as a leader would want to encourage members to share with one another?

5. How does a person decide how much commitment to make to a particular group? Have you ever stayed in a group that you were unsure about at first? If so, what happened for you as a result?

6. As a group leader, what are some of your main concerns about maintaining an ethical group practice in the real world where profit and loss sometimes take center stage for administrators?

7. As a developing specialist in group leadership, what qualities might assist you in promoting ethical practice, even in situations in which you may feel yourself in a lower power position in relation to individuals who have no knowledge or understanding of group leader ethical principles?

8. In which group specialization do you have the most interest? Least interest? Why?

9. What are some ways that you might be able to increase your familiarity with each of the four group specializations?

10. What are your deepest concerns at this point about screening and selecting members who will be appropriate for a group that you intend to start?

LEADING THE FIRST SESSION

A good start is half the success of any endeavor. Then, every small dose of success breeds further success. The same principle applies to the group. The first session sets the tone for the rest of the group's course. If a sense of connection, trust, and hope are fostered in the first session, the group will be launched in a successful direction. The first session, therefore, is a crucial one in the life span of a group. If you are a group leader for the first time, this first session may prove challenging for you. You will have to make many adjustments as you change from individual counseling mode to group counseling mode. You may feel an initial "group shock" (described in Chapter 2).

This chapter presents ways to structure the first group session and areas to consider to ensure its success. It covers:

- Leadership and the forming stage
- Structure of the first session
- Leadership considerations for the first session
- Reflections on first sessions

LEADERSHIP AND THE FORMING STAGE

Five Stages of Group Development

Groups tend to move through stages during their life spans. Some group models identify four stages (Corey & Corey, 2002; Gladding, 1999), while others recognize five stages (Lacoursiere, 1980; Tuckman, 1965; Tuckman & Jensen, 1977). In this text, we adopt the five-stage model, as it corresponds more precisely with the framework and the skills that we employ.

The first stage of group development is called the initial, or *forming,* stage. This stage is characterized by setting goals and boundaries. The group very much has to depend on the leader for structure and active facilitation. The second stage, the *storming* or *transition* stage, is the time when covert and overt conflicts within the group become undercurrents that the group has to process. The third stage is called the *norming* stage; in this stage, a growing sense of cohesion develops as members start to gain confidence and take risks to work toward their goals. The fourth stage is the *working* or *performing* stage. This is the most productive time. Deepened self-disclosure, honest feedback, caring confrontation, a sense of humor, reality testing, and here-and-now intense work are most likely to happen in this stage of the group. The fifth stage is the *termination* stage, where members say good-bye to each other and prepare to move out into their own lives with a newly developed sense of competence.

Although the stages sound discrete in group development theory, in a live situation, they are rather fluid and are seldom definite or linear. One stage is often still present when the next stage comes into view. Indeed, groups are likely to recycle through the various stages as the members move through their journey. As a group recycles, it is important for the leader to guide and support it if members are to stay on course with their interpersonal learning tasks.

The Forming Stage

This chapter will focus on the *forming* stage of group development. The forming stage of a group parallels the childhood of a human life. Its features include looking forward, setting goals, a need for structure, and a dependency on the leader for active facilitation. In the forming stage, the leader's task is to provide structure to foster a sense of orientation (Lacoursiere, 1980) and to reduce anxiety about the unknown.

People often are anxious and apprehensive when attending a new group. What is the group going to be like? Who else will be in the group? What is going to be talked about? What is expected of me? All sorts of questions go through people's minds. Members in a new group must learn about the work of the group and how the group will go about accomplishing that work. In this forming stage, they especially depend upon the leader, holding an expectation that the leader will be more or less an expert on group building.

Two Keys of Group Work: The Task and the Relationship

A time-limited group has pressure to get down to business as quickly as possible. The two keys to getting down to the business of group work are task and relationship (Bales, 1953). Granted, the group is gathered to accomplish its predesigned task. The task drives the group's conscious energy. However, in their wish to cast out their sense of uncertainty and ambivalence, members in a new group are often all too ready to latch onto the task without fully realizing how to actually get there. Given this, the responsibility of the leader is to provide a structure through which members can achieve the task. Providing them with structure will make new members feel relaxed and productive.

While providing a structure within which the group can launch its task, the leader also needs to get members to forge relationships with one another in order to foster a sense of connection, trust, acceptance, and hope. This relationship aspect is the second key to group work. The leader needs to not only develop rapport with his group members, but also to facilitate cohesive relationships among members themselves. Understandably, connection among a group of relative strangers will not happen automatically. This is where group leadership skills are important. A good deal of leadership is about forging relationships among members that have a therapeutic effect for them.

The best way to apply these two keys in the first session is to have members share their problems and goals with one another. When people start to share their difficulties, issues, struggles, and the areas they desire to change, wonderful things can happen. A sense of universality (Yalom, 1995) starts to seep in as members listen to their fellow humans' struggles. Their typical sense of aloneness and isolation in the world is likely to melt away. Herein a sense of bonding starts to build. Helping members introduce their goals, therefore, should take the bulk of the first session.

The Need to Be Included

Schutz (1958) pointed out three universal individual needs that exist for all people: the need for inclusion, the need for control, and the need for affection. These needs are central in the interpersonal process and the development of groups. The need for inclusion is especially prominent in the forming stage of the group (the needs for control and affection will be addressed later in Chapters 7 through 9). Addressing the need for inclusion is the first task in the forming stage of a group. As soon as a group starts, its members need to get to know their fellow members with whom they will be in close association. To fulfill this need for inclusion, the group leader needs to create a structure that makes it easy for members to show mutual interest in one another.

On a different note, when a leader starts a group anew, his own need for inclusion will be fulfilled automatically, as he will be ushered into the very heart of the group and the members will depend, to a great deal, on his expertise as a leader. However, if a leader must enter an already intact group, his own concerns regarding "being included" may be larger than they are in a newly formed group, since he will be the "new kid on the block." Members may test him to find out if he can handle it. In these situations, the best way to respond is with openness, authenticity, a reasonable level of self-confidence, and clarity about the particular role you are playing.

Structured, Semistructured, and Nonstructured Groups

To address members' needs for inclusion, the leader needs to create, in the first session, a structure that is conducive to members showing mutual interest in one another. An exercise you can use to provide structure in the first session is called "go-around." This go-around exercise will make sure that every member is included in the sharing and will reduce the anxiety of members who otherwise might feel nervous and awkward in the new situation.

Generally speaking, an interpersonally focused process group is unstructured or at most semistructured. A group with minimum structure is known for its power: The lack of structure creates enough ambiguity to allow members' interpersonal styles to manifest themselves. The interpersonal styles and patterns, when emerging, become the grist for the mill of group work. However, the first session must be an exception. The first session needs a lot of *structure* so the group will begin on good terms with the *task*-related aspect (Hetzel, Barton, & Davenport, 1994).

Starting with the second session, an experiential group will take on a style of minimal structure so as to allow maximum room for members' interpersonal styles to emerge. Taking turns and predetermined topics or structured exercises are best not relied on as crutches, although the opening and the closing of each session are exceptions to this rule. The opening and closing structure provides a bridge into and out of the intensity of interpersonal interaction that occurs in the session.

STRUCTURE OF THE FIRST SESSION

The structure of the first session may follow this sequence: (1) welcoming and names; (2) breaking the ice; (3) introducing members' personal goals; (4) summarizing members' goals in terms of common themes; (5) discussing emerging group ownership issues; (6) wrapping up the first session; and (7) giving reminders. This is just a suggested structure; you may tailor it to best suit your group's needs and conditions. Following are the details of this structure.

Welcoming and Names

Welcome the group in a warm and professional manner. For example,

> Hi, everybody! Welcome to our first group session! I'm glad that every-
> one made it here tonight. We have about 90 minutes together. During
> this time we'll start learning a little bit about one another. Since I know
> all your names, but you haven't met one another yet, let's go around
> and use our names and one sentence or so to introduce ourselves.

Breaking the Ice

People often come to a new group with mixed feelings. If not expressed,
these feelings may detract from their mental presence in the group. As a
principle, expressing feelings of the present moment can serve as an ice
breaker. In this ice-breaking exercise, which requires five to ten minutes
to complete, you may ask members to have a go-around using a few sentences to describe the feelings they have about coming to this new group.
You may say,

> Thank you for sharing your names. Before we start our first session,
> maybe it will be helpful for all of us to share where we are and how we
> feel at this moment. Whether or not this is the first group experience
> for you, most of you carry mixed feelings about coming to the first ses-
> sion. Your feelings, whatever they are, are important to share. We may
> spend 5 to 10 minutes doing this. So let's have a quick go-around,
> where I would like the group to respond to this question: *What emo-*
> *tions are you experiencing at this moment? I will begin with myself,*
> *then we'll continue from this direction."* (with hand gesture)

It will not be surprising if the issue of confidentiality comes up as the
immediate concern. Should a member address this concern, the leader
may simply acknowledge his feelings and facilitate the group to discuss
this issue:

> So Judy, it sounds as though you're worried that what you say in the
> group may get passed to others outside the group. This certainly will
> make you feel unsafe. [Turning to the group] At this moment, I would
> like the group to talk a bit about where each of you stands on the issue
> of confidentiality and what each of you is willing to do to protect the
> others' right of confidentiality.

When the issue is exhausted, the leader may say,

> Where are we on the subject of confidentiality? Can we move on now?

To go back to complete the ice-breaking exercise, you may say,

> Now, we all seem to be on the same page regarding confidentiality. I
> would like to go back to the question of how you feel about being in
> the group. Who is next?

After this ice-breaking exercise, leaders can summarize the common feelings to forge a sense of universality:

> It sounds like most of you feel excited about the group, and some of
> you feel ambivalent about what challenges might be ahead of you.

This ice-breaking exercise not only addresses the immediacy in the group, but also forges the beginning of group cohesiveness. As one leader reflected, "I found that through the initial disclosure of feelings by everyone, we had begun a bonding process."

Introducing Goals

The most important task of the first session is for members to introduce their personal goals. To ensure the success of the first session, leaders need to use the bulk of the session on this task. Although the leader has previously interviewed each individual member and learned of her goals, other members in the group do not know what their fellow members are in group to work on. Without knowing the others' goals, members cannot help one another in future sessions. The most important task in the first session, therefore, is to introduce the goals that members want to achieve by the end of the group experience.

It might have seemed easy for the leader to help a member narrow down his goal in the screening interview. In that one-to-one screening interview, the setting was relaxing and more conducive for self-disclosure. However, that relaxing comfort level can disappear into the thin air in the first group session. Feeling overwhelmed at the presence of a roomful of strangers, many new members have difficulty sharing the goals that they had articulated so well in the screening interview. They may become vague and elusive in their sharing. They may want to retreat to a safe corner with as little self exposed as possible. This presents a challenge for the leader in the first session.

To reduce anxiety, you can again use the go-around format for the task of goal introduction. Be cautious in choosing who will start the go-around, though, because the first person sets the tone for the rest of the group. If the first person in the go-around is emotionally open in sharing her issues and goals, the rest of the group will follow suit. If she is emotionally blocked or superficial, however, you will find the group fumbling through a big portion of the first session. So, try to recall, from your memory of the screening interview, who is the most open and aware person, then invite that person to start the go-around.

To initiate the goal introduction, you may say:

> We have 70 minutes left for today's session. During this time, I would
> like for each of you to introduce your personal goal in the group.
> [pause] Since we have 8 members in the group, each member will

take about 8 minutes, give or take a few minutes. [pause] Although each of you discussed your goal with me in the interview, other group members haven't had a chance to learn about it. As we only have 12 sessions for our group, it is important that everybody knows the others' goals so that you can best help one another achieve those goals. [pause] Therefore, I would like each of you to respond to these three questions: *First, what is the issue you want to work on? Second, if this issue is not worked through, what do you predict will be the possible negative consequence? And third, what improvement would you like to set as your goal at the end of the group?* Let's start with Jeff and then go this direction. [indicating the direction]

Again, make sure that the person you choose to start the go-around is emotionally open in sharing his issues and goals.

Four Tasks of Goal Introduction

When a member introduces his goal, the group task is to (a) help the member present the issues, (b) help the member shape up the goal, (c) maximize group interaction with the member, and (d) steer away from problem solving and rescuing. Following are the specifics of these four tasks of goal introduction.

Presenting the Issues   The first task of goal introduction is problem presentation. Goals can best be understood when we know the issues and problems in which the goals are embedded. Therefore, you want to invite each speaking member to first present the issues that are behind her goal so that other members understand why the goal is so important.

Some uncomfortable situations can arise unexpectedly. Some members may hold back a lot of information due to the anxiety of exposing personal information in front of the group. Fear of exposure leads them to present themselves in a way that is impersonal. At the same time, the rest of the group may feel inhibited, not knowing how freely they can interact with one another. This can be especially true of those individuals with cultural and familial experiences that discourage them from sharing personal information outside their own family. These scenarios are common challenges in the first session. A leader needs to be equipped with sufficient basic facilitative skills to handle these situations. These facilitative skills will be presented in Chapter 5.

When a member introduces her goal, both the leader and the group can help the member describe more fully what the issues are by asking:

Would you like to tell us a bit about where this issue came from?

What have you tried that did not work?

How has this problem been influencing your life or relationships?

"If change doesn't happen, what will be the consequences?

Shaping up the Goal The second task in goal introduction is to help members shape up their goals. It cannot be stressed enough that successful group work is possible only when members start with clearly defined goals (Haley, 1976). As stated in the previous chapter, goals are a basis for human motivation—goals direct our behaviors. To be conducive for client change, goals must be defined in such a way that other members can clearly see whether or not the goals have been achieved at the end (Barker, 1985). Goals must be shaped up to be meaningful, specific, and at a moderate level of difficulty to achieve. That is, they must be challenging, yet realistic and reachable within the life span of the group.

Setting goals in this manner helps members create a vision—a clear and concrete picture of intended results—that is understood by the whole group. If the vision is clear enough, it can chart the course, perk up commitment, and produce a needed momentum for the image to become a reality. Given this, leaders strive to facilitate the group to help one another shape up goals that are workable and challenging. If group members do not know how to do that, this responsibility falls on the shoulders of the leader. Members will take their cues from the leader and assist one another in setting clearer goals.

Looking back on his group experience, one member, who originally had difficulty in setting a personal goal for himself, realized the virtues of goal setting. He wrote:

> I have found the group experience to be compassionate and fun rather than confrontational or intrusive, as I had previously feared. Certainly this is due to the emphasis on empathy and respect and my fellow members being so sincere, forthcoming, committed, and generous. But most importantly, the whole idea of "having a purpose—a personal goal" is the key that accounts for this success of the group. I think that there is a lesson in this goal-setting thing in the group—even in life. If you have a purpose, a stated goal, your personal experience is transformed.

Two skills are involved in helping members shape their goals: The leader must help members define their goals in (1) positive terms, and (2) behavioral and visible terms.

DEFINING GOALS IN POSITIVE TERMS To make their goals reachable, members need to define their goals in positive terms, rather than in negative terms. According to Barker (1985), "many people come to therapy with negative goals. They want to feel less depressed, or to stop eating so much, or to stop smoking. Or they want their children to stop fighting, or their teenage daughter to stop refusing to eat the food they provide. These are all good reasons for seeking professional help, but they are not adequate as outcome frames" (p. 67). A description of the goals "requires more than a statement of what you *do not* want to be happening"; rather, it is critical to get "a comprehensive picture of how you *do* want things to be" (p. 67). To help a member define her goal in positive language, you may ask,

If you don't want to feel depressed, how do you want to feel?

What will replace smoking (or eating) in your life?

What will your children be doing instead if they are not fighting?

DEFINING GOALS IN BEHAVIORAL AND VISIBLE TERMS   Even when members' goals are stated in positive terms, frequently they are vague and ill-defined. For example, clients may say that they want to "feel happier," "have more energy," or "be able to decide what I want to do with my life." Barker (1985) pointed out: "Such statements are all right as starting points for the discussion of treatment goals, but they are not in themselves adequate outcome frames. What does 'feel happier' mean? Happier than what or who? Under what circumstances does the person want to feel happier? How will the client and the therapist know that the desired degree of happiness has been achieved?" (p. 68). So it is important to get the member to describe, as much in behavioral terms as possible, what things will be like when his goal is successfully achieved.

For example, to the member who says he or she wants to feel happier, the leader may ask:

When you feel happier, what will you be doing exactly?

When you have more energy, how will you act differently from how you act today?

What will you be doing differently when you reach your goal?

When you know what you want to do with your life, what will your life be like?

How will we be able to see that you are reaching your goal?

Group Interaction   The third task in goal introduction is to maximize group interaction. The power of group lies in group interaction. Without interaction, a session will soon turn disinteresting and lifeless. To make the first group session an engaging, interesting, and bonding experience for members, the leaders need to facilitate as much group interaction as possible. Usually members in the first session do not know what is expected of them when they listen to others introducing their issues and goals. The leader can facilitate interaction by encouraging the group to give comments or ask clarifying questions spontaneously. The leader may say,

I want to remind the group that while one member is introducing his issue and goal, the rest of the group can feel free to make supportive comments, to acknowledge his feelings, or to ask him clarifying questions. You don't need to get permission from the leaders. Is this clear to everyone?

If members still do not feel free enough to chime in with comments and questions, the leader can draw out group interaction by asking the group:

> Do any of you have any clarifying questions that you would like to ask of Julie?
>
> Do you all understand what Joe is trying to say?
>
> Do any of you get the point that Mary is trying to get across?
>
> Can any of you restate what Joe is trying to work on?

Talking about one's issues in front of a roomful of people can be nerve-wracking. Therefore, it is especially comforting to hear others disclose similar concerns. When the speaking member feels that she is not alone and sees that others share similar dilemmas and experiences, a sense of trust and bonding will naturally build. This is the therapeutic factor of universality in action. To develop this norm of sharing commonalities, the leader may elicit common experiences from the rest of the group by saying,

> Do any of you have similar struggles in your own experiences?
>
> Who else in here has similar concerns?

If a member is skeptical or resistant in sharing, do not work too hard in the first session to draw him out. Give him time to watch and observe the group until he feels comfortable enough to get his feet wet.

Steering away from Problem Solving and Rescuing   The last task in goal introduction is to steer the group away from problem solving and rescuing behaviors. People often feel compelled to give reassurance, offer advice, or problem-solve upon hearing about others' problems, as though they are afraid of appearing indifferent if they failed to do so. In a new group, members are highly likely to exhibit this zeal to help by jumping in to offer reassurances, and even advice.

For example, suppose a new group member, Katie, expresses concern that her brother might be drafted and says she is worried about his safety. As she continues speaking about the subject, she becomes visibly upset. Another group member, Julie, feels compelled to rescue her by saying, "I don't think the war will happen. The danger is not that great, so you don't need to be worried." Even though Julie's reassurance is given with the best of intentions, it has the effect of dismissing or discounting Katie's fears. Interestingly, this is exactly the response that Katie has been getting from her father and her friends—a response that negates her feelings as illogical. With redirection, the leader can interrupt this rescuing behavior and prevent it from cascading. The leader may redirect by saying one of the following:

> I wonder, do any of you understand what makes this event so difficult for Katie?
>
> Katie, how would you like the group to be helpful for you?

Upon hearing the second prompt, Katie expresses a desire to work on giving herself permission to experience her own feelings more fully because she often suppresses them. This becomes her goal within the group.

From a member's perspective, the experience of being rescued and reassured will hardly make her feel good. It is validation of her pain that will offer the support she needs. Here is another example: A new member, Judy, shared her painful experience of breaking up three months previously with her boyfriend of five years. She appeared teary-eyed as she talked about how she had never been met with this type of rejection in a relationship before. She wanted to come to terms with the breakup and be able to move past it. Job, in trying to make her feel less pain from the breakup, said, "It is just part of life. Everyone experiences it." After the session, Judy reflected in her journal:

> When it was my turn to introduce my issue and goal, I announced my issue and felt somewhat belittled or insignificant when Job said that my issue was "just part of life" and that "everyone experiences it." Even though I knew Job was trying to make my issue seem normal so that I don't feel rejected for being "dumped" (how he referred to it), I felt as if I shouldn't have admitted feeling so bad for the breakup because "breakups are normal and happen to everyone." Ken, however, kept saying that "it's hard" and acknowledged that "it must have affected all the other areas of your life," which made me feel like he understood why this was such a painful issue for me.

Clearly, members are able to judge by their own reactions whether particular kinds of responses are truly altruistic in nature, or whether what is communicated is something not for another member's benefit after all.

Summarizing Members' Common Themes

After all group members have introduced their personal goals, the leader may want to summarize the common themes emerging among members' issues and goals. This can foster a sense of bonding for the members. For example:

> Thank you, everyone, for sharing your personal issues and goals with one another. From what you have said, I sense that a lot of you in this group share a common desire to work on some unresolved issues from the past so that you can live more fully in your present relationships. Are there any other themes that you noticed as well?

Discussing Emerging Group Ownership Issues

Frequently, time is too short in the first session to discuss group rules. It may take many sessions for the group to make their own rules. But if any issues related to group ownership emerge, the leader may want to give some time for the group to come to an agreement about those issues. Typically, the collective issues that concern group members may include:

- Confidentiality
- Attendance
- Tardiness
- Smoking and eating in the session
- Recording
- Socializing outside of the group with other members
- Getting involved intimately with other members
- Members' rights and responsibilities

You may summarize the discussion, if any, by saying,

> These issues we've just discussed are very important for all of us. Since the group is what we create it to be, I would like for us to continue to address these issues as they emerge.

The leader should remind the group that it could take a few weeks for the group to complete the list of rules and encourage them to feel free to continue adding to the list any rules they consider important so as to ensure their sense of boundary and safety.

Wrapping Up

Successfully closing the session is an important leadership skill. A quick go-around provides an opportunity for each member to express her experience of this first, usually exciting but apprehension-producing, group session. The leader may say,

> We have 5 minutes left for today. Before we leave, I would like to have a quick go-around and have each of you share how you are feeling at the end of today's session. How about starting with Katie, and then going around this way.

The leader may also include his own response in this final go-around:

> I feel very good about our first meeting. My respect goes to all of you who have taken a lot of risks today to let others know about your issues and your goals. And I am impressed by the vastly different experiences that members bring to this group.

Reminders

A reminder can serve as a guidepost, giving members a sense of how to prepare themselves for the following sessions.

> Thank you, everybody, for all the hard work today. Before we leave, I just want to remind you that beginning next week, we will spend considerable time in each session helping members work on their identified

struggles and goals. I would like to encourage you to take some time *during the week* to think about the issues you would like to present in detail in our next session. Okay, have a wonderful week!

LEADERSHIP CONSIDERATIONS FOR THE FIRST SESSION

To ensure the success of the first session, the therapist should give attention to the following considerations.

Avoiding In-Depth Therapy in the First Session

The first session is not the time to jump in to do "in-depth" therapy. This means the therapist should avoid spending an extended length of time, for example, more than 15 minutes, focusing on one single member, digging into the deeply rooted issues. It might be tempting to jump in to explore what is behind the tears when a member is visibly distressed or tearful as she shares her issues and goals. However, most members are not ready for this type of in-depth work during the first session. This is not to mean that the session should stay shallow and superficial. Just the opposite is the case: the first session must be made as engaging and interesting as possible, and bonding among group members should be encouraged. But exposing members to in-depth therapy too early, in the first session, can actually frighten them away. The fear of exposure can be illustrated by a member's reflection:

> Although I'd heard about how powerful group sessions have the potential to be, I was not expecting my own reaction to the event to be so strong. I was the last one to introduce my goal. I surprised myself by starting to cry almost immediately after I started talking about my goal in the group. I was, of course, aware that this was a painful issue for me to talk about, but honestly I didn't think that I'd break down this way and during the first session, no less! I have to admit I felt pretty embarrassed by my outpouring of emotion. I felt extremely vulnerable and naked in front of a roomful of group members. Although I trust some of them, I still felt really exposed and kind of silly and overly dramatic.

As illustrated by this reflection, one can feel rather vulnerable when exposing difficult emotions, especially when a deep trust has not been established in the group. If a member is visibly distressed when introducing her issues and goal, the leader can simply acknowledge her feelings and provide a sense of direction:

> Amelia, I can sense how hurt you feel to be so rejected by your own parents. The group is an excellent place to explore such issues. Maybe

you can spend some time working on this issue in future sessions when you're ready.

If a member is already in tears, you might reduce her sense of embarrassment by saying,

> Tracy, it is totally okay to cry. We all have these moments. Please take your time to stay with your feelings for a moment. We are in no rush.

After this, proceed to acknowledge her feelings and provide a sense of direction, as shown in the previous example.

Explaining Ground Rules as Situations Arise

The leader should not wait until the end of the session to discuss ground rules for the group. Rather, the rules should be addressed as situations arise. If the leader lets undesirable behaviors become entrenched in a group, they will become difficult to change. When ground rules are established in due time with all members' consent, they are more likely to be followed in the later sessions. For example, if during the ice-breaking exercise, a member reveals apprehension about confrontation, you might want to take the opportunity to address the ground rule of confrontation:

> [To the whole group] What Jamie addressed is an important concern. I would like to comment on that. I would like our group to establish a ground rule that no one is allowed to attack another member. We are here to learn from one another, not to attack those who differ from us. How do all of you feel about having that as a group rule?

If a member brings up a concern of trust, you may take this opportunity to address the ground rule of trust:

> Ken, thank you for mentioning this; it is a legitimate concern. [Turning to the group] Before anyone starts to share something personal, I want to emphasize the rule of confidentiality that we briefly discussed earlier. If we want to build a group where everybody can trust one another and feel safe, it is imperative that we keep confidential the personal sharing within our group. Can everyone commit to this rule?

If members ask about whether or not they can share what goes on in the group with a significant other, you may use this opportunity to educate them:

> I see a difference between sharing with your significant others about what you are working on in the group and talking to them about what your fellow members are working on. Keeping confidentiality means that you don't share any group member's information with any outsiders. How does the rest of the group see this issue?

Goals and Issues Must Go Hand-in-Hand

During goal introduction, it will be productive to invite members to put their goals in the context of interpersonal issues. The group must understand what each speaking member's issues or struggles are in order to help one another change. In other words, the goal must be an offshoot of an embedded issue. Without knowing what the issues are, attempts to understand the goal are like trying to see an entire picture in a puzzle with missing pieces. Goals must be understood in light of the issues underlying them. For example, a member who was being very short in her goal introduction said, "I want to learn to be more emotionally open with others." Then she stopped. The group tried to probe for more details but got only fragmented answers. At this juncture, the leader asked,

> Would you tell us what makes this goal so important at this stage of your life?
>
> What issues in your life are the background of this goal?

Such questions are not for the purpose of doing "in-depth" therapy, but rather are aimed at getting a clear picture of the issues within which the goal is embedded.

Time Management

Time management within group sessions proves to be a challenge for new leaders. Sometimes they overdo an activity, leaving the group rushed to finish its more important sharing. For example, a new leader might use an extensive ice-breaking activity that leaves insufficient time for goal introduction, which is the major task of the first session.

Another difficulty in time management for new leaders is that they may not feel comfortable redirecting the flow of group interaction and may instead let some members ramble on and on, without getting to relevant points. The failure to intervene by the leader can result in precious group time being wasted. The facilitating skills presented in Chapter 5 should help leaders increase their capacity to redirect the group toward more productive interaction. If, in the first session, a member starts to ramble and tell his stories, the leader can simply acknowledge his issue and redirect the group interaction:

> John, it seems like a complicated situation; I hope you will bring it up again in a future session so the group can help you. [turning to the group] Before we move on to the next member, I want to make sure that everyone understands what John's goal is. Could anyone summarize what John wants to achieve in the group?

Being Active and Directive

In individual counseling, the therapist can afford to be nondirective and take time to build rapport with her clients. In group counseling and therapy, however, the therapist needs to be more active and directive. You need to use a lot of facilitating skills to make the group interact. If you forget to facilitate group interaction, members' interest may soon fade. And whenever situations come up, the leader needs to intervene quickly. If you wait, the interactions will have moved rapidly forward, and the moment for proper intervention will be lost.

Promoting Group Interaction

Promoting interaction among members is one of the most important responsibilities of group leaders, especially in the early stages of group development. The leader should promote group interaction by inviting members to freely comment or clarify as they participate. Turn-taking and silence are common obstacles to group interaction. Therefore, you should not let the group slip into a habit of taking turns to talk. Encourage the group to spontaneously interact. The only time when the group takes turns to talk is when the leader uses a go-around as an exercise, especially for the purpose of efficiently opening or closing a session. At other times, the group will function better with no turn-taking. In the first session, the leader can spell out this expectation of spontaneous interaction before members introduce their goals:

> After one member introduces his or her goal, I would like the rest of you to feel free to jump in to relate, to empathize, to make a comment, or to ask a clarifying question. I hope you interact spontaneously with the speaking member without first seeking my approval.

Linking Similar Experiences

Yalom (1995) points out that most people experience a basic sense of inadequacy, a deep concern about sense of worth, a sense of interpersonal isolation, or a concern about their ability to relate to others. But most of them come to group thinking that they are the only ones who experience this distress. This sense of aloneness increases their social isolation. It is healing to hear other members disclose concerns similar to one's own—to discover that one is not alone and that others share similar dilemmas and experiences. Members experience a sense of relief and a lift in their spirits when they realize that "we are all human." To create an environment for this healing effect, the leader can solicit members to share similar experiences. To do this, the leader may say,

> Would anyone like to share any reaction or experience similar to what Tracy just shared?

To create the environment of we-are-all-human, the leader also can summarize the similarities of members' experiences every now and then:

> It seems that many members in our group experience a similar fear of losing a loved one.
>
> There is a real theme in this group of feeling unimportant in your life.
>
> I am hearing how people in the group want to feel more powerful and important. And I also hear Chris talking about wanting to be more real.

Watching How Members Are Responding

In group sessions, the leaders should avoid making constant eye contact with the member who is speaking. If the leader maintains steady eye contact with the speaking member, as a therapist usually does in individual counseling, she will encourage that member to speak to her, and not to the group. This can easily turn the conversation into one-to-one individual counseling. To avoid falling into this pattern, the leader should move her eyes slowly around the room, taking note of how other members are reacting to the speaking member, and noticing what their body language is saying while they are listening. People's body language tells more about them than their verbal language.

When the leader notices a consistent body language in any member, she can use it as a cue to invite that member to share what he is responding to:

> Mike, you look touched by what Sue just said. Would you like to share a few words with Sue?

Being Sensitive to Multicultural Dimensions

The background experiences that group members bring to the group will greatly influence the participation and response patterns within the group. Multicultural dimensions that exist in the group often include culture, ethnicity, language, gender, socioeconomic status, and the particulars of family life. These dimensions will affect members' willingness to disclose, response to conflict, and openness to differences.

For a group to be effective, members need to be able to appreciate similarities and accept differences so that they all feel included (Conyne, 1998). The leader can model the norm of celebrating cultural differences by saying,

[To the entire group] Now that we've heard a bit from all of you in the group, I can tell you that I'm seeing some similarities in what you're wanting to do. I'm also very excited about the potential for us to learn from the variety of experiences and cultural backgrounds that all of you are bringing to the group.

Minority group members may not receive the same degree of inclusion as majority group members (Barker et al., 2000). As a result, their experiences of the group may be less satisfying. Given this possibility, group leaders must be aware that members may treat one another in ways that are less than conducive to creating a trusting group environment. If you have minority members in the group, you may make the following statement to create a group that will be more inclusive for them:

[To the entire group] I'm aware that many of us have had too few opportunities in the past to share experiences with people of different cultural backgrounds and experiences. In this group we are now presented with great opportunities to do so. I hope that we will find many similarities in our basic human needs, and I hope that the variety of perspectives will offer us a richer array of options for understanding and addressing our life issues.

Sitting the Group in a Circle

People feel more relaxed about talking when they are sitting around a small circle, and thus able to see each member of the group. Before the session, leaders should arrange the chairs in a way that will put no three members in a straight line. If members are sitting in a straight line, they will not be able to see one another. Groups are of many different sizes. While some psychoeducational groups involve dozens or even hundreds of members, experientially oriented groups are primarily small groups. A small group offers advantages that are pivotal to interpersonal learning. Sitting in a small-group circle, members can see and observe one another, which builds a sense of cohesiveness as the group matures.

For most cultures, the circle is a symbol of wholeness, completeness, and fulfillment. Native-American cultures often regard the circle as a sacred place, capable of holding all the divergent elements of life. In a similar way, Tibetan and Hindu cultures identify the mandala as a sacred circle in art, able to simultaneously depict multiple aspects of wisdom. These qualities that the symbol of the circle represents are part of the nature of an experientially focused group (Arrien, 1992; Mullin & Weber, 1996; Neihardt, 1959).

REFLECTIONS ON THE FIRST SESSION

New leaders may benefit from reading about real group experiences as described by the people who had the experiences. This section offers reflections on first session experiences from both members' and leaders' points of view. All names are fictitious.

Reflection One: Louise

After the first session, Louise reflected:

> I went into the first session thinking this process would be easy, especially after having worked on my issues in individual counseling. I now know that the hurt surrounding my issue with my family is far from over, and continues to live just below the surface. I surprised myself when some emotion started creeping in as I described the issues surrounding my goal. What surprised me most was my ability to identify with something each member said when describing their issues; I was able to connect to some aspect of each and every person's issue. . . . After the first session, I feel positive and optimistic. I really trust everyone in our group and feel a sense of security. I left the session feeling that each member has the best interests of the group at heart. But I am also realistic, knowing that it is inevitable that conflict will arise, but I am very interested and curious to see what will develop as we begin to challenge one another to work and delve deeper into our core issues.

Following is the leader's reflection regarding the part shared by Louise:

> Louise's goal is to gain a means of not relying on approval from others. I was touched by her openness about her struggles with her feelings concerning her father not showing the slightest trace of approval to her accomplishment in life. The group seemed to understand what she was dealing with. After some group interaction and clarification, Louise's goal seemed to change to achieving inner approval instead of from others. Emotion swelled in her as this notion of inner approval struck a chord in her and she seemed to make a valuable connection. As I looked around the room, I noticed that many members had a pensive look on their faces and nodded their heads as if in agreement to Louise's restated goal.

Reflection Two: Karen

Here is a first session reflection by a group member named Karen:

> The first session for me was very intense and scary. I started out feeling that no one would be able to relate to anything I was going through. This was the first time in my life that I ever had a chance to sit down

and talk about things that were happening in my life. I was very nervous and a little apprehensive about talking. My mind was racing with thoughts of how the group would react to the things I would say and of their views of me after I spoke. But when Louise began speaking, I found myself really in tune to what she was saying. My thoughts were, "finally, someone is having similar issues and goals as me." When it was my turn to speak, I became very nervous. But as I started talking, I tried to observe everyone's reactions and nonverbal expressions. The group's responses were making it easier to express myself. My goal is to have the ability to find someone in my life that I can talk to and feel comfortable when talking to that person. I want to be able to trust that individual. After I finished introducing my goal, I thought this was the first step in me developing trust in myself to develop trust within the group. . . . Even though this is my first group session, I felt a sort of peace, sitting listening, learning, and observing the group of relative strangers who I will be interacting with for the next 11 weeks. I have to give positive recognition to the leader of the group for setting the tone and keeping the interaction flowing.

The leader's reflection regarding this particular member was as follows:

Karen spoke cautiously as she revealed to the group that her goal was to gain trust from others. I sensed that she had been hurt many times by people she placed her trust in. Knowing this made me feel even more privileged that she was able to open up and trust in the group. This was a step she took which demonstrated her strength of character despite the wounds and hardships that she had to go through. She admits that she began building walls around self to protect her feelings ever since she realized, as a child, that her mother would never be there emotionally to support her. The group listened quietly and I wondered if they ever had to deal with this type of mistrust before. I also wondered if this first session gave enough "water" for Karen to test her trust in us? Nonetheless, this first session is a good beginning. It allowed the members to share a glimpse of their lives with one another. I believe that a small increment of trust gained from this session will create a bond among members that will continue to strengthen and grow throughout further sessions.

SCENARIOS FOR YOUR PRACTICE

1. It is the first session of a personal growth group. As the group leader, you've invited all the members to share their identified goals for the group. Lou, Sally, and Bill offer fairly focused behavioral changes that they want to work on during the group. When it comes time for Sue to speak, she begins very slowly, "Well, when I was six I had to go live

with my grandmother for two years while my parents divorced and my mom found a good job. . . ." For another ten minutes, Sue continues to describe her painful feelings at age six about this experience. What would be a helpful response that you could make at this stage?

2. After you have explained the group ground rules to everyone and each person has identified a goal for the newly beginning group, Jared comments to Alphie, "I think that everyone in the group has identified a solid goal except you. Your goal is silly." How might you respond as a group leader who wants to set useful and effective norms for the group?

3. In the first session of a new group, after each of the members has identified a goal for the group, Curtis asks you directly, "I hope that you will be instructing us just what to do. I can't see much benefit in following a policy of 'letting the blind lead the blind.'" What are some possible responses for the group leader?

4. Mary states that she felt reluctance to come to the group, but that her husband Phil encouraged her to come because "he feels that I will learn to better fulfill my duty. In fact, Phil said that he would call the leader from time to time to make sure that these matters receive enough attention." What aspects of this statement would you want to address? Why? What would you say?

5. Sylvia says she learned of this group through her individual counselor who encouraged her to come to the group. She says that she doesn't understand how a group is going to help her, because she is a shy person. How might you want to speak to Sylvia to help her find a way to work within the group?

SELF-REFLECTION

1. What are your personal experiences concerning the issue of inclusion? What would you do to make every member feel included? What would you do with members who seem to be shy?

2. As a group leader, you are responsible for screening potential members to determine which ones would be appropriate for a particular group. As an interviewer, perhaps you won't have the same level or type of anxiety as the prospective members who are interviewed. How might you stay in touch with and be sensitive to their anxiety and need for inclusion within the group?

3. There are times when you may enter an already established group as the "outsider" to lead or consult with the group. How do you envision working through your own need for inclusion and other expecta-

tions with a group that could be mistrustful or even hostile, depending on the circumstances? Perhaps your coming into the group may even represent some threat to the established roles and feeling of inclusion for current group members. How might you sensitize yourself to the underlying concerns that members may have about your presence in the group?

4. Think back to some recent time when you've set goals for yourself. What was helpful for you in clarifying those goals? How did you find resources that assisted you in clarifying your goals?

5. For goals that you've been able to attain in recent years, what factors do you think contributed most to your success in reaching those goals? Support from others? Sheer perseverance? Wise plan of action?

6. What principal emotions tend to be stirred in you upon entering a new group? What thoughts tend to accompany these emotions? How do you react to these thoughts and emotions? Do you act or react in certain ways in order to deal with any discomfort?

FACILITATING, OPENING, AND CLOSING

The Foundation of Group Skills

Before getting into the essence of group work, which is to help members work through their issues and goals, in the next chapter, we will focus on the leader's need to be equipped with a foundation of group skills. The foundation of group skills is what most group workers know as "facilitating skills." Facilitation refers to the art of helping people communicate more easily. Without facilitation from the leader, a group may fall into states of turn-taking, silence, one-to-one conversation, boredom, frustration, or dominance by a few members. Facilitating skills enable a leader to get the group members actively engaged with one another. These skills get the group going. Regardless of the type of group involved, a leader must be equipped with these skills before she walks into the group. Without them, she might find herself unsuited to lead the group and overwhelmed by the group's complex and ever-in-a-state-of-flux characteristics. This phenomenon, as we discussed previously, is called group shock (Zaslav, 1988).

Some neophyte leaders cope with group shock by addressing each individual member, using their favorite individual counseling techniques such as probing, reflection of feelings, paraphrasing, and interpreting. This coping mechanism might reduce new leaders' own anxiety as they stay within their comfort zone, but it inevitably results in a series of leader-to-member or member-to-leader dyads that resemble a matrix of individual counseling. Although each member is actively engaged with the leader, the combination of a series of dyads is itself, unfortunately, not group counseling, because it robs the group of the member-to-member interaction that is so essential for group counseling. This coping strategy tends to create a group atmosphere that is detached, lethargic, or intellectualized.

The best way to minimize the group shock experience and maximize group energy is for a leader to master facilitating skills. This chapter presents these skills. It covers:

- Leader as observer-participant
- Skills of facilitating group interaction
- Skills of opening a group session
- Skills of closing a group session
- Using structured exercises with precaution

LEADER AS OBSERVER-PARTICIPANT

The most basic facilitating skill a leader needs to develop is being in the role of both a group participant and a group process observer. Indeed, Yalom (1995) calls the group leader an "observer-participant in the group" (p. 140). This dual role may sound demanding, but with time and practice, it becomes natural and allows the leader to be the best of who she is in the group. In the following text, we explain this dual role and process.

Leader as Observer

In conducting the group, the leader often needs to step back and observe the group dynamics and interpersonal process. She must be the process observer. When you step back a bit, you observe the relationship dynamics that are unfolding at the moment. You observe how one member is having difficulty in owning up to his own feelings by talking abstractly. You notice that another member feels compelled to rescue any member who is getting in touch with deep pain. You see how yet another member becomes defensive when challenged by the group. And so it continues. You observe all the relational dynamics that are going on when members are interacting with each other. The patterns you witness then become the data that guide you to intervene and facilitate.

This role of observer—of stepping back, observing, facilitating, and intervening—requires a great deal of mental alertness and clinical objectivity on the part of the group therapist. It requires you to "squirm loose" whenever you find yourself "hooked" or sucked in by members' interpersonal pulls. Unhooking yourself is imperative if you are to effectively facilitate the group and get to the heart of the issues at hand.

Leader as Participant

In the midst of process observation and facilitation, the leader also needs to participate in whatever activities she directs the group to do. If you ask the group to make a wild guess at what feelings a specific member, say Tracy, is experiencing, then you also need to participate in getting into

Tracy's inner world, sensing what she might be feeling, and then verbally conveying that understanding to Tracy. If you ask the group to disclose their reactions toward a particular member, say Jose, then you need to disclose your feelings toward Jose as well. If you want the group members to share their observations of Jose's behavioral pattern, then you also must participate and give your feedback to Jose. You need to be a participant as well as an observer. By doing so, your warmth, understanding, and insight will radiate to the group members. You are part of the group!

Group-Centered Leadership

Some beginning group leaders forget to be participants as well as facilitators. They do all the facilitating and intervening activities but forget to engage themselves in the process. They have no problem with drawing out responses from members, but they tend to shy away from joining in the action. The result is a group leader who seems remote and separate from the rest of the group.

To balance the dual process of leadership, a group therapist might want to follow this principle: Facilitate and have group members contribute first, and then participate yourself. You want to give members a chance to contribute first because you want the group to experience the power of altruism by giving something to one another—you want to have a "group-centered" session. Once the members have shared their contributions, then you as a leader can join in to give empathy, understanding, reactions, insight, or whatever is missing from the group contribution. You are both a participant and a process observer.

When new leaders immediately engage a group in dialogue without giving the members time to share first, the session becomes "leader-centered" or "leader-dominated" and regresses to a form of individual counseling. In this situation, the power of interpersonal learning that a group has to offer is lost. To avoid this, the leader must facilitate first, and then participate.

THE SKILLS OF FACILITATING GROUP INTERACTION

The power of a group comes from member interaction, in terms of both quantity and quality. Hearing alone is not enough. Member-to-member dialogue must follow. Since the group itself is a living organism, its communication flow resembles a network wherein every component has a way to communicate with the others. The networked system must be highly interactive.

An elementary task of the leader is to "host" the member-to-member conversations and nurture member-to-member dialogues. The following text presents the skills needed to facilitate group interaction.

Simple Acknowledgment

Simple acknowledgment serves as a sort of group lubricant, helping to move things along. When a member finishes speaking or a leader wishes to stop a member's talking without being abrupt, the leader may simply say,

> Thank you!
> All right!

Observing Group Reactions

As an observer-participant, the leader cannot afford to fixate her eye contact on a speaking member. Rather, the leader must slowly glance around the room to observe the reactions of the other members when one member is speaking. This does not mean you avoid eye contact with the member who is speaking. Rather, you establish adequate eye contact and rapport with the speaking member first, and then slowly scan the room, coming back to make eye contact with the speaking member now and then. Maintain a view of the room that is as broad as possible. Observe everything curiously, and at the same time, stay focused mentally.

Scanning the room is difficult for many beginning group leaders. Since members in a new group tend to speak to the leader, beginning leaders often feel they need to keep exclusive eye contact with the speaking member. They may fear it would be rude to look away from a speaking member who is talking to them. But if the leader does not break free of eye contact with that member and shift to observation of other members, she will create problems such as these:

- Other members will feel excluded and will lose interest.
- The leader will fail to notice how other members are reacting to what is being said.
- The leader will have no idea about which member in the group may want to speak next.
- The leader will nonverbally encourage the speaking member to go on and on, even when it might be more beneficial for that member to hear what other members have to say.

By scanning the room, the leader obtains a broad picture of the group dynamics and learns which members want to add comments or respond. This makes leading a lot easier. It does take practice to learn to break free of eye contact and scan the room while a member is talking to you, but once you learn to do it, it will seem natural to you.

Using Nonverbal Cues to Invite Sharing

When you scan the room, you will see nonverbal cues such as leaning forward, head nods, facial expressions, and body shifts. You can use these cues as a guide to invite member interaction if members do not initiate it by themselves.

Leaning Forward   The forward lean usually indicates that the person has something to say and is ready to speak. You can go ahead and invite the member to speak by saying,

> Linda, you seem ready to say something. What would you like to say?
>
> Tracy, I noticed that you were leaning forward and nodding your head while Jean was talking about her efforts to reconnect with her cutoff family. I wonder whether you could identify with some of the things that Jean was talking about?

Head Nods   Head nods may indicate understanding or that the person is relating to the speaker's words because of having had similar experiences. When the leader sees a head nod, she can invite a contribution by saying,

> Jane, I see you nodding; what are your thoughts right now?
>
> Matt, you were nodding when Sue was mentioning her anger. Would you like to share your reactions?

Facial Expressions   Facial expressions usually suggest disapproval, confusion, or some other reaction. The leader can open a space for members to express their inner reactions by saying something like the following:

> Lily, by your expression, I guess that you have some reaction to what Matt and the others are saying. Would you like to share your thoughts?

Body Shifts   Shifts of body posture during the group frequently indicate confusion, boredom, or irritation. When a leader observes this, she may want to invite members to openly talk about how they are feeling:

> [To the group] I sense that the group is getting a bit confused at this moment. Would any of you like to share how you are feeling right now?

Allowing Adequate Time to Respond

When facilitating a group, the leader needs to make sure that adequate time is given for members to respond. The session should not be a rush from one intervention to another. If the group has only one or two members who are responding to the leader's prompt, the leader should ask for more responses. Sometimes members need just a bit more time to ponder and to formulate what they want to say. This is especially true for members who are not quick-paced or aggressively expressive. Quieter members may have something to say but are waiting for their turn. If the wheel of conversation is turning too fast, they may never get the chance to speak because they are not people who can spontaneously jump in at any point. It will serve the whole group well if the leader makes the following inquiry part of the leadership habit:

> Does anyone else want to respond to the question I just asked?

Paying attention to see whether the quieter members have had a chance to speak is very important. The stress of not being able to get a turn to speak is well demonstrated in a member's weekly journal:

> When Ann began telling her issues with weight, I could really identify. I have serious struggles with my weight also. I have every intention to exercise daily and it just does not seem to happen. I wanted to express this, but it was so hard to get a chance to chime in. I am now nervous about the next session because I am afraid that I will be still unable to speak up because I am just not as vocal and fast as others.

Getting All Group Members Involved

When a member presents her issue, the group can easily focus its attention on that particular member to such an extent that she may feel overwhelmed. To avoid this, a leader should think up ways to get everyone involved without focusing exclusively on one member. To get the whole group involved, the leader can periodically fan out or spin off to other members after a member has been sharing for a while. By doing so, the leader ensures that all members feel included and no one feels neglected by the group. To spin off from one speaking member to other members, the leader may say,

> Matt, at this time I would like to invite you to reflect on what you have just said in the past 15 minutes, and then we can come back to you later. Right now I want to shift gears by hearing from the rest of the group. [turning to the group] What kind of issues or reactions did Matt's sharing bring up for you in your own lives? Would anyone want to share what feelings or memories were triggered just now?

Blocking and Redirecting

Some people tend to indiscriminately speak up first on any issue. Other people tend to become negative or long-winded. These behaviors are rather counterproductive to group interaction. The leader must discourage such behaviors and facilitate productive behaviors. This requires the skills of blocking and redirecting. Blocking means stopping members from doing what they have been doing. Blocking probably is the toughest technique for new leaders because they fear it might hurt the feelings of those who are interrupted. They fear that those who get cut short may become angry. These fears are understandable. Yet, the leader is responsible for the group's outcome, so she cannot possibly allow counterproductive behaviors to continue in a group. She must intervene.

Here are some principles for leaders to consider when blocking a member: First, stop members quickly before they have rambled on too long, before they have argued for an extended amount of time, or before they have offered unhelpful advice. Second, do not use a criticizing voice. The goal is to stop, not to criticize. Third, explain to the members why you are stopping them and what behaviors you are stopping. Finally, if you want to block in a subtle way, you may use avoidance of eye contact to hint that talkative members should wind down, or you may use your hand to give them a nonverbal signal. Many times, a slight gesture is all that is needed.

Leaders must block certain counterproductive behaviors, such as member rambling, arguing, or rescuing, in a timely fashion (Jacobs, Masson, & Harvill, 2002). Blocking and redirecting can be used to do so. These techniques are also used in other situations, such as when there is a need to shift topics, or when the session is approaching the end. Following we detail each of the circumstances that require blocking and redirecting and describe how leaders can use these techniques in different situations.

When a Member Is Rambling   A leader may want to avoid eye contact with a member who goes on and on without focus. Rambling members frequently wind down if the leader does not encourage their comments. The leader can block without appearing abrupt by summing up the member's core message and then turning to the other members:

> Thank you, Dale! It seems that you are saying that all of us fear being taken advantage of by others. [summing up the member's core message] [turning to the group] Would the rest of the group like to share some of your similar fears, whatever they are? Does anyone want to start? [Finish the invitation by fixing your eyes on one of the quieter members.]

When Wanting to Shift Focus to Another Member   While a member is talking, another member might react strongly to the topic being discussed. The leader can block the floor action and shift the focus to that member:

> Jim, may I stop you for a moment? I notice that Bruce has been trying to say something. [turning to Bruce] All right, Bruce, could you tell us what you were just trying to say?

Lily, let me stop you before you get into the details of another story. It seems that Jane is reacting to what you just said, and I want to give her a chance to comment. [turning to Jane] Jane, would you like to share what's going through your mind?

When Near the End of the Session   Sometimes members are unaware of time running short toward the end of a session. They may start digging into a complicated issue just when the end of the session is near. If the leader lets such members continue, the group may not close on time, and it will not be able to help the members explore the issues at hand. The better alternative is to block the action. The leader may say,

> Barry, this seems like an important issue. May I ask you to hold this until we meet next week? We don't have enough time now to really deal with the issue. How about waiting until the next session when we have more time to explore it in full? Is it okay with you? [turning to the group] Now with five minutes left, let's wrap it up by having each of you share your reactions to today's session.

When Members Are Arguing   Arguing or attacking one another is not productive for group work. To turn the counterproductive into the productive, a leader needs to stop the action immediately. Chapter 7 details the methods of working with conflicts, whether covert or overt, within groups. For the purpose of facilitating a productive session, a leader just needs to remember that when arguments or attacks happen, the leader's best response is to block the negative exchange and invite the rest of the group to share their observations of what happened. For example,

> John and Jeff, let me stop you for a moment. You two are trying so hard to make the other see things from your own point of view. But I don't think that either of you are hearing each other out. So please stop for a moment, and I would like both of you to hear what the group has to say. [turning to the group] I would like the rest of the group to share your observations of what is going on between John and Jeff. Does anyone want to start?

Alternatively, the leader could ask:

> John and Jeff, I'd like you to each pause for a moment, and then do your best to reflect back what you have heard the other say up to this point. [pause] John, would you like to go first and state what you heard from Jeff?

This intervention can facilitate mutual hearing for those who are in conflict with each other. For more details on this skill, refer to "Facilitating Mutual Hearing" on the book's Web site (see Preface for URL).

When Members Are Rescuing   Why do rescuing behaviors need to be blocked? Rescuing is not the same as helping. To rescue is to smooth over the painful or negative emotions that someone is experiencing. To help, on the contrary, is to help someone resolve the painful feelings by experiencing them fully and working through them. This subtle difference needs to be heeded. Most new members will not be able to differentiate between rescuing and helping initially. Many of them will get into the business of rescuing. When that happens, a little instruction followed by redirecting may go a long way. For example,

> Sue, may I stop you for a moment? I see that you are very eager to cheer Jane up so that she won't feel so much pain. I appreciate your good intention. I believe that what is helpful for people doesn't always involve making them feel better immediately, but rather we can help by allowing them to experience the pain fully, no matter how uncomfortable it is to witness. [turning to Jane] Jane, would you please tell the group what kind of support you need most from the group?

Drawing Out Quiet Members

In leading, the leader basically respects each member's pace and avoids pushing for premature participation. This said, it is sometimes wise to invite quiet members to speak. Quiet members usually desire to participate but do not know when is the appropriate time to do that. The leader can help by drawing them out. Following are some things to consider when trying to draw out quieter members. First, do not draw people out unless it is needed. Members may develop a dependency on the leader if the leader extends an invitation too frequently. Second, do not try to draw out uncommitted members. Let them watch other members working until they feel ready to participate. Finally, be sensitive to multicultural dimensions with respect to participation patterns. Members from some cultures may need more time to observe before jumping in. Of course, the leader can invite them to share, but only on a level that feels comfortable to them. If they hesitate, do not push them to immediately engage in the group's interaction. Be supportive, and allow them time to watch and learn.

Basically, the leader may use simple encouragement to invite quieter members, for example:

> Jeff, it looks like you are thinking. Would you like to share your thoughts?

> You are nodding. Go ahead, Matt.

> Sue, you seem to be reacting to something. Is there anything you would like to share?

> John, I notice that you have been quiet in this session. I am not sure whether I should comment on this or not. Certainly we'd like to hear from you, but only if you feel comfortable.

Fred, I've noticed how attentive you have been in today's session to all that's been happening. If you feel comfortable, would you share with us some observations that you've made?

Looping Back and Refocusing

When the group is flowing, the interaction can stray into social chatting without a focus, or it can become lost in some topics irrelevant to the group's purpose. When this happens, the leader has to act quickly to redirect the group's focus. This action is called refocusing. It is better to get into the action of refocusing before too long because the longer the group strays, the harder it will be to bring it back to focus. To bring the group back to focus, the leader may try saying something like:

> [To the whole group] It seems that somehow we have gotten away from something that Judy just said which seemed important. Can we go back to where we were five minutes ago? [to Judy] When you were talking to George, you seemed to be near tears. What was happening inside of you?

> Let's spend the next 10 minutes talking only about our reactions triggered by Matt's sharing. Anyone wants to share how Matt's experience affected you?

> Let's go back a moment and stay with Mark for a few more minutes. Mark, would you say again when you started to feel that way?

Summarizing Themes

The leader is wise to periodically summarize the themes of group discussion before moving on to the next topic. Summarizing group themes helps members internalize the learning they draw from the shared discussion. The leader may summarize the themes by saying something like:

> [To the group] Many members have shared the experiences of growing up in an alcoholic family. It seems that the anxiety of not living up to expectations, the angst that things are ready to fall apart at any point, the need to be overly responsible, the need to be perfect, and a tendency to be mistrustful, are themes that run through our discussion.

The leader may also ask group members to summarize the themes for themselves:

> [To the group] We have had a great deal of personal sharing for awhile now. I wonder whether anyone in the group can summarize the themes that seem to run through our discussion?

When Group Members Cry

Members may cry or tear up when they are speaking or listening to others. Crying often indicates that the topic is touching a deep reservoir of emotion. The leader should avoid being socially correct by helping the specific member stop crying. Quite the contrary, the leader may encourage the member to feel all right about crying and to get more in touch with what is causing the tears. Following are different circumstances requiring different responses from the leader.

When the trust level within the group is high, the leader can encourage members to plunge deeper into the emotions. For example,

> Please don't feel that you need to rush through this. Stay with that feeling for as long as you can.

> Don't feel guilty about taking the group time. Your feelings are very important to the group.

After the member has gone through the waves of emotion, the leader may encourage him or her to talk about it. For example,

> Mike, would you like to share what your tears are trying to say?

> Susan, try to continue to talk to the group. See whether you can put your tears into words.

As the trust in the group matures, the leader can go one step further to explore the member's feelings about crying in general:

> Jean, thank you for the intimate sharing. How does it feel to cry in the group's presence?

When the group is still young and trust has not been firmly established yet, the leader may simply acknowledge the tears or just let members express their pain silently through tears. The leader may say,

> Dale, I can sense how much it hurts to lose something so important when you were so young! The group is very touched by your tears.

> Mike, please take your time to stay with your pain. We are in no hurry. Please know that we are here to support you.

There is always the question: to offer or not to offer the box of Kleenex? People in the field debate whether or not to give a box of Kleenex to a group member who is crying. There is no definite answer. The leader can only be sensitive to how members interpret the offering. Some members might feel comforted by the soft tissue as they dry their faces, while other members might interpret the giving of Kleenex as an indication to stop crying. Some might feel distracted by the passing of the box, as shown in one group member's reflection:

When I began to speak in the group, something unexpected just happened inside of me and I began to cry. I became a little upset when people quickly moved to offer the box of Kleenex because it distracted me from what I was trying to say, and I also saw it as an effort of trying to stop my tears.

As a leader, you cannot predict how a specific client might respond. In general, we prefer to wait awhile so that a crying member can fully experience his own pain while the group is fully present in the sacred moment. After the crying has subsided, the group then can go ahead and pass the box of Kleenex.

Member-Member Empathic Responses

Reflecting clients' core messages and emotions is the grain of a therapist's everyday life. This is groundwork in individual counseling. In the group setting, however, the leader must not take the entire responsibility of empathy on his own shoulders. If he does, he will turn the group session into multiple individual counseling; he will be dominating, not leading, the group. Many leader-centered groups fail to bring the best out of members because of leader domination. Of course, the leader should reflect members' emotions and core issues at times, but primarily for the purpose of modeling.

We encourage leaders to try group-centered leadership. People need to receive empathy, but empathy should not come solely from the leader. Empathy proves much more powerful for the group when it comes from fellow members. The leader's job is to make sure that this happens by inviting members to participate in giving empathic responses. For example,

Gina, it seems like not only did you lose your father through the car accident, but you also lost your relatives because of the cut-and-dried way they treated your loss. [turning to the group] Right now, I would like to see if anyone can imagine what feelings Gina might have had under those circumstances. Please speak directly to Gina when you are ready.

Leader Modeling of Empathic Responses

If no one in the group is able to convey empathy for Gina in her struggles, the leader can step in. This will provide modeling for members regarding how to express their empathy to one another. The leader may say this to Gina:

Gina, I sense that you feel reinjured each time when you run into those relatives who stir this pain in you. Their cut-and-dried treatment makes you feel invisible. You feel hurt and lonely.

Here is another example of a leader providing modeling of empathy:

> Sue, it seems that you feel inhibited in your current life, not knowing how to express yourself, especially when strong emotions are involved. And you felt sad growing up in a household where there was no verbal expression [leader modeling empathic response] [turning to the group] I would like to ask the group whether anyone can tell Sue what other feelings she might have had under these circumstances.

Addressing Group Members Instead of Talking about Them

When the leader speaks to the group, he should not address the group with words like *they* or *their*. The group members are in the room right in front of the leader; therefore, the leader should address them in the language of *you*, as if the leader were saying "you guys" or "you all." For example, the leader should avoid saying,

> Many members look thoughtful. I wonder what *they* think George was trying to say?

> Some members are nodding *their* heads. I wonder whether any of *them* would like to share *their* experiences with George.

Instead, the leader should use "I-Thou" conversational language. For example,

> Many of *you* look thoughtful. I wonder what *you* think George was trying to say.

> Some of *you* are nodding *your* heads. I wonder whether any of *you* would like to share *your* experiences with George.

Handling Silence

In the early stages, the group frequently may encounter silence. There are two types of silence: productive silence and unproductive silence (Jacobs, Masson, & Harvill, 2002).

Productive Silence   Productive silence happens when members are quietly taking in what has been said or done in the group. This type of silence has a sense of energy and a depth of connection. It allows members to fully feel their feelings and to honor what is happening in the group. When the leader encounters a silence, it is best to let it last for one or two minutes, or for as long as members need it for their internal processing. If a member starts to speak when everyone else is still deep in processing, the leader may say:

[To the group] Let's wait for just a couple more minutes. It looks like people are still processing.

This waiting may test the leader's faith of the inner workings of silence. Many new group leaders are not comfortable with silence and may hasten to fill it up. This should be avoided. It is better to wait a few minutes, and then break the silence by drawing out members. The leader can say:

[To the group] We have just had a moment of silence here. I would like the group to share what was going on inside of you in the moment of silence.

[To the group] I am very touched by this moment of silence. I wonder if any of you would like to tell the group about what went through your mind in this silence—what you thought about saying, but didn't.

Nonproductive Silence   Nonproductive silence happens when members are bored, confused, or afraid to talk. This kind of silence has a sense of tension that makes people ill at ease. When nonproductive silence happens, the leader may summarize what has been covered and find a new intervention or a new entry point for discussion.

Handling Advice-Soliciting

Exchange of advice and information may prove helpful when group members have a thorough understanding of the nature of one another's issues. Prematurely given, however, advice tends to be unhelpful. Almost every group has some members who habitually solicit advice from others as a way of relating. They may say something like:

I have this problem, and I just want to hear what advice you all have so I can make a decision about what I should do.

As open to others' input as these members appear, they may not really be ready to implement whatever advice is given. Often their way of soliciting advice is their way of relating to people. The leader needs to discern whether the request is genuine or habitual. When a group is faced with pressure to give advice that is habitually solicited by a member, the leader may say,

[To the group] Although we all want to help Denis solve this problem right away, what we know about the nature of her issue is very limited right now. So let's try to understand more before we jump in to resolve the issue. [turning to the soliciting member] Denis, the group will be willing to give you some fresh perspectives if you allow the members to gain some insight into the nature of your problem. This will take a bit of exploration. When you are ready, the group will be most happy to help you work it through.

SKILLS OF OPENING A GROUP SESSION

The ability to open each group session effectively is an integral part of group work. To open a session without any structure or direction is to risk chaos. Whatever is on the floor may turn to dominate the group's energy. In the end, the group may regret that time has been wasted on irrelevant topics.

To effectively open a session, leaders may use the method presented in this section. This method allows the group to efficiently make connections from one session to the next, bringing group energy into focus. A quick go-around provides just a minimum of structure to ease the group into working mode. After the opening, the group session can then be non-structured or semistructured to allow interpersonal processes to emerge.

The method of opening a group session can be broken down into three sub-steps: (1) a brief relaxation exercise; (2) a check-in; and (3) a request for agenda items.

Brief Relaxation Exercise

The first step in opening a session can be a brief relaxation exercise. Members often come to the session after a hectic day, exhausted by their daily hassles. A brief relaxation exercise can do wonders to set the mood for the session. A three- to four-minute relaxation exercise can guide members to feel more centered and focused before diving into the session. Following are two examples of such relaxation exercises. Leaders can choose one of these to open the session or take the liberty of tailoring one of them to suit their own groups' needs.

The first relaxation exercise combines a body-centered breathing technique with guided visualization. Leaders should use a slow, soothing, calm voice to guide this exercise:

> I'm glad that we were all able to make it here today. Before we dive into the session, let's spend three to five minutes on a relaxation exercise. Please find a comfortable sitting position. When you are ready, take a quiet and slow breath. Notice your stomach rise. Then notice your stomach slowly descend as you exhale. Take another quiet and slow breath. Again notice the air flowing in . . . and out . . . of your body. [pause] When you feel comfortable, slowly close your eyes. Concentrate on your body sensations as you breathe. If your mind begins to wander, just allow the competing thoughts to dissipate and bring your focus back to your breathing sensations. Just notice your breath, notice how it is in . . . and out . . . in a rhythmic and relaxed pattern. [pause]

> As you are feeling relaxed, imagine that you are walking quietly on a beach, watching the waves in the lake going up . . . and down . . ., up . . . and down. . . . As you continue your walk, you notice the warmth of the sunlight, the gentleness of the breeze, and the color of the sky. You notice the sounds of the birds and the smell of fresh air. You notice you feel totally relaxed and calm throughout your entire body. Allow yourself to remain in this total state of relaxation for a while. [pause] As your eyes remain closed, feel free to shift your attention from the beach and come back to the room. Allow yourself to gather thoughts about whatever you would like to share or to accomplish today in the group meeting. [pause] When you are ready, you may open your eyes.

The second example of a relaxation exercise involves reprogramming the mind in order to override the stress caused by the daily hassles of life. Again, the leader should guide this exercise with a slow, rhythmic, calm voice:

> Before we start today's session, let's do a simple relaxation exercise. Please sit comfortably on your chair. Close your eyes and breathe slowly. Let your arms and legs go limp. [pause] As you continue to breathe in and out slowly, notice your arms and hands begin to feel heavier and heavier. [pause] Next, notice your legs and feet begin to feel heavier and heavier. [pause] At the same time, notice your arms and legs begin to feel warmer and warmer. [pause] Your heart is calm and relaxed. Your heartbeat is slow and relaxed. [pause] Your breathing is slow and comfortable. Your stomach is calm and relaxed. Your forehead is cool and calm. Your entire body is calm and relaxed. [pause] Allow yourself to be in this total relaxation for awhile. [pause] While you are relaxed, let your attention go to the thoughts, feelings, or issues that you want to share with the group today. When you are ready, please open your eyes.

Check-In (The First Go-Around)

The second step in opening a group session is the check-in. In this step, the leader uses a quick go-around to invite members to share any lingering feelings or unfinished business from the previous session. If members do not have unfinished business from the previous session, they can share how they were during the week or what skills they practiced outside the group. It is important to mention the time frame because otherwise some members may ramble and chat away valuable session time. To initiate this check-in go-around, the leader may say,

> [To the group] Let's start today's session with a quick check-in. We have about 5–10 minutes for this go-around. If you have any lingering reactions or unfinished business from the last session, please use a

few sentences to share what it is. We will spend some time to process
your lingering feelings if necessary. [pause] If you don't have any unfinished business, please share how you have been during the week.
[pause] If you don't have unfinished business or any significant event to
share, then please share what new behaviors you have been practicing
outside the group. [pause] Okay, let's start with Jeff and then go in this
direction. [hand gesture]

Let me add that while you are listening to the other members checking
in, please feel free to respond to one another if you feel a need to make
a comment.

If the group is in a later stage of development, the leader may start the
check-in by saying,

Let's start our session with a quick check-in. Last week, several of you
shared difficulties that you've experienced in your lives, and you were
able to gain insights into these difficulties in the group session. I've
noticed that some of you have tried out some new approaches here in
handling difficult issues. I'm wondering whether anyone here has been
able to test out new approaches in your life. If so, I hope you will share
your experience with the group and talk about how those new
approaches have worked for you.

Asking members to report on new behaviors that have been practiced
outside the group is quite important. As one member reflected in her
journal:

I am glad the leader asked the group to talk about the new behaviors
they have been practicing outside of the group. Since I joined the
group, I am becoming more conscious of my interaction with others. I
am also making progress toward strengthening my interpersonal relationships with significant others in my life. Since I notice a difference
in myself, I am curious to know whether other members are making
progress toward their goals in their lives outside the group as well.

Handling Issues That Emerge during Check-In

While the group is doing the check-in, unpredictable things may happen.
When members are commenting on unfinished business from the previous week, some intense emotions and interaction may emerge.
Occasionally, open conflicts may even surface. The principle of leadership
in these circumstances is to handle the hot emotions with care. The leader
should stop the check-in and give priority to processing the emotions. The
key is to engage the whole group in bringing the issue to a closure. For
example, the leader may say,

[To the group] I sense some tense emotions at this moment. Let's stop
our check-in for the moment and give our priority to resolving this issue.

If a member starts to feel emotional when sharing an event that happened during the week that does not involve other members in the group, the leader can invite the member to take some time from the group, that is, to put it as an agenda item to work on during the session. Working on the agenda will be presented in the next chapter.) The leader may say,

> Susan, this seems to be an important yet complicated issue for you. Would you like the group to work with you to help you get a clear perspective about it? If you would like to pursue it, we can put it as an agenda item later for today's session. Would you like to do that?

If a member is absent from any given session, it is important to acknowledge the absence of the member and ask the group whether they have any reaction to that:

> I just want to acknowledge that Patty is not with us today. If you have any reaction to Patty's absence, please feel free to share it with the group.

Requesting Agenda Items (The Second Go-Around)

For Initial Stages of Group Development   The last step in opening a session is requesting agenda items. In this step, the leader has the group do a quick go-around for the second time, engaging all members to briefly say what they want to gain from this specific session. This is the time when members can identify personal agenda items (Yalom, 1983) that they will work on during the session. The function of this second go-around is to have an overall picture of what members' needs are in a given session. It also puts members in a position where they have to own up to their responsibility for creating the experiences they want in the group. To request agenda items, the leader may say:

> [For initial stages of group] Thank you for your sharing during the check-in. Next, we have about 70 minutes left for us to work on our goals. This is your group, and all of you help create the kind of group experience you want to see happening. So, let's have another quick go-around. In this go-around, if you have a personal agenda item (a stressful, patterned, interpersonal issue) to work on, please indicate that you do and use one or two sentences to say just what it is. After the go-around, we will work on the agenda items on the table in much detail. [pause] If you don't have an agenda item, please use a sentence or two to tell the group what interpersonal skills you are willing to put to practice in today's session so that you can take baby steps toward change. [pause] Okay, let's start with Jen and go in this direction. [hand gesture]

If time is pressing, you may combine the unfinished business, outside practice, and agenda item request in one quick go-around:

> We are going to combine the check-in go-around and the agenda go-around today. Let's spend a few minutes to have just one go-around. In

this go-around, please share any unfinished business from last week and any progress you have made in practicing your new behaviors in your life. If you have an agenda item to present, please say so; if not, please state what new interpersonal skill you would like to put to practice in today's session. Okay, let's start from this direction. [hand gesture]

For Later Stages of Group Development   In later stages of group, especially during the working/performing stage (see Chapters 9 and 10), when group members' anxiety has subsided and the trust level has been developed, the leader may open the session without requesting agenda items. In so doing, the leader is leaving the session totally open. This type of open session will provide wide and wild opportunity for members' interpersonal styles to emerge. Though somewhat anxiety-provoking, this type of totally nonstructured session is purposeful and is much celebrated for its power in helping members become more aware of their interpersonal characteristics in the here-and-now of the group setting. Once aware, members are more able to make conscious choices about change. After the check-in, the leader may open the session by saying,

> [For later stages of group] Thank you, everybody, for sharing. Okay, we have 70 minutes left for today's session. Today, we are not going to request any agenda items. Rather, we will let today's session be totally open. That is, we will let the group decide how you are going to spend the time today. If you want the group to give you some input on any issue, please feel free to take the group time. If you have had any feelings or reactions about the group or about certain members within the group, please feel free to address them in the group. We will work together as a group to see what we can learn in our time together this evening.

Practicing Interpersonal Skills

You probably have already noticed, in reading about the agenda item go-around method, that in each session members are either working on their personal agendas or practicing an interpersonal skill of their own choosing with one another. You probably have also noticed that the leader has the members decide what personal agenda items or interpersonal skills they wish to work on or put into practice. This way the leader can put the ball in the members' court. For group counseling to work effectively within a brief time frame, leaders must put members in a position where they have to assume a great amount of responsibility for their progress in achieving their goals.

Most members know what issues they want to pursue as their personal agenda item because they know what brought them to the group. However, members often struggle to come up with an interpersonal skill to "test-drive" within a group session. After a while, most members get a sense of areas of interpersonal functioning in which they need to improve. Through our experiences with groups, we have been privileged to hear members choose many types of interpersonal skills to test-drive within the group laboratory. These interpersonal skills can be categorized into nine areas:

1. *Maintaining one's center and identity in interpersonal relationships*

    In this session, I want to try to articulate my feelings, whether they are positive or negative, to the person I am interacting with.

    In today's session, I want to try to take good care of myself and be truthful about my feelings, even if that requires me to bring up difficult subjects.

    I want to resist my tendency toward withdrawal and try to stay engaged with people, even if I feel nervous or rejected.

    I want to lower the wall I build in my relationships with people. I want to be able to show others who I really am, without being controlled by fear of rejection.

    I want to respond nondefensively when I face criticism.

    I want to be my true self without always wearing a smiling persona or constantly trying to change my behaviors to please or control others.

    I want to stand comfortably for myself, without second-guessing or worrying about what others think of me.

    I want to say no to what I don't want, without feeling guilty.

    I want to express my feelings, positive or negative, diplomatically without worrying about others' approval and without making others feel defensive.

2. *Comforting and soothing oneself when faced with stress or difficulties*

    In today's session, I want to try to use my inner resources to calm myself and step back from interactions when others are in the midst of anger and hostility, or step back from situations that can cause trauma.

    I want to slow down, instead of leaping into an argument or losing my temper.

    I want to stay present with my own feelings when under stressful interaction, instead of engaging in compulsive or addictive behaviors.

3. *Having one's self-esteem and mood remain constant in the presence of others' anxieties and worries*

    In this session, I want to try to remain empathic and supportive without feeling compelled to rescue others or worry for them when they are anxious, depressed, or going through a hard time.

    I want to remain a loving witness to others' struggle and growth, without absorbing their painful feelings or feeling responsible for fixing the problems for them.

4. *Knowing that one's values are a given*

In today's session, I want to try to let my sense of self-worth remain stable whether I am praised, criticized, making progress, failing, in pain, or in a cheerful mood.

I want to hold the ground that my value is inherent in being who I am and being alive, without needing to please others.

I want to foster my self-worth through internal validation. I won't let my self-worth rely on what kind of praise, grades, status, looks, or weight I get.

5. *Being able to self-assert and self-confront*

In this session, I want to try to routinely reflect on my behaviors and confront myself. I want to be able to stop and ask myself, "How did I contribute to the problem in this interaction?"

I want to keep the focus inward, own up to my own mistakes, apologize when appropriate, and stop other people when they are hurtful to me.

I want to set boundaries for myself. When an interaction is intruding into one of my boundaries, I want to be able to say no and leave that interaction without fear of feeling alone.

6. *Asking for and receiving support without feeling weak or compromised*

Today I want to learn to accept help from others without feeling indebted.

I want to reach out for help when I am in need.

I want to connect with others through receiving. I want to experience that my ability to receive allows someone else to experience the gift of giving.

I want to ask for what I desire, without feeling embarrassed.

7. *Developing a set of values through reflection, awareness, learning, and experimentation*

Here in this session I want to practice trusting my own inner wisdom that comes through my experiences and my own personal reflections, instead of relying on my family, school, or religious institutions to determine what is important for me.

8. *Feeling comfortable with different belief systems and perspectives*

Today I want to try to feel comfortable, whether or not anyone agrees with me. I want to learn to appreciate differences as unthreatening, enriching, and interesting.

I want to allow myself to be curious, rather than jumping into self-defensiveness immediately when differences surface in my interactions with people.

9. *Seeing others clearly*

> In this session, I want to practice dropping my preconceived beliefs and expectations about people. I want to get to know the persons in front of me as who they truly are, allowing myself to feel close to their unique idiosyncrasies.

Toward a Higher Level of Self-Differentiation

One can see that the interpersonal skills listed in the previous section characterize the functioning of a well-differentiated person. In other words, most of the interpersonal skills that members want to practice serve the purpose of moving them toward a higher degree of self-differentiation. This is of no surprise. If we look deeply, we often find that the source of anxiety that makes us so "radio-reactive" consists of any number of hot issues we have carried from our first families but never processed or resolved. We often repetitively do the same old things to snap ourselves out of anxiety, only to find our old patterns perpetuated and our growth stymied. We rely on withdrawal or cutting people off as ways to reduce our anxiety without really addressing the issues that cause our anxiety. These easy-way-out coping strategies only make us even more reactive in other areas of our lives (Goldhor, 1989).

To stretch our potential for interpersonal competency and self-intimacy, we need to work on doing something different, something new. This something different and new is to clearly state just what we believe and what we feel. To become a more solid self or to tone down our reactivity, we first need to learn to stay emotionally connected to significant others even when things get intense. Goldhor (1989) puts it so well:

> Family connectedness, even when these relationships are anxious and difficult, is a necessary prerequisite to conducting one's own intimate relationship free from serious symptoms over time and free from excessive anxiety and reactivity. The more we manage intensity by cutting off from members of our own kinship groups, the more we bring that intensity into other relationships. (p. 98).

To become a more solid self, we next need to address difficult issues and take a position on things that are important to us. We need to focus on the self, not on others. We need to learn to state our different opinions and allow others to do the same. In sum, we need to learn how to stand on our own feet and own up to our own personal truth. With this vision in mind, the leader should strive to enable group members to practice something new in each group session. This is the reason why leaders should ask members at the beginning of each session, as discussed previously, to state just what interpersonal skills they want to practice during the session. As members own up to their own responsibility for practicing the interpersonal skills they most need to develop, they take gradual steps toward a greater level of self-differentiation.

The following journal entry by a group member demonstrates the benefit members gain when leaders ask them to take responsibility for practicing new interpersonal skills in each group session:

> Each risk that is taken in the group is a springboard for more risks to be taken, which continues to bring the group to a deeper, more honest level. Such is the risk I took with Matt tonight. After I asked Matt to clarify the meaning of his laughter which seemed to target me, I felt ready to cry. In asking Matt I was letting the rest of the group see the neurotic, self-conscious side of me—the side of me that I usually go to great lengths to hide. This exposure was a huge risk for me. What a relief it was, however, to hear from Matt, rather than allow myself to misconstrue his smile. In the outside world, I fear being laughed at. I have a tendency to "read into" or misread other's behaviors, and then withdraw from them. Perhaps if I start to take the risk of asking people the meaning of their behaviors, it will help my relationships reach a higher level of honesty and closeness. When I first began the group, I admit to feeling very skeptical that I would ever feel a change in my behavior. Now each time I practice stating my feelings or ask for clarification with someone, I am beginning to feel a bit closer toward reaching my goal. I have seen small, continuous improvements that I have made in the past three sessions. Especially tonight! I left the session feeling very charged, ready to go out in the world and practice these new skills.

SKILLS OF CLOSING A GROUP SESSION

Closing a session effectively is another important part of group work. Most often, the group has more issues to work on than time allows in a session. Closing the session on time is important. When groups stay past the session closing time, unnecessary resentment or a sense of blurred boundaries can be created in the members. To close the group effectively, the leader can use the method presented in this section. This is a three-step method: (1) announcing the closing; (2) the check-out; and (3) the reminder.

Announcing the Closing of Session

Announcing the closing of the session allows for a sense of transition. The leader may make the announcement with an acknowledgment or a brief summary:

Thank you, everybody, for your active participation! We are approaching the end of the session, so we need to call it a day. I know that we don't have time to get to Miki's agenda today. [turning to Miki] Miki, would you mind if we table your agenda and make it the first priority of our next session?

We are approaching the end of the session. We all worked hard today. When I look back, I see that a sense of loss—be it loss of job security, attachment to loved ones, or untapped potential—has been a connecting theme in today's session.

Check-Out (The Third Go-Around)

To give group members a chance to review their progress and to clear up any unspoken reactions, the leader may use a quick go-around to have members share one of the following:

- How they feel about the interpersonal skills they practiced during the session and any unexpressed feelings from the session.

   Let's use a few minutes to wrap up today's session. Before we leave, I would like each of us to do a quick check-out, that is, to share how you feel about the interpersonal skill you practiced in this session. Remember that the focus is on you and your interpersonal skill. If there is any reaction you would like to say but did not have a chance to say during the session, please take this time to express it. Okay, let's start from Jean and go in this direction. [hand gesture]

- What they liked or did not like about the session.

   This was a very emotional session today. We have five minutes to wrap up for today, so before we leave, let's have a quick go-around and each of you can share what you like or dislike about how we are working and relating today.

- What they learned about themselves.

   We have five minutes to wrap up the session. Before we do, I would like to hear from the group about what you have learned about yourself in your interaction with other members.

- What progress they made in the session.

   Research shows that members who set goals and report on their progress in weekly sessions show greater therapeutic success than those who do not (Hart, 1978). To maximize this effect, leaders can ask group members to reflect on their progress when wrapping up a session. The leader may say,

> Before we wrap up for today, I would like each of us to share your progress. Please tell the group what little steps you have taken in this session toward reaching your goal.
>
> I was aware that a number of group members took some important risks here in the group today relative to your goals. Can we do a quick go-around with each of you giving a short description of how you worked on your new skills today?

Some members have a habit of waiting until the last minute to pour out a significant disclosure, and then the group is confronted with a difficult situation just before closing. When this happens, the leader can acknowledge the issue and table it until the next session. The leader may say,

> Steve, that seems like an important issue for you, yet we are running out of time today. If you will bring that up at the next session, we will certainly spend some time on that.

The Reminder

The last step of the closing is a reminder. A reminder serves to encourage members to continue their personal work during the week. The leader may say,

> Thank you for all the hard work today. Before we say good-bye, I would like to encourage each of you to practice, in your own lives, those new behaviors that you have learned in the group. And if you have not yet presented your personal agenda item, I would like to encourage you to take some time during the week to think about the issues that you may want to explore in the next session. Thanks, and have a wonderful week!

USING STRUCTURED EXERCISES WITH PRECAUTION

During the initial stage of group counseling and therapy, there is a high possibility that members will experience a "letdown." A letdown is especially likely in the second session. The first session is often filled with a lot of sharing and excitement as members get acquainted with one another and discuss why they are in the group and what their experiences have been. This level of sharing and excitement, however, is not always present in the second session. Further, when members sense in the second session that their sharing will start to reach a more personal level, they get nervous and become hesitant to participate. This phenomenon is called "second-session letdown" (Jacobs, Masson, & Harvill, 2002).

Beginning group leaders usually find this letdown to be very stressful. Neophyte leaders often think the energy of the first session will continue through the rest of the group's life. This wishful thinking leads them to fail to plan the group adequately or to fail to anticipate the change of atmosphere. Having a framework to guide the group in the second (and later) sessions will help to lessen the impact of the letdown and help the leader steer the group members toward doing productive work. (Chapter 6 presents such a framework.)

One way to deal with letdown is to set aside some time in the second session to mention the potential decrease in enthusiasm from the first session. Another way is to use warm-up exercises, for example: (1) sentence completion; (2) lists; (3) one-and-another; (4) inside-and-outside; and (5) expressiveness. (These are described fully later in this chapter.) Such exercises get members to talk to one another and to share information about themselves. Note that the exercises are not helpful in and of themselves; rather, it is the time spent personalizing and processing the exercises that is helpful.

Misuse of Structured Exercises

Even though exercises are valuable, leaders should beware of their drawbacks. Many inexperienced leaders do one exercise right after another. This misuse of exercises can cause members to become bored or resentful of what they may feel is a gimmick. The leader can use the exercises to get members focused, but not just to fill the time.

A common myth among prospective group members is that group is a fake environment (Carter, Mitchell, & Krautheim, 2001). This myth or negative expectation is caused and reinforced by some group leaders' overuse of structured exercises because they take away a sense of ownership and autonomy for group members.

Good and Bad News

Generally speaking, there are two sides of using structured activities in group work.

The Good News   Yalom (1995) and his colleagues have done extensive research on the effect of structured exercises on group outcomes. They found that leaders who used many exercises were popular with their groups. Exercises create immediate results that lead members to perceive the leaders as more competent, more effective, and more perceptive than leaders who do not use many exercises. However, the long-term outcome showed the opposite. Members of groups with the most exercises had significantly lower outcomes and fewer behavior changes, and even when there were some changes, they were less likely to be maintained over time.

These research findings suggest that if leaders primarily want their group members to think of them as competent, then they may use as many structured interventions as they wish; in doing so, they will fulfill members' fantasies of what leaders should do.

The Bad News   The outcome of group work is not improved with structured exercises. In fact, too much reliance on these exercises makes a group less effective in the long run. Yalom's (1995) research showed that structured exercises plunge the group members quickly into a great degree of expressivity and bypass the anxiety and the difficult stages. This immediate result seems to be wonderful, but the group pays a price for its speed. The speeding-up bypasses many developmental tasks of the group, and as a result, the group does not develop a sense of autonomy and potency.

Another barrier is that the structure of the exercises makes it difficult for members' interpersonal styles to emerge. Thus, the group cannot move to the here-and-now of interpersonal learning. Hetzel, Barton, and Davenport (1994) concluded in their study that unstructured sessions were more helpful than structured ones. One of the members in their study commented, "I feel like the group really took off once we stopped doing exercises" (p. 59).

On the leader's part, leading a group with structured exercises and predesigned topics is less challenging and less anxiety-producing. Many untrained paraprofessionals lead groups with the help of structured exercises and topics. However, for a well-trained group leader, leading a structured group is less gratifying. There are fewer insights and less depth of interpersonal learning generated in such a group.

The Procedures for Conducting Structured Exercises

The general consensus among group specialists is to use structured exercises as little as possible. Hetzel, Barton, and Davenport (1994) contended that a few structured exercises during the initial session can be helpful, as they may help ease the group into a trusting mode, but that no more than one such activity should be included in a session. If the leader decides to include a structured exercise in a session, he needs to make sure to follow the procedures detailed in the following text.

Introducing the Exercises   The leader needs to first introduce the exercise and explain what the group is to do in the exercise. The leader may say,

> Let's shift gears a bit. In a minute, I am going to ask the group to do an exercise that should get you in touch with your feelings and thoughts about. . . .

Conducting the Exercises   The second step is to actually ask the group to do whatever activity is designed. The leader needs to ask members if they need to have more time in response. In conducting the exercise, if a member refuses to participate or has a negative attitude, the leader can just move on to the next person, but make a mental note about the problem with that member. Rarely should a leader push someone into participating. If a member is not ready to join the activity, the leader may simply tell the member that she will come back to him at the end, and then make sure she does so.

Exercises can stir up intense feelings. If the leader sees that a member is experiencing a strong emotional reaction, she can simply acknowledge that she will come back to him later and then proceed to the rest of the group so that no one feels "stranded" while waiting. After all is shared, the leader can go back to that specific member. However, if the leader sees a member crying, attention should be given to this member immediately. The leader can ask the group how they feel about stopping the exercise so that the group can help the troubled person.

The leader has the option of participating or not participating in an exercise. As a rule, leaders do not participate in exercises that might cause them to focus on their own feelings, thoughts, or unfinished business that have nothing to do with the present members.

Processing the Experiences   The third step is processing. Processing is by far the most important phase in using structured exercises. Group processing gives members an opportunity to discuss what has just happened inside of themselves during the exercise, and to put the feelings they experienced into words. Exercises merely act as catalysts for initiating discussion and interaction among members. If well designed, they may trigger ideas and feelings within members that will energize the group. The actual learning comes only through processing the internal awareness triggered by the exercises. Therefore, it is important for leaders to help members look inward and explore their feelings at a deeper level once they have completed the exercise. Leaders need to have some questions prepared beforehand and use them to stimulate the expression of experiences and feelings in the group. Questions the leader might ask include:

What feelings came to you during the exercise?

What part of the exercise stood out to you?

What thoughts do you have about this experience?

Would anyone like to respond to what Matt just said?

Examples of Structured Exercises

When choosing structured exercises, it is important to match the intensity level of the exercise with that of the group. The emotional intensity of the interaction tends to increase gradually as the group develops over time. Exercises of too low or too high a level of intensity are not helpful for members (Corey, Corey, Callahan, & Russell, 1992; Jones & Robinson, 2000).

Written exercises are both versatile and useful, and they have the potential to help members become focused in the beginning stages of a group. When members are finished with the written exercises, they have their responses in front of them, available to share. This eliminates members' anxiety of having to "perform" on the spot. Some of the most popular written exercises are sentence completion, lists, two-paper exercises (e.g., one-and-another, inside-and-outside), and expressiveness. These are described more fully in the text that follows.

Sentence Completion   In this exercise, you make up a sentence stem and leave the rest of the sentence blank for the group members. Examples of sentence completion are as follows:

When I enter a new group, I feel _____.

In a group, I am most afraid of _____.

When people first meet me, they _____.

I trust those who _____.

I regret _____.

If I had to do it all over again, I would _____.

Lists   In this exercise, you ask the group to make a list of things. Examples of lists are:

List things that are stressful for you.

List the feelings you feel most often recently.

List the recent problems that concern you most.

One-and-Another   This is the type of exercise that can help group members reflect on their preferred life outcome. For example:

On the first piece of paper, draw a picture of your face that reflects how you think it appears to other people. Please remember how you feel inside as you are drawing this picture." [after a while] Now, on another piece of paper, draw another picture of your face that reflects how you actually feel.

On one piece of paper, draw a picture or write key words to illustrate how you are now—that is, how you are feeling and what your current life situation is. Don't be concerned about being artistic. Just let your pen lead you! [Wait until members finish.] Now, on another piece of paper, draw or write how you wish to be in the future.

Inside-and-Outside   This is one type of structured exercise that may help members clarify what they want to keep in their lives and what they wish to change. Here is one example:

> On your sheet of paper, draw a big circle. Think of those things in your life that you are proud of or delighted about, and then write or draw these things inside the circle, regardless of whether they are people, objects, or ideas. [Wait for a while.] Now think of those things that bring with them a feeling of uneasiness and inadequacy, and add those things outside the circle.

Expressiveness   In this exercise, you offer a context in which members can express what is happening inside them. Examples of expressiveness include:

> I would like the group to take a few minutes to write down on a sheet of paper some of your hopes and fears surrounding your being a part of this group.

> Maybe each of you can take a few minutes to think of an animal with which you identify. Then write a few sentences to describe how this animal deals with change and uncertainty.

Other expressive exercises involve storytelling, poetry, drawing, and music. They are all catalysts to open members to their inner experiences.

SCENARIOS FOR YOUR PRACTICE

1. About halfway through the second session of a personal exploration group for laid-off white-collar workers, Bob states, "I don't know why we must listen to all these tales of woe from everyone here. What we need to know is how to find a new job." What are some possible group leader responses at this stage?
2. About 30 minutes into a group session of an experiential group, Joan directs the following question to you: "I don't think that what Melanie has been talking about is relevant to what our group is doing. Don't you agree?" What would be an appropriate response from a group leader?
3. At the start of the fourth session of a grief group, there is a great deal of silence and a lack of responsiveness to your general invitation for someone to begin. As you scan the group members, you notice that most of them are avoiding eye contact and gazing into

the distance. You also notice that Molly is red-eyed and is twisting a handkerchief in her hand. You recall that in the last session, she was the focus for most of the group in what you perceived to be an especially productive session with much input from others. As the group leader, what would be a helpful response that you could make at this stage?

4. Ten minutes before the end of a group session with ten group members, Alice makes the following statement: "Well, I've been thinking that half of us are much better at this than the other half." You notice that all of the group members sit upright at this statement. Wayne expresses agreement with Alice and states that he has been better at group than some of the others. He then asks, in a demanding tone, "What do you quieter members have to say about *that*?" Given the short amount of time left in the session, what would be a helpful response that you as group leader could make at this stage?

5. In an experiential group, Jeff describes a painful experience with his supervisor at work. As he speaks, you notice that Walt gets an angry-looking expression on his face but does not say anything. What are some of your options for dealing with this? Why might you make these choices?

6. As you begin a session of a growth group, you invite members to comment on unfinished business with respect to the group. Instead, the members begin a lackluster discussion of recent controversial decisions made by city officials. How would you respond?

7. As the second session of a personal growth group gets under way, one group member, Hilda, waves an inch-thick packet of photos in the air. She says, "Wouldn't everyone like to see the photos of our family's camping vacation from last summer?" What would you want to consider in formulating a response?

8. As you are concluding a session for an experiential group, you ask for a quick go-around for each member to briefly comment on what they learned or experienced during the session. Most comments are fairly positive, but Wally blurts out, "You know, I wasn't given a chance today to tell you of the traumatic experience I had this afternoon." As the group facilitator, what are some of your options for responses?

9. Just as you are concluding a session of a personal growth group, Joe makes a statement with a sharp tone in his voice: "I just don't like how some people dominate the discussion in here. What about the rest of us?" What things would you need to consider in your response to Joe, and what response might you offer?

SELF-REFLECTION

1. How comfortable are you in dealing with silence? Do you tend to feel anxious to "do something"? What cues help you to distinguish between productive and unproductive silence?

2. What personal concerns might you have about stepping forward as a group leader to block rambling, counterproductive, or argumentative behaviors by group members?

3. What difficulties do you anticipate having with scanning the room and being aware of what is happening with all the members in a small group of, say, 12 members?

4. What have been your personal experiences with structured exercises? Under what circumstances did you find them to be especially useful? Under what circumstances might such activities actually take something away from the group experience?

WORKING ON AGENDAS

Basic Framework of a Group Session

The group has now started. The first session, with the help of a predesigned structure, went surprisingly smoothly. Now the leader is facing the second session. This session can be the most challenging session in the life of a group, because as the group launches into its second session, it is hard pressed with the two demands of group work—the task and the relationship. A wide array of issues and goals has been entrusted to the group in the first session. Now, how do the group members go about helping each other achieve their goals? Beginning leaders obviously need a framework to get a sense of how a session can flow. This chapter provides such a framework to give leaders a road map of how to go about helping members work through their issues and achieve their goals. This framework will enable the leader to initiate high-level interaction among members, make more effective use of group time, and increase members' sense of responsibility. This basic framework has helped numerous new leaders develop a sense of direction and flow in the initial stages of group life. This sense of direction and flow builds their confidence and competency when they are faced with the towering challenge of working with a group within a limited time frame.

Of course, a framework is just a road map; it can never delineate for the leader the interplay among elements in each given moment of a group session. The leader must rely on her own clinical intuition and judgment for that. But the framework will help leaders slowly shift toward a more intense here-and-now focus (see Chapter 8) when the group passes the initial stages. And later, when the group is mature enough, the framework gives way to a totally unstructured mode with a pursuit of immediacy within group (see Chapters 9 and 10). So this framework grows in steps with each stage of the group development.

This extended chapter presents the essentials of a comprehensive framework. The reader can gain a clear vision of the framework through an examination of Figure 6.1 near the end of the chapter.

This chapter covers:

- Key to the group session framework
- Getting an agenda contract
- Presenting an agenda
- Creating a safe environment
- Facilitating feedback-giving
- Working with grief and crisis
- Making the transition to the next agenda item
- Principle of half-and-half
- Cases in point
- Overview of the group session framework

KEY TO THE GROUP SESSION FRAMEWORK

As the group dives into its work in the second session, members may feel unspeakable tension in facing the unknown. Most members have no pre-existing notion of what to expect in a real working session. The tension can be contained by using this framework, the key to which lies in "working on agendas." When members' personal agenda items are put on the floor, both leaders and members get a sense of what work will be done in the session, and the session starts to flow.

Agenda as a Springboard

Many people are surprised when they hear, for the first time, that groups work on each member's personal agenda. They do not know what *personal agenda* means. In process-focused groups, leaders do not design topics for members; rather, members have to take responsibility for bringing up *personal issues* they want to work on. These personal items are called "agendas." Agendas are members' self-acclaimed programs for particular sessions. Agendas are closely related to members' issues and goals (Kivlighan, Jauquet, Hardie, Francis, & Hershberger, 1993).

A member's personal agenda often involves distressing issues or events happening in the member's life outside the group. These issues tend to be there-and-then focused, and are closely related to members' presenting problems—the very issues that have brought the members into therapy. Typical agenda items may include but are not limited to: depression, interpersonal conflict, addiction problems, relationship problems, anxiety, low self-esteem, and employment difficulties. Members experience these issues in their lives at large, and, over time, they tend to establish patterned behaviors. Some personal agendas involve situations in members' lives or members' concerns about how they are perceived by others (Ferencik, 1991). Some personal agendas, however, may be here-and-now focused if they involve events and relationship issues within the group.

In sharing their personal agendas, group members are offered a medium through which they can see that all of them share common struggles, as if they are "in it together." They feel a sense of inclusion. This sense of inclusion, of feeling included, is the first universal need (Schutz, 1958). By allowing each member to decide when to begin substantive work through presenting his agenda, the leader shows respect for the second universal need—the need for control (Schutz, 1958).

Working on members' agenda items is not an end in itself. Nor is it a format for solving members' problems one at a time. Rather, agendas are used as a *springboard* to bring about energetic interaction among all members. Working on agendas requires that the whole group become engaged, regardless of whose agenda is on the floor. The engagement of the whole group provides the exact seed needed for interpersonal learning. When an agenda is presented, the group members have a chance to become actively involved with one another. As they do so, their interpersonal styles and the roles they habitually play in their own lives are activated within the context of the group. Once activated, these interpersonal processes become grist for the mill of group work. Great insight and motivation to change can result from such group processing. Therefore, it is not only the member presenting the agenda who benefits from working on the issue, but all the members benefit by becoming more aware of and more motivated to improve their interpersonal functioning. This is the ultimate purpose of working on members' agendas.

With personal agendas serving as a springboard, the group leader can initiate high-level interaction among members, make more effective use of group time, and increase members' sense of responsibility. Simultaneously the group can attend to the task aspect (achieving members' goals) and the relationship aspect (fostering trusting relationships and group cohesiveness) of the group process. All of this can be achieved without the leader deciding on specific topics and exercises for the group each week. This ability to address both the task and the relationship aspects of group work is the strength of this framework.

Balancing Two Elements: Support and Challenge

The group members' involvement with one another's agenda-working is a powerful avenue to interpersonal learning because working on agendas involves balancing two elements. The first element is *support*. When presented, each agenda is treated with sensitivity and explored until a full picture is revealed. While one member is working on her agenda, the whole group engages with this specific person in helping her achieve goals. The energy of the group is invested in giving responses in empathic, supportive, and honest ways—the kinds of validation and understanding that the specific member normally does not have the chance to receive in daily life. This fosters a safe environment in which members can bond with one another.

The second element of agenda-working is *challenge.* Getting support by itself is not what helps people heal. Support needs to be balanced with challenges. The working of the agenda is initially geared toward there-and-then stories, but very soon the focus shifts from outside events toward interpersonal perceptions within the group. There will be various degrees of here-and-now interaction. The group will examine actual reactions evoked during group interaction in the hope of shedding light on maladaptive behavioral patterns. It is this action of mutual challenge that ultimately brings about insight and change. In order for any member to reach this point of illumination and change, a series of group interactions, sometimes across several sessions, may be required.

Although some members need more support and others more challenges, the leader is wise to balance support and challenge within the group. Most members' experiences can be promoted to the optimal level when challenge is balanced with support.

Getting An Agenda Contract

Requesting personal agenda items is a prerequisite to plunging into the work of a group session. This section covers a method for asking members to put their agendas on the table.

Agenda Contracts

Before the group starts to dive into any member's issue, the leader must first get an *agreement* (or *contract*) from the individual. That is, the member has to agree to become the focus of the group's attention. Without explicit permission from a given member, the group should not dig deeply into a member's issue for an extended length of time.

Many new leaders make the mistake of focusing on a member when she is not ready to work on an issue. The situation usually goes like this: A member will be describing a problem or concern that appears to be dramatic and that captures the attention of other group members. The leader assumes that because the member tells dramatic stories and appears to need support from others, she must want to work on her problem. Acting on this assumption, the leader and the rest of the group dive right in to address the problem, eagerly offering suggestions to that person, only to be met with "Yes, but" responses or resentment. The rest of the group simply feels frustrated.

This kind of "Yes, but" response is quite understandable. Some members have a history of externalizing their problems or blaming others for them and have no desire to take charge of their own lives. Some are frightened of committing themselves to a plan of action in front of others. Others have worked through their concerns and are simply sharing a past experience for whatever it is worth. Still others just want to vent the feelings associated with a situation but are not yet ready to move on to any type of personal growth work.

To maximize group effectiveness, the leader must make sure that an agreement is garnered from a particular member before diving in to his problems. This agreement is called an "agenda contract." How does the leader get an agenda contract? There are two ways to go about it: (1) through check-in, and (2) through agenda request.

Through Check-In   The first way of getting an agenda contract is through check-in. When the leader opens the group, he usually opens it with a relaxation exercise and then with a first go-around for check-in, as demonstrated in Chapter 5. During this check-in, if a member reveals any crisis or stressful event that needs the group's attention, the leader might invite him to offer it as an agenda item. The leader may say one of the following:

> Jeff, this event seems to bother you very much. Would you like to offer this concern as an agenda item to work on today?

> Jeff, this seems to be a complicated issue. Would you like to wait for a few minutes and present it as one of today's agenda items?

> Jeff, would you like to use some group time to explore this issue a bit further so that you can understand it better?

If the particular member does not want to offer his issue as an agenda item to work on, the leader should simply respect his wish and move on. If he does want to pursue the issue, the leader has made an agenda contract with the member.

Through Agenda Request   The second way of getting an agenda contract is through an "agenda go-around" devised by Yalom (1983). Yalom uses this ritual in the beginning of each session when group members are asked to formulate their agendas. The purpose of this agenda go-around is to formally bring agenda items to the forefront. Since leaders cannot impose agendas on group members, the agenda go-around serves to ask members to make explicit the issues they would like to work on. This round also asks those who do not present agendas to commit to practicing their interpersonal skills during the session. By doing this, the leader puts the ball in the members' courts. Everyone in the group must take responsibility for deciding on the kinds of group experiences desired for that particular session. (For a recap of how to conduct an agenda go-around, read Chapter 5.)

If several agenda items are put on the table, the leader needs to warn the group that it might not be possible to work on all of them in a given session. The leader needs to do this so that those members whose agenda items get tabled until the following week will not feel neglected. The leader might say:

> Okay, we have a number of agenda items on the table today. We will work as hard as possible to cover all of them, but please remember that realistically we may not be able to bring all of them to closure in one session. If that is the case, we will continue working on the agenda items in the following weeks.

When several agenda items are on the table, the group may decide who is to go first by judging the urgency of each issue. The basic principle is to let the member whose emotions are running highest go first. The leader might say,

> Jane, you seem to be already in the depth of your emotion. Why don't you start first?

If no particular issue is pressing, the leader may ask those who have presented agenda items to decide who should start:

> Since no agenda item is especially pressing, we will let those of you with issues to work decide who will go first. So who would like to start?

If by the end of the session only some of the agenda items have been covered, the leader needs to carefully handle the feelings of the members whose agenda items will be delayed. The leader might say:

> We are running out of time today, and we haven't had a chance to work on Tom's agenda item yet. [turning to Tom] Tom, would you allow the group to put your agenda item as the first priority in the next session?

In the following session, the leader may want to remind the group of Tom's agenda item:

> Last week we did not have a chance to work on Tom's agenda item, so today we will put Tom's agenda item first. [turning to Tom] Tom, would you still like to pursue your issue today?

If in the following session someone is experiencing a crisis and needs the group's immediate attention, the leader will need to consult with Tom to see whether the member in crisis may go first. The leader may say,

> Tom, I know that your agenda item was tabled last session and we should give yours the first priority. But Betty is having a crisis today and is quite shaky right now. She seems to need the group's immediate support. Would you be willing to allow Betty's issue to be addressed first and yours second?

When There Is No Agenda: Dealing with Reluctance

A dreadful event that may occur in the second session is that there may be no member who wants to present an agenda item. This kind of hesitance or reluctance happens most frequently in the initial stages of the group because of members' fear or distrust. Many times members who seem unwilling to participate are really fearful, awkward, anxious, or skeptical; they are not necessarily "resistant." Fear and hesitance are normal emotions that often surge before major learning. What these indicate is that the members exhibiting these reactions are "not ready." They are not ready to put themselves on the line and risk exposing themselves in front of others. Inexperienced group leaders must be careful not to personalize members' reluctance as a personal failure on their part. Members' unwillingness is not rejection of the leader, but a reflection of the members' fear.

To encourage risk-taking, the leader must create a group atmosphere that is safe and nonjudgmental. If no one wants to present an agenda item, the leader may lead the group to explore the reasons underlying the members' reluctance. Is it possible that members do not feel safe? Having members discuss their feelings helps them break out from their sense of aloneness. If members admit reluctance, the leader needs to applaud their honesty. If members know they are not alone in their feelings and that it is common to feel reluctant about exposing oneself in front of others, they will be more willing to open themselves to the group. To help members talk about their fears, the leader may say something like,

> No one appears eager to present an agenda item at this moment. It seems like many of you still feel apprehensive about presenting your issues in the group. I wonder whether we can spend some time talking about these feelings. And we can also talk about how to make this group a safe place for all of you to share your private struggles and feelings. Would anyone want to say a few words about this?

After members have fully expressed their fears, the leader can reinforce the need for a safe environment. The leader may say,

> I am glad that feeling safe is a priority of the group. I'd like to see all of us in the group make a commitment to making everyone feel safe and supported.

Besides issues of vulnerability, some members may hold back because of a deeply entrenched sense of low self-worth that discounts the importance of their issues. If this is the case, the leader may say,

> George, I just heard you say two things. The first was that it bothers you that sometimes you don't choose to express yourself in your personal life and at work. The second thing I heard was that you think your issues are not as important as those of others within this group. I wonder whether you might have discounted the importance of your issue, thinking that since it is not a severe problem, it has no place in this group. I would like to challenge you about that part of what you said, because group is not reserved only for extreme problems. All kinds of interpersonal concerns are appropriate for this group and are worthy of the group's attention.

PRESENTING AN AGENDA

After agenda items are put on the table, the leader should encourage members in self-disclosure, that is, presenting their agenda items. To present one's own agenda in front of the group is to disclose oneself in front of the group. Following are things a leader should consider when helping a specific member present her agenda.

Disclosing One's Problems and Struggles

To present one's agenda is to tell one's story. The member first describes the problem: what it is, how it got started (the history), and the impact the problem has on his life. Then, if the person is aware, he may talk about his involvement in the problem: how he reacts to it and how he gets entangled in the depths of it. The telling of the story is like peeling the onion of one's self; there are many levels to the stories, and many levels of the self. Often the telling starts with the outer, less sensitive layers, but self-disclosure is absolutely essential in group counseling and therapy. No member will benefit from such counseling and therapy without honest self-disclosure (Yalom, 2002).

Self-disclosure in front of a group of people requires courage and risk-taking. People who have not been in counseling and therapy previously often find it frightening to reveal themselves in the group setting.

To encourage genuine self-disclosure, the group needs to provide a safe environment that establishes trust. This aspect is discussed in detail in the next section. At the starting point, the leader can help members relate the outer layers of their stories by asking them to restate their goals. Restating goals helps members situate themselves in the context of the problems and issues that led to the goals they set. The leader may say something like,

> Before you start, Matt, maybe you can remind the group what your goal is. Then, you can go ahead and tell the group about the issues and struggles behind your goal.

Members frequently change their goals after being in the group for a few sessions. Other members' work or their own reflections can lead to such alterations in goals. Regardless of whether a member has changed her original goal, the leader's question will give the member a chance to state what she wants to work on during the session.

Providing Help with Self-Disclosure

Ideally, all members would know how to cover all aspects of their presenting problems, but some members express themselves ever so vaguely. They say things like "I'd like to stop playing all these games with myself," "I want to feel not so distant with my sister," or "I want my wife to be more understanding." They may give little or no further information beyond such a simple statement. A presentation like this does not give the group any material to work on. When an agenda item is presented with major pieces of the puzzle missing, the leader may engage the rest of the group to help the person get to the heart of the story. To engage the group, the leader might say one of the following:

> [To the group] Do the group members all understand why this issue is so troublesome for Matt?

> [To the group] Some of you look puzzled. Would you like to ask Matt some clarifying questions so that you can get a clearer picture of what Matt's underlying concern is?

The leader may also participate in clarifying the picture by making a comment like one of the following:

> Matt, you said that you are hurting. I have been listening attentively to that feeling, yet I am not sure I get it.

> Matt, has that sense of feeling like an outsider ever happened in other situations?

Directing Clients away from Storytelling

Some members have difficulty getting personal in presenting their agenda items. They may talk about life situations in a way that focuses on others and on what others have done to cause them difficulties without revealing any trace of themselves in the picture. They are basically "storytelling." Their inner reactions remain hidden from the listeners. This kind of storytelling does not facilitate self-awareness. The leader may steer such members to talk about their experiences on a more personal level by saying something like,

> Matt, I am aware that you are talking a lot about several important people in your life. They are not here, so we aren't able to work with them. But we can work with your feelings and reactions toward them and how these reactions affect your life and relationships.

Listening for the Core Issue

While a member is presenting his issues, the leader needs to listen carefully to identify the core issue. The leader needs to listen with purpose. Effective listening is a fundamental part of leadership. Listening requires that the leader focus intently and sort through the member's experiences and interpersonal relationships in her own mind. The leader should listen for clues to the underlying message, the hidden dynamics, and the implications of the dynamics.

To listen in such a way, the leader must be emotionally and mentally present in the conversation at hand. She must be focused. When a leader listens without focus, she will blur and dilute the information and derail the conversation. The leader must listen with an effort at understanding in order to identify where a member's patterns need to be changed if they prove to be maladaptive, or where patterns may need to be increased in sophistication if they prove to be too provincial. Once the leader has a sense of the whole picture, she can facilitate the group to help the member see the situation as it is.

CREATING A SAFE ENVIRONMENT

In having members work on agendas, the leader must create a safe environment where sensitive issues can be explored without fear. As mentioned, the unfolding of a member's story is like peeling an onion; several layers must be removed to reach the core. Peeling one's own onion in front of a roomful of people can feel threatening. Thus, the leader must help the group build a safe environment to becalm the members' fears. This safe milieu is the bedrock for deeper exploration of any issue. Group cohesiveness is enhanced when trusting relationships among members are established. It is only through the evolution of a trusting atmosphere that members can strive to reach their goals. The level of intimacy and trust that the group attains will ultimately determine the group's outcome.

The leader can use the skills presented in this section to create the much-needed safe environment for group work. These skills include: (1) understanding the blocking effect of fears; (2) avoiding a rush to solve problems or give feedback; (3) drawing out empathy; (4) linking similar reactions; (5) connecting relevant issues; and (6) bringing back focus whenever it is lost.

Fears That Block Sharing

Fear is a strong human emotion across cultures. There are common fears that block people from going deeper into interpersonal work. Some members dread drawing attention to themselves. Some are afraid that once the gate is opened, their emotions may surge out of their control. Many people are blocked from making themselves known because of their fear of:

- Rejection
- Judgment
- Pressure to perform
- Looking stupid
- Burdening others
- Discovering abnormal patterns
- Attack
- Not being able to cope once opening up

These fears may prevent members from plunging deeper into personal levels of disclosure. However, these fears and apprehensions are developmentally appropriate and healthy (Leszcz, 1992). To create a sense of safety, leaders must acknowledge members' fears and help members work through them in the beginning sessions of group. The leader needs to build a group culture that invites members to move at their own pace, respecting the differences in the rhythm of individual engagement (Leszcz, 1992). Trust takes time to develop and can be achieved only through gentle facilitation.

Some people believe that group is a place where people can readily practice honesty. They believe that group members should start, as soon as possible, to confront one another with their immediate honest feelings. This is a dangerous belief. People need to feel safe to be able to open up deeper levels of themselves to one another. It takes time to build that sense of safety. Premature honesty only bruises the tender skin of a group in its infantile stage.

Avoiding Overstimulating Clients Too Soon

In the early stages of group, members often focus more on there-and-then stories, seeking relief rather than growth. Members are within their comfort zone when focusing on the there-and-then, avoiding those emotions that might be present in the here-and-now group setting (Shapiro, 1979). This avoidance is normal. Leszcz (1992) states: "Frequently this resistance centers around the issue of subjective feelings of safety and vulnerability" (p. 56). The leader can allow some time for members to dwell on the "there-and-then" of their stories. There is no need to push them into the immediacy issues at this early time. It is unwise to stimulate too much too soon. The main task of the leader in the initial sessions is to maintain an environment that is accepting enough to allow for meaningful exploration of the individual idiosyncrasies within the interpersonal fields (Karterud, 1988).

Focusing on there-and-then stories can help in avoiding overstimulating the members' affect beyond the capacity of the group as a whole (Leszcz, 1992). In their extensive study of effective and ineffective groups, Lieberman, Yalom, and Miles (1973) found that those groups that had a moderate level of emotional stimulation tended to be the most effective as compared to groups that were either high or low in the level of emotional stimulation.

Although process groups are grounded in the philosophy of the here-and-now (the immediacy of interpersonal learning), the here-and-now focus must be achieved in the right time frame; otherwise, it will overstimulate the group. The issue of timing is essential for almost all powerful intervention techniques. Friedman (1989) states, "knowing when to focus on here and now and when to focus on there and then is something of an art born of experience, sensitivity, and good instincts" (p. 115). This is true for the beginning as well as the later stages of group development.

Avoiding Premature Problem Solving and Feedback-Giving

Most people have a tendency to feel responsible for solving any problem presented to them. People in our society are well trained to attack problems head-on. Too many times we witness this phenomenon: After a speaking member presents her problem, the rest of group, and even the leader, rush in to provide advice or a solution, only to be met with resistance, resulting in mutual frustration. The purpose of group counseling is not to help any given member solve a specific problem, but to help members gain self-awareness through discovering their own interpersonal functioning. A tone of premature problem solving will jeopardize any chance for change as the working member undergoes this self-discovery process. A person's self-awareness is pivotal in moving beyond old ineffective defensive behaviors and into a new realm of long-term resolution. The goal of a process group is to put the client back on track through this journey of self-awareness.

When presenting her agenda, what the working member most needs is the group's help in exploring her issues at a deeper level. This is not the time to give feedback, either. Any feedback or new perspective that is provided before the underlying issue is fully explored tends to be superficial, lacking the penetrating power of insight. Therefore, after a member has presented her agenda, the group should not rush into a problem-solving session. The leader should not say to the group, "What do you think Jane can do to eliminate her stress?" Rather, what the working member needs is a warm and nonjudgmental acceptance so that she can go deeper into her issues to achieve a more complete understanding and a motivation for change. This involves validation, which will be covered later.

Power of Giving: Altruism

If advice and feedback are premature at the time the member is disclosing his agenda, then what is the group to do? Many things! The group can (1) tune into the speaker's spoken and unspoken emotions, (2) communicate understanding, and (3) connect to the person in a meaningful way. When the group does these things, the members feel better about themselves. The most fundamental way of leading a group is to facilitate the group to give what comes from the authentic self. The act of giving makes all parties involved feel better. The receiver feels validated, understood, and even enlightened. The givers feel that they have offered something precious to others—something that wealth and status cannot buy. They feel a sense of "altruism." As discussed in Chapter 1, altruism is one of the key therapeutic factors for a group (Yalom, 1995). This sense of "having something to offer" raises group members' self-esteem; they feel better about themselves. A sense of meaningfulness and deep connection starts to build. *Giving validation* and *giving feedback* are the cornerstones of interpersonal learning, and the whole group benefits from such giving.

Importance of Giving Validation

People want to be heard. People want to know that others understand what they are going through. And yet many people seem to have a hard time opening up to others. Most people have been hurt in relationships. Paradoxically, however, relationships are required for healing (Chen & Giblin, 2002). What we do in the process-focused group is to offer something that people are unable to get in the world at large. Most people, when wounded, have to lick their wounds alone; they do not have the luxury of receiving validation. Indeed, underlying many people's developmental problems and their insecurities and inadequacies is the agony produced because they felt invisible in their home lives as children. A powerful antidote to that occurs in groups where members feel they are truly seen by other human beings because the members validate each other's emotions and acknowledge the reasons behind these particular emotions. We all need to remember the power of giving others an opportunity to feel heard, seen, and understood. The power of the group comes from this feeling of being psychologically visible.

When validated, the working member feels at home in the group and is able to form meaningful relationships with other group members. This feeling of being accepted can be especially important for those who are minorities and for those who have had many past experiences of being rejected or excluded. Receiving acceptance and validation is an essential part of Yalom's (1995) concept of corrective emotional experience. The healing power in the affirmation of a group of people far exceeds that in the affirmation of a single therapist.

For the group members, to practice giving validation is to exercise a skill that is the foundation for interpersonal intimacy. In order to give validation, one has to be attuned to the nonverbal metacommunication in another's message. Practicing this kind of attunement in a group setting provides excellent interpersonal learning. Validation and empathy bring compassion and love to the group members, enhancing group cohesiveness. It is at this level that the third universal need, the need for affection (Schutz, 1958), can be fulfilled.

Giving Validation through Naming Feelings

Members in a new group do not always know what to say to show validation and empathy. The leader has to set the stage for empathic interaction. There are two types of empathy: basic empathy and advanced empathy. Advanced empathy is covered in Chapter 8. This section focuses on basic empathy. To give *basic empathy* is to convey our understanding of what the member *evidently* has gone through. How do we convey our understanding? We do so through naming others' feelings. When a feeling is not named, it becomes submerged. Often in group, a range of superficial feelings is expressed, revealing only the tip of the iceberg. The facades remain incongruent with the depth of the emotions that are actually stewing inside the group members. Unless their feelings are legitimized, members will continue to hide their emotional pain and doubt the validity of their emotions. Therefore, members' feelings need to be named so they can begin to pay respect to their own emotional depths. Naming the feelings is the first step toward conveying our understanding of people's experiences. Naming permits people to feel more fully those feelings that are part of the human condition.

To facilitate empathy, the leader can ask the group to name the feelings that a particular member might be having inside. Some new leaders, however, have a habit of asking the group, "Can any of you relate to what Matt was saying?" The word *relate* may only prompt the group to share similar experiences and stories, which may make Matt feel less alone, but which also may remove some of the intensity from Matt. This kind of sharing does not necessarily make the receiver feel psychologically visible because such responses fail to openly acknowledge the person's difficult emotions.

Other new leaders stumble by asking the group, "Would any of you like to say anything to Matt?" The word *anything* is so inclusive that it might not direct the group to the desired empathic expression. Often this question prompts further questions, information, or advice that quickly derails the group from the track. To facilitate giving validation and empathy, the leader needs to be specific in his prompt. There are two ways to do that: (1) by using a sentence-completion exercise, and (2) by guessing at and naming the working member's feelings

Sentence-Completion Exercise   The first way to help the group name a working member's feelings is by using a sentence-completion exercise. Sentence-completion exercises are covered in the structured exercise section of Chapter 5. The leader should not overuse structured exercises, as they tend to confine members' free expression, but sometimes an exercise like the following is helpful in a new group:

> [To the whole group] Matt has been talking about his wife's feelings as she goes through the cancer treatment. But it seems that he has difficulty taking time to feel his own feelings. So I would like the group to try to complete this following sentence. The sentence is, "I am Matt, and I feel _____ because _____." When you complete the sentence, please address it directly to Matt. Okay, whoever is ready, please jump in. Let's try not to take turns.

One of the principles in using a structured exercise is to follow the exercise with group processing (see Chapter 5). After members have responded to an exercise, the leader may ask them to talk a bit about their experience in doing the exercise. The leader may say,

> [To the group] Thank you all for participating in this exercise. I would like to take another step forward and ask you to share what you were going through internally when you said what you just said to Matt.

What memories or reactions were triggered inside of you? Would anyone like to share?

This processing will bring out a lot of deep feelings and touching stories
that will warm group members' hearts.

Naming Feelings by Guessing   Another way to help the group name a
member's feelings is to have the group guess or imagine what the speaking member's feelings are or what the personal struggle really is. This is a
powerful way to prompt the group to show basic empathy to one another.
To use this intervention, the leader may say,

> [To the group] Now we have a pretty good picture of Matt's story. I
> wonder, as you were listening to Matt, what feelings did you guess Matt
> might be experiencing under these circumstances?

Other examples of prompts not related to Matt's agenda include:

> [To the group] Rick has opened up to us about the abandonment issue
> and how it ties to his constant struggles in his current life. At this
> moment, I would like the group to imagine what it would have been
> like to grow up as Rick did, in the circumstances he has described.
> When you are ready, please feel free to jump in and speak directly to
> Rick. If you prefer to pass, that will be respected.

> [To the group] If you were Bill, how would you be feeling after you
> experienced this loss of marriage and his two near-death events?

> [To the group] "What feelings did you sense in Sue as she explained
> how she grew up in a family affected by her father's alcoholism?

Most members do well in naming the working member's feelings if the
leader gives them specific and clear prompts. Upon feeling heard and validated, the working member usually feels safe enough to plunge into the
deeper levels of her story that were hidden in her initial self-disclosure.
This is the reward given to an empathic group.

Giving Validation through Sharing Similar Experiences

A less powerful, yet still meaningful, way of creating a safe environment in
the group is by linking together similar experiences or reactions. Most
people experience a certain sense of interpersonal isolation. As humans,
most of us think that we are alone in experiencing problems and distresses
in our lives. This sense of aloneness increases our social isolation. This
aloneness dissipates as soon as we hear others disclose similar reactions,
dilemmas, and life experiences. Other group members' revelations of
similar thoughts and struggles that reflect the human condition are
extremely soul-comforting, as they offer a sense of universality. They provide a "You are not alone!" and "Welcome on board!" kind of experience

(Yalom, 1995; 2002). This certainly helps to relieve the sense of vulnerability that a member feels when exposing the self in front of others. To foster this sense of universality, the leader may invite members to share their common distresses and similarities. In the case of Matt, the leader may say one of the following:

> [To the whole group] As Matt dug deeper into the anxiety that he is experiencing in his life, how did this notion of anxiety strike a cord with any of you?
>
> [To the group] I wonder what issues of your own may have been awakened as you heard Matt's story?

Other examples not related to Matt's issue include:

> [To the group] I can see that Jackie has a sense of being out of control. I would like the group to stop for a moment while all of you try to recall an instance in your lives when you knew you shouldn't be doing something and yet you couldn't help doing it. When you are ready, please share these experiences with Jackie so she sees that you understand her struggle.
>
> [To the group] It seems that Maria's sharing about her fear of being judged has struck a chord in many of you. Would any of you like to say a few words to Maria?

The leader may also summarize the similarity of members' experiences periodically:

> [To the group] It seems that many members in our group have experienced a similar fear of losing a loved one if we feel we don't do enough or aren't good enough.

The powerful effect of receiving validation through a sharing of similar experiences can be demonstrated by Matt's reflection:

> I felt especially warm and grateful toward Dory, since she was the only one who described a similar experience to my own. Hearing that someone else felt some of the same things had a powerful effect on me. I felt some of my own self-judgment melt away in being reminded that I was not so terrible to the extent that no one else could possibly relate to my experience.

Connecting Two or More Members Together

Working on a member's agenda is not a linear procedure. Rather, it is more like weaving a web. Often a member's presenting issue may make another member aware of some of her own issues that she has previously neglected. Many members' issues are connected in a surprising way. The relevancy of these issues makes us realize that we all share in the human condition. To make the group a safe environment for expression, the leader may identify themes that connect intimately to the issue being described. One member's issue can be integrated into another's right away, so that the group reaches a complex and profound level of experience of the issues at hand. If time allows, the leader might try connecting two members' issues and see whether the group can help both individuals at the same time. Sometimes even a third member's issue may be connected to the other two. To weave the web of connection, the leader may say,

> [To the group] It looked like Karen was in touch with something painful when she responded to Matt's sharing. Did anyone notice how Karen's reaction was connected to Matt's experience? Would anyone like to say a few words to Karen at this moment? Then we'll go back to Matt.

When a leader connects two or more members together, he must remember to go back to the person who originally presented the agenda item, lest the focus get lost. The leader may loop back to the focus by saying,

> We have had quite an intense exchange about the issue of loss. Many of you have shared how this issue has triggered deep feelings inside of you. Your comments have been very helpful for all the group members. Right now, though, I am aware that Matt's agenda hasn't reached closure, so let's go back to Matt for awhile.

Leader Participation in Reflecting Feelings

While busy facilitating the group to give validation to member experience, the leader should remember that she is an "observer-participant in the group" (Yalom, 1995, p. 140). With group-centered leadership, the leader gives the group members prime opportunities to validate one another's feelings, but if an opening arises she may also participate in reflecting feelings. If group members are short on words to convey their understanding to one another, the leader certainly needs to take the lead in validating members' feelings.

The leader may reflect members' feelings on two levels: feelings of individual members, and the group's collective feelings.

Feelings of Individual Members   If the leader asks the group members to imagine what feelings a specific member might be experiencing, the leader should also participate in getting into the member's inner world and verbally conveying that understanding to the member. If the leader asks members to share their reactions toward a particular member, then the leader also can share his feelings toward that member. The warmth and understanding of the leader will radiate when he participates in validating individual members' experiences. For example,

> [To an individual member] Matt, you feel hurt to see your daughter so stressed out by your wife's illness. You wish she could just talk about

her feelings instead of yelling at her brother, yet you don't know how to talk to her about this and it makes you feel powerless.

Group's Collective Feelings   The group as a whole often possesses collective emotions and consciousness, although such feelings may not be explicitly articulated. The leader can put these unspoken feelings into words. Openly acknowledging these feelings, positive or negative, helps the group to develop cohesiveness more quickly. For example,

> [To the group] It seems like the group is deeply touched by Matt's struggle. There is a sense of connection in this room right, now as if all of us are in touch with similar longings and pain buried somewhere inside of us.

> [To the group] I sense that the group is very tentative right now and does not want to address Tracy's deeper feelings for the moment. I can see that the group cares about Tracy very much and does not want to make Tracy feel even more vulnerable than she already does.

Redirecting Unhelpful Behaviors

As the group helps the working member with his agenda, group members' many interpersonal styles will emerge. The leader should keep half of her attention on the working member's issues and half on the rest of the group. This is called the "half-and-half" principle and is expounded in a later section of this chapter. Basically, the leader must remember not to focus exclusively on the working member and inadvertently allow ineffective interpersonal communication patterns to be used among the other group members.

Should a member give premature advice, the leader may intervene by saying,

> Jeff, I appreciate your good intentions in trying to solve Matt's problem, but at this moment I don't think we know enough to do that. So let's try to understand a bit more of what's underlying Matt's struggles. How does that sound?

If a member rushes in to stop another member from fully experiencing painful or undesirable emotions, the leader may intervene by saying,

> Let's allow Matt a moment to be with his pain. I think he knows that we care. [turning to Matt] Matt, please realize that we care and we are supportive of the emotions you are feeling right now.

Should a member talk *about* Matt rather than *to* him, the leader may intervene and say,

> Lisa, since Matt is here, would you please talk to him directly, instead of talking about him?

FACILITATING FEEDBACK-GIVING

The third element in working on an agenda is facilitating feedback exchange. Feedback is important in the later steps of working on a member's agenda. As the group successfully gives validation and empathy to the working member, with each sign of acceptance, the working member typically will peel his "onion" one layer deeper until he gets close to the core. This allows the group to have a better comprehension of the nature of his struggle. At this juncture, the working member is more receptive to insight-oriented input, so this is time to move the group to the action of giving feedback. This section presents a method for facilitating a group to give feedback in an effective manner.

Reality Testing: The Power of Receiving Feedback

People want to experience themselves and know themselves through feedback. They crave learning about how they come across to others. They want to knock down the walls that separate them from others and feel closer to others. Most people come to group counseling and therapy to resolve long-standing difficulties that are embedded in certain behavioral and thought patterns. Self-awareness is critical to moving beyond ineffective or defensive action and into the realm of long-term resolution. There is no better way to gain self-awareness than through receiving feedback.

The power of a group comes particularly from feedback—sufficient and honest feedback. Receiving feedback of this sort allows the member to see herself as others see her. The feedback is like a mirror, reflecting back images of the person's reality. Most people in our society have little chance of getting honest and open feedback from daily encounters, except in intimate relationships. Consequently, they continue to conduct themselves in the same manner, unaware of the influence their behavior has on others. Interpersonal learning is possible only when there is accurate interpersonal feedback. The group strives to provide abundant interpersonal feedback. With the help of feedback, members' defense mechanisms and relationship patterns are brought to light. Personal strengths and other characteristics become visible. Thus, honest feedback provides *grounds for reality testing*, leading to lasting therapeutic change.

Self-Esteem Boosting: The Power of Giving Feedback

Feedback not only benefits the receiver, but also the giver. People who suffer from low self-esteem often feel they have nothing valuable to offer to others. Many people are so self-absorbed that they cannot step outside themselves to see the greater needs of others. The more they are self-absorbed, the less they give, and the lower their self-esteem. To help group members increase their sense of self-worth, the leader can invite members to *offer* feedback to one another. Members begin to feel better through the action of giving.

Under this principle, the leader must avoid taking the responsibility of giving feedback onto his own shoulders. Otherwise, the leader will appear too much like an expert, and the group will become a leader-dominated group. Instead, by letting group members have the chance to give feedback before the leader does, the leader lets group members feel they are needed. Through *giving,* the members boost their self-esteem and achieve some sense of self-actualization. Indeed, Toth and Erwin (1998) showed that most members prefer to receive feedback from fellow members rather than from the leader.

Principles of Feedback-Giving

It cannot be emphasized enough that the group should not provide feedback before the members have gained a comprehensive understanding of the working member's story and validated her struggles. Feedback, when given prematurely, tends to be superficial. Only when the working member has received enough empathy and support can feedback be given.

Giving feedback is an art. Most important in giving feedback is a willingness to be honest, even if the feedback given may appear to be off-target. Members and leaders cannot remain removed from the group. It is better to make a contribution and risk being off-target than to withhold true feelings. The art of giving feedback can be learned through specific instructions. Leszcz (1992) gives us three ingredients of feedback that are necessary if feedback is to have any value in terms of reality testing. These ingredients are:

1. Feedback needs to contain an emotional component on the part of the giver.
2. Feedback needs to convey some message about the relationship between the giver and the recipient.
3. The giver of the feedback needs to take some risk in disclosing this communication.

These three ingredients will be covered more fully in Chapter 8, but in the early stage of group development, the leader should heed the fundamental elements of giving feedback. The following discussion contains some suggestions for the leader.

***Do Not Use General Terms, Such as the Word* Feedback**   To invite members to give feedback, the leader should avoid general terminology such as, "Would any of you like to give Matt any feedback?" As a psychological term, the word *feedback* carries a definite connotation in therapy. But in our society, laypeople often use the word *feedback* in such an overarching way that it conveys almost everything, and thus nothing. Members in groups do not usually know what *feedback* implies, or what kinds of feedback are helpful. In spite of their good intentions, members often give feedback that consists of stories, advice, or quick solutions. This kind of input is not helpful. The leader is responsible for clearly directing group members in how to share their observations. The key is to invite feedback without using the word *feedback*.

Be Specific in the Prompt   The leader should provide *specific* instructions by telling the group what kind of response he wants the group to offer. Examples of how to give specific prompts are discussed next.

Three Types of Basic Feedback

In the early stages of the group, three types of basic feedback are appropriate: (1) identifying old patterns, (2) connecting seemingly unrelated issues, and (3) providing a vision of the future.

Identifying and Thanking the Old Pattern   Identifying a behavioral pattern that runs through a member's problems can help the member understand his issues more deeply. When given gently and with care, group feedback can soften the grip that the coping pattern has on the member. The best way to soften the grip of an old behavioral pattern is by thanking the function it has served in the member's past. It is only when the grip of the old pattern is softened that a new and more effective coping skill can replace the old one. This kind of feedback is a gift that the group freely grants to the individual members.

To initiate this kind of feedback, the leader may say one of the following:

> [To the group] It seems that Matt feels well heard and supported by the group. Now I would like to take things a step further. I wonder, after listening to Matt's stories, what pattern you see running through Matt's life. What would you say to thank this pattern that has served Matt well by assisting him through his past difficulties? And how do you think this old pattern might hinder Matt in his current life? [Allow a moment for the group to ponder what they want to say. Scan the group for cues from members who might have something to say.]

> [To the group] "Thank you all for your empathic support for Matt. It would now be appropriate to give Matt some of your insight. So my question is: After listening to Matt's multilayered story, what patterns do you observe in his behavior or relationships? How have these patterns

helped Matt in the past? And how are these old coping skills working or not working for him in his current life?

Another example not related to Matt's issue is:

> [To the group] Julie and Mary seem quite moved by the group's empathy and support. Let's see whether we can go further to offer some insights for them. My question for the group is: After listening to Julie and Mary's stories of growing up in alcoholic families, how would you appreciate and honor the different coping pattern each has used with the same situation? And how are these coping skills working or not working for them in their current lives? Your perceptions will add some new self-awareness for Julie and Mary. Is anyone ready to start?

Connecting the Dots   The second type of basic feedback is one that connects seemingly unrelated issues with a theme. Some members may bring to the group what they see as a plethora of seemingly unrelated phenomena occurring to them and around them. The group can help by piecing together the underlying theme that weaves through the array of experiences, offering a whole new level of insight to the member. With a deeper level of insight, the receiver is more likely to experience a sense of leverage in her situation. Instead of having to deal separately with numerous and diverse of interpersonal issues, the receiver can shut off the single source of fuel that feeds all the fires. To initiate theme-focused feedback, the leader can give precise instructions to the group by saying something like this:

> [To the group] Let's shift focus a bit at this moment. Tracy seems to feel distressed and ashamed by the fact that she could not help but slip into affairs with other men whenever she was bickering with her boyfriend whom she loves very much. We also heard Tracy say that she has cut off contact with her father for many years. Do any of the group members see any connection between Tracy's cutting off from her father and her difficulty in handling tension in her intimate relationship? [pause] If you do, please talk to Tracy directly about what you see is the connecting theme between the two seemingly independent events. And please tell Tracy how you honor her old way of coping with this theme. [pause] Who would like to start?

Many surprising insights can come out of feedback-giving. The leader's job is to trust that the group has the ability to see things from a different perspective that is fresh and insightful enough to help the recipient of the feedback.

Providing a Vision of the Future   The third type of basic feedback is one that provides a vision of the future for the recipient. Here, the leader asks the group to project the member into the future and to consider what challenges the recipient has to take on now so that years from now he will be able to look back without regret. This kind of feedback can motivate a member to take responsibility for his own change. For example, the leader may say,

> [To the group] I wonder whether the group can envision what Lisa's life can be like five years from now and, most importantly, what must happen if she is to get there? In other words, what responsibility must Lisa take for her own change so that she won't be crying over the same distress as she did today? Does anyone want to start?

Leader Participation in Feedback-Giving

When a leader facilitates the group to give a member feedback, she also needs to participate in that action of giving. The leader's participation provides modeling as to how to package the feedback in a way that is helpful for the receiver. Advanced feedback techniques will be presented in Chapters 8, 9 and 10, but in the early stages of group development, a moderate level of intensity in the feedback is adequate. Following is an example of a leader offering feedback to a member:

> Tracy, I noticed that your legs would not stop shaking when you said that you cut off contact, many years ago, with your dad, who you called a loser. Minutes ago you also said that whenever you had a fight with your boyfriend of seven years, you would pick up the phone and set up an intimate meeting with another man afterward. It seems that the common thread in both situations is a desire to run away from the anxiety that any conflict arouses. I appreciate how important this running away has been in helping you. It helped you go through those disappointing moments in your life, some of which caused you unbearable pain. Yet I also see that the more you try to run away from confronting the issues, the more the anxiety seems to catch up with you. It's as if the anxiety is a reminder that something in your life needs to be resolved rather than being run away from.

Redirecting Unhelpful Feedback

Leaders must focus half of their energy on processing the agendas on the floor and the other half on attending to the interpersonal behaviors of all the group members. Even with leaders providing specific prompts, some members may still stray into giving advice, making interpretations, or asking impersonal questions. These responses are not helpful. They do not bring the receiver any helpful insight. When this happens, the leader may need to intervene and redirect the conversation. For example, the leader may say,

> [To the group] The purpose of giving feedback is not to solve a specific problem, but to help the member gain insight into the rut he or she has been unknowingly trapped in. So please don't feel compelled to solve Matt's problem in a session.

Jeff, you asked Matt a question just now. Would you please state what you were really trying to say to Matt behind your question?

Nita, when you give feedback to Matt, please tell him how you personally perceive him rather than telling him what he should do.

Teaching Members How to Receive Feedback

Frequently when members are receiving feedback, they are also busy thinking of answers to give, thinking of things to say back. Thus, their minds are constantly chattering as they carry on an inner dialogue. This kind of rehearsal or immediate response often curbs members from really hearing what is being said. If this continues, the session may become an extended dialogue between one specific member and a few of the other members. If this happens, the session will stagnate.

It is important for the leader to coach the recipient on how to listen to feedback. The more silent one's inner dialogue becomes, the more one is able to become aware of how the body and emotions are affected by the feedback. When coached wisely, recipients can practice trying not to respond to anything being said to them, but rather simply becoming aware of what's been said and of the energy in the feedback at a level beyond words. In so doing, the recipient may find a wealth of information flowing to him.

To coach a member to listen reflectively to feedback, the leader may say,

> Matt, the group seems to have several areas of feedback for you. While they are giving you the feedback, you may just simply listen for awhile without thinking about what to say back. Also, you don't need to accept all the feedback wholesale. You don't need to reject some feedback immediately, either. Just allow some time for the feedback to sink in, and notice how it affects you later. If you want to respond to the feedback today, there will be time for you to do that when the feedback has been completed.

To make sure that feedback has been understood, the leader can ask the receiver to paraphrase what he has heard. This serves both to reveal misunderstandings, which can then be corrected, and to encourage internalization of the feedback by having the receiver state it in his own words. The leader can say something like this to the recipient:

> Matt, maybe you can just listen for the moment. After the feedback is done, please paraphrase the feedback that you have heard from the group. Does that sound all right with you?

If a member dismisses similar feedback from many members, the leader needs to intervene by asking the member to consider how the feedback might fit him or her:

Jane, four members have made similar comments to you. It seems that you have difficulty listening to this feedback. I would like to invite you to pay attention to any consistent feedback because feedback that comes from so many people is likely to have a certain degree of validity.

Seeking Consensual Validation of Feedback

Sometimes insightful feedback can be hard to hear. When a receiver minimizes or discounts valuable feedback, the leader can seek consensual validation of that feedback. First, the leader restates that feedback concisely, and then he asks the rest of the group if they also observe the same patterns. Faced with a consensus of fellow group members, the recipient tends to reconsider the feedback. For example, you may say,

> [To the group] The group has provided Matt with a lot of interesting feedback. Among the various comments, Tom's feedback stands out. It seems that Tom is saying that Matt has a tendency to push people away by his people-pleasing behaviors. [leader restating insightful feedback]. I wonder, do other members also see this pattern in Matt? [seeking consensus]

Inviting Reaction to Feedback

After the group has offered feedback, the leader can invite the recipient to share how this feedback affects him. This creates a complete feedback loop. The leader might say one of the following:

> Matt, the members have shared with you some of their observations and comments. I wonder, among all this feedback, what strikes you the most?

> Matt, I wonder where you are now after listening to all this feedback? How are you feeling right now?

> Matt, it sounds like there is a lot for you to take in right now. Since our time is running short, I invite you to reflect on this feedback during the week. When you come back next time, would you share with the group what feedback fits you the best, and what insights have come out of this feedback that has been given to you?

WORKING WITH GRIEF AND CRISIS

When members present an urgent or unresolved grief issue, it's often because it triggers recurring crises in their lives. Leaders must think hard, in this situation, about both the short-term and the long-term needs of the member. The short-term need of the client in a grief case is definitely support, not challenge. Providing support alone, however, does not make the best use of a process-focused group. The grief issue itself is not related to any patterned or maladaptive behaviors, and thus is best worked through in a designated support group. However, grief issues are at times presented in a process group. When that happens, the other group members often do not feel comfortable challenging the presenter in any way. The group often stays in an empathic mode, unable to move on to the deeper feedback need-ed for the member's personal growth, which is exactly the client's long-term need. This section presents ways of dealing with grief and crisis issues, with-out shortchanging the power of the process-focused group.

From Grief and Crisis toward Personal Growth

Some members present urgent or unresolved grief issues because these issues are affecting their current lives. Others are tempted to present a grief issue as a way out through the "back door" because they assume that no one will feel right about giving the grieving member challenges for growth. In both situations, these members are denied challenge and con-structive confrontation, and thereby miss out on opportunities for self-exploration and a full group therapy experience. This dilemma is illustrat-ed by Jenni, as reflected in her journal near termination:

> When I presented my agenda to the group, I was in a time stricken by grief. I couldn't take that time to focus on my original interpersonal goal that I set for myself. It was a good experience hearing affirmations of my feelings. Looking back, however, I wish I had time to explore my original goal (which is to be more assertive and to learn to stand up for myself). At the beginning of the group, I do not think I was ready to hear people's feedback and the patterns they might see in me. The idea of someone exposing me was like pouring salt into an open wound. Now, I am hungry for that kind of feedback. I feel that I could have grown much more had I not let my fear of exposing take over. I wish I still had an opportunity to hear honest responses about myself from other members. That is one regret that I will carry with me. Because I presented a grief issue, I was not able to gain the maximum amount of insight about myself and make the growth interpersonally in the way that other members were able to.

From what we have observed, a group needs to work within the mode of emotional integration that is the key for any healing experience if the group wants to progress from one of grief support and crisis support toward one of personal growth.

Repairing Emotional Wounds

We believe that most mental issues have unresolved grief as the backdrop. This backdrop is brought to life in the group setting. Something about the group seems to stir up certain primitive emotions inside of people.

Members' pain and traumatic memories often resurface when they are working on their issues. Original wounds caused by past disrespect, rejection, and even abuse, are reexperienced. The resurfacing of strong or painful emotions is a sign that the core of some significant issues has been touched. Gaylin (2000) states that changes that are most significant and long-lasting are "those that engage the most profound emotions of the patient" (p. 218). When these painful affects resurface, the group must provide an environment in which the members can reexperience these strong, essential emotions without fear. Bloom (1993) states: "We cannot change the past, but we can change the way the past is constantly relived" (p. 264).

Changing "the way the past is constantly relived" is achieved when the group offers members empathy, acceptance, and validation (as discussed earlier in this chapter). This kind of response is totally opposite to the neglect and dismissal that members may have experienced in the past. For people who have experienced little unconditional acceptance in their lives, this emotional atmosphere is no small experience—but can be utterly reviving. The emotional solace and acceptance that members experience often represent their first experience with unconditional acceptance. Such acceptance repairs the emotional wounds that have been carried by the clients.

The repairing of wounds starts when the group relates to the member in a way that gives the member a unique opportunity to experience an atmosphere in which familiar painful patterns from her past interpersonal relationships are not repeated. Under the more favorable circumstances provided by the group, members are able "to face those emotional situations which were formerly unbearable and to deal with them in a manner different from the old" (Alexander & French, 1946, p. 67).

When members present grief issues, the group usually encounters no problem in offering validation and unconditional acceptance to the presenter. The atmosphere is usually emotional and moving, but the next element of challenge leading to personal growth is often lacking.

Healing and Restoring Perspective

For certain members, receiving empathy and affirmation is sufficient to start a healing process. For others, however, it takes more than that for change to occur. Previously held *misconceptions* must be reflected on, and *new perspectives* must be formed so that new attitudes, choices, and behaviors can be integrated into the wholeness of person. In grief and crisis cases, the feedback must not focus on maladaptive patterns, but rather on perspectives that can heal the wounds and restore the faith and trust that clients need in life.

In a short-term group, the pace of change is fast. To speed up the process and help members with unresolved grief issues to integrate new hope and trust into their whole being, the group leader may need to provide a catalyst. This catalyst is an experience wherein the members are given the very thing the outside world or their early environment failed to give them, thereby allowing them to experience a closure to an unacknowledged pain. Without this experience, they will remain somewhat unchanged. To guide the group to this healing action, the leader can ask the other group members to give a client what the outside world has failed to give him. Following are some examples:

Gina told her group about her unresolved grief that was repetitively stirred up whenever she ran into the daughter of the man who killed her father in a car accident and whenever she was reminded of the crude treatment her relatives gave to her family after her father's death. In Gina's case, pattern-focused feedback was not what she needed for emotional healing; she needed something else. In Gina's group, the leader might ask the group to do the following to give Gina a healing and restoring perspective:

[To the group] We see clearly that Gina is carrying an unbearable pain. She is repetitively injured by the cold attitudes of the people who ran over her father. She lost not only her father, but also the relatives who treated her family's grief in a cut-and-dried way. There are so many feelings of anger, hurt, pain, and sadness that keep Gina from moving on. At this moment, I would like all of you to imagine that you are Gina's father, and you are in this room now, facing your daughter's pain. What would you say to your daughter so that she can resolve this intolerable pain caused by her sense of injustice and move on with her life? Please take a moment to reflect on what you would say. When you are ready, please speak to Gina directly.

Joe (see the Cases in Point section later in this chapter) was experiencing panic and anxiety related to an unresolved past trauma. The leader of Joe's group might ask the group to do the following to bring emotional integration for Joe:

[To the group] Joe has talked about a long history of betrayal and abandonment by his supervisor, families, and friends since he came out as a gay man and a recovered alcoholic. In light of the panic attacks that he has been experiencing, I would like the group to try out an exercise with Joe: I would like each of you to choose the role of one of the persons (either his boss or his father, mother, or friends) who have betrayed or abandoned Joe in some way. As you put yourself into that role, say something to Joe that your heart wants him to hear so that a healing can begin. When you are ready, please jump in and speak directly to Joe.

Shina, a self-proclaimed perfectionist, had practiced keeping her illness (muscular dystrophy) a secret all her life, fearing that others would react with pity toward her if they knew of her illness. The leader of Shina's group might say,

[To the group] We have heard Shina share her fear of disclosing her illness, muscular dystrophy. I wonder, how does the group feel toward Shina now that you have come to know this "messy" part of her, the part of her that she has tried so hard to keep hidden? Please speak directly to Shina.

When Kathy presented her issue, it seemed to be clear that she had never experienced nurturing love and acceptance from her mother. The leader of Kathy's group might say,

[To the group] We all feel deeply touched by Kathy's struggle. She feels so beaten up and belittled by the most important person in her life, her mom, and she feels so stifled and lonely as a consequence. I would like to engage all of you in an imagery exercise. Imagine that Kathy's mom can speak through you. What would you say to Kathy about her strength and quality, based on your direct personal experience with Kathy within the group, that Kathy has never been able to get acknowledged from her Mom? What are the truths about Kathy that she has the right and need to hear? When you are ready, please speak to Kathy directly. Who wants to start?

Allowing Clients to Express Newly Surfaced Feelings

To complete the experience of emotional integration, the leader may ask a client to express any feelings that surfaced after she received the feedback offered by the group. Here is how the leader might prompt the client:

Kathy, now that you have listened to the group speaking in the voice of your mom, I wonder, what would you say to the part of your mom that will listen? What are the things you wish to say to your mother based on the new feelings that are welling up inside of you right now?

MAKING THE TRANSITION TO THE NEXT AGENDA ITEM

The last element to discuss about working on agendas is transition. The leader must be able to make effective transitions from one agenda item to the next. Ideally the group should work on multiple agenda items simultaneously, but new groups may not have the capacity to handle multiple agendas concurrently. For such groups, the most important task is to find a sense of direction and build a sense of competency. Working on one agenda item at a time helps the group to achieve just that. As the group matures, it will increase its capacity for working with multiple agenda items simultaneously, and may be able to work in a totally unstructured format. This mode of working on multiple agendas without structure will be detailed in Chapters 9 and 10.

As a new group works on one agenda item at a time, it must transition from one agenda to another. However, members in new groups often do not know how to do that. Sometimes they will continue discussing the same issues after those issues have been worked out. Such a group simply needs clear direction from the leader so that they can move on. To help the group make the transition to a new agenda, the leader might say something like:

> [To the group] It seems that some of you are directing the conversation to Matt again, but I thought he said that the group has done a pretty good job on his issues and now he needs some time to take it all in. I'm also aware that Mary has identified another important agenda item for the group. [turning to Matt] Matt, do you feel that the group can move on to the next agenda?

> Matt, thank you for your hard work and your trust in the group. I hope you have something to take home to reflect on during the week. Is it okay that we move on to the next agenda now? [pause] All right. Who is next?

PRINCIPLE OF HALF-AND-HALF: THE TASK AND RELATIONSHIP ASPECTS OF AGENDAS

Working on agendas provides a "launching pad" or "springboard" for interpersonal learning. It is not an end in itself. The core value of working on agendas is that it allows every member's interpersonal style and patterns to play out in the group interaction. Indeed, whenever a group of people is put together, the interpersonal pattern of each person will be carried into the group to cast its dynamics. One cannot predict how things will happen because when the interpersonal patterns are enacted within the group, anything can happen.

In each session, the group has two major things going: (1) the *task* of working on agendas, and (2) the *relationships* among members, with all their interpersonal styles being invisible players in the room. The leader must intervene on both the task and the relationship level. The principle is a balanced half-and-half approach: about half of the group's energy should be spent on working on the presenting member's agenda items, and the other half should be spent on helping members raise awareness of their interpersonal process and communication styles that shape interpersonal relationships.

This chapter has already presented a comprehensive method of tackling the task aspect of working on agendas. In this section, we will start to focus on the relationship aspect. Ways of helping members learn more effective relationship styles will be presented.

Importance of Balancing the Task and Relationship Aspects

Spending half of the group energy on agendas and half on group dynamics and interpersonal patterns is extremely important. First of all, intense focus on a given member's agenda may create a "hot-seat" effect, making the member feel overwhelmed by the attention. To reduce this effect and, most of all, to build a sense of responsibility in the group, the leader needs to provide balanced intervention to highlight what is going on among other group members, especially when their ineffective patterned behaviors occur in the midst of group interaction. This takes away the hot-seat effect from the presenting member and shifts the focus toward more members of the group.

Secondly, while the rest of the group interacts with the working member, they are practicing new interpersonal skills leading to their goals. They are taking little steps in achieving their goals. A wise leader will pay attention to the progress that members make and applaud them.

Interpersonal Process as the Gold Mine of Group Work

Interpersonal process and relationships within the group are the gold mine of group work. As members are working together on agendas, the leader might, for example, notice how one member, Brenda, jumps in to rescue Susan when Susan reveals painful issues. The leader might notice how Mike cannot speak directly to Susan. The leader also might notice how Brenda shuts down when Tracy confronts her rescuing behavior. The leader must be ready to take members' recurrent patterns by the horns, making the interpersonal process the grist for the mill for group work. Sometimes she should just keep these data of members' interpersonal styles and her own personal reactions to them in her mind. Sometimes the leader should use self-disclosure to share her insights with the group. Other times the leader simply redirects members.

In the initial stage of the group, the leader primarily uses various *redirecting* techniques to intervene as members' maladaptive interpersonal behaviors occur. Redirecting arouses less intense affects, and thus is more suitable than confrontation in the initial stages of group development. When the group matures, however, the leader will use a wide range of stimulating intervention strategies (see Chapters 8 through 10) to render the interpersonal process the material for group work. The matter of proper timing must be considered when the leader decides which level of intervention is appropriate.

Applauding Members' Progress and Effective Behaviors

In regard to the relationship aspect of group work, the leader does not focus her attention only on maladaptive interpersonal styles, but also targets the positive behaviors she observes. As discussed in Chapter 1, Yalom's (1995) research shows 12 factors as being responsible for the therapeutic effect of group. The first factor is instillation of hope. Group becomes a powerful instrument for change because it restores hope in people. To maximize the power of hope in the group, the leader needs to track the progress that each member makes, however small it is. Whenever there is any sign of a member's inner strength, wisdom, sense of humor, or creative talents, the leader needs to call on it, affirm it, amplify it, and celebrate it. As other members see a member improve, hope for their own improvement is increased.

To comment on a member's progress, the leader may say,

[To the group] Something very important just happened here. Lee just said something that he never told the group before. I would guess that is a very big step.

In order to acknowledge members' progress, the leader needs to be a group historian. He needs to remember each member's goals and how each specific issue has developed. To build a sense of hope, the leader may share how he sees the member progressing from original issues to desirable outcomes. For example,

Jim, I remember that your goal in the group is to work on being more willing to share your vulnerability with others. You have had difficulty with this issue. Yet, today you took risks to reveal something so personal and so delicate about yourself. I am impressed by the risk you took today. It is a step toward reaching your goal.

Phyllis, you really took some risks today by sharing your feelings of anger toward Bill, who wanted to move past your issues before you were ready to move on. This seems to relate to your goal of wanting to become more assertive. How was it for you to express yourself in this way today?

Intervening When Members Exhibit Domineering Behaviors

As the leader pays attention to members' positive behaviors and progress, she also needs to heed those ineffective behaviors that block members' growth. When the leader notices them, she must gently redirect the members. Gentle language is extremely important in this kind of intervention, since those whose behaviors are being redirected may feel sensitive. For example, when one or a few members dominate the interaction, the leader may intervene by saying,

Mary, let's hold on for a moment. I notice that many members in the group are trying to say something. Let's give everyone an equal chance. [turning to the quieter members] Who would like to make some comments to Matt?

Let's stop for a moment. [using hand gestures] I have heard a lot from this side of the group, but I haven't heard much from this side of the group. Let's have a change and hear more from the members who haven't had much chance to talk yet.

Correcting Impersonal Language

People use generalized language to avoid being personal with others. When a person uses terms such as *we, you,* or *people* in talking about herself, she is avoiding owning up to her personal experiences. This serves to protect the person, making her feel less exposed. Habitual use of this kind of impersonal language, however, tends to become a self-defense mechanism that prohibits others from feeling close to her. It is a type of self-defeating behavior. When members use a generalized *you, we,* or *people* to describe their "I" experiences, the leader can simply ask the members to repeat what they said, but in "I" language. For example, the leader might say:

Jeff, I have a sense that you are making this comment from your own personal experience. Yet I am confused when you use the general "you" statement rather than the "I" statement. It will be helpful if you can make your comment once again, but this time change the word *you* into the word *I.* Would you please try that?

Karen, could you clarify what you just said by rephrasing it with an "I" statement?

If the member being addressed still does not understand how his use of a generalized statement influences his relationship with others, the leader may call upon the group to give him feedback. The leader may say,

[To the group] I notice that Jeff has used the word *you* several times in describing his personal experiences. I wonder how the group has responded to this? It will be helpful if you can share with Jeff some of your reactions.

Redirecting Members Who Talk about, instead of to, Other Members

When interacting in the group, some members talk *about* one another rather than *to* one another. The reason for this behavior is that it is less intense to talk about another than to talk directly to that person. Yet this kind of indirect talk often seems like gossip, making the person who is talked about feel disrespected. To get members to interact with one another with more personal presence and in a more direct manner, the leader should guide members to talk *to* one another. For example, the leader might redirect the impersonal behavior by saying,

> Sue, since Dale is right in front of us, would you talk to Dale instead of talking about him?
>
> Reggie, I noticed that you just spoke *about* Frank even though he is sitting right here with us. Would you speak directly *to* him?

Intervening When Members Exhibit Rescuing Behaviors

If a member begins to cry, it is often unhelpful for another member or the group to immediately rush to the person's side and try to comfort him. Therapeutically, the member needs to fully experience his own pain, rather than be "rescued" from the pain. Certainly the group members should be free to show support, care, and concern, but they should not rescue the member who is feeling pain. The leader can prevent such rescuing by saying:

> [To the group] Let's allow David to be with his pain at this moment. I think it is important for him to experience this part of him. [turning to David] David, please know that we care and we are supportive of your emotions and the work you are doing right now.

If some members still jump in to rescue the person, the leader may need to explain why rescuing is not helpful. The leader may say,

> [To the group] Let's stop for a moment. Usually when a member is struggling with some issues that are painful, he doesn't need our sympathy or advice. The best way to show that we care is to let him feel that his emotions are important in their own right, that we are willing to listen to him and support him in whatever he is going through.

Correcting Labeling Behaviors

When members unknowingly practice labeling, such as calling themselves "loser," "victim," or "wimp," the leader needs to remind them to confront the behavior patterns themselves and avoid cementing labels to their personalities. For example,

> Steve, I notice that you have used the word *wimp* to describe yourself two times thus far. I hate to see you categorize yourself with such a label. I want to invite you to confront the behavior pattern itself rather than assign a label to your own personality.

Inviting the Isolated

Quiet people come to the group and continue to be quiet. The isolated come to the group and continue to be isolated. Such people need help from the leader to break through their habits of isolation. The leader may invite their participation when appropriate by saying,

> Pat, is there something you would like to say to Jennifer?

> George, I noticed your eyes tearing up as Clarissa described her mother's death. Would you be willing to share more with Clarissa about your reaction?

Redirecting Attention away from the Leader

Group members usually speak mainly to the leader unless the leader encourages them to speak to the entire group. If the leader allows them to speak only to him, the group will develop a leader-member, almost one-to-one, interaction pattern. This will make leading the group much more difficult. In order to get more members involved, build group interest and cohesion, create an atmosphere of support and belonging, and have members care for one another, the leader must redirect members to speak to the whole group, instead of just to the leader. To do this, the leader may:

- Slowly scan the room. The talking member will get the cue and start to look at other members.
- Signal the member to talk to everyone by making a sweeping motion with his hand.

CASES IN POINT

Case One: Sara

Sara's original presenting problem was self-censorship in her communication with people in general, and with her father in particular. Her goal was to become more self-assured and confident in her communication. In the fourth session, Sara presented a problem that had been causing stress for her recently. She spent quite some time speaking about her complicated and stressful relationship with her supervisor at work. As she spoke, it was obvious that she wrestled hard to control her bouts of emotions—the hurt, the sadness over loss of trust, and her devastation over lack of support in her job.

Since Sara's story was quite complicated, the group made several clarifying inquiries to get the full picture of the situation. Mindful of Sara's obvious struggle in letting her emotions be known, the group made an effort to give her empathy and genuine understanding about the difficult feelings that she was not yet able to articulate. As empathic as it was, however, the group became caught up in the particular dynamics between Sara and her supervisor and was unable to go beyond this. Just as the group was about to glide into problem-solving mode, the leader navigated the members to help them provide connection-focused feedback instead:

> I am very touched by the support the group gave to Sara. As I listened to the group, I started to remember that Sara's original goal was to develop a better relationship with her father without censoring her own voice. Although her difficulty with her supervisor seems to stand as a separate issue, I am wondering whether any of you see any parallel between Sara's relationship with her father and that with her supervisor?

Sara was already fully in tears, but this question opened the floodgates to some deeper level of emotions.

The group was jolted awake by the leader's question and by Sara's immediate reaction to it. Several members commented on the similarities they saw between the two relationships. These comments led Sara to a sudden realization that took the group by surprise. It went like this: In the first group session, Sara had said that her father suffered from chronic depression. Under the spell of depression, he was usually self-centered and harsh. This was very oppressive to Sara, since she had to censor her own voice and walk on eggshells around him. The way Sara dealt with her father had become so entrenched that she often censored herself around others. But during Sara's emerging difficulty with her supervisor, her father had conveyed to Sara, though in his own idiosyncratic manner, that he felt for her. He noticed her pain. He was, to her surprise, sensitive to her sadness even when what Sara expressed was only irritation. As Sara shared this realization about her father's new emotional availability to her with the group, her emotions escalated rapidly. She was very moved and shaken by how her father was able to step out of his own depression and show her the affection that she had been longing for all her life.

Watching Sara become engulfed in her deep emotions, the group felt unspeakable tenderness toward her. For the first time, they felt close to her, and so they went one step further. They gave Sara their perceptions about her interpersonal patterns. Alice hinted that frequently Sara did not get the kindness she needed from people around her because of her habit of silencing herself. Julie wondered whether Sara's voice of amicability kept her from expressing her true feelings, particularly in situations involving authority figures who were harsh and unfair like her father and supervisor.

After the session, Sara wrote in her reflective journal:

This fourth session was unlike any event I have witnessed and/or experienced in my life. It's an amazing feeling to have each member's complete understanding and empathy. Most importantly, the directing of my thoughts toward my father's recent efforts of connecting with me was extremely powerful for me. This was an evening I will be hard-pressed to forget. I am forever grateful to each group member, to this experiential group, and to the leader. Each member attempted to give me thought-provoking insight. It was enlightening. I had felt a slow tension building within me over the past few weeks since the start of my work situation. But as today's session progressed, a sense of calmness came over me. I was able to get a better perspective of the situation. I'm hoping that as I have more time to contemplate the empathic remarks, themes, and patterns that my fellow members offered, I will be able to alter my coping pattern and be the person I have the potential to be. Lastly, I was moved when some members of the group gave me hugs after the session. My only regret is that Kathy was not present to share in this event. I missed her contribution.

Other members also wrote about this event in their reflective journals. Lori wrote:

This was, without a doubt, the session that made me feel that our group was building trust and cohesiveness. It was full of emotions. As Sara shared her agenda, the group could sense her frustration, anger, sadness, resentment, pride, and pain. She was, evidently, fighting hard with her tears when she spoke of her father's unexpected support during her time of struggle. It was at this point that I became tearful because I, too, have a similar relationship with my father. Near the end of the session, I told Sara that this instills hope not only in her relationship but also in mine with my father. I felt very close to Sara at that moment. In the next session, I will continue to work on sharing less people-pleasing remarks with others. I am feeling more confident of myself so I am looking forward to the next session with anticipation.

Rose wrote:

As I listened, I noticed how Sara kept her body in control. Usually when Sara talks, she uses her hands. This time her fingers and hands stayed interwoven in her lap. I don't remember seeing them move, even when she was in tears. With the leader's prompt for feedback, I began to see the connection between the current situation and Sara's goals of building a better relationship with her father and of being more assertive. As Sara began to see how the relationship with her supervisor was so closely connected to that with her father, her eyes began to tear again. As Sara worked on her agenda, I found myself reflecting on the relationship with my dad, and I told her so. At the end of the session, I noticed a smile appearing on Sara's face. It indicated new hope and new strength!

Case Two: Anne

Anne's original presenting problem was discussed in an example of intake summary in Chapter 3. During the check-in of the third session, Anne reported on a weekend visit to her family. There seemed to be some turmoil during the visit, and the leader could see that Anne was struggling to keep a smile on her face when speaking to the group. Anne agreed that she might be up for the evening's agenda. After completion of the check-in and all other business, Anne started presenting her agenda. As she unfolded her story, Anne got tearful and really struggled with her tears. It was obvious that she felt very vulnerable in her pain. She seemed to want to hide herself, as she brought her hands up to her face and nervously chewed on her fingers and looked down. The group became very still and quiet. At this moment, the leader broke the stillness by saying,

> It's perfectly okay to cry, Anne. We are all supportive of what you are struggling with right now.

Anne felt somewhat relieved and gathered her courage to reveal to the group that she felt like something was wrong with her and that she thought others looked upon her as if something was actually wrong with her because she seemed to be unable to have a long-term relationship.

In response to Anne's revelations, the leader tried to make Anne feel safe by drawing out empathic responses from the group. Feeling understood and validated, Anne went on to tell the group how she grew up as her mother's confidant, with her mother unloading her feelings about her troublesome marriage to Anne. As Anne peeled layer after layer of her story, she continued to be tearful. She constantly apologized for her tears, and at times she would try to make a joke about her tearfulness. It was obvious that when confronted with uncomfortable feelings, Anne had a pattern of joking to distract herself or others from her feelings.

At this moment, the leader asked the group to do a sentence-completion exercise that successfully initiated an animated exchange between the group and Anne. The leader said,

> I would like the group to complete this sentence: *When I see you crying, Anne, I feel _____ toward you.* Please jump in when you are ready, and please speak to Anne directly.

The group members stated that they felt drawn to, and closer to Anne, and had a desire to nurture and reach out to Anne when she showed her vulnerable side instead of her all-smiling side. Anne was surprised to hear these positive responses. It was then that the group felt a sense of cohesiveness. There was a bonding of trust and a sense of safety in the group that allowed Anne to continue disclosing more about her issue with intimacy.

Ran said that he felt drawn to Anne because of his own feelings and experiences. He revealed his past experience as a member of the clergy and discussed how he learned to build walls that did not allow others to see who he really was. Ran actually moved his chair closer to the circle and leaned forward when he spoke. He expressed fear, loneliness, and resentment at having to hide himself. His tone of voice had much emotion and kindness in it when he spoke to Anne. Ran, who made several insightful observations during the session, suggested that Anne had also built a wall around herself and was not allowing people to get to know the real her, and that perhaps she used her listening skills to focus on others because she did not feel worthy of being the topic of discussion. Ran then asked Anne why she felt so undeserving. This insight obviously hit upon another sore spot in Anne, as she nodded in reflective agreement and shed more tears.

As the group strived to give Anne feedback about the pattern they saw in Anne's life, the leader created a hypothetical situation for the members to respond to. The leader said:

> I would like the group to respond to this hypothetical situation. If you were an invisible light and you were allowed to follow Anne to a date that she has with a man, what would you be likely to see happening during the date? You can be spontaneous, but please speak directly to Anne.

One member said that Anne probably would use her listening skills as a wall to keep the man at a distance so he would not get to know the real Anne and reject her. Another member stated that she saw Anne using humor as a way to deflect the focus off herself. Another member stated that if Anne turned the focus of conversation back onto the man when things got too revealing, the man would wonder what he did wrong and beat himself up over it. The response was spoken humorously, and the group laughed. Still another member shared with Anne that she thought Anne would get resentful after awhile because she would do so much listening and feel that nobody listened to her; her needs would not be met, and so she would become frustrated and end the relationship. At this point, Anne's face resonated with insight. Anne agreed that what was said was true. She admitted that often she just wanted to tell people to shut up and listen to her for awhile.

As the group wrapped things up, Anne was grateful for the words of insight and felt she needed some time to absorb everything. The leader encouraged Anne to write down her thoughts and spend some time during the week reflecting on what had been exchanged in the group. Following are Anne's reflections:

I came into the third session not sure whether I was ready to open up or not. It has always been easier for me to focus on others' problems than to talk about my own. I knew what I needed to get off my chest was a very emotional issue for me. But the thought of maybe getting upset in front of a roomful of members in the group made me very uneasy. I surprised myself when I put my agenda out on the table when the group was opened. And I panicked inside when I went first for the night.

Even more, I was surprised by my tears. They seemed to come almost instantly as I began to talk. I am the type of person who tries to keep a smile on my face even if I am upset. I cover a lot of emotions with humor, most of it self-deprecating. I was instantly worried about how everyone in the room was seeing me. I did not want them to pity me or think that I was a total nut case. It seems weird to me, since I would never think that about anyone else if they shared a problem or cried, but I could not help thinking that about myself. Once I began crying and struggling with talking to the group, the leader told me that the group was with me in my pain. Seeing and hearing the sincerity in her voice made me feel a little bit more comfortable. As comfortable as I was, I still could not stop fidgeting, biting my nails, and avoiding looking the rest of the group in the eyes.

When I let the group know how unnerving it was to get so much focus put on me, Ran made a comment that stuck in my head. He asked me why I felt so undeserving. I had never thought of it in that way. When I went home I could not stop thinking about it. I realized that there have been many times in my life where I have wanted something but have made excuses why I shouldn't have it. Or if I did get it, I would give a million reasons as to why I did not deserve it. For instance, when I won teacher-of-the-year award at my school, I felt guilty and could not enjoy it because I thought others were thinking of the same thing—my undeservingness. I wondered what made me act this way.

In this group, I felt a real connection with Ran. I remember hearing him say that one reason he had joined the clergy was to avoid relationships. When I heard this, I felt that he could understand where I was coming from. At first I found it a little odd that the group felt drawn to me when I was being so vulnerable. I had never had anyone relate to my emotions in that way or with those words. I really felt like the group heard me and understood. It was a nice feeling—one that I do not get to experience often, especially lately. Everyone in the group was so encouraging to me. I was especially touched by Joe, who gave me a hug before I left. This was an exceptionally helpful session. I know that my journey has just begun.

Ran wrote:

Today I decided that the interpersonal skill I wanted to practice in the group was to really try to listen, not only to the words, but also to the feelings, and to let myself feel without going to my head and being clogged by my thoughts. As Anne shared how she would not let people see her real self, I could relate with that behavior very much. I could also understand her fears. Instead of jumping in to tell her pieces of my story, as I used to be inclined to do, I remained reflective and tried to become even more intensely focused on what Anne was saying. As she was talking, I responded and reflected back to her the loneliness that I also have felt, since I am used to keeping things on the surface, and not letting others in to see the real me behind the facade. I had that same fear very often. But the result was a huge hole in my life that created a sadness along with the loneliness.

I was surprised at the interconnection of Anne's story about her family and the image of her family being "all together," even though they were not, which they always presented when going to church. I saw the connection right away and shared with the group and with Anne that it seemed like Anne lives her life as if she is "in church"— presenting herself in a certain way and not being able to just be herself and let others see the "not so together" side of herself. After all, it isn't appropriate to be naked (not literally) in church.

Anne mentioned that she was surprised that others would be drawn to her when she felt so open and vulnerable. I do hope that sharing in the group like this might be a big step in learning that she can be vulnerable and open and let others in to see her deeper self. When I left the session, I sensed a feeling of "togetherness" that was exhibited by the whole group walking together and talking together as we left the building. I am pleased with my practice in the group this session, and I think I made progress on my own awareness. Anne's sharing has served to open me up to look at myself more deeply and to recognize the patterns of my relationships and the fears that cause me to control so much. This recognition challenges me to let down the walls I build.

Case Three: Joe

Joe's original presenting problem was a sinister anxiety that he had not been able to shake. In the ninth session, Joe decided to pursue his anxiety issue, hoping the group would help him to reduce his anxiety problems. Joe told the group that approximately two years ago, he suffered a panic attack in the middle of a session with a family and ended up in the emergency room of a hospital. After that he sought individual counseling and continued to suffer minor bouts of panic. From time to time, he found himself losing control of his emotions, particularly nostalgia, sentimentality, and melancholy. The September 11 terrorist attacks triggered major anxiety and agitation at his job and in his personal life, as it stirred up memories and feelings from a tragic school fire when he was 11 years old. More than 100 children died in that fire. He was an unwitting hero, leading three classrooms of other children to safety. He described how he had to kick one of his female classmates down a flight of stairs when she grew hysterical and blocked the way out of the deadly, smoke-filled floor she had inadvertently trapped them on. When he went home, his mother did not acknowledge his actions but only reprimanded him for not finding his sister earlier. His father failed to defend Joe against his mother. He felt a mixture of hurt and disappointment because he never received any acknowledgment from his parents for his actions. His bout with PTSD (posttraumatic stress disorder) was aggravated by his supervisor's handling of an incident at work when Joe grew short with a colleague who was playing the self-absorbed obstructionist on 9/11. His supervisor reprimanded him for the emotional display. Joe was threatened with a demotion of his job or a lowering of his status.

Joe's voice quivered when he talked about his fear that he was becoming like his parents. Joe then went on to disclose more pain in his life with regard to alcoholism and losing friends, being abandoned by his significant other, and his homosexuality. As Joe told his stories, it was obvious that a theme of emotional abandonment ran through his life. He felt abandoned by his parents. They were not emotionally available to him, and indeed, Joe had to become a caretaker to his mother. At an early age, his father put Joe in charge of taking care of his mother, who was mentally ill, and reporting back to him about what went on in the house. He felt abandoned by his two ex-wives in that they were overly dependent on him and were emotionally unavailable to him. He was always the caretaker and never received the nurturance of being taken care of. When he hit bottom as an alcoholic, his friends with whom he drank vanished into thin air and were not there to support him on his road of recovery. More recently, he was left hanging out to dry emotionally by his supervisor when he was sobbing uncontrollably in her office after the 9/11 bombings. All of these abandonment and betrayal issues combined to create an undercurrent of anxiety in him that was about to surface with any trigger. Joe was terrified of having more panic attacks.

As Joe told his stories in a "raw" way, the other group members sensed a deep anguish tossing about inside him, a churning tide of pain, sorrow, suffering, and torment. Many members in the group found it hard to listen to his remarks. They did not know what to do with all the information Joe laid out to the group. They did not know which issue to pick to try to remedy. Joe seemed to recognize the pattern in his life so clearly. He had tremendous insight into his childhood trauma and how it continued to influence his current life. He did not need more insight of any sort. So how could the group help?

The group worked hard to try to give Joe empathy. They reflected the fear and vulnerability Joe was feeling inside. But any empathy they could give seemed feeble in light of the massive suffering that Joe continued to carry with him. The group was at the edge of anxiety, and a sense of powerlessness could be sensed in the air. At this moment, the leader asked the group to do an exercise so Joe could experience some emotional healing and integration. The leader said,

> Joe has talked about a long history of abandonment and betrayal by his supervisor, family, and friends since an early age, as well as since he came out as a gay man and a recovered alcoholic. In light of the panic attacks that he has been experiencing, I would like the group to try out an exercise with Joe: I would like each of you to choose the role of one of the persons (either his supervisor, or his father, mother, ex-wife, or friend) who abandoned or betrayed Joe in some way. As you take on that role, I would like you to say something to Joe that your heart wants him to hear so that a healing can begin. [pause] So when you are ready, please jump in and speak directly to Joe.

Everyone in the group took on the role of a specific person who had let Joe down at some time in his life and movingly apologized to Joe from their hearts. Many members had tears in their eyes as they spoke from the role they picked. After each member offered a heartfelt apology, there was a moment of silence. The emotional level in the room was very high. Joe was visibly emotional. His face got flushed, and he appeared to be struggling to control himself. He admitted afterward that he was trying not to cry. Joe had difficulty speaking at first because he was so emotional. It was obvious that the group had struck a chord with him. He stated that Kim, Shina, and the leader affected him the most with their portrayals of his parents and his supervisor.

After the session, members reflected on what had happened in their journals. Joe wrote:

> I had an "aha" experience when the group addressed my own agenda. I was able to take a vague and unspecific problem such as anxiety to something more concrete and deeper emotionally. What really brought it home for me was listening to Shina portraying my father and the leader portraying my former supervisor. Somehow Shina's (my father's) asking my forgiveness for not protecting me enough from my mother's emotional excesses and dramas really got to me. I felt like I was going to lose it right then and there. The leader sensed it and asked me to close my eyes. I was then able to pull it together and listen further to Shina. When the leader took the role of my supervisor, I was amazed at how perceptive she was. She asked for forgiveness for shaming, blaming, and threatening me for how my September 11–related PTSD had affected my workplace. For months, I had been struggling to have a reprimand removed from my file. When the leader approached the

situation by having my supervisor apologize for causing me so much anguish, fear, and pain, I realized how much that was what I had wanted and needed all along. It was truly amazing to me how much an apology could mean to me. The fact that I was hurt and harmed and I deserved an apology was such a simple fact. However, it had somehow escaped me as I lived my everyday life. Kim summed it up for me by portraying my mom with a simple, no frills message, "I am sorry, and I love you even though I could not express it at times!" I had come a lot further along in forgiving my mother than I might have thought. Everybody surprised me that night! My sibling rivalry with Jim and Ron in the group ended that night. My transference with the leader melted away when she reached out to me in her role-play as my supervisor. I am so moved that for all their own struggles with their own issues, all members stayed real, empathetic, caring and often very wise and perceptive throughout.

Anna wrote:

When the leader invited the group to pick a role in Joe's life and say something to him, I struggled with it. I felt tears in my eyes and I still am not sure of the reason. Maybe I feel as if I need an apology from people who hurt me in my past as well. In the session, I tried hard not to problem-solve, as that is what I tend to do. I felt close to Joe during and after the session. In the lobby I hugged him. I realized my own need for some sort of apology, but am not brave enough to ask.

Ron's reflections were:

As Joe shared the horror of not being able to find his sister and feeling so responsible and scared about how his parents would react if he didn't find her and watch out for her, I felt angry. When he related his mother's response when he did show up with his sister, I was very angry. I could only imagine being that scared little boy and getting a totally inappropriate response—not getting what he needed—to be held and cared for. I was very aware that the anger feelings related to my own feelings about the lack of love, understanding, and being cared for in my own early life. I felt sad for Joe. I was deeply moved as each group member took the role of a person in Joe's life and responded to him. I was especially moved as Shina took the role of Joe's father. As it turned out, that was one sharing that touched Joe deeply. I later realized the "father" piece in my own life that is still unresolved. I learned so much from Joe's sharing regarding my own self. I wanted to go back to the experience in the fire and the feelings in that situation created by the chaos and trauma where Joe seemed to be all alone.

Jim's comments were:

When Joe said that he wished his mom could be made aware of her past transgressions, I remarked that she probably never will be cognizant of those past events. I was comparing my mom's similar reactions when I have brought my past up to her. My mom has total amnesia about my childhood emotional distress. "That never happened!" she would say. My mom never came to my rescue either. My stepfather was very authoritative and oppressive in his parenting style. He was also very distant with feelings, and I cannot remember to this day one nice thing he ever said to me. So, when Joe brought up this issue of abandonment, it started to hit home! This really shed new light on my own unresolved issues of abandonment. I wonder if this has any bearing on my being emotionally distant with my wife and kids? I felt drawn closer to Joe. I felt like I wanted to be his mentor. I wanted to educate him to be wise and selective about his disclosure at work. Joe thought that boldly disclosing his sexual orientation and recovery at work would be rewarded with newfound freedom and would be a cleansing catharsis for him. Instead, he encountered betrayal! I saw a similar fellow at my agency do that and he experienced the same "fall from grace" at my agency. I was thinking to myself, "My god, Joe, don't you realize how open you are to the wolves, sharks, and jerks out there?" I wanted to educate Joe about human nature and office politics, but I realize that this insight must come from his own personal life experiences.

AN OVERVIEW OF THE GROUP SESSION FRAMEWORK

This section provides you with an overview of the framework for early group sessions in the form of a chart (Figure 6.1). The purpose of this chart is to give you a quick glimpse of the basic procedure for leading a session in the early stages of a group. By presenting this procedure in such a simple fashion, we run the risk of oversimplifying group action and reducing complex leadership practice to a simple linear procedure. Remember, a chart is just a chart; it can never represent the reality of the multiple actions and circular interactions that often occur simultaneously in any moment within a live group.

SCENARIOS FOR YOUR PRACTICE

1. In a group session, after several members have put their agenda items on the table, Bo states, "I'm just here to learn what I can. My wife joined a group like this a couple of years ago, and she thought it was great—all the feeling of support that she got. She said that it would be good for me and for our relationship. So here I am." As the group leader, how might you respond to Bo's comments?

A. Opening the session
- Relaxation exercise
- Check-in
- Requesting agenda items

B. Working on first agenda item
- Member self-disclosure (member presenting the agenda) and group interaction
- Group giving empathy (creating a safe group environment) and member deepening self-disclosure
- Group giving feedback and member responding to feedback
- Transitioning to the next agenda item
- All along, the leader following half-and-half principle of balanced focus on both task and relationship

C. Working on next agenda item
D. Closing the session
- Announcing closing
- Check-out
- Reminder

FIGURE **6.1**

BASIC PROCEDURE FOR SESSIONS IN EARLY GROUP STAGES

2. In the third session of a group, Stephanie recounts at some length her difficulty in expressing herself and feeling heard by others. Stephanie reports, "It's as if others sort of hear me, but then discount what I say by going on to some other topic that they prefer." She pauses, and then adds, "It makes me feel . . ." Her voice breaks and her lower lip trembles. Without waiting for more than a few seconds, Wayne interjects, "Well, that must be pretty annoying, but, hey, I get annoyed at work all the time. Like today, a coworker jumped all over me just because my cell phone rang a couple of times during our department meeting. Well, duhhh, people want to talk to me." As the group leader, how might you respond?

3. In a subsequent session of the group, Stephanie makes the following statement, and you notice several others in the group nodding their heads in apparent agreement as she says it: "Wayne, I have something to say to you. You have yet to acknowledge any of the comments that several of us have made to you about how we experience

what seems like your lack of listening." Wayne instantly responds, "I think that it is just the other way around in here. It's none of you who are bothering to listen to me. I think that I've had some pretty good insight into what's wrong with people here, and yet no one seems to notice." As a leader, how might you respond to further this feedback exchange?

4. During a session of a group for interpersonal skill development, Jamie says to Bhavani (who is from India), "Bhavani, I don't know if you are afraid of talking in this group, because you haven't said very much. I just don't know what you're thinking over there half the time." Bhavani looks puzzled but does not immediately respond. As a facilitator, how might you work with this issue from a diversity perspective?

5. It is the third session of a personal growth group. While mostly looking at you, Bill describes in lengthy detail his troubles and fears at work, but he doesn't pause or ask the group for any specific input. What are some of your options for response as the group leader?

6. During a session of a personal growth group, Sue describes her feelings of missing her father and home life after her parents divorced. Alphie expresses her feelings concerning her husband's unexpected death. Bob mentions how he felt betrayed by his company when they gave him his layoff notice. What links could you, as the facilitator, make between these experiences?

7. In the third session of a group, Max asks Faroud, "Can I offer you some feedback?" Without pausing to wait for an okay, Max continues, "You seem like a very timid person because you don't say much in this group." As a facilitator, how would you respond to this kind of feedback statement?

8. It is the fifth session of a group for laid-off white-collar workers. Tina took the first job that became available to her but is having some second thoughts about whether it is a good fit for her and whether she can accept the questionable business practices of her new employer. Sheila asks Tina, "How can you look at yourself in the mirror while working for an outfit like this? I would never take a job with a company like that. What were you thinking?" As a leader, what issues would you identify in this exchange? How might you want to manage the discussion?

9. After Martha gives a very brief outline of a dilemma with which she is struggling at work, Jill stares right at Martha and says, "That is just immoral." As the group leader, what options do you have for handling this type of encounter?

10. It is the fourth session of a personal growth group. Marie has described some of her relationship struggles, including those with her spouse. You've heard Bonnie (who was only recently divorced) make a statement implying that if Marie had any courage, she, too, would seek a divorce. What are your options, as the leader, for directing feedback around these issues?

SELF-REFLECTION

1. If you were to join a personal growth group now, what are some of the agenda issues that you might formulate for yourself? As you envision setting out these agenda issues in front of strangers, what feelings are evoked for you?
2. Imagine yourself as a group member. What kinds of feedback would you like? Would it all be positive and supportive? Would you prefer to receive challenges along with support from the group to help you develop new alternatives?
3. Think back to some of your own significant emotional experiences in your life. What factors were present that made those emotional experiences significant to you? What were you able to learn from them? How were you able to implement changes in your thoughts and/or behaviors as a result?
4. When family and friends are experiencing difficult times, how do you react? Do you tend to jump into a problem-solving mode and tell them how to fix things, or do you tend to respond more by acknowledging their feelings and understanding their reactions?
5. Envision yourself as the leader of a group being faced with unhelpful group member actions. What frame of mind will help you to assist the members in redirecting their behaviors to more positive channels?
6. Imagine yourself as a group leader receiving various kinds of feedback from group members. How might you react to positive feedback? Negative? Mixed? How would you like to respond to each type of feedback?
7. Are there any unresolved strong emotional issues in you life? If so, how might you respond to clients with similar unresolved issues?

WORKING WITH TENSION AND CONFLICT

Anytime a group of people is put together, tension and rift may develop sooner or later. Tension is inevitable in all relationships, including those within groups. Without a doubt, the process group, with its open structure, is a fertile soil for conflict to sprout. Indeed, tension may be apparent as early as the second session. When tension starts to bubble, many new leaders feel threatened or take it personally. They feel that the strain in the group is an indication that they have failed in their leadership. This distress is normal, yet unnecessary. The leader does not need to be intimidated by members' expressions of frustration and dissatisfaction. Indeed, to make the group grow into a cohesive unit, group members need to express and resolve whatever negative feelings stand in their way. No group can grow until its members are able to express the full range of their group experiences. Given this, tension and friction should be seen as a potential source of learning rather than as a problem to be avoided.

This chapter aims to help leaders manage tension and discord and make the experience of conflict resolution an integral part of interpersonal learning for members. It covers:

- Dissatisfaction and the transition stage
- Managing unspoken tension
- Handling member negativity toward leaders
- Working with issues related to cultures and diversity
- The paradox of open conflicts
- Managing open conflict
- Leader, cure thyself

DISSATISFACTION AND THE TRANSITION STAGE

Groups may launch into their "transition" stage as early as the second session. The transition stage is the second stage of group development. This stage is featured by projections, tension, and conflict due to power struggles and competition that are inherent in a group that is relatively young (Corey & Corey, 2002). This stage of a group parallels the adolescence period of a human life. Parents who have adolescents in their household know well of their teens' furious struggle for independence and self-identity. They are quite familiar with the tension and conflicts that often arise in the house. Because a volatile and disquieting quality is at the core of this group transition stage, Tuckman (1965) coined the term the *storming* stage to describe it.

Throughout various stages of group development, members need to learn to resolve conflicts and tension among themselves in a constructive manner. The transition stage marks the first step of such learning. In the transition stage, the leader can expect many phenomena that pose a challenge for leadership. Following is a discussion of some of these:

A Sense of Relative Dissatisfaction

In the early stages of group, members tend to resist therapeutic work for fear of losing control. They dread exposing their vulnerabilities, or they feel unsafe. Lacoursiere (1980) observed that a group often moves into a stage of relative dissatisfaction once it has passed the initial stage. At this juncture, members seem to stumble over a number of issues: the perceived untrustworthiness of other members, a perceived lack of competence in the leader, and serious self-doubt about their own abilities to change. In one way or another, group members may feel that the group is not turning out to be quite like they had anticipated or hoped. Therefore, the members feel anxious about what actually will ensue.

In reaction to this internal frustration, members may begin to express negativity or antagonism toward other members and the leader. Yalom (1995) noted that members' yearning for acceptance is so strong in the forming stage (first stage) that they often martyr their own feelings in the cause of group cohesiveness. These martyred feelings, however, can mutate into disappointment for the therapist and the group during the transition stage.

Struggle for Control

The source of member dissatisfaction has a great deal to do with struggle for control. Our need for control is manifested in our desire to be able to influence others and to negotiate influence coming from others. This need for control is an integral factor in tension and discord. As one of the three universal needs (Schutz, 1958), the need for control is likely to activate itself once the issue of inclusion has been satisfied to a certain degree.

When members' preoccupation for approval shifts into preoccupation for control, their desire for control can be enacted in the form of aggression, scapegoating, silence, storytelling, and the pursuit of secondary gratification. Leaders may find themselves leading the group in an edgy environment, even when nothing is said explicitly.

Indirect Power Displays

The distribution of power in a group is often not even to begin with. Some members tend to dominate, others get silent; some cut people off, others censor themselves; some get praised, others get ignored; some do all the work, and others let everyone else do the work. These power issues usually are not openly commented on, but are played out indirectly in the form of interpersonal tension.

Power display comes in different shades, but however it is manifested, indirect behaviors such as the following tend to block group progress:

Domination: In all interpersonal interactions, not just those in group, certain people tend to dominate with louder voices, or quicker response speeds. Some people dominate to win. Others dominate simply because of temperament or some cultural factor. Whatever the cause, when one dominates, others in the group are deprived of equal opportunity to air their concerns.

Interruption: Some group members empower themselves by interrupting others inappropriately. They interrupt by changing topics, talking over others, or taking away a critical emotional moment with a joke or an irrelevant comment.

Withholding: As the opposite of domination, some members gain power by withholding what they think and feel or by keeping peace. They may not feel safe enough to speak truthfully about themselves. When some members withhold, however, the group misses important input and energy from them, and trust and group cohesiveness are hampered.

Anxiety-Provoking Differences

When the group has not yet developed a high level of trust, members are likely to focus on real or perceived differences among themselves and with the leader. Differences in values, beliefs, communication styles, mannerisms, and cultural backgrounds can easily breed anxiety and negative projections. Unchecked negative thoughts breed contempt.

The element of differences touches again on the aspect of inclusion, identified by Schutz (1958). Group members grapple with issues such as whether they want to be a part of the group and to what extent they will accept other members as full participants. Each member confronts questions such as: "If I am a part of this group, which includes people who are different from me, will my needs be sufficiently addressed?" In any event, what emerges from elements of difference will become a key issue for the group in its development.

Projection and Misinterpretation

The filters that we bring with us from our past experiences influence how we interpret others' intentions, feelings, and messages to us. These filters cause projections and misunderstanding among group members. Heitler (1990) observed that people's unresolved inner conflicts often become intertwined with their interpersonal conflicts. If significant issues from one's past remain unresolved, any traces of familiarity in mannerisms between someone in the group and someone in one's past may beget unconscious reactions that are out of proportion to what has been done or said. For example, someone with a strong personality may remind a group member of an authoritarian or even abusive figure from the past, even if the association is completely unfounded. Members may even project unrealistic and irrelevant qualities onto other members with unfamiliar characteristics. As an example, those who have unresolved anger or disdain within themselves may project these qualities to others.

The inextricable relationship between inner and outer conflicts will eventually be expressed in some way in the group (Yalom, 1995). More often than not, members are quite unaware of these inner conflicts, which typically stem from their family of origin experiences, and they are unconscious of how they project them onto others (Daniel & Gordon, 1996; Ogden, 1979; Yalom, 1995). When projecting unresolved inner conflicts onto others, these members may see in others characteristics and qualities that they despise but do not acknowledge within themselves. When others in the group refuse to accept the mantle of these projected qualities, a conflict ensues.

The phenomenon of projection kicks in fairly early in group, as demonstrated in Jill's journal reflections about her second session:

> When the group started in our second meeting, I felt fairly open and able to share. But after I made one comment to another member, I felt, based on her facial expression and the fact that she didn't say anything back to me, that she didn't value or appreciate what I had to say. I felt really hurt and immediately began to withdraw. For the rest of the session, I could feel myself more tuned in to what I was feeling and not into what others were saying. I felt alienated from the group in a way, even

though I rationally knew that it was only my reaction to this feeling of being rejected. At first, I got caught up in thinking that she didn't like me and that's why she acted that way. Then I realized that this member probably did not mean it, but it had already set off all these other emotional reactions that I could not control or rationalize myself out of. I also was surprised by my physiological reaction of a headache. I did not feel able to share this with the group at the time because I don't feel trusting enough yet to be honest with feelings. The other thing I didn't expect was that I recognized this pattern within myself in relationship to my extended family. I know that this is exactly how I felt as a child and even as an adult when relating to my dad's side of the family. I am surprised that I am having such strong reactions to these memories or patterns related to my extended family. Today's session has brought up some extremely painful memories for me. I never would have thought that this would have been what would be brought up for me so early in the group.

The phenomenon of projection also came up in Jim's third session:

I was aware of Ron's effect on me, or rather, transference between him and me. I felt challenged to argue when he spoke. I think he appears resentful toward me when I share after he does. That perception, be it true or not, bothers me. I made a special effort to control my emotions when he spoke, so I acted kind and supportive of his input to Anne. I cannot yet figure out what my part is in this transference. I do not think it is his being a former priest. It would be hypocritical of me if it were. I think it is because I want acceptance and approval from him. His facial expressions and tone of voice toward me caused me to think he does not like me. This may or may not be true; however, they are the real cause for my anger.

Cultural Stereotyping

Cultural stereotypes may be another source of discord in the group process. A member may stereotype another member who is from a different cultural background. These stereotypical impressions may be created by a negative past experience and transferred unknowingly to the present member. Often those who harbor such stereotyped feelings will not say how they feel; they keep such feelings inside. Their attitudes, however, are demonstrated in their body language and manners and are clearly seen by the rest of the group. These unchecked reactions and behaviors can open the door to friction.

Additionally, group members with differing cultural, family, and ethnic backgrounds are likely to have different values and preferences, including ideas about the expression and handling of tension and conflict (Halverson & Cuellar, 1999). For members from certain ethnic groups, such as Native American and Mexican American, rates of verbal participation may be lower. They may be reserved and indirect in the way they handle conflict

(Shen, Sanchez, & Huang, 1984). For other members, open expression of conflict may be part of daily life. At this transition stage of group, members often size up each other on many fronts, including styles of expression. Leaders must help all members move past snap judgments and learn to express their experiences in a manner that will ultimately contribute to trust and understanding of one another.

Transition Stage as a Necessary Step

As tension and conflict bubble, the group's task-related processing will backslide. Members' attention shifts to personal matters, such as a sense of safety, leader competence, trust, and interaction undertone (Gladding, 1999). This backslide is natural. People often look hard before they leap into the process of change. The tension of the transition stage certainly feels uncomfortable, but this stage serves as a necessary stepping stone to the next. The built-up tension prompts members to finally speak the truth about their reactions, which is vital for group aliveness. As a group learns to deal with dissatisfaction and frustration honestly and constructively, the very energy that drives their negative responses will become the energy that brings the group closer and sharpens the self-awareness of their interpersonal functioning.

Not infrequently, leaders gloss over the conflict that members are struggling with so that members can immediately feel better and the group can feel more at ease. This is unfortunate. Literature in group therapy repetitively emphasizes the importance of addressing conflicts within groups. Kraus, DeEsch, and Geroski (2001) go so far as to say that conflict, when embraced, can serve as a change agent in group. McClure, Miller, and Russo (1992) note: "The successful resolution of this stage provides a bridge between the superficial conversations of the first stage and the more direct expression of feelings in the later stages" (p. 268).

Leaders must become comfortable with the idea of tension and conflict, embracing them as a necessary part of the human experience. By doing so, they will be more able to develop skills that can create an environment in which discord is allowed and dealt with effectively. Leaders must have faith in the group process, trusting that even interaction that begins with annoyance can lead to group cohesion and growth.

MANAGING UNSPOKEN TENSION

Group members tend to experience unspoken discontent more often than open conflict. What is left unsaid is covert. While boiling underground, these feelings will have an impact on the group indirectly. Wheeler and Kivlighan (1995) point out that angry and frustrated feelings are more often left unsaid than expressed during conflict. Because of the negative connotations associated with such feelings, members tend to avoid voicing these emotions aloud to the group. As a matter of fact, not all unspoken discontent and tension can be resolved during the transition/storming stage. Many of these emotions will not be effectively addressed until the group matures into its working stage (Chapters 9 and 10), at which point members grow more confident in speaking up about their truthful observations and impressions.

In this section, we will focus on the management of unspoken discontent in the initial stages of group development. First, let's learn to recognize the many forms by which unspoken discontent can be manifested.

Avoidance and Distance

Unspoken frustration and tension can be observed through subtle nonverbal clues, such as evasion of comment, avoidance of eye contact, momentary looks on faces, and positioning outside the circle of the group (Osbeck, 2002). Other kinds of avoidance-related behaviors include reminiscing about issues that have little connection to the group, joke-telling that pulls the group away from moments of intensity, pointless gossiping about people or events outside the group, and making ambiguous statements (Agazarian & Simon, 1967). As indirect and subtle as they are, these behaviors provide unmistakable hints about the undercurrents within a group.

Frozen Silence

As mentioned in Chapter 5, there are two types of silence: productive silence and nonproductive silence. Nonproductive or frozen silence is likely to happen in the transition stage when members are struggling with the issues of power, projection, differences, and stereotypes. Sporadic attempts may be made to break the frozen silence, but only through terse comments, stilted attempts at humor, or nervous nonverbal behavior such as restless shifting of feet and body positions.

We need to remember that not all silence is a form of tension. Members of certain ethnic groups may be much more comfortable with silence and find it normal and productive. Leaders need to be able to grasp the meaning of silence from the members' perspective, and not just from their own.

Covert Conflicts

Covert conflicts may boil underground. Issues of power struggle, distrust, and misunderstanding may be repressed. The group may attempt to act as if these processes do not exist. This pretense is very uncomfortable, yet acknowledging the hidden issues can be anxiety-provoking for members.

Covert conflict may occur within a group due to a perceived lack of cohesion or inclusion. Group members who do not feel a sense of "we-ness" with other members may experience an increased level of negative affect (MacNair-Semands, 2000). Members may attempt to redress this lack, but perhaps not knowing just how to do so, these members may express their negative feelings in indirect ways. If this occurs, the simmering issues must be brought out into the open so they can be dealt with in a way that not only will help the individual member experience the feeling of being included and belonging, but also will help the group as a whole increase the level of closeness and intimacy.

Managing Unspoken Tension

Any emotions that block group work are better acknowledged than brushed under the rug. That being said, group leaders should gauge which issues at hand are most important to focus on at a given time. The following are some options for managing covert conflicts.

Postponing   If a group is just beginning, the leader may choose to focus on the need for inclusion and the need to foster hope, a sense of universality, and cohesion—and postpone dealing with the tension simmering in the group. Tension and covert conflict, with their power of making people feel extremely uncomfortable, are dangerous waters to navigate. The group may not be ready to deal with them at its young age. In choosing to postpone digging into the covert currents, the leader is not avoiding dealing with conflict, but rather, buying time for the group to mature until it builds the necessary interpersonal infrastructure to manage the conflict (Kormanski, 1982, 1999).

Illuminating the Process   Sooner or later, covert currents need to be addressed. A ripening conflict cannot be left unaddressed for too long; otherwise, the tension will be likely to hamper the group. Breaking the silence can help the group reduce its tension. The leader can break the silence by bringing the hidden tension or repressed emotions to the forefront for members to explore and examine. In doing so, the leader is navigating the group to the *meta-communication* level of discussion of group interaction and relationships. Bateson (as cited in Perlmutter & Hatfield, 1980) noted that all communications include *meta-messages*, a form of *unconscious communication*. The unconscious level of communication only maintains the group in the status quo; it does little to bring people closer. It is only when the meta-communication is brought to the conscious level that the door to true intimacy can be opened (Marshak & Katz, 1999; Perlmutter & Hatfield, 1980).

The skill used to bring meta-communication to the conscious level is called *process illumination*. The leader steers members to look at what has been communicated in hidden or unconscious ways. Such a discussion may help members better understand the impact of their behaviors, verbal or nonverbal, on others. For example, members may become aware that silence or repressed hostility can inadvertently brew high levels of anxiety, helplessness, and lack of control within the group. As a result, members can bring to a conscious level their patterns of covert behavior in dealing with interpersonal problems outside the group (Swogger, 1981). More on the skill of process illumination will be presented in Chapters 9 and 10. In the beginning stages of the group, the leader may use a simple process illumination to help the group explore covert currents existing at the meta-communication level. The leader may say,

> Jeff, I heard frustration in your voice when you gave feedback to Noel. I wonder what it is about Noel that makes you feel frustrated.

> [To the group] I notice we are off to a slow start. I wonder what has brought about this heavy silence.

Using Writing as a Tool   If process illumination is not effective because the group is too young to dive into the level of here-and-now conversation, therapeutic letters or documents may be used. Therapeutic documents allow the leader to provide observation and feedback without the pressure of face-to-face statements. For details, please read Chapter 12.

It may prove helpful for group members to look into their emotions after the session and report back to the group in the following session. Writing reflective journal entries can be a rewarding tool for change. More details on reflective journaling are provided in Chapter 12.

HANDLING MEMBER NEGATIVITY TOWARD LEADERS

Sometimes the tension in the transition stage is manifested in the form of member attack on or negative reactions toward leaders. Members may openly challenge leadership, complain about group rules, or act in passive-aggressive, even antagonistic, ways. Sometimes this negativism comes from members' projection and transference. Other times, members' criticism is based in reality and, thus is a genuine reaction to the leader's behaviors or attitudes. This section addresses how to deal with the member-leader relationship when such tensions arise.

Transference

Members bring to the group their own unique developmental histories, including their own blind spots, self-limiting views, tendencies toward avoidance, and self-defensiveness about issues related to authority and parental figures. These histories often reflect lifelong interpersonal patterns of self-protectiveness, such as avoidance of intimacy and reluctance to take interpersonal risks to build relationships. They may also reflect patterns of internalized oppression that are not based on reality, but instead on a negative message that has become deeply entrenched.

These particular patterns may be played out to other members in the group, and especially to the leader, in the form of attacks or negativism. Members who harbor hostility toward the leader may express it by making outright critical or sarcastic remarks, by refusing to participate in group discussions, or by nonverbal cues such as rolling the eyes or clenching the jaw. Miller and Springer (1996) point out that clients often use their defense systems—such as becoming evasive, argumentative, resentful, and contemptuous—to oppose change. Understandably, the leader will feel distressed and anxious when combated or criticized. Such a reaction is part of being human.

Yalom (1995) points out that most clients, to a certain degree, perceive the therapist incorrectly because of *transference distortion.* Sullivan (cited in Yalom, 1995, p. 21) used the term *parataxic distortions* to describe our tendency to distort our perceptions of others based on our early experiences. The dynamics of a group, which are similar to those of a family, often put the leader in the position of being the parent while the members are the children. Every member, whether aware of it or not, longs for the affection and approval of the leader. This is the area in which the member's birth order is most likely to play out. The youngest readily expects to receive most of the attention, the middle child easily feels ignored, and the oldest child is perceptively left to manage on her own. In addition, any unresolved issues from members' relationships with their parents, or any hints of leader imperfection, can evoke strong reactions from members toward the leader.

Transference as a Pathway to New Solutions

Transference can be grist for the mill of therapeutic work or a troublesome shackle that hinders every move the leader makes (Yalom, 1995). How transference is dealt with ultimately depends on the degree of client insight (Gelso, Hill, & Kivlighan, 1991). Since the fertile soil of member insight is in the here-and-now, the leader's primary task is to allow this transference to play out in the present moment without taking it too personally. As the pattern is played out, the nature of the group's dynamics can be explored and illuminated in the moment as events occur, allowing members to work through unfinished business from the past.

A leader needs a great deal of patience and willingness to deal with transference. The benefits of this work, though, are enormous. If worked through, transference can become a pathway to client change. As

Alexander (in Alexander & French, 1946) stated: "Reexperiencing the old, unsettled conflict but with a new ending is the secret of every penetrating therapeutic result. Only the actual experience of a new solution, in the transference situation or in his everyday life, gives the patient the conviction that a new solution is possible and induces him to give up the old neurotic patterns" (p. 338)

Handling Negative Transference

Given the fact that transference can become a change agent for members, group leaders need to learn productive ways of dealing with negative transference. A leader who is easily threatened by negativism and hostility, who needs group approval, or who is hypersensitive to negative feedback will have a difficult time dealing with transference. It is important to remember that the leader is the consummate model for members; the way the leader deals with a negative transference will set the tone for the group. Following are some things for leaders to consider when facing negative transference.

Equality   As humans, leaders are subject to personal preferences, to their own likes and dislikes, when it comes to their relationships with group members. No leader can be totally neutral at all times. Yet, the leader can limit negative transference to a certain extent by becoming aware of the fact that members are especially sensitive to favoritism. If the leader can treat all members as being equally lovable in her eyes, this unconditional acceptance can have a therapeutic effect for many members.

Nondefensiveness   Being attacked will bring out the vulnerable part of the leader. He may be tempted to defend himself. However, even the worst situation, if handled nondefensively, can become an educational moment for the members and serve to increase group cohesiveness. Members may verbally attack the leader as a result of an unspoken power struggle. When attacked, the leader should not attack the member in return. The best way to handle the attack is to defuse it by requesting feedback from the group. The leader may say,

> [To the group] I would like to get some feedback from the group. Whenever I share my observations, Jason always questions me or rolls his eyes. How do the rest of you see the dynamics between Jason and me?

Staying Open   If a member is hostile toward the leader, the leader should express her here-and-now thoughts and feelings authentically and continue to stay open to the attacking person. Staying open means showing acceptance and patience as much as possible. After the leader has shared her genuine thoughts and feelings, she can invite the hostile member to share what he expects from the leader. For example, the leader may say,

> Dale, it looks like you are upset with me for some reason. I apologize if I have said or done anything to offend you. Would you please help me understand exactly what I said or did today or earlier that made you feel so irritated?
>
> Ned, I hear an edge in your voice, which tells me that you are upset with me right now. I want you to know that all along I have valued your presence in this group. You've been able to bring a unique perspective to our group that adds to our understanding. I am very interested in hearing what your concern is toward me at this time.

If the leader keeps the communication open, she may discover what actually is bothering the agonizing member. The leader's willingness will break down the hostility of the member and earn the trust of the group. In addition, just having an issue verbalized and raised to group consciousness can have an energizing effect on a group.

Self-Transparency   Yalom (1995) stated that increasing a leader's degree of transparency can help to address the transference issues. The leader does this by gradually revealing more of his self—such as his motives, feelings, life experiences, and especially his here-and-now reactions—when doing so would prove beneficial to the group. Such sharing can make members look at the leader more realistically and can disconfirm their distortions about him. Sharing the therapeutic document (see Chapter 12) with all members is also an excellent way to increase the leader's transparency and defuse transference.

When Negativity Is Not Transference

All negativity from members is not transference. Sometimes a member's reaction to the leader is an authentic response based on an actual observation of the leader's attitude or competence. Transference or nontransference, a consensual validation will reveal the truth. When the group discussion reveals serious limitations on the leader's part, supervision and personal development are strongly suggested. Consensual validation, and supervision and personal development, are further explained in the following text.

Consensual Validation   In consensual validation, the leader seeks the group's input about their perceptions of her. This will help the leader discern whether a hostile member's negative reaction to the leader is genuine feedback or a negative transference. For example, the leader may say,

[To the group] Joe said that I play favoritism in the group, especially favoring Ron. I wonder whether other members in the group have observed the same problem? Your input will help me realize if I do have a favoritism problem. And it will give me a chance to change so that I can better serve the group. Would anyone like to share some observations regarding this?

Supervision and Personal Development   Leaders are human beings with their own limitations and with buttons that will be pushed if they are not prepared. The push will have an impact on both the group and the role of group leader. When this happens in your group, do not repress your emotions, since they may actually offer rich clues about areas in which you need to grow. When a leader finds that his own emotional reactions run especially hot or cold toward certain group members, it is time for him to examine the possible meanings of his reactions. Supervision can be used at this time to provide a safe and trusting forum in which to explore the possible meanings. In Chapter 2, we offered suggestions for personal and professional development that will help leaders work on their personal limitations.

WORKING WITH ISSUES RELATED TO CULTURE AND DIVERSITY

Tension in the group is sometimes caused by issues related to culture and diversity. The factors of culture and diversity can contribute to power differentials and to misunderstandings within the group. Group leaders need to learn how to work with these issues to promote optimal group functioning during the transition stage of the group.

Culturally Bound Behaviors: Sources of Misunderstanding

Many underlying cultural norms and values held by members may not be articulated accurately in the early stages of groups. Often members are not aware of their own emotions, and sometimes they cannot identify the nature of their discomfort. Many of our behaviors are culturally bound. These behaviors can range from those associated with concepts of time and punctuality or the degree of openness and emotional expression, to those that are concerned with willingness to expose personal issues outside the family.

A group member from a culture that entertains a more flexible orientation toward time may not always come to group meetings punctually. This lack of punctuality may be interpreted as irresponsibility by those members who come from cultures that place a high value on punctuality (Kluckhohn & Strodtbeck, 1961; Hall, 1983). By the same token, members from cultures that encourage openness and self-expression may not appreciate the reservation demonstrated by members whose cultures teach them to keep feelings and reactions to themselves (Hofstede, 1991). The expressive members may even misinterpret less expressiveness as a sign that the less expressive member is closed off or distrustful.

When different cultures meet, the lenses of value and expectation are put into use as interpreters for all sorts of behaviors. For example, blunt behaviors may be construed by one member as purely honest but by another member as thoughtlessly rude. Likewise, face-saving behaviors may be construed as thoughtful and mature by some members, but as avoidant and deceitful by others. As such, culturally bound differences easily become fertile soil for misinterpretation and misattribution when each party assumes that the other party entertains the same norms and values.

Tension Caused by Diversity Factors

Besides culturally bound behaviors, diversity factors in the group also can be the source of distrust and tension. Diversity includes such aspects of human difference as socioeconomic status, educational attainment, language, gender, disability, and sexual orientation. Members who come from the dominant or privileged groups often find it difficult to understand the subjugation that many minority members experience in their lives. They may be skeptical of the validity of oppression experienced by the minority members, or simply gloss over the minority members' experiences (Ting-Toomey & Oetzel, 2001). For example, should a gay member in the group allude to discriminatory experiences at work, some group members may attribute the problem to the individual in question. Instead of acknowledging the pain and injustice experienced by this member, they may say something like, "Perhaps you are just a bit too sensitive about that."

Members who come from low socioeconomic backgrounds, who are female, who are not strictly heterosexual, or who speak with an uncommon accent can be wounded once more when other group members minimize their experiences of subjugation. With each distress being invalidated, the mistrust grows. These minority members become even more reluctant to disclose significant issues. The anguish of being glossed over within the group is devastating because it reminds the minority person of the chilliness he experiences in society at large. Insensitivity to diversity issues, however unintentional it is, can impede the atmosphere of openness and tolerance that the group works hard to build.

The Subtle Dynamics of Power Imbalance

Culture and diversity factors can contribute to power differentials within the group. Many of the tensions and impasses experienced in the transition stage of the group are the result of an underlying imbalance of power. Ting-Toomey and Oetzel (2001) assert that group leaders need to know the group composition and balance of power. However, the power dynamics are likely to be subtle. The balance of power can be observed only when the dynamics are in action. A group leader needs a large amount of mindfulness to observe such subtle dynamics in action. Conyne (1998) suggested a number of ways by which leaders can become cognizant of the existence of power dynamics within the group. Following is a summary of Conyne's suggestions:

1. Observe whether members of differing backgrounds can openly disagree with one another or whether such disagreements are expressed in indirect ways.
2. Notice whether members of diverse backgrounds have their issues heard, or whether they experience getting interrupted, cut off, or avoided within the group—and are somehow kept outside the "inner circle" of the group.
3. Be mindful about whether certain cultural values held by diverse group members may clash with preferred group behaviors.
4. Notice whether all group members are invited to participate in the conflict-resolution process. Observe how inputs from diverse group members are received by others within the group.
5. Observe whether culturally sensitive topics that may play a part in the group conflict are acknowledged. If the group skirts around issues of ethnicity and similar topics, notice which group members seem to support the avoidance.
6. Observe whether certain members convey a tone of superiority about their own preferences while expressing contempt for the approaches of others.

Culturally Sanctioned Responses: This Is the Way We Battle

Culture often shapes the way people respond to disagreement or tension. For example, when friction arises, members of Western and individualistically oriented cultures tend to focus on the *outcome* of the event. This orientation toward outcome energizes them to take actions that seek to preserve self-esteem as well as gain individual power and status in the group. They will defend their own positions and challenge those of others with passion when circumstances warrant it. Members from collectivistic cultures, on the other hand, may focus more on the *process* of getting through the discord. Whatever action they take to settle the discord is likely to be geared toward promoting harmony within the group and preserving the dignity or "face" of people in the group. Such members often try to avoid the issue, find someone to mediate the dispute, give in, search for a compromise, offer apologies, or set up a private time to address the issue one-on-one (Oetzel, Ting-Toomey, Masumoto, Yokuchi, & Takai, in press, as cited in Ting-Toomey & Oetzel, 2001; Shen, Sanchez, & Huang, 1984; Ting-Toomey, 1999; Ting-Toomey & Oetzel, 2001).

No sense of shame or guilt should be involved in how members settle disputes because this is the way they have been taught to fight their battles. For members of individualistic cultures, the action of defending oneself involves self-respect. For members of collectivistic cultures, the effort to reach harmony, though long-winded, is a form of art. Therefore, there is neither a right nor a wrong way of responding to discord, only culturally sanctioned way.

Looking for Common Goals That Transcend Individual Cultures

It may take more effort for a culturally diverse group to work through issues that are sensitive in the group. Ting-Toomey and Oetzel (2001) emphasize that it is important to help members bridge gaps by looking for common goals that transcend individual and cultural differences. One way of bridging gaps is to draw attention to one of the group goals in promoting understanding despite differences. To attend to this overarching group goal, the leader may say,

> [To the group] There seems to be a lot of tension here. Let's slow down for a moment and recall our original goals for this group. I recall that one of our goals is to improve communication with others who are different from us. Let's look back and reflect on how we have been doing so far in our efforts to achieve this goal.

Helping Members Build Culturally Sensitive Listening Skills

Many things that are shared in the group can be difficult for a member to talk about and difficult for others to hear. One of these topics is the pain of subjugation experienced by some diverse members (Comacho, 2001; McGoldrick & Giordano, 1996). How that experience is communicated within the group can make a difference in the degree to which the other members will be able to listen and acknowledge the existence of such issues. When a minority member struggles to share a difficult-to-listen-to experience, the leader may need to help the member feel heard by asking the group to reflect on the pain that is expressed. This will help the group build culturally sensitive listening skills. For example, the leader may say,

> [To the group] Barry has just shared with us some very painful experiences. Although his experiences are difficult for some of us to take in, I think that it would be helpful for Barry right now if several of us can reflect back to him some of the things he just shared or some of the feelings he has been struggling with in these experiences. Who will start?

One of the benefits of building culturally sensitive listening skills is that sensitivity to the suffering of others is a small step toward bridging differences. Groups that can acknowledge differences will be better able to work toward common goals that transcend their individual differences. At the same time, members can honor who they are without feeling shame or guilt (Comacho, 2001; Ting-Toomey & Oetzel, 2001).

Managing Tension Caused by Culture and Diversity Factors

It may take some time for the group to bridge gaps and build sensitivity to suffering. Meanwhile, the leader needs to rely on mindful observation to better understand the nature of any discomfort or tension within the group. Such observation may give the leader clues to what needs to be addressed in the group. For example, if a leader notices that members of different backgrounds seem unable to openly disagree with one another or that their disagreements are being expressed in indirect ways, he may say something like the following to address this issue:

> [To the group] I understand that we carry into this group a variety of ways of responding to disagreement and tension. Perhaps it would be useful for us to stop for a moment and just share with the group our preferences and methods of managing conflicts.

If the leader observes that certain cultural values held by diverse group members clash with preferred group behaviors, he may say,

> [To the group] I know that in the group we tend to advocate the free sharing of emotions and reactions. Yet I also know that such feelings are handled differently in some of your homes and communities. I'd like for us to share what it has been like to come to this group and talk about these things that are not easy to talk about.

If the leader notices that members of diverse backgrounds are not having their issues heard, are getting cut off, or are being avoided within the group, the leader may address this issue by saying,

> [To the group] I noticed that a couple of times when Arturo stopped talking, he actually hadn't quite finished his sharing. I wonder whether the group can honor some members' need for longer pauses.

If the leader notices that certain members convey a tone of superiority about their own preferences while expressing contempt for the approaches of others, something like the following may be said to address this issue:

> George, I noticed that you seem very certain about your view of this situation to the extent that you have not been able to take in the other views expressed here by Arturo, Li, and Sanjay. I wonder if you would be willing to take a closer look at some of their comments. What is it, do you think, that they have been suggesting to you?

All these interventions help members air their ways of dealing with friction, become more aware of other members' unique needs, and see a broader variety of possibilities. This may pave the way for members to understand one another on a more realistic level. Regardless of cultural background, many group members are open to expanding their possible means of dealing with dissent.

THE PARADOX OF OPEN CONFLICTS

Some conflicts in the group are subtle and covert, while others are intense and openly explicit. Intensity is shown through tone of voice, expression in the eyes, body language, breathing patterns, and the use of words. Open conflicts make the heart beat fast and the adrenaline shoot high. They stir up a great deal of emotional distress for members, and certainly for the group leader. This section explores the impact of open conflicts and their potential as a creative force within the group.

Common Fear of Open Conflicts

On a societal level, open conflicts have led to war and other types of violence. Within certain families, conflicts have led to quarreling members cutting themselves off from one another, and sometimes refusing to speak to one another for decades. Unfortunately, conflicts are often settled through the force of might rather than through a true understanding of differences. Hocker and Wilmot (1985) identified some of the common images that people associate with conflict. These images include: "conflict is war," "conflict is explosive," "conflict is a mess," and "conflict requires a hero." Clearly these images are associated with destruction, and with conquering or being conquered. Such images of conflict arouse fear in people.

Members, as well as the leader, come to group with an array of memories of how conflicts have been handled in their past. In facing conflict, most people react with fright. The results of conflict are often unpredictable, and the experience of conflict is nerve-wracking. Too many people in our society have not experienced a situation in which a conflict has been handled in a constructive manner.

Fight-or-Flight Response

When conflict arises, people naturally fall back on the responses to it that they have previously learned. Many times, those responses are based on the fight-or-flight reaction. Seaward (1999) expands the fight-or-flight response into four modes, mostly maladaptive, that people use to handle interpersonal conflicts:

1. **Withdrawal**: With this style, people handle negative emotions by walking out, taking a circuitous route, or remaining silent. They withdraw out of fear of direct confrontation. This is a flight or avoidance response that allows them to avoid dealing with the conflictual issues at hand. Withdrawal is a maladaptive coping style, for it tends to prevent resolution, to breed resentment, and to prolong hostility.

2. **Surrender**: To surrender is to give in to the will of others. This is also a flight or avoidance coping style. Habitually using this strategy to manage conflict tends to make one feel like a victim, hampering one's self-esteem.

3. **Hostile aggression**: When using this style, people confront conflict with verbal intimidation, including yelling, pounding fists, and throwing objects across the room. These behaviors fall under the fight response. They are aggressive in nature and aimed at making the other party submit to agreement. Without a doubt, aggressive behaviors—whether verbal or physical—seldom resolve any conflict. Rather, they worsen the tension, fear, and hostility between people, making conflict into a wheel that rolls on with no end.

4. **Persuasion**: Persuasion is a verbal expression aimed at changing another person's beliefs, attitudes, views, decisions, or behaviors. This mode of coping with conflict also belongs to the fight response. In this style, the conflict is negotiated head-on, as though it is a win-lose game. When used only to win in a conflict, at any cost and without willingness to hear the voice of the other side, persuasion is a maladaptive coping style.

The approaches group members take toward conflict may have served a function in the members' lives. Some may not have had any other choice available at a given time in their developmental history. For example, if a young child is confronted with an abusive parent, withdrawal may be the only strategy possible; there may be little opportunity for that child to develop other responses to conflict. As a result, withdrawal and/or surrender may become equivalent to survival. Some of these individuals continue to feel that withdrawal or surrender is the only response available; other approaches may feel too risky to them. Other individuals internalize hostile or aggressive behaviors to the extent that when they grow up, they find themselves employing the same strategies in their own relationships.

Conflict as a Dialectical and Creative Force

Although some conflicts are inevitably destructive, most of them propel the engine of change. Conflict can actually contribute to creativity and growth. The wonderful views available in the Himalayas are the product of the conflict among tectonic plates. The result is land being pushed higher and higher toward the sky—a beautiful transformation. Likewise, water sometimes conflicts with land as spring rains bring inundating floods to river valleys such as that along the Nile River. One result is the depositing of enriching soils on the floodplain so that nourishing crops may continue to be grown. In response to the struggle with England in the 18th century, American colonists reflected deeply on their values; gathered many of the best democratic ideas from many cultures, such as the model of the Iroquois Confederacy (Weatherford, 1988); and articulated a plan for a union, recognizing a need for continuous discussion, participation, and ultimately change. Clearly, these are all processes of creative transformation that continue to unfold.

In the same vein, human conflict is a dialectical process, but too often conflict is viewed in highly dualistic terms as to who is right and who is wrong rather than as a dialectical process that can release the creative potential of all participants involved (Fox, 1983). For conflict to result in constructive outcomes, it cannot be managed on a "win-lose" basis, but instead must be based on the expectation of a "win-win" position.

It is only when awareness is raised that the outcome of interpersonal conflict may prove to be win-win or constructive. The constructive aspects of interpersonal conflict, as identified by Kottler (1994), include: encouraging growth, opening doors to greater intimacy, and establishing boundaries within relationships. When these aspects are present, conflict is a force that, as described by Lewin (1951), serves to unfreeze established patterns. This unfreezing opens the door to new ways of interacting.

Conflict Management: Part of Interpersonal Learning

Group is a powerful laboratory for interpersonal learning because it provides people with opportunities to learn a deeper level of self-disclosure and to receive feedback lacking in their own world. This kind of learning is especially crucial in situations involving uncomfortable feelings and the simmering tension of conflict. Instead of closing up (not disclosing) or shutting down (not receiving feedback), people in the group learn to resolve conflict constructively. Instead of seeing anger as just anger, people learn to see it as a cover-up for fear, guilt, or hurt.

Conflict management requires people to uncover areas that have been kept deeply hidden within them for many years. It allows all parties to get beyond the surface in order to deal with the depth issues. Conflict experience is a critical component to the overall interpersonal learning in the group. It is so critical that Yalom (1995) went so far as to assert that the absence of conflict implies impairment of group development.

Power of Conflict Resolution

All leaders need to learn how to create an environment in which group members can engage in conflict without the stigmas and pressures that life places on us. The group becomes an experimental laboratory where members are encouraged to communicate disagreement in constructive ways that enhance the likelihood of their being heard. In the group, people learn to approach issues in a caring and sensitive way. They learn to be receptive, rather than defensive, in listening to difficult feedback. When conflicts are resolved, people have less chance of distorting their interpersonal perceptions or hindering their psychospiritual growth.

Developing group cohesiveness is crucial for group success. Cohesiveness, however, does not mean comfort. A cohesive group displays support, acceptance, intimacy, and understanding; and it allows expression of hostility and conflict among members (Yalom, 1995). To make the group cohesive, the leader must help the group accept conflict and derive constructive benefit from it. The leader is wise to view open hostility and tension as a sign of increased trust and risk-taking among group members.

When the group starts to embrace conflict, the members will soon learn that conflict enhances self-disclosure. As conflicts happen, each member tends to reveal more and more to clarify her position. As more information is revealed, each member comes to understand more of the others' experiential world.

MANAGING OPEN CONFLICT

The management of open conflict is solely the responsibility of the leader. One of the primary tasks of the leader is to teach members the value of working through conflicts in constructive ways. Once the open conflicts have been resolved, members will have more knowledge about one another's realities and can use that knowledge to give further productive feedback. Each member also comes to realize that his or her relationship with the other is strong enough to take up honest challenges. The working through of open conflict with another person within the group is an experience of great therapeutic power. This section specifies intervention strategies for managing open conflicts in the group.

Resolving Conflict by Establishing a Dialogue

In an open conflict, Yalom (1995) states, communication often breaks down. The antagonist develops a belief that he is right and everyone else is wrong. The opponents stop listening to each other, and each unintentionally distorts what the other has just said. If not managed, conflicts tend to result in defensive behaviors, hostility, and a general lack of trust. However, unrestrained expression of anger will not result in successful resolution of conflict, either. One of the tasks of the group leader, therefore, is to guide members to work through conflict in a constructive way.

Seaward (1999) points out that the most effective strategy for conflict management is dialogue. In dialogue, the voices, views, perceptions, and beliefs of all parties are taken into consideration, opening the room for greater understanding of the spectrum of issues at hand. Studies have shown that communication alone is not sufficient to resolve conflict, but that trust and interdependency are essential determinants (Deutsch & Kraus, 1962). Trust and interdependency are the primary features of dialogue.

Key Element: Empathy

The real issues that drive any open conflict are seldom the obvious ones. What one sees in conflict is much like what one sees in an iceberg: The biggest chunk of its mass is below the water line. Hidden under conflict are often unresolved disappointments and resentments from previous encounters. It is this deeper level of energy that drives the conflict. Once you scratch the surface of most difficult behaviors that seem defensive, combative, bullying, hostile, or alienating, you are likely to find underlying suffering—feelings of violation, betrayal, hurt, abandonment, neglect, or rejection that have been simmering since a tender age.

Empathy is the key element in conflict resolution. Understanding another person's past often plays an important role in the development of empathy. Yalom (1995) stresses that once a member appreciates the aspects of an opponent's earlier life that have contributed to the current behaviors and stance, the opponent's behaviors and position not only make sense but may even appear right. If you notice issues buried in a member's iceberg, search for a caring, empathic, and sensitive way to bring them up, using the right timing.

Method of Conflict Resolution

When open conflict occurs, the physical and emotional tensions of those involved tend to rise. As the emotional temperature rises to a certain point, cognitive processing begins to bog down. This is typically observed when participants repeat the same arguments again and again, but at louder volume and with less explanation. The task of the group leader is to help the members learn first to modulate and regulate their emotional tension and, second, to process the issues of conflict in a way that could lead to a mutual solution. Rather than watch the conflict boil over onto the stove, the leader helps group members turn down the heat so they can look closely at what is fueling the fire. To do this requires a shift from an emotional mode of handling the issues toward a cognitive understanding of both the issues and the dynamics involved.

This is not to say that emotions are in any way unimportant. On the contrary, emotional reactions point to what issues are important to group members. Once the heat is identified, however, it is time to think of ways to cool down the reactions and to heal the burn that has occurred among members.

The following is a five-step method of conflict resolution. Some conflicts take several sessions to resolve. The leader should adopt whatever method is appropriate and tailor it to the group situation.

Stop Any Task at Hand and Give Priority to the Intense Emotions

The group's ability to resolve open conflict relies heavily on the leader's ability to recognize the signs that indicate a conflict is arising. The strength of members' voices alone may not be the best indication of a conflict. Some members become loud when they are excited or enthusiastic. Following is a list of signals that indicate that emotions have reached a certain threshold and some form of aggression is present:

- Tense or twitching muscles
- Staring or lack of eye contact
- Closed defensive postures
- Shallow breathing
- Quivering
- Clenched fists
- Angry words

Overwhelmed by such emotional intensity, the group may feel flooded and the leader shell-shocked. But the leader must recover from the stress reaction and take action immediately. The first thing the leader must do is to stop any task at hand, be it the check-in, the agenda, or an activity in which the group is engaging. Then the group can make dealing with the emotions the top priority. To do this, the leader may say,

[To the whole group] Okay, we all see the tension in the room right now. It's important that the group devotes some time to resolving this conflict. So let's stop our check-in for now and give our priority to the issue between Alice and Dale.

Facilitate Open Dialogue   One of the most common causes of conflict is miscommunication. People involved in a conflict often focus on their own assumptions and have difficulty hearing each other out. To resolve the conflict, the leader must first facilitate both parties to talk to each other openly about what is actually bothering them. When the issues are placed on the table, the group as the observer can get a clear picture of where both parties are coming from. To encourage both parties to talk openly about the issue, the leader may say,

[To the parties involved] I hear that both of you feel irritated by what was said to you, but I'm not sure whether either of you is hearing the other person. So I would like both of you to take turns explaining how you feel and where you are coming from on this issue. Okay. Alice, would you go first and explain how you feel and where you are coming from? Then we'll go to Dale.

The leader also may use a paraphrasing exercise for the parties involved to facilitate mutual listening. The details of the exercise and an example to illustrate it can be found in "Facilitating Mutual Listening" on the book's Web site (see Preface for URL).

Involve the Group in Offering Validation   As the involved parties begin a dialogue, they will probably still feel too tense to articulate and listen well to how each feels and what each assumes. When the heart is pounding and all the other physical stress reactions are taking place, people's ability to process information is reduced. If the stress reactions are not cooled down, the members will find it hard to pay attention to what each other is saying, and therefore productive problem solving will become virtually impossible. To help both sides cool down, the leader can involve the group in giving both parties validation and affirmation. When validated, both parties will feel heard and affirmed; then they usually can calm down and become more able to resolve the disparities. To involve the group, the leader may say something like:

[To the group] Alice and Dale are still trying to straighten out this issue between them. I wonder, can the rest of you share how you imagine each of them might be feeling under the circumstances? Can any of you see where each of them is coming from? Please speak directly to Alice and Dale.

Facilitate Self-Reflection   After each party has heard the other out and reached a certain degree of understanding, the leader may facilitate both parties to reflect on what lies under their conflict. Too often tensions and tempers flair when conflict arises, preventing people from reasonably examining the issues that are contributing to the conflict. Kleinberg (2000) suggested that the particular context of the conflict must be identified and examined. It is only after such an examination that awareness of the participants can be raised and factors contributing to the conflict can be understood.

The best time to facilitate self-examination is after both parties have felt heard and validated. At this juncture, the leader may ask both members to reflect on the possible meaning that the conflict might hold for them. Questions the leader may use to raise awareness include:

> Alice, what issues are being drawn to your awareness through this conflict that you might not have noticed before?
>
> Dale, what did you learn from the experience of this conflict?

Entire Group Processing   The last step in resolving an open conflict is an entire group processing. Systems theory teaches us that the actions of one member influence the rest of the group's interaction. A member cannot be conceived of as an independent individual, but rather must be seen as an integral part of something larger, which is the group (Donigan & Malnati, 1997). The member or members who display aggressive or hostile behaviors must be understood in the context of the whole group. When managing open conflict, the leader should focus not only on the specific member or members, but also on the group's interaction. The leader must think about what is best for both the members in conflict and the group as a whole.

This systemic perspective calls for a further processing that will engage the whole group in exploring the impact of the event. The use of group processing to gain insight into any event is called *process illumination* (Yalom, 1995). Here the leader may initiate process comments by saying,

> [To the whole group] I'd like to invite everyone in the group to share your thoughts and feelings about how our group worked on managing the conflict in this session. How did you personally experience the conflict? What did you learn about yourself and others in working through today's conflict? Who would like to start?

A Case in Point

It was the fifth session of a twelve-session group. The session started as usual with a check-in. Group members looked calm, relaxed, and enthusiastic for the session to start. What happened that night was something that took the group by surprise. During the check-in, a conflict arose between Sue and Loretta. Sue said she was thinking of quitting the group because she was angry and hurt by something Loretta said at the end of the previous session. As she expressed her anger, Sue's face became stern, her eyes got intense, and her voice fluctuated. Sensing the emotions coming from Sue, Loretta rose to the occasion to meet Sue's confrontation.

The confrontation between Sue and Loretta soon led to high-flying emotions in the group. Many members were stunned by the intensity of Sue's reaction. Few had picked up on how Sue felt toward Loretta's comment in the previous session. As the tension rose, the group felt paralyzed. It was obvious that if the conflict was not attended to by the entire group, it could cause a serious rift within the group. Therefore, the leader informed the group that they would stop the check-in and allow both Sue and Loretta adequate time to air their feelings and work through the conflict. The leader said,

> [To the group] What happened between Sue and Loretta is very important. Let's stop our check-in for the moment and give our priority to resolving this issue.

Sue came from an alcoholic family where she was hurt repetitively by the loud voices of family members and their insensitive comments to each other. Loretta came from a family where her parents constantly battled, leaving Loretta feeling powerless despite her frequent protests against their behavior. Sue and Loretta locked horns with each other when the roles they played in their families of origin were enacted in the here-and-now context of the group. The comment Loretta had made in the previous session, while seeming so innocent to other members, had triggered Sue's feelings of being ostracized. Loretta had, in a way, filled the role of Sue's family of origin through her challenging comment to Sue. On the other hand, the intensity of Sue's reaction during the check-in triggered Loretta's feeling of powerlessness that was so familiar from her family of origin.

As Sue and Loretta were trying to resolve the friction, both of them seemed to repeat, in a circular manner, the points they desperately wanted to get across. The leader noticed this and realized that each party needed a sense of validation from the other. Validation is difficult to come by when emotions are crowding the cognitive processing, however. The leader, therefore, steered the group to validate both members' experiences by saying,

> [To the group] I can imagine how vulnerable and stressed both Sue and Loretta are feeling right now in trying to put themselves in line to straighten out this conflict between them. I would like to invite the rest of the group members to share your understanding of this event. What I think would be most helpful is for you all to share how you understand the way both Sue and Loretta might be experiencing this event.

This intervention brought the group together to make both Sue and Loretta feel validated and affirmed regarding their feelings and positions. It was a successful intervention, as evidenced by how the tension gave way to a sense of relief. The conflict between Sue and Loretta was resolved. During further group processing, the entire group had an "aha" experience in terms of how well all the members worked together. The icing on the cake was when Sue and Loretta hugged each other at the end of the session, which indicated they no longer had hard feelings toward each other.

Both parties and other group members wrote journal entries after the session. Loretta wrote:

> This session was a real breakthrough for me personally because it showed me how processing issues openly in group can provide multiple viewpoints. This process gave me much insight into how I am perceived by others. Many in the group showed compassion for me and told me that I was courageous, and they were careful to protect me as they empathized with Sue's pain. Through the group processing, I now know that talking nondefensively can work to resolve conflict. All along in this group I have been struggling with how I would come to self-awareness and what my role will be in my own issue, and now I am somewhat satisfied. From this experience of resolving the conflict with Sue, I think I am now willing to confront someone if I am truly convinced that it can help them. Also, the importance of being genuine became obvious to me tonight when Sue searched my face endlessly for the "truth" of my feelings for her. I feel so fortunate to be so personally involved with tonight's experience because the strong emotions I felt helped me more fully understand the interpersonal processes. My hope is that in the future I will never again lose sight of the person I am responding to and I will endeavor to keep in touch with the emotions that they carry.

Sue wrote:

> Group session five was very surprising for me because I did not know that my issue would surface in the group. I had many lingering feelings about the fourth session. I was angry because I was criticized by Loretta at the end of the session. What I wanted at the end of last session was reassurance that I had in fact done a better job in terms of the interpersonal skill I said I wanted to practice during the session. But what I got from Loretta was the opposite. It was like sideswiping me. There was nowhere to go with the feelings that got triggered in me. The timing of the confrontation was inappropriate. I had to sit with my confusion, anger, and hurt all week. In our open dialogue tonight, Loretta said that she felt very ashamed of what she said to me. She said that she had caught herself on more than one occasion being critical in her responses toward others. As Loretta was talking, I realized that she was in the same boat as I was when interacting with others in the group. It feels like once you are in the group process, you are caught in a spider's web, and there is no escaping what will transpire.

Kim's comments were:

> This group session was very interesting for me. I first felt apprehensive when it was Sue's turn to check in with her reaction from last session. I

wondered what she was going to say and was afraid she would be angry. Anger has always been a difficult emotion for me to both feel and to deal with when it is from others. When Sue started to express her anger, my heart started pounding and my breathing got shallow. If the anger had been directed at me, I would have gotten paralyzed with fear. I would have been unable to respond and would have shut down completely until it seemed safe again. When someone is angry with me, I tend to feel great shame because I take this to mean that I have caused them great harm and therefore must be a terrible, thoughtless person. I remember as a child being terrified of angering my parents. I have to admit that I still carry the same bodily reactions and fears in dealing with my parents and others close to me, although I tend to move through my fear now and am more likely to deal with anger directly instead of hoping it will go away. When it comes to my own anger, I tend to keep it buried and hold onto frustrations and resentments. Lately, though, I have been working on owning my own anger and using it as an indication that my boundary has been crossed, and then decide what to do to maintain my boundary intact. This has helped me to feel more in control of my anger and use it as a source of power rather than seeing it as something scary about to take over me.

Jullie's journal entry read:

I thought it was very interesting that many people in the group perceived Sue as being very strong despite her confession of being cautious and afraid in group situations. At the first session, Sue said that she has always been very cautious in group situations and is very concerned that people in this group may hurt her. In the last session when Sue asked for feedback from the group, I began to formulate something positive to say to her because I knew about her feelings regarding groups. When Loretta burst out with her response to Sue at the end of the session, I felt like the air had been knocked out of me because I knew how painful it would be for Sue; however, at the same time, I felt admiration for Loretta because she was being honest and rising to the request. I think this week's session was very healing for both Loretta and Sue. They both seemed to feel a lot of gratitude that we as a group would take the time to understand where each was coming from during the interaction and their resulting reactions. I was so fascinated by what other people had to say and by what they thought about what had happened, that I just found myself listening to everyone. I was also interested in how Sue and Loretta responded to what everyone else was saying. I was so glad to see both of them relax a lot as they heard the group members share empathy and show that they understood each of their points of view.

Lisa wrote:

During the session I was impressed by how straightforward the interaction was between Sue and Loretta. It was truly a productive process that

I admire. But my feelings came flooding up when I was barely out of the driveway and on my way home. I felt a deep sadness that, all too often, my husband and I don't resolve things or talk the way Sue and Loretta did. They "fought" fairly by sticking to the subject, validating each other's feelings, and not making threats or accusations. I felt sad also that, rather than argue in what I call an unfair situation, I just retreat or go my own way when I feel frustrated by my husband, and thus our communication diminishes.

Finally, Sam's journal entry read:

I thought it was fascinating to watch Sue and Loretta fight. They both started out so angry and hostile, and yet ended the evening by being relaxed, friendly, and laughing. They seemed to come full circle within the 90-minute session. It was interesting to me that although Loretta continually states that she does not like confrontation, she provoked a confrontation by making the initial remark to Sue at the end of last session, and then rose to Sue's confrontation immediately in this week's session. It was also interesting that Sue fears being ostracized from the group, but initiated an interaction that had real potential of forcing the group to cut her off. The group had to make a choice this evening regarding Sue: to come to her defense and include her fully in the group, or to side with Loretta and confirm Sue's worst fears—that the group could reject her. It's interesting that Sue would bring that circumstance about. I thought the group handled the situation beautifully by supporting both women and rejecting neither one. Speaking further of personalities coming to the fore, Jean's tough exterior was preventing her from empathizing with Sue. Her "suck it up" attitude really did not allow much softness for Sue. Jim innocently provided the comic relief that we all needed. This session showed beyond doubt the value of humor to defuse tension in the group. When it is genuine and not meant to make fun of anyone, humor can be a wonderful tension reliever. I am so glad we had it tonight.

LEADER, CURE THYSELF

Centered and Grounded Leader

It is difficult to maintain a clear perspective in the midst of an emotionally charged situation filled with tension and conflict. One must be centered and grounded so that the erratic acts of others do not throw one out of balance (Heider, 1985). The leader who stays centered does not get drawn into triangulation with members who may try to sway the leader to take sides regarding who is right and who is wrong. The centered leader can, instead, see those emotional tugs as opportunities for members to explore their patterns of relating with others. A tide of emotion from members can be seen as a signal that the members need increased awareness in that area of life. Tensions and conflicts contain a golden opportunity for members to have a "corrective emotional experience" (Yalom, 1995).

The leader's personal developmental work partially determines his competency in managing tension and conflict within a group. Personal work increases self-awareness. The more leaders grow aware of what drives them, the less likely they are to be caught by surprise when hot issues arise in a group.

In their research on group leaders' development of comfort in managing conflicts within groups, Secemsky, Ahlman, and Robbins (1999) found that the personal growth of group leaders had a strong positive influence. As leaders gain experience in leading groups and obtain supervision to become more effective leaders, it is important that they also continue their personal growth work.

Leader's Transformative Self-Care

A variety of approaches exist for increasing and transforming a leader's level of consciousness. These may include individual counseling, group counseling, journaling, art therapy, music therapy, meditation, yoga, physical exercise, and just about any other activities that bring a disciplined and consistent measure of self-reflection to the process. This list certainly includes several things that counselors and therapists might suggest for their own clients. If these practices are useful in developing self-care in clients, they are certainly useful for counselors and therapists.

Whatever means of transformation are employed, the goal is to attain a greater degree of wholeness through increased consciousness. Transformative practices may initially lead to the identification and experience of internal conflicts. If these internal issues are not worked through sufficiently, they may inappropriately engage one's attention while one is leading a group during conflict. Such unresolved issues are potential "hot buttons" that clients are likely to press.

Personal development is an avenue to achieving higher levels of integration. *Yoga* is a Sanskrit word meaning "oneness." The practice of yoga is directly concerned with increasing a sense of wholeness. Although it has been popularly associated with certain types of physical poses, yoga can be a way of yoking our perceptions to the wealth of experience within a group. The experiential approach described in this book is pointed toward achieving oneness or wholeness of experience in the present. As we become more aware of each present moment, we become more conscious of all the emotional, physical, intellectual, social, and spiritual currents held within us and of our own relationships with others.

SCENARIOS FOR YOUR PRACTICE

1. In the fourth meeting of a group, Joshua looks at you and states, "You are just like my dad, expecting me to be a clone of yours instead of who I really am." What is possibly happening here? How might you want to address this within the group, and especially with Joshua?

2. In a personal growth group, Wayne looks at Martha and states, "You cannot scare me with your short hair and your heavy shoes. I know your kind. I know people like you just want to put others down." What type of process is at play here? What would you do to de-escalate the situation? What might you say?

3. You are meeting with a group that includes two members from the Middle East and one member from Asia. The group is focused on increasing personal communication skills and awareness. In the third session, Myra emphatically states, "Non-Christians are untrustworthy sinners. They should all become Christian if they are going to stay in this country." What are some of your options as the group leader for responding to Myra?

4. In a group meeting, after a brief heated exchange with Martha, Gertrude turns fully away from Martha and, facing Patty, says (with a little smile and nudge), "Do you believe that she's actually saying this stuff? I'm sure that you agree with me that she's dead wrong." What type of conflict statement is this? How would you respond?

5. In the third meeting of a personal growth group, with a scowl on her face, Jill says, "Glen, last time you missed our meeting, with some built-up excuse. You always hang on every word the group leader says, like you're some kind of teacher's pet. You try to act like you're best friends with everybody in the group, like you're so sincere [said thick with sarcasm]. You're such a fake!" What are your options for intervention?

6. A strong disagreement has occurred in the group just a few minutes before the end of the session. You suggest that the group table the discussion until the next meeting because of lack of time to explore the issue. In a sharp tone, Tony objects: "Wait a minute. I'm not going to let you weasel out of this. Before we leave here tonight, I need to know that you all agree that my view prevails." What are your choices for responding before you leave this session? What are your choices for responding when you begin the following session?

7. As the group moves into the final half hour of its third meeting, you have a sense that group members have mentally left the group for the day, as it begins to feel quite lifeless. You are aware that an energy drain seems to have hit the group just after Verla very obliquely contrasted her view of the growth process with Hugo's. What are some of your options at this point for helping the group to identify what is actually happening?

8. David, who has been a bit emotionally removed from the group up to this point, looks at Reggie, who originates from Alabama and who has been quite active in the group, and says: "Do you actually expect anyone to consider your suggestions seriously when you state them with such a drawl?" As the group leader, what issue would you want to highlight? How might you engage the group to address this dynamic?

9. Marvin is just divorced from his wife, who recently came out as a lesbian. During group, he addresses Willis, who is gay, as follows: "I don't think you get the picture here. There are two sexes, forming the cornerstone of our society, which will soon fall apart if undermined by you people." What is the underlying issue? How would you engage the group in addressing it?

10. During the fourth session of a group for interpersonal skills development, you notice that Wayne is starting to tease and mock Bhavani about his foreign accent, although he always does it with a big smile. Bhavani looks a little annoyed by this but does not say anything. As the leader, how might you work on this issue from a diversity perspective?

SELF-REFLECTION

1. What have been your experiences with conflict? Have most of them been harmful and destructive, or have you had some personal experiences with conflict that resulted in positive outcomes? What factors contributed to the resulting outcomes? What were your contributions to the outcomes?

2. What approaches to dealing with conflict were most prevalent in your family of origin? Do you find yourself continuing to use these approaches in your own day-to-day conflicts? If not, what influenced you most to incorporate different approaches to conflict?

3. What transformative activities do you engage in to promote your personal growth and increase your level of self-understanding?

4. What activities do you consider to be important for your continued personal growth in the future?

5. In your personal life, what signs do you look for to help you recognize covert conflict with your family and friends? How do you act once you are aware that covert conflict is present?

6. As a developing group leader, how can you ascertain when you might be expressing countertransference or projection onto group members?

7. What is your own level of awareness, knowledge, and skill in working with diverse individuals? What is the range and depth of your personal experiences in building relationships with others of different cultures, ethnicities, sexual orientation, socioeconomic level, educational attainment, age, and ability/disability? How do such factors influence your views of diverse members?

8. What personal experiences have you had in shifting worldviews in order to "live in more than one world" as members of many nonprivileged groups have done?

ADVANCED LEADERSHIP SKILLS: GETTING THE GROUP TO UNCHARTED WATERS

TAKING RISKS IN COMMUNICATION

Toward Greater Group Closeness

The life of a group is ever complex and evolving. As the group grows past the transition stage, its momentum and intensity increase. The framework of agenda-working presented in Chapter 6 can give the leader a sense of direction, rhythm, and flow when leading a group. But the framework is just the basis of group work. To ensure that the group remains vital and continues to move forward, the leader must help the group increase its collective achievement. In this exhilarating journey, the leader needs to push the group members into exploring new territories, session by session. In order to meet this demand, leaders must continue to advance their level of intervention skills and techniques.

This chapter is designed to help group leaders move toward a higher level of leadership skills and techniques. It covers:

- Leadership in the norming stage
- Increased risk-taking in self-disclosure
- Greater risk-taking in group interaction
- Advanced empathy
- Greater risk-taking in feedback-giving
- Leader's self-involving disclosure
- Constructive confrontation
- Teaching members to request feedback
- Enhancing member ability to receive feedback
- Cases in point

LEADERSHIP IN THE NORMING STAGE

Norming Stage

Once the group has learned how to tackle members' agendas in a safe environment and how to deal with tension and conflict, it is progressing into its "young adulthood." This period is called the *norming stage*. In this stage, desired norms of group culture and behaviors can be solidified (Tuckman, 1965; Tuckman & Jensen, 1977). Group norms serve as guideposts, navigating members to communicate in effective ways and make productive use of group time. The building of group norms is a continual process that starts at the beginning of the group, but intensifies in the norming stage.

During the norming stage, members' dissatisfaction tends to dissipate while positive feelings increase. The experiences of supporting one another in the midst of handling rift and tension should have contributed to a sense of *group potency*, a sense that the group can be a powerful and constructive force (Jung & Sosik, 1999; Lacoursiere, 1980). Increasingly, members will see the group with greater clarity and have confidence about how to accomplish their goals. A greater sense of hopefulness will be exhibited.

Group Cohesiveness and the Need for Affection

The leader's task in the norming stage is to help the group establish a solid foundation of cohesiveness. Group cohesiveness is a sense of "group-ness" or "we-ness"—a level of intimacy and caring in members' relationships with one another (Schutz, 1958; Weber, 1999). Among the three universal needs referred to by Schutz (1958), the need for affection tends to surface once the needs for inclusion and control have been sufficiently met. Affection concerns the degree of intimacy and caring that people express to one another. Affection is deepened by increased depth of personal sharing among group members. Of course, the three universal needs cannot be completely addressed at any given stage. As members deal with issues of affection, the issues of inclusion and control may recycle to the forefront.

The primary tool that leaders use in building group cohesiveness and affection is a higher quality of communication.

Three Classes of Communication Quality

Interpersonal closeness and cohesiveness are nursed by high-quality communication. Quality of communication can be classified into three categories (Agazarian & Simon, 1967):

1. **Approach**: The highest quality of communication is a result of the approach communication style. This style promotes interpersonal closeness.

2. **Contingent**: The neutral style is termed contingent communication. Whether this style brings about interpersonal understanding depends on each situation.

3. **Avoidance**: The lowest quality of communication occurs with the *avoidance* style. This type of communication brings about interpersonal distance and inhibits mutual understanding.

If a group is to enjoy greater cohesiveness, the members must increase their approach-style statements and decrease avoidance communication. Members in the group, however, rarely know how to make approach-style statements. They need a bit of help from the leaders.

Increasing Risk-Taking in Communication

Classic studies show that the best way to increase approach-style communication in a group of people is by taking their interaction to a more personal and riskier level (Hill, 1965; Agazarian & Simon, 1967). The Hill Interaction Matrix identifies five styles of interaction: responsive, conventional, assertive, speculative, and confrontive (Hill, 1965). The first three are as follows:

1. **Responsive**: The responsive interaction style is the least personal style of interpersonal communication. This interaction style is passive and reactive; people using it take little initiative in the communication.

2. **Conventional**: The conventional interaction style is the second lowest level of interpersonal communication. At this level, people share things that are minimally personal.

3. **Assertive**: The assertive level of interaction is marked by a willingness to reveal at a greater personal level, but people communicating at this level still operate very much from a self-protective and safe stance.

Hill clustered these first three levels under the term *prework,* suggesting that people are still testing each other out in their interactions for trustworthiness before disclosing riskier personal information. Within the group setting, the prework level represents the relative absence of openness and lack of risk-taking by group members. Hill's last two levels are as follows:

4. **Speculative**: The fourth level of interaction is known as speculative. This level is demonstrated by people's willingness to guess or speculate out loud about one another's issues and internal experiences, but only at the request of a person who wants such input.

5. **Confrontive**: The highest level of interaction is referred to as confrontive. It is exemplified by people's willingness to take risks in self-expression and in sharing their observations and reactions, without a specific request coming from others first.

These last two levels are identified together as the *work* level, since they represent the kinds of interaction demonstrated in a well-functioning group. Within the group setting, the work level represents member openness and willingness to take risks (McCarty, 1969).

In the norming stage, the leader can navigate the group members to an increased use of approach-style communication by guiding them to step up to the speculative and confrontive levels of communication through increased risk-taking. Only through this increased risk-taking practice can the group prepare itself for its next stage—the here-and-now stage—where the most intense interpersonal learning hopefully will occur. (See Chapters 9 and 10.)

Two Axes of Communication: Self-Disclosure and Feedback

Communication in the group can be boiled down to two categories: self-disclosure and feedback. How much others understand about who we are and where we have come from hinges on how much we are willing to reveal to them. Low self-disclosure leads to misunderstanding whereas high self-disclosure leads to greater support and understanding. Further, our self-awareness about the way our behaviors affect others is proportionate to the feedback we receive. Low-level feedback leads to low self-awareness while high-level feedback leads to high self-awareness.

In general, people rarely have the luxury of receiving honest feedback from others, nor the faith to disclose their vulnerable parts to others, resulting in a massive unconscious part of the self. The price of having such a massive unconscious part of the self is that the person does not know how she is living her life. The unconscious part of the self actually dictates, to a great degree, our behaviors and relationships. The more massive the unconscious part is, the less available are behavioral options to the person. Therefore, a small conscious area accompanying a huge unconscious area alerts us that a person is in great need of psychological help. Usually this is a person who suffers from low self-awareness and low levels of intimacy. When a person is not aware of her impact on others' reactions, she tends to view herself as powerless prey for others. When a person feels that no one really understands her, she becomes lonely and is unsupported.

The effects of various levels of self-disclosure and feedback can be seen clearly in a "Johari window" (Luft, 1966). The ultimate goal of group work is to increase a member's conscious area and decrease the member's unconscious area. If a group is successful, its members' profiles might appear like that shown in the Johari window in Figure 8.1. To see how such profiles differ depending on the degree of feedback and self-disclosure that is present in the group, please see "Johari Window" on the book's Web site (see Preface for URL). In order to increase the open or conscious area, the group members need to take greater risks in the areas of feedback and self-disclosure. The following sections explain how leaders can facilitate members to take such action.

INCREASED RISK-TAKING IN SELF-DISCLOSURE

Self-disclosure is a sign of mental health. Research has found that people who disclose themselves are more content, adaptive, competent, perceptive, and trusting toward others, when compared with nondisclosing persons (Johnson, 1981). Johnson noted that sharing our emotions improves our health, helps prevent disease, and lessens our interpersonal problems. Further, self-disclosure serves to increase our self-awareness (Bach & Deutsh, 1970). In describing ourselves, we sort out our feelings, get a clearer view of our inner needs and fears, and take ownership of our choices. The sense of shame and guilt that often lurks underneath is decreased, and interpersonal closeness is deepened.

In group counseling and therapy, not only does self-disclosure create more meaningful relationships within the group, but this effect also carries over into relationships outside the group. Self-disclosure is such an important part of group counseling and therapy that it overrides many other elements. Without effective self-disclosure, other key therapeutic factors, such as universality and interpersonal learning, cannot be achieved. Therefore, self-disclosure is the first area in which the leader should encourage members to take more risks.

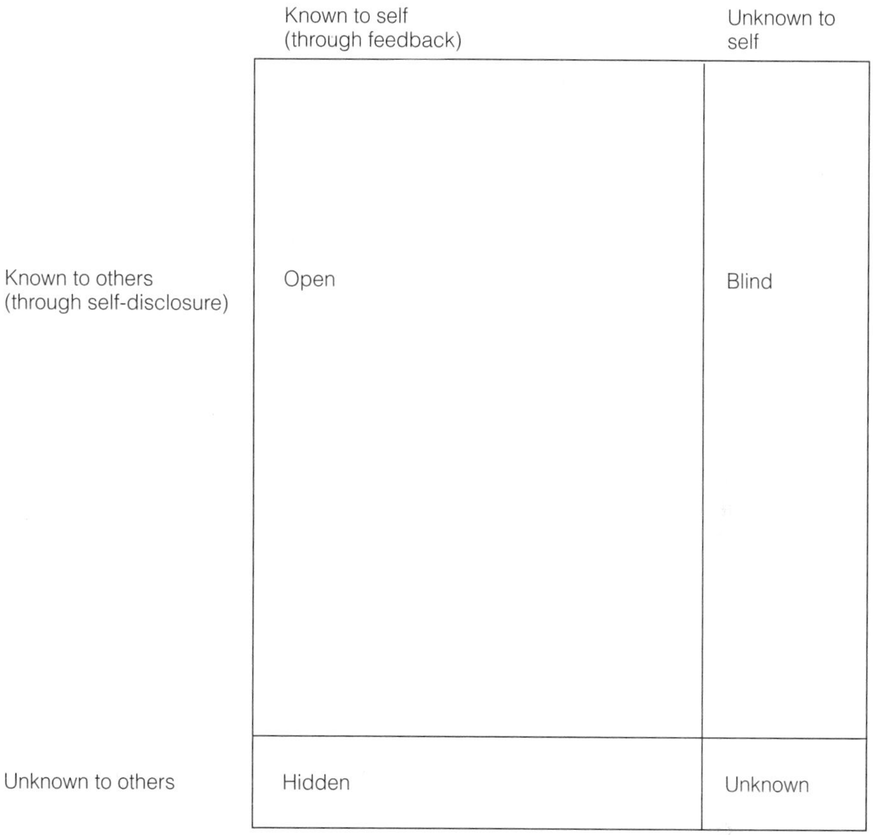

	Known to self (through feedback)	Unknown to self
Known to others (through self-disclosure)	Open	Blind
Unknown to others	Hidden	Unknown

FIGURE 8.1

POSSIBLE GROUP MEMBER PROFILE DEMONSTRATED WITH A JOHARI WINDOW

Presenting Agenda: Importance of Self-Disclosure

If the ultimate goal of the group is to immensely increase a member's open or conscious area of the self, then all members need to learn how to disclose themselves and be more open with others. Presenting one's agenda is itself a form of courageous self-disclosure: It is a courageous act because it involves revealing personal information. Revealing oneself at such a personal level involves risks. One can actually feel naked and vulnerable, not knowing whether others might judge or reject one for what is disclosed. One cannot know whether that fear is real or not until a risk is taken. Chances are good that taking such a risk will allow one to reap the harvest of openness within one's relationships, strengthening trust and intimacy with others. A person who withholds himself from others, on the other hand, may well keep himself unknown, thereby closing off opportunities for establishing close relationships with others.

Self-disclosure and a sense of closeness tend to increase over time in a process-focused group. This progression, however, is not achieved automatically. Many self-disclosures are superfluous or irrelevant; some people talk just to hear their own voices. Such disclosures tend to slow the group down and annoy others. Ultimately, the group becomes frustrated and impatient with those who hold back from personal disclosure. The group may start to target the discussion on the members' reactions to those who are unwilling to disclose themselves to the group.

Many barriers have to be overcome before members can share themselves at a more personal and meaningful level. Among them is the tendency for people to talk about things that are not relevant to what is happening in the relationship. Another barrier is the tendency people have to tell stories and stay stuck on the surface.

There-and-Then Disclosure: It Is Just a Start

When members present their agendas or share their issues, they typically start by telling something external about themselves, something from outside the group. This external event may be a crisis in their life or an event that happened in the distant or recent past. Basically, members tell their stories about the events that led them to seek group counseling. This kind of disclosure is called a *there-and-then disclosure,* or a *vertical disclosure* (Leszcz, 1992). The telling of there-and-then stories is important. The action of telling may be cathartic itself. When the audience is attentive, it can even be therapeutic. The group ought to allow members to tell their stories in an unhurried fashion.

As important as it is, however, this kind of disclosure does not make the group feel connected. In fact, if it goes on and on, there-and-then disclosure can render the group listless and disconnected. A group functioning in this manner will not develop a feeling of "we-ness" or cohesion. The possibility that such a group will disintegrate is increased (Slavin, 1993). Hence, there-and-then disclosure is the first barrier to be overcome before members can share themselves on a more personal and meaningful level.

Stuck in the Stories and Surfaces

To feel connected with the others, group members have to become more open and honest in their self-disclosure. Many members, however, face another barrier: They often get stuck in the facades of their stories. They may confuse self-disclosure with storytelling (a pseudo self-disclosure) or with secret-telling. They may tell the group facts and details from their past without making any connection to their present struggles or their inner feelings. Storytelling, as a form of pseudo self-disclosure, does not promote interpersonal intimacy and group cohesiveness. Pierce and Baldwin (1990) state: "Appropriate self-disclosure is not revealing one's innermost secrets and digging into one's past, it is not expressing every fleeting reaction toward others, it is not telling stories about oneself, and it is not letting group pressure dictate the limits of one's privacy" (p. 152). Rather, appropriate self-disclosure occurs when the depth and pace of disclosure matches the group's capacity. The kind of self-disclosure that has depth usually has to do with current struggles; unresolved personal issues; fears and expectations; sorrows and joys; a sense of inadequacy or self-doubt; inspiration and hope; and strengths and weaknesses.

Often fear restricts members from disclosing personal reactions in group. Members fear being negatively evaluated, losing control, and damaging relationships with other members. When gripped by fear, people use a number of devices to avoid revealing their feelings. These devices include: asking questions, using the editorial "we," and changing the subject. If members use avoidance tactics chronically, they will be alienated from their inner experience.

People's ability to self-disclose depends on their own self-awareness and the degree to which they are comfortable with themselves. If members are not self-aware, they will not have much to disclose because they will not feel much. They do not have an awareness of their own inner experiences and therefore are unable to reveal them to the other group members.

Facilitating Disclosure at a Personal Level

As the group progresses to the norming stage, the leader can help members step up to a more personal level of self-disclosure. For example, if a member has a tendency to tell stories without revealing personal feelings or reactions, the leader may intervene by saying,

> Julie, I am very interested in hearing about the events that have happened in your life. They help the group get a sense of what your life has been like. However, please help us see how what you just described relates to your present struggle.

> Jeff, when you tell your stories, would you please direct them toward issues that are relevant to the changes you wish to achieve in this group?

Encouraging Measured Risk-Taking

Revealing oneself on a personal level involves risks, as it can make one feel naked. The best way to learn risk-taking is by first taking a measured risk. The leader can encourage members to take measured risks by saying something like:

> Julie, I know it is not easy to open up to other people. But we need to take some measured risk, because if we don't, we leave room for misunderstanding. We also remain mysterious, and people can readily project their own feelings and assumptions onto us. Most importantly, if we don't share things at a personal level, it is very difficult for other people to care for us.

Promoting Here-and-Now Disclosure

The most productive form of self-disclosure is revealing the feelings that are evoked in the here-and-now immediate setting—the I-Thou relationship disclosure. It is more meaningful and intense than revealing feelings from the remote past. Yalom (1995) states: "What is important is not that one discloses oneself but that one discloses something important in the context of the relationship with others" (p. 172). This type of here-and-now, I-Thou reaction talk can lead the group members to experience a sense of increased intimacy and transparency with one another. To promote I-Thou relationship disclosure, the leader may say,

> Julie, you said you struggled with a sense of insignificance while growing up. How do you feel about sharing this with the group today?

> Jeff, how difficult was it for you to tell the group about this today? How did you anticipate the group would respond?

Suppose Julie shares her fear with the group. The leader can then invite the rest of the group to respond to her here-and-now self-disclosure:

> [To the group] I wonder, would any of you like to respond to Julie's fear about taking too much time from the group?

Respecting Individual Pace

As the leader encourages members to take risks in self-disclosure, she must be careful to respect each individual's pace. Each member's pace of self-disclosure is different, and therapists need to respect the unique pace of each member. When too much self-disclosure is pushed for too soon, before the member is ready, the person will feel vulnerable and feel a need to withdraw. If a member is pressured to disclose too much before she is ready, the leader may intervene and reassure the member that she is the ultimate authority who decides how much to disclose, and how soon, by saying one of the following:

> [To the group] There are obviously some things that Julie does not yet feel like sharing. Although most of us are eager to understand Julie more, Julie does not feel comfortable enough yet. So let's respect her pace for now.

Julie, I sense the group is eager to know exactly what made you decide to leave home at such an early age. However, don't give in to group pressure. You are the only one who can judge for yourself when and how much to disclose.

[To the group] Self-disclosure is very important, but it is imperative that people disclose things and feelings only when they are ready.

GREATER RISK-TAKING IN GROUP INTERACTION

As a particular member discloses her stories, strong inner reactions might be triggered in the other group members. These reactions are important materials for sharing. The sharing of inner feelings and reactions within the group can create an intimate, supportive environment, encouraging the working member to dig deeper into further layers of self-exploration. This is the second area in which the leader should encourage members to take more risks to promote effective communication. This section presents intervention techniques and skills for leaders to consider if they want to steer the group interaction to a deeper level.

Tapping into the Group's Inner Reactions

What is usually missing in dysfunctional communication is authenticity—the honest engagement of one's self in the interaction. Group is a perfect setting in which to unlearn dysfunctional communication as members learn to verbally respond to others in an authentic way. A lot of reactions get stirred up as the agenda on the floor unfolds. These inner reactions may be appreciation, resonance, surprise, shock, or concern; they may be positive, neutral, or negative. Most people do not know whether it is appropriate to express these reactions unless the leader invites them to do so. Or they may respond in vague ways that reveal nothing about themselves. If members respond with vague statements such as "I can really relate to you" or "I understand how that feels," the leader should not accept such statements as they are; rather, the leader should ask the members to be more specific and open. For example, to draw out more authentic inner reactions, the leader may say,

Jim, would you be more specific about what you mean when you say "I understand how that feels"?

[To the group] Many of you seem to be quite affected by Julie's story. I wonder, what reactions were triggered when you listened to Julie describe her struggle?

Who else feels like Jim does? [effort to draw more members out]

Sharing Recurrent Feelings

The group is a rich environment wherein certain member interaction repeatedly triggers strong feelings in others. If the leader observes reactions to be recurrent or persistent, something significant is definitely going on. Common persistent feelings may include:

- Boredom
- Anger
- Disappointment
- Feeling touched
- Amazement
- Respect
- Closeness
- Powerlessness
- Irritation

These feelings, when shared in an honest and caring way, provide opportunities for members to know how their interpersonal styles affect others. Leaders can encourage members not to hold back these feelings by saying:

> [To the group] I sense some unspoken feelings going on in the group. I wonder what the group is feeling at this moment. If you have felt a certain way more than twice, I invite you to trust your feelings and try to express them in a way that is easy for others to hear. [pause for the group to comprehend these words] Would anyone in the group like to share some unspoken feelings you have had about certain things at this moment?

Getting into the Real Thing: I-Thou Immediacy Issues

Immediacy issues involve raw emotions and dynamics happening in the I-Thou relationship. Since these immediacy issues are so personal, they are the most powerful and stimulating aspects of group life. Most immediacy issues, however, remain unspoken in our society because it is considered to be too direct to tell another person how we are affected by his personal demeanor. In the group, immediacy issues may happen in member-to-member relationships or in member-to-leader relationships. Talking openly about I-Thou relationship issues is most instrumental for group work. Through sharing such intensely intimate feelings, the group members practice a form of interaction that gets them to the pot of gold at the end of the rainbow—an increased intimacy and transparency with one another. Because most people are not familiar with talking about these I-Thou relationship topics, the leader must facilitate this meaningful sharing. Following are some ways to lead members into a discussion of immediacy issues.

If, say, the leader interrupts a member who is giving advice or dominating the conversation, the leader may bring up the I-Thou immediacy issue by asking,

Bill, how did you feel about my interrupting you just now?

If the group gets bogged down, the leader may explore what I-Thou relationship issues have been swept aside to contribute to this difficulty by saying,

[To the group] For the last several minutes, we have been discussing
"safe" issues, but I sense that some of you have feelings about one
another in the group that you are not openly discussing. I know it's not
easy, but let's try to take some time to talk about these feelings about
one another that are difficult to share.

If a member is cut off while sharing her reactions, the leader may intervene by saying,

Barbara, you said that you feel strongly sometimes when people cut you
off. Do you feel this way right now?

[To the group] I wonder, if you were Barbara, what would it feel like to
be cut off while sharing your feelings?

ADVANCED EMPATHY

A powerful effect occurs in groups when members feel truly seen by other human beings. When their difficult-to-understand experiences are recognized and their hidden struggles are acknowledged, members' self-awareness is expanded, leading them to a deeper contact with their own psychological selves. People experience optimal self-awareness and psychological visibility through the experience of advanced empathy. This is the third area in which the leader, in order to promote more effective communication, should encourage members to take more risks.

Empathy on a Deeper Level

Advanced empathy is a deeper level of empathy in which the group communicates the meanings and feelings of which a speaking member is *not yet* aware. This kind of empathy is advanced because the group has to delve deeper into specific members' underlying struggles. The group crawls even deeper under the skin of the working member and senses what he is not fully aware of or is only half saying (Chen & Giblin, 2002). The group is one step ahead of the member regarding awareness of his underlying struggles. If the group can tune in at this level of subtlety to identify unspoken materials and reflect them back to the working member, the receiver will be surprised by how much he feels heard, validated, and seen at such a deep level.

Receiving such advanced empathy can be a truly liberating experience. Feelings that were originally blocked are now named. Once the underlying feelings have been named, they become possible to deal with. Deep listening is required on the part of the group if members are to be able to give advanced empathy.

Giving Advanced Empathy

To give advanced empathy is to take a great amount of risk. One risks making mistakes in guessing what the other person's hidden feelings might be. Fortunately, cues help us understand other people's underlying emotional struggles. These cues include tone of voice, facial expression, nonverbal cues, and hidden messages. The leader can encourage the group to take the risk of empathizing with a person in her struggles by saying,

> [To the group] Okay, we just listened to Julie's story. Let's pause for a moment and let our reflections sink in. [pause] Now, I would like the rest of the group to imagine that you were Julie in that situation. I would like you to guess what Julie might be feeling but has not yet been able to articulate. [advanced empathy] When you are ready, please speak directly to Julie.

> Can any of you help Mary identify what underlying feelings or struggles she is really battling with?

> Beyond the sense of loss and abandonment that Bruce has shared, do any of you sense any other emotions that he may be struggling with but is not aware of at this time?

> I would like everyone to try to guess what Linda is struggling with that she has only half communicated to the group.

GREATER RISK-TAKING IN FEEDBACK-GIVING

Of all the group interventions, feedback in particular serves to help people see their own role in their problems. Feedback helps people see how their behaviors are viewed by others, how their behaviors make others feel, and how their behaviors influence others' interactions with them—as well as how their own self-esteem is, in turn, influenced by the way others interact with them (Yalom, 2002). It helps people understand how and why their emotional experiences are being created in their lives. This is the force that will bring about client change and growth.

Giving feedback, however, is a complex art. Feedback is most useful when it brings to the surface a person's outdated coping or defense patterns.

It takes courage to give others feedback that touches on this level of self-awareness. In the norming stage of group development, this is the fourth area in which the leader should encourage members to take more risks.

Changing Interpersonal Patterns, Not Symptoms

Most people come to group counseling and therapy to cure whatever symptoms concern them—stress, anxiety, depression, sleep disturbance, relationship problems, eating disturbance, health issues, career dissatisfaction, and so on. But the truth is: Therapists cannot cure clients' symptoms, and neither can groups. Symptoms are just on the surface; they are the products of an underlying problem. Scratch the surface, and you will find maladaptive interpersonal patterns that sustain or perpetuate the symptoms.

Therefore, groups cannot treat symptoms, but they can translate members' symptoms into ineffective interpersonal behavior patterns and coping mechanisms that can be changed (Yalom, 1995). Once this life-support system of the symptoms—that is, the maladaptive interpersonal coping patterns—changes, the symptoms naturally subside. For example, a member's symptom of depression may be perpetuated by his coping pattern of discounting his true feelings, trying overly hard to please others, and not honoring his own needs. Only when he starts to change these ways of coping can his depression be lifted. In another instance, a member's stress may be perpetuated by her avoidance of emotional intimacy through overinvolvement in an excessive number of activities. When she changes her way of handling intimacy, most likely her stress will be reduced.

All You Have to Know Is within the Group

How does a group recognize a particular member's underlying interpersonal patterns? This is nothing to be worried about. Sooner or later, members' interpersonal patterns show up within the group for everybody to see. Yalom (1995) pointed out that the group is not an artificial organism, but a social microcosm. Masks of social politeness and sweetness drop as a group moves along, and the interpersonal patterns used outside the group are used within the group as well. This feature makes the group an excellent setting for adjusting oneself interpersonally.

Feedback as a Corrective Force

As long as clients continue to believe that their problems are caused or perpetuated by the actions of other people or external factors, they will not change. Unless clients are helped to see how they themselves contribute partially to their distress or coconstruct their own reality, no significant change will occur for a long while. It is only when clients see how their own role, however limited, plays a part in the sequence of events that they will start to take responsibility for changing that which is within their power to change.

Feedback, in its true sense, serves as a challenge to open members' eyes to the roles they play in their life events—to help them see those roles as clearly as others see them. The insight derived from feedback is the driving force that helps members to drop their blinders and finally see the impact of their own behaviors. They start to see themselves as co-creators of their own reality.

A word of caution: Some groups get too excited about the power of feedback and jump the gun by skipping the empathy step and moving directly to corrective work. These groups nail down each member's self-defeating behavior patterns with zeal in an effort to help members see their own demons, only to receive defensive responses from the recipients of the feedback. Presenting challenges through feedback without the balance of empathic support only creates hostility and defensiveness.

Greater Risk-Taking in Giving Feedback

Feedback can be a catalyst for change only when the group knows how to give useful feedback. The truth is, without guidance, most people do not know how to give feedback. They end up giving advice or information, or taking over the floor by telling their own stories. Although everyone's feedback is appreciated (Leszcz, 1992), not all feedback leads in a productive direction. The leader must help the group members offer productive feedback to one another.

There are two levels of feedback aimed at increasing awareness in group members. The first level is less intense than the second. The first level of feedback helps members become aware of the interpersonal patterns/themes *in the members' lives outside the group.* Pattern-focused feedback is an example of this type. The leadership skills needed to facilitate this kind of feedback were covered in Chapter 6.

The second level of feedback is higher than the first in both intensity and risk. This type of feedback is aimed at helping members become aware of the interpersonal patterns they display *in the here-and-now within the group.* Giving this kind of feedback involves a substantial amount of risk, as the giver of the feedback may expose himself in giving it. Once a group has progressed to the norming stage of development, it is ready for this type of feedback. To move the members toward a greater level of communication, the leader can direct their comments toward two types of high-risk feedback: (1) here-and-now focused feedback, and (2) feeling-focused feedback. These types of feedback are explained in the following text.

Giving Here-and-Now Focused Feedback

Here-and-now focused feedback, a higher-intensity type of feedback, is valuable for reality-checking. In here-and-now feedback, *members tell the receiver how his interpersonal pattern affects them personally, right here and right now in this group.* This kind of feedback is quite intense because it touches on the immediacy issues in the group, but the reward is that it helps the receiver see, maybe for the first time, how he has created a reality of his own. Giving here-and-now feedback, however, involves a risk— the giver must expose her own personal perceptions, impressions, and reactions in the context of the group. It takes courage to share here-and-now feedback.

To facilitate here-and-now feedback, the leader simply asks the group members how they experience the recipient firsthand in the group. For example, if a member, say Julie, tells the group that she has had a problem of low-grade depression, the leader may guide the group to risk revealing how Julie's behavior patterns that they have experienced or seen within the group might have perpetuated her low self-esteem. The leader might say one of the following:

> [To the group] From Julie's story, it is obvious that she often discounts her true feelings in her interactions with people in her life. [summing up the point] I wonder if any of you ever found Julie doing that with you? [here-and-now focused feedback] If you have, please share your experience with Julie.

> [To the group] It seems apparent that Julie takes on the responsibility for everything that goes wrong in her relationships. Have any of you seen this behavior pattern manifested in the group? If so, what impact does it have on your relationship with her?

Other examples:

> Debbie is obviously concerned with her almost fanatical need to stay in tight control in her relationships. Have any of you seen this pattern in her as she has interacted in the group?

> As you listen to Bill, do any of you see any parallels between how he acts in the group and how, as he told us, he runs into problems in his relationship?

Feeling-Focused Feedback

Another powerful way of giving feedback is for the group members to talk about how they feel. The members can reveal how they feel about a given member's repetitive behavior, for example, whether they feel shut out and disconnected from the member or closer to him because of it. When the feedback is packaged in a way that involves self-disclosure on the part of the giver, it will feel more caring and acceptable to the receiver. This will enhance the chance of it being heard. An example of feeling-focused feedback is:

> I feel disconnected to you when you go on and on about how your colleagues accused you for nothing. I cannot get a sense of your inner experiences in the situation. I don't feel you with me!

Sometimes members downplay the intensity of their feedback by asking questions or making intellectual comments. Lacking the emotional component on the part of the giver, this kind of feedback loses its reality-testing power (Leszcz, 1992). Without the honest engagement of the giver's self in the interaction—that is, without the authenticity—the interaction resembles dysfunctional communication. When this happens, the leader can gently redirect the giver of the feedback to take greater risks by giving feeling-focused feedback. The leader may say,

> Nina, please share how you see Julie's personal style and how you feel toward her, not how you think.

> Marcy, I noticed that you have asked two questions of Julie. I sense that under each question there is something you wanted to say. Would you share any reactions you were having as they are, rather than as a series of questions?

Here is a reflection from Matt after the members of his group took risks to give him honest feedback:

> It was something I had been wondering about for a long time, so tonight I decided to ask the group how I came across to them. I was left feeling overwhelmed with the inputs I received from the group. Virtually everything they shared had at least some truth about me in it, but I also imagined some members' own issues coming into play. Perhaps the most important feedback for me to hear was not what others have found difficult about me, but that they still like me with all those parts of my personality and behaviors. When people began to focus on showing me this unconditional acceptance, I felt that it was the most important part of the session for me. The unfortunate thing was that the session was running out of time and I left feeling hungry for more.

LEADER'S SELF-INVOLVING DISCLOSURE

A special type of feedback that has the potential to increase members' self-awareness has to do with the group leader. It is not therapeutic for the group if the leader remains opaque and concealed behind a professional mask. When the group leader discloses something personal and meaningful, especially something that involves how members' behaviors have affected him, he immediately gets the group's attentiveness. This kind of self-disclosure dramatically draws members' attention to their own interpersonal patterns. The leader's disclosure becomes one type of powerful feedback. The focus of this section is on how leaders can use self-disclosure to help clients gain insights about themselves.

Timing and Content

When it comes to therapist self-disclosure, many new leaders become vigilant, as they have learned to refrain from making inappropriate self-disclosures to clients. Yet, research shows that therapist self-disclosure with the right timing may alleviate feelings of isolation and despair in clients. Therapist self-disclosure can provide a sense of the universality of shared experiences, normalization of members' feelings, and reassurance that they are not alone, all of which make the clients feel less helpless (Chelune, 1979). The key is in the timing and in what is being disclosed.

To be appropriate, the leader's self-disclosure must not take the focus away from a group member. Not all the floating feelings of the leader should be disclosed. Before the leader makes any disclosure about her inner reactions, she should ask: Will this disclosure serve the clients' best interests? Leaders should self-disclose only to provide feedback to clients. When done appropriately, the action provides an excellent modeling of transparency for the rest of the group. Therapist/leader self-disclosure is especially valuable in an interpersonal process group for helping members become aware of their interpersonal styles. Many leaders fear they might disclose too much, but in fact, most new leaders disclose too little. A principle to keep in mind is that the leader can disclose as much information as is needed to help the clients.

What kinds of information are appropriate for leaders to disclose? In general, any persistent feelings that members evoke in the leader are appropriate for disclosure. This kind of disclosure is called self-involving disclosure.

Making Self-Involving Disclosure

Part of the success of the communication within a group depends on the degree to which the group leaders are committed to communicating to the members openly, directly, and unambiguously about how the leaders are affected by members' behaviors. As mentioned, the leader's self-disclosure should not take the focus away from group members. The most productive leader self-disclosure, therefore, occurs when *the leader reveals how members' behavior patterns have evoked certain persistent feelings in the leader.* Any incessant feelings that the leader has about a member or about what is happening or not happening within the group are generally best revealed. Since this kind of disclosure has to do with the leader's feelings and how the leader has been affected, it is called *self-involving disclosure* or *impact disclosure* (Kiesler, 1982b; McCarthy & Betz, 1978). This kind of communication is confrontive in nature because the leader needs to tell the truth as it is, yet it is also supportive and protective of members' self-esteem when the leader uses sensitive language to increase the recipients' receptivity (Kiesler, 1982b).

To make this kind of self-disclosure, leaders must have in-depth self-awareness and must be willing to take risks. The rewards of self-involving disclosure, however, are worth the effort, since McCarthy and Betz's (1978) study showed that therapists who used self-involving disclosure were rated as significantly more expert and significantly more trustworthy.

Following are examples of leaders' self-involving disclosures. In the first example, a member was crying, but her emotions did not match her stories. The feelings seemed to be "produced" because they lacked authenticity and did not seem natural. The feelings were actually being produced in the service of something else, namely, the need to dramatize. As a result, the other group members felt frustrated. Until the leader addressed the real issue, the process was going nowhere. In this case, the leader gently addressed the issue by using self-involving disclosure:

> Ellen, I am feeling lost here. I want to understand what's bothering you, but for some reason, I don't feel the emotions behind the tears. [turning to the group] I wonder, does anyone else in the group feel the same way?

Such disclosure from the leader is likely to give other members permission to comment on the truth of how they experience the working member without fear of being considered callous.

Another example involved a situation wherein a member told a painful story with a smile on her face, which really had the group baffled. The leader self-disclosed how this incongruence affected him:

> Maria, I am hearing you share some very painful experiences, yet I am seeing a constant smile on your face while you are talking. It makes me feel out of touch with your pain. [turning to the group] I wonder whether other members feel the same way.

Although leader self-disclosure is important, the leader should not feel compelled to be transparent about every reaction. He does not want to overwhelm the group prematurely (Leszcz, 1992). This is especially true in the early stages of group development when the group needs the leader to provide structure and to set appropriate norms for the group. As the group becomes mature, it will become ready for the leader's self-disclosure.

But even at the later stages, leader self-disclosure should seldom be an end in itself but, rather, should be a means to serve the members (Block & Crouch, 1985).

Radiating Support and Concern

Leader self-involving disclosure should be purposeful, caring, and responsible. The sharing of unprocessed emotional reactions on the leader's part are not likely to be helpful to the group. For example, anger/dislike toward a member, or boredom/frustration with the group, is probably not going to be helpful if the leader does not know where they come from. Therefore, the leader needs to process her own feelings first, before she reveals them to the group. That is, she needs to first "get unhooked," and then she can move on to "analyzing his or her emerging emotional reactions, processing them, and putting forward feedback in a fashion that is workable for the member" (Leszcz, 1992, p. 55). This is the responsible way to use leader self-disclosure.

After the leader has fully analyzed her own reactions, then she can put these emotional reactions into words that demonstrate her concern and support for the members. Following are some examples of a leader's self-involving disclosures that show care and concern:

> Jamie, I felt closer to you when you revealed this very vulnerable and open part of you to the group. I feel I have come to know you on a much more intimate level. And I believe that when you feel safe enough to show this part of you to people outside the group, they may feel drawn to you as does the group today.

> Helen, I appreciate your faithfully coming to group every week. However, I am a bit worried that you are silent during most of the meetings. As much as I want to help you and have tried to bring you into the group and help you talk, today I decided to resist bringing you in. I know that by continually bringing you into the group, I am doing something that you can do for yourself. It will be much better if you can initiate participation by yourself. [The leader revealed her inner struggle between wanting to draw out the member and desiring to give the member a sense of autonomy. This disclosure also served as feedback about the client's style within the group.]

The following is an example of a leader's self-involving disclosure that encouraged other members to also reveal their honest reactions:

> Julie, I find that you are always ready with a response to help with the issue or problem at hand. Yet, I find myself puzzled by the uneasiness I feel when I talk with you. I find it difficult to be as humorous with you as I am able to be with other members. I feel as though you are trying

> so hard to be on target, to be correct, to be perfect all the time in your actions within the group. Might this perfect role be how you see the way you ought to be, that is, the perfect friend to the troubled couple with whom you are entangled? Might this need to be perfect also connect to the performance anxiety you presented originally as your long-term issue?

With this, members were stimulated to offer their own self-involving disclosures. Kelly said:

> Julie, I often feel protective of you because your mannerisms and the way you go about doing things remind me of my grandmother. I was taught to be frightened of her and to be on my best behavior with her. She was a woman who was respected and feared. I was always taught to wear my best clothes around her and to stay at a safe distance. As a consequence, I never really got to know her. In the same way, I feel like I never get to know you, as if there is a veil of something covering the person you really are.

And Sara offered:

> Julie, I find you to be able to speak from your heart and choose words very effectively. Yet, as I listened, I saw your body tighten up as you sat on the edge of the chair, and your eyes fell upon your hands holding your glasses. This makes me feel protective of you. I have tried previously to give you some feedback, but I didn't feel heard. You have a way of deflecting what I try to say. I am struggling as I tell you this because I don't know whether this will cause conflict between the two of us.

CONSTRUCTIVE CONFRONTATION

The word *confrontation* stirs within most people a sense of anxiety because most people's experiences with confrontation have been associated with tension, conflict, or withdrawal. In the group setting, confrontation, when done in a sensitive and constructive manner, does not lead to conflict or withdrawal. The idea behind confrontation is for members to challenge one another and examine the discrepancies between members' words and actions—that is, to challenge members' maladaptive interaction styles. Confrontation provides constructive information that serves as a catalyst for changing unproductive client behavior. This kind of constructive confrontation becomes one of the most powerful types of feedback that members can receive. As a result, members become more aware of and thoughtful about the way they interact with others, which ultimately increases their interpersonal effectiveness. In this situation, confrontation is just another type of feedback, but one that requires a great deal of risk on the part of the person who is confronting another.

Fear of Confrontation

When someone displays unproductive behaviors—for example, dominating the group, telling others what they should or should not do, or attacking others—the group may feel irritated but may not feel comfortable enough to confront this particular member. Most members are afraid of confronting others for the following reasons: (1) Confrontation is a high-level interpersonal skill that most people have not learned in their lives; (2) members' past experiences with confrontation, due to lack of skills, have tended to be damaging to relationships or hurt others' feelings; and (3) people are afraid of retaliation. These are exactly the reasons that make members shy away from confrontation, making them choose an indirect way to get their messages across. The consequences of this avoidance strategy are: (1) The same problem remains; (2) members feel frustrated and powerless; and (3) resentment builds.

Given this fear, it is the leader's responsibility to model effective confrontation. Once the group members have learned it, they will have a powerful way to solve problems and will be able to speak up for their own truth.

Confrontation as Corrective Feedback

Confrontation is nothing mysterious. As stated earlier, it is but one form of feedback: a corrective feedback, or a so-called negative feedback. Without question, most members have no difficulty in giving and receiving positive feedback. It is corrective feedback that is a challenge. Generally speaking, people in our society are uncomfortable with expressing negative reactions. Added to this discomfort is the fear of being wrong.

However uncomfortable, corrective feedback is imperative for interpersonal learning. Feedback that focuses solely on positive aspects is limiting and unreal. It does not open space for self-examination that is essential for interpersonal learning. Corrective feedback, on the other hand, illuminates the unproductive behavior and helps the member become aware of it. As Toth and Erwin (1998) state, corrective feedback "provides information about a group member's behaviors that interfere with his or her interpersonal relations or that have other negative consequences" (p. 295). Therefore, the leader must model giving corrective feedback in an effective way. This is most appropriately done when the group progresses into the norming stage.

Seven Principles of Constructive Confrontation

Constructive confrontation is the highest form of effective communication. A person takes a great degree of risk in confronting another. To perform it well, the person making the confrontation has to follow the laws of effective communication. These laws are similar to the principles of corrective feedback. An important thing to remember is that good timing is everything. Confrontation can be more readily accepted when the timing is right. The only proper time to deliver or encourage confrontation in the group is during the middle and later stages of the group (Toth & Erwin, 1998). Leaders should restrain the group from getting into heavy-duty confrontation when the group is still tender in its skin.

Our observations constantly confirm that people receive confrontation as constructive, instead of destructive, when certain principles are not violated. The seven principles of effective confrontation are:

1. Own up to one's own part in the dynamics of the relationship.
2. Give a positive comment prior to making a negative comment— "First a stroke, then a kick."
3. Avoid "you" statements.
4. Describe specific behaviors. Do not make personality judgments.
5. Tell the receiver how you feel rather than what you think.
6. Avoid asking questions.
7. Avoid sarcasm.

In the following text, we explain and provide examples for each specific principle.

Principle 1: Owning Up to One's Own Part in the Dynamics of the Relationship   What happens frequently in failed confrontation is that we see only how the other person is making us feel, and not how we ourselves play a part in the dynamics. When our focus is exclusively on the other's deeds and we do not reveal where our own feelings are coming from, our feedback will sound like we are blaming the person, no matter how tactfully we phrase it. To avoid this, the first rule of thumb in confrontation is to reveal how we also have contributed to the situation that has aroused undesirable feelings in us. For example, a member named Jen who had been intimidated by a monopolizing member named Michael confronted him finally after she had felt frustrated with him for several months. She prepared well for the confrontation and carefully followed the first law:

> Michael, this is very difficult for me to say, but I am going to try it. I have been wanting to say this but didn't quite have the courage to say it. But I feel dominated in the group by you because you frequently take charge of the group and chime in quickly to respond to whatever is going on in the group without giving the quieter members a chance. So often I wish that you would notice other members' need to also share. [describing specific behaviors] I guess I myself also play a part in this feeling of being dominated. I have been struggling with a sense of feeling unworthy since I was very little. Speaking up has always been difficult for me. So here in the group, I also feel as if my opinions and

inputs do not matter. And when you monopolize the group, leaving no chance for others, my difficulty with speaking up just gets worse. [owning up to the part one plays in the dance]

Michael was dumbstruck by this confrontation. Until then, he did not know that he was monopolizing the group and taking away others' chances for sharing. But Jen's confrontation was well received by Michael because she owned up to her own part in the situation. Afterward, Michael started to change; he became more considerate of others' needs. The successful confrontation of Michael also boosted Jen's self-esteem. She started to come out of her shell more frequently, with measured risk-taking, both in the group and in her life.

Principle 2: "First a Stroke, then a Kick"   Confrontation is effective only when the recipient is receptive to the input. So the second rule of thumb in confrontation is to avoid making the recipient defensive. In confrontation, it is not just honesty that counts, but honesty expressed in a way that the receiver can tolerate. To be better received, each confrontation must include two components: "first a stroke, then a kick" (metaphorically speaking). This principle originated with Salvador Minuchin, a structural family therapist, who used it as leverage in challenging and confronting his clients about their dysfunctional interaction patterns (Nichols & Schwartz, 1998). The principle can certainly be applied in the group setting. In the group, this principle is applied in the rule that each confrontation must include an acknowledgment of a positive aspect of the receiver's behavior, and then an honest expression of how the same behavior might have a negative impact on others. In this way, the confrontation is offered in context and does not sound like an accusation. Following are examples of this principle in action:

> Claire, I appreciate your willingness to participate and talk about yourself. [stroke] However, I am concerned because I have heard very little from several others in the group, and I want to hear from them, too. [kick]

> Mark, I know that you are eager to figure out why you relate to people in general differently from how you relate to most women. You are very articulate about what model of communication is most effective in interpersonal relating. [stroke] Yet, I am afraid that the very way you theorize yourself without revealing your inner feelings may make it hard for others to feel close to you. [kick]

Principle 3: Avoiding "You" Statements   Here is an example of a "you" statement: "Kelly, *you make me* feel agitated." When we say, "You make me feel . . . ," we are putting blame on others for our feelings without owning up to our own responsibility. Indeed, other people cannot make us feel a certain way unless we allow them to. In order to make confrontation constructive, we need to change the "you" statement into an "I" statement. For example:

> Kelly, I *feel* quite on edge *when you* keep talking during the session *because* it keeps me from hearing from other members. ["I" language, similar to self-involving disclosure]

Principle 4: Describing Specific Behaviors and Avoiding Personality Judgments

An example of making a personality judgment is: "Why do you have to be *so domineering?*" Another example is: "Peter, you are *so self-centered!* You get what you want here and leave nothing for others." Here again is the "you" blaming language, and the "why" language in the first example surely invites the receiver to argue back. Added here are judgments and the criticisms about the receiver's personality. A confrontation like this will certainly invite defensiveness or hurt feelings. To be constructive, the confrontation should be changed to *a description of the behaviors* that the speaker wants the other person to change. For example:

> Peter, I appreciate your contribution to the group; you are very verbal and very assertive. [positive feedback] However, at almost every group interaction, you begin with your agenda. [describing specific behavior] The group always waits for you to start. I certainly feel relieved when someone is willing to start, yet I also feel frustrated that other members are not given the opportunity to take initiative. [describing the impact:; self-involving disclosure]

Another example of describing behaviors is:

> Jim, I appreciate what you have to offer in the group. But there have been many times when I have felt frustrated because the group was experiencing a deep emotional connection and you said something totally irrelevant to break that connection [describing the behavior] I don't know whether you have noticed it or not, but this really took away the feelings that I was experiencing at those moments. [describing the impact]

Principles 5 and 6: Describing Your Feelings, Rather than Your Thinking, and Avoiding Questions

Here are two examples of the kinds of questions people use to disguise confrontation: "Sue, how many times have you caused people to shy away from you by giving too much too soon?" and "Brenda, is it safe for you to reveal so much about yourself so quickly? Do you think that it might scare some people off?" The use of questions, as an indirect way of performing a confrontation, is often met by the receiver with a need to rationalize her behavior. The questions only turn the interaction into more intellectualization and defensiveness. Instead of asking questions, in effective confrontations, we should *make a statement of our feelings, not our thoughts*. When we state our thoughts, receivers are inclined to want to explain and reason about their behaviors. But by telling our feelings, we can make the statement much more personal. For example:

> Brenda, you have revealed yourself more openly than anyone else in the group. [stroke] And now, in this our third session, you have begun to explore your sexuality. [behavior description] Frankly, I feel concerned when someone moves that fast. Also I am worried that other group members may feel pressured to match your level of disclosure. [describing feelings, not thoughts]

Principle 7: Avoiding Sarcasm and Cynicism   Sarcasm is often used as a way to confront. For example: "Boy, Dale! You really know how to be honest!" Such sarcasm and cynicism often stir defensiveness in the receiver without the benefit of leading to change. A better way to confront someone is to describe the behaviors without slipping into cynicism. For example:

> Dale, there is something significant going on here between you and Jean. I see tears in Jean's eyes. She seems to be feeling very hurt. I respect your honesty when you told her that her choice of relationships is dumb and self-destructive, yet you told her this with little emotion. [describing observation] I find myself feeling humiliated for Jean. [describing feelings]

Redirecting Unhelpful Confrontation

Obviously, most people are not well versed in the art of confrontation. Often they finally decide to take a risk and become more honest with someone, only to have what they say hurt others. Confrontation without tact will happen in groups sooner or later. When it happens, the group may be daunted and not know how to ease the resulting tension. It will be the leader's responsibility to repair the damage, and the leader needs to do two things at this juncture: (1) acknowledge the receiver's feelings, and (2) direct the contributor to restate the message.

Acknowledging the Receiver's Feelings   The person who is on the receiving end of an untactful confrontation may feel any of the following reactions: hurt, offended, annoyed, shut down, humiliated, or ashamed. These feelings need to be acknowledged so that the person can feel supported and validated. The leader may say something like:

> Jean, you look upset by what Tom just said.

Directing the Contributor to Restate the Message   After acknowledging the feelings of the affronted, the leader needs to coach the offender to restate the message in the correct way. Usually the confrontation is delivered out of good, rather than malicious, intention, and the contributor cares enough to want to help the recipient change. Lack of tact, however, gets in the way. The leader may seize the opportunity to coach the contributor by asking him to restate the message in a way that will be easier for the recipient to hear. The leader, for example, may say one of the following:

> Tom, it sounds like you feel strongly that Jean is not making the best choices in her life. Yet, it seems that what you said was difficult for Jean to hear. Would you try to state your comment in a different way, starting with an "I" statement instead of a "you" statement, so that your message can be heard more receptively? Would you like to try it?

> Tom, it sounds like you care very much about Jean and want her to make the best choices in her life. Yet, the way you said it was difficult for Jean to hear. Would you please try to make your point again, but this time speak from your own personal experience? Would you like to try it?

A Group Member's Reflection on Confrontation

To demonstrate the psychological inner work that a member goes through in learning to confront others constructively, we provide the following reflection from a group member named Lori, describing what she learned in the group and how her learning took place:

> My goal in the group was to be able to confront people, without fear or embarrassment, when their negative actions had an impact on me. My goal remained the same throughout our group life, but my motivation changed. Originally, my motivation was to tell the most difficult person in my life—my sister—how her unpleasant behavior affects others and me. But now, she is no longer my motivation. I am my motivation. I have discovered that I feel liberated when I speak what is in my heart and on my mind. It is, indeed, very therapeutic as long as it is done tactfully, the way I learned it in the group.
>
> Before this group, I had bad experiences with confronting or simply being honest with others. My comments were not readily accepted. Too many of these situations occurred to me, so I just closed down. I refrained from speaking any "evil" about others and focused on "pleasant" things. This is how I came into our group. I recall during many earlier sessions wanting to share some negative reactions about others but not doing it due to my fear of being attacked. I really was afraid.
>
> During one group session, the leader told me that I write excellent reflections, which are full of insights, but then I get into the group and disconnect from my feelings. She said I needed to allow my emotions to surface and speak to others as I did in my reflective journal. My first

response to her comment was resentment. I resented her because I felt she did not know me well enough to see things like that in me. I felt angry because her comments penetrated my soul. That was the turning point in the group for me. Later I knew why the leader's comments affected me so strongly. They were 100% true and I had never acknowledged them to myself. After that realization, a transformation took place in me. I felt determined and motivated to practice my skill. I was still afraid of being attacked, but I was more afraid of staying the same.

I took enormous steps in practicing the skill of confrontation in the eighth session. In leaps and bounds, my progress grew when I confronted Rose. I continued to make huge strides when Eve presented her issue. Since then, I have felt more empowered with each passing session. Currently, I feel very confident about myself. I don't worry or become anxious when I am experiencing a negative feeling about someone. I now know that it is not what you say to others, but it is how you say it. I have learned a plethora of tactful ways of speaking my mind. I know that, internally, I am equipped with a variety of means that will allow me to share my "true" self with others. This group experience demolished my old facade, which had become my coping mechanism. The group experience reconstructed my method of communication as well as interaction. It has helped me become a stronger and more truthful person. I have a newfound sense of gratitude toward other group members and the leader for "opening my eyes" and pushing me. I am very proud of all of us.

Teaching Members to Request Feedback

One sure way to raise a member's consciousness is to help him learn to request feedback when it is not forthcoming. This is a simple leadership intervention that will make a big difference in the group and in members' lives.

When members do not know how they come across to others or how their interpersonal styles influence others, the leader can invite members to request feedback, and then discriminate between that which is helpful and that which is not. Some examples follow:

Pat, you said you don't know why people tend to take you for granted. Maybe it will be helpful for you to ask members in this group how they see you. [Pat nods] Okay, go ahead and ask the group.

Kelly, there are many people who know you very well in this room. Why don't you ask each of them? Okay, go ahead and ask!

June, it is most helpful if you can ask the group for feedback about your interpersonal style. You can say to the group, "I would like to know what I do that puts people off."

ENHANCING MEMBER ABILITY TO RECEIVE FEEDBACK

Listening to feedback is an important part of effective communication and interpersonal learning. It enables one to become aware of where one needs to better manage one's impact on people and where the assumptions of others are erroneous and need to be addressed. Not all people have the same ability to hear feedback. The ability to hear feedback is related to one's self-esteem. People with a higher self-concept are usually more able to accept and integrate corrective feedback (Kivlighan, 1985), and vice versa. Teaching members how to hear feedback is essential work for the leader.

Enhancing Ability to Listen to Feedback

Many people hasten to reply or to explain whenever others give them feedback. This kind of reaction prevents them from hearing fully what others have to say. If a member is feeling compelled to reply immediately without being able to listen nondefensively, it is the leader's task to ask the receiver to just listen without reacting immediately. The leader may say,

> Julie, when people give you feedback, I would like you to listen reflectively without rehearsing how you are going to reply next. After we finish the feedback, the group would love to hear your reactions to the feedback.

> Tom, the feedback given to you by many members seems to be consistent. It would be helpful if you would take them seriously, consider the validity and the significance of the message, and then decide what you are going to do with this new self-knowledge.

Enhancing Ability to Evaluate Feedback

When feedback is finished, the leader can then ask the receiver to comment on the feedback. To help members differentiate unhelpful from helpful feedback, the leader may ask the receiver to tell the group what feedback (including members' and leaders') was most helpful for them and what feedback caught them by surprise. The leader may say one of the following:

> Julie, a lot of members, including me, have given you some strong reactions. What is your reaction to our comments?

> Julie, now that you've gained insight into how others in the group feel and react toward you, can you share with the group how this influences your opinions about yourself?

Other examples:

> Peter, which of the comments made here struck you the most?
>
> Helen, I can see that you have been wanting to talk about that issue for a long time, and until today you have not been able to. Somehow Nelson helped you to open up. What did he do?
>
> Jane, this week I have seen you listening to the group with less arguing. You have even said "thank you" twice. I wonder whose comments have been particularly helpful in silencing the voice of anger so that you could hear those comments for which you are grateful?
>
> Jake, you've received some fairly direct feedback from the group. How are you putting all these remarks together for yourself?

CASES IN POINT

Case One: Kelly

Kelly's original presenting problem was her tendency to act as if everything is okay when in truth it is not. Her goal, thus, was to be able to be herself as she desired to be. In the fifth session of her group, Kelly presented an agenda. Interestingly, the agenda was presented as a career decision-making struggle. Kelly explained to the group how she was torn between completing her graduate program and pursuing a long-standing dream of stand-up comedy. As she talked about the stand-up comedy, her face became illuminated, even glowing. Excitement and enthusiasm were present in her voice. The bottom line of her struggle in this decision-making process was the lack of support from her family, who seemed to have made this clear: Pursue your dream, and all financial and emotional support will be cut off; follow the expectations of the family, and you will be accepted and supported. Kelly described feeling tremendous pressure to live up to her family's unreachable expectations. In Kelly's words, "I made another screw-up." In fact, she used this expression several times.

As Kelly spoke, any pain she might have been experiencing was hidden behind a smile. Her speech was rapid and upbeat. Several times, she used the word *closet* to explain the place to which she retreated to lick her wounds. The leader noticed Kelly's use of the word *closet* and asked the group to take a risk and give *here-and-now focused feedback* by linking their personal experience of Kelly at the present moment to their perceptions about Kelly's life struggle. The leader said,

> [To the group] While I was listening to Kelly's stories, I noticed that she used the word *closet* several times to describe her struggle, and she also smiled and laughed a lot throughout. I wonder, how does the group

experience Kelly at this moment in this room? And how might your experience of her run parallel to the way she copes with the outside world? When you are ready, please talk directly to Kelly.

In responding to this prompt, a member named Lori commented that she experienced Kelly as a person who hides herself behind the closet of smiling and laughing while telling a story that is painful in nature. Peter told Kelly that her main emotional energy seemed to be a rush of excitement, but said he wondered what was beneath it. He also told her that he liked her way of communicating, but he guessed there were more levels beyond the smiling, joking, and fast talking that she showed to the group. In Peter's own words, "By keeping the band of emotions so narrow, it was limiting to *me;* it was as though you were controlling, not your emotions, but *me.*" Rose said that she experienced Kelly as a clown who is laughing on the outside, yet crying on the inside. This seemed to tie in to the stand-up comedy, where she could continue to laugh and not show the side of herself that is hurting.

At this point, the floodgates opened; Kelly's smile gave way to tears on the words "my family." She then revealed her sexual orientation as a lesbian and her pain over the lack of acceptance by her family, and society in general, on this front. She described feeling shame when walking with her female companion on the streets of the city. As she exposed this part of herself, Kelly's overly enthusiastic persona was scaled off, and she became more calm and vulnerable. The group was enlightened to see this inner side of her, which they liked much better than her facade. They felt closer to her, and they told her so.

After the session, Kelly wrote in her reflective journal:

> This was an extremely helpful session for me. I learned a lot about how I don't present my true self to people but just show enthusiasm and a smiling face. I was aware that I do that sometimes but was not aware of the extent of it, and certainly not aware that people could tell and were thus limited in their experiences around me. It was a bit uncomfortable for me to be given all this feedback all at once. But it was such powerful feedback. Because of this I would like to try in the group a different way of being around people, not to be afraid of showing my authentic self. I have a different sexual orientation from everyone in the room and have a radically different home life than people in the group. Growing up I learned to pretend that everything was okay and wonderful because that was how I could get people to accept me. I think that is why I started crying in the session. I will say that I have experienced a lot of abuse, and I really feel as if I am a person who doesn't have the freedom and privilege to be herself. At the same time, I feel that my background has made me a very strong and aware person. To be honest, I often look at people and think that I have a lot more experiences in living because I have been through a lot. Some people will take who I am and see it as

someone who must be crazy. For example, my family thinks I am crazy. I therefore am very scared about the notion of really showing myself to people. However, now I feel I want to start being myself and learn to differentiate with whom I should shield myself and with whom I can let my guard down.

Peter reflected in his journal:

I felt very connected to Kelly, and I told her so. I felt that I really shared myself with Kelly. I empathized with her, and I challenged her in ways that weren't always easy for me. I felt that Kelly saw herself in our session today. But it was after the group that I fully realized the connection between Kelly's need to joke and laugh for her parents, and her need to be an entertainer.

Eve reflected in her journal:

I'm not sure what it was about this session, but I had great difficulty transitioning out my feelings of overwhelming sadness. I cried all the way to the parking lot. Although I have tried to figure out what happened and why the session affected me that way, I haven't reached any conclusion. I felt that Peter was so insightful that he was able to make the most poignant statements to Kelly. I remember at one point Lori and I looked at each other and said, "Wow!"

Kelly's transformation has an interesting ending. One month later, right before the group ended, Kelly wrote in her journal:

When I presented my agenda, I was struggling with my career path. In that session, through fellow members' feedback, I learned that I am constantly hiding who I really am from others. I was hiding many things and trying to be someone that people wanted me to be. I was trying to hide the fact that I was a lesbian without really understanding what this was or what this meant. I was hiding the fact that different relatives had abused me because it was not okay for me to shame my family by telling the truth. I had hid behind a smiling face for a long time. I had forgotten that I was doing this. It had already served its purpose, but I continued to do it. In the group, I learned that I do this to people, and now I feel I can make a choice about whether to hide behind my smile or to be myself. As a consequence of learning this, my life path has evolved to a new height. I have been writing a great deal on stand-up comedy, and for the first time in my life I am not ashamed of my work. In addition, I have been able to really talk about myself and my life and am starting to find my voice as a comedian. I don't think three months ago I would have been able to talk about being a Latino, Jewish lesbian on stage. Now I can. In the group, I have been challenged to be myself and to stop hiding. I know that is what has been keeping people away from me. I have always had a hard time getting close to people beyond a superficial level. I never understood why. And now I know. My challenge to myself now is to let people in behind my stoic smile. I wish the group could run for another three months so that I could continue to work on this skill, but I hope to take what I have learned and really apply it to my everyday life.

Case Two: Amelia

Amelia's original presenting problem had to do with a deteriorating relationship with her husband. Her goal was to improve her ways of handling the problems with him. In the sixth session, Amelia presented an agenda on a recent event where she and her brother got extremely upset. She described how her parents were supposed to go to Iowa to visit her brother and his family, but once again, her parents' drinking problems interfered with their obligation. They made up an excuse to stay home. Amelia stated, "What makes it difficult to distinguish the truth from lies is that what they say is often partially true, just not entirely true, and this is a repetition of a previous pattern." The group was supportive and considerate while listening to Amelia's story. After a while, the leader led the group to give Amelia a *here-and-now focused feedback.* The leader said,

> [To the group] It seems that Amelia felt supported by the group's understanding of what she has gone through. At this point, I would like the group to tell Amelia how you experience her firsthand in the group.

This brought the group discussion from an outside focus toward something more relevant, that is, the group members' subjective experience of Amelia. Later, the leader asked the group to give Amelia *connection-focused feedback:*

> [To the group] Okay, let's take this another step to see whether we can give Amelia some insight. My question is, what connection do you see between Amelia's experiences with her parents and her current difficulties with her husband?

The interventions prompted a discussion that turned out to be a very enlightening experience for Amelia, as shown in her reflective journal entry:

> When the leader talked about how each of them "experienced" me within the group setting, I was a bit apprehensive, but due to the bond I have built with them, I did not feel threatened. Jenny stated that she experiences me as defensive and that she sees me as a person who "takes on" everything. She associated that with my pattern of being a caregiver and feeling responsible for things or people whom I cannot control. I know that last week I was certainly defensive during my conflict with Anna. It's helpful that Jenny pointed this out to me. By giving me this feedback, Jenny provided me with the impetus to be aware of my own defensiveness in the future and possibly nip it in the bud. I appreciated her candor very much.

The rest of the feedback given by the group really warmed my heart and made me feel like the group members really understand the "real me." Keith commented that he feels I am a giver but that maybe I'm not as comfortable receiving care as I am giving it to others. That's pretty much in line with how I am. I often feel guilty when others do things for me and am constantly "keeping score"—something my husband always chides me for. Mary shared that she experiences me as caring and sensitive. Mia stated that I seem strong on the outside but inside there is a sensitive and vulnerable little girl. I felt this was right on. I feel this way a lot. I have always been an extremely sensitive person and feel myself "regressing" when I get very upset about something. Although living and working in New York served to help me develop a thicker skin, obviously there are still times that I feel like that oversensitive little girl again.

The most important part of the session for me was when the group was asked to identify the underlying connection between the ongoing issue with my parents and the difficulties in my marital relationship. A connection was proposed between the loss I experienced due to my parents' alcoholism and my fear of intimacy with my husband. This was a really enlightening thing for me to hear, as I have never had this association so clearly defined before. Not being able to count on my parents is a huge disappointment for me, and it hurts to know that I cannot really go to them for anything. My parents can't be there for me. Instead, my brothers and I have had our roles prematurely reversed, and *we* are the caregivers. My parents can hardly remember to ask what is going on in our lives, as they are so busy complaining about all their ailments, which then serve as their excuse to keep drinking. This relates to my fear of intimacy in general and to that I am currently experiencing in my relationship with my husband because *I am afraid of getting too close*. Subconsciously I reason that if I am too close to someone, then when that person "leaves" me, I will get hurt as I have been hurt by my parents. The *abandonment* I would experience could be in either an emotional or a physical sense, or both, which is beyond what I can handle, and I would fall apart. *I feel like we entered a new territory when we connected my parents' alcoholism with my fear of intimacy. We really went to a deeper level than we had been before.* I appreciated everyone's honesty and directness. It was so helpful for me to hear these potential connections being stated out loud. Some of the insights were new; others were ones I had speculated on before but never had a "test" by which to validate them. This group session was that test for me.

Jenny reflected on the session in her journal as follows:

I empathized with Amelia. I too grew up in an alcoholic home and from that learned that my father was not one who could follow through with commitments. I learned at an early age not to trust men and that I could not depend on them. It is an issue that I continue to work on to this day.

Amelia touched on the fact that she did not like to feel vulnerable, and I too could relate to this. I keep myself at a distance when intimate with my husband. *I subconsciously think that if I don't give myself completely, I will not get emotionally hurt or rejected.* This, too, I continue to work on. I am making progress, and I shared this with Amelia during the group. After listening to Amelia, I realized how far I have come in my self-actualization. I am becoming healthier in my relationship with my husband. Keith stepped into the conversation and shared that he, too, came from an alcoholic home and that he goes to Al-anon. I was shocked by this comment. In past sessions, Keith painted a picture of having a perfect family. Thinking about Keith's behavior and the way he is living his life, I realize that this self-denial is common for an individual who grew up in an alcoholic home. I was glad that Keith opened up and shared this information with the group.

Keith's reflective journal entry read:

In this session I aimed at working on the skill of saying what was on my mind. I have a tendency not to say what I am really feeling or ask what I really want to know. Oftentimes I catch myself not being as forthright as I could be at the moment. By the end of the session, when we shared how we reacted to the session, I have to say, I was speechless and it was hard for me to describe. *At that moment, I realized that the reason I have a problem expressing how I feel is because I also grew up in an alcoholic family and have emotionally detached from my own true feelings surrounding the subject. So, when I was asked how I felt, my mind drew a blank and I conveyed this to the group.* I expressed to Amelia that I didn't detach from her; in fact, I was very much in tune to her message and her feelings regarding it. But *when it came to my own feelings, that was another story.* Amelia's life story certainly makes me think about my own root problems. I guess you never know what you are going to work on in a group. I came to the group tonight to work on a skill but ended up facing a discovery that will become my agenda for the next session.

The leader reflected:

As I took an opportunity to bring the group into the here-and-now focused feedback, I was anxious about how this would change the group's dynamics. I realize this was very risky, but I felt it was the right time to do so. During the group's session, we started to see how members changed their original stories as they presented their issues and opened up to the group. We saw a different side to Amelia's story about her relationship with her husband. We also saw a different side to Keith's family, which we were not aware of before. This is what makes the here-and-now feedback such a powerful experience.

Anna, who was seen as cold and aloof in the group, confessed the following in her journal:

When wrapping up the group, Mia said that she often wondered where I was during the session. I thought about this statement a lot and realized that I had not let people know my internal states. I was in extreme pain for the entire session. I had a severe illness as a child. Well, that illness is a chronic bowel disorder, and I will always have it. In February I had a surgery. Since then I have been ill off and on. When I was a teenager, I resolved not to complain to others about my chronic pain because I strongly felt that people backed away from me and perceived me differently when they knew about my health. However, now I realize that my way of dealing with pain may have become self-defeating. *When I am quiet, it comes across to others as being disengaged or cold.* I should perhaps rethink my nondisclosure strategy and perhaps take some risk to let people know what is going on with me.

SCENARIOS FOR YOUR PRACTICE

1. During a session of an interpersonal skills building group, Emily makes the following statement: "I really don't feel like saying much about myself." As the group leader, how might you handle this in a way that both encourages greater self-disclosure and shows respect for Emily's right to choose her own pace of disclosure?

2. During the seventh session of a group for interpersonal skills development, you realize that you're becoming a little frustrated with and feeling distanced from Jamie. Sometimes she does not respond to the issues you raise, but instead quickly changes the direction by asking another group member about some issue they raised in another session. How might you effectively disclose what you're experiencing?

3. Ricardo talks about how, in his relationships, he feels that people retreat from him, and how he then responds by chasing them more aggressively. He says he doesn't know how this cycle started or how to break free of it. He looks directly at you and asks, "You are the expert here. What should I do when people run away from me?" What might be a helpful response that you, as the group facilitator, could make?

4. As the group begins, William states, "I usually just prefer to be an observer in groups. I feel that I learn so much through watching the interactions of others." What are some key issues associated with this type of stance? What are your options as a group leader for handling this situation?

5. You become aware that Jim continues to question Phil about factors that entered into his decision to quit his job and how Phil's family has responded to that decision. Although you are aware that the

discussion may be of some benefit to Phil, you are also aware of your own feeling of discomfort with this exchange, especially with Jim asking several very pointed questions of Phil. What might you want to say to Jim or ask of him?

6. As Curtis opens a session with a long and detailed description of a disagreement he had with his mother over the weekend, you become aware that he is asking for validation from you and the group. You also are aware that there may be some parallels between what is happening in the group and what happens for Curtis with others outside the group. How would you choose to help Curtis become aware of this?

7. In a support group for caregivers, Josephine has been very attentive to other members and supportive of their issues in the group. Although Josephine has asked for nothing from the others in the group, you recall that she entered the group partly at her adult son's urging because she does not take any time for herself, and her son is concerned about this. How would you help Josephine see this possible connection?

SELF-REFLECTION

1. Think of your own level of awareness as represented by the Johari window. What relative sizes would you assign for each of the windows? Would they all be the same size, or would some be larger than others? If they would be of different sizes, which windows would be larger?

2. What methods do you tend to use in your life to increase the size of the Johari window area that is labeled "known to others, but not to self"?

3. Do you have any strategies or approaches in your life for decreasing the size of the area that is "unknown to self"?

4. How easy do you think it will be for you to use primarily *approach* and *contingent* comments in the groups that you lead? What level of awareness do you think you have with respect to your own use of *avoidant* statements?

5. What type of self-disclosure do you think is most appropriate for a group leader? To what extent might you expect group members to meet your level of risk-taking and self-disclosure?

THE HOT-SEAT METHOD

A Knee-Jerk Experience

As the group continues to work on the two fronts—that is, the task and the relationship—members' anxieties start to subside and a sense of trust begins to build. The group is now mature enough to tackle those crucial dynamics previously put aside. The crucial dynamics are the group dynamics happening within the here-and-now that lurk beneath the surface. They represent the real challenge that makes group work exciting and intriguing. It is easy for groups to spend most of their time reflecting on members' past experiences, and fail to draw parallels between what happens in members' lives and what happens in the present interaction of the group. In so doing, however, many subtle issues in the group get sidestepped. If the leader of such a group looks back carefully, she may find that many relationship dynamics between members have not been fully processed; that some perceptions and reactions to certain members have long been simmering; and that some difficult personalities or disquieting behaviors have not been openly addressed. Unexpected episodes that happen may prove to be especially difficult, but as long as the group addresses them in a timely fashion, they can become turning points for members' growth.

The challenge of working with here-and-now group dynamics will be the focus of the next step of group work. This chapter is designed to address that challenge. It covers:

- Unstructured sessions and the working stage
- Interpersonal enactment
- The hot-seat method
- Process illumination and change
- Process illumination techniques (I): Go where the reactivity is
- Process illumination techniques (II): Whatever is hidden is worth pursuing
- Process illumination techniques (III): Linking the inside to the outside

UNSTRUCTURED SESSIONS AND THE WORKING STAGE

Halfway through the life span of the group, members are likely to become more trusting, more cohesive, and more willing to take risks in their communication. It is at this juncture that the group enters a mature stage called the *production* (Lacoursiere, 1980), *performing* (Tuckman, 1965), or *working* stage (Corey & Corey, 2002). The working stage marks a major shift in group energy, leadership focus, and in member responsibility. Many wonders can be achieved this stage.

Characteristics of the Working Stage

The working stage runs parallel to the stage of adulthood in a human's life, featured by its highest level of productivity. At this stage, the group is mature enough to put forth the most intense form of interpersonal learning. Hill's (1965) description of member-to-member *speculative* and *confrontive* statements will be much more evident and applicable in the working stage than in norming stage. At this time, members become willing to speculate about one another's inner dynamics when a group member requests input. More impressively, members are now freer to challenge and to offer insightful feedback to one another without specific requests. The increased frequency of speculative and confrontive statements exemplifies that members have developed a strong trust in one another and are much more open to the unknown (McCarty, 1969). These strengths make the working stage the most invigorating and exciting stage of the group.

The excitement of the working stage lies in the fact that vital, yet charged, work that was previously put aside in favor of establishing group function and norms can now be rigorously pursued. The group can afford to bring up those unprocessed perceptions and relationship issues that have been a running undercurrent until now. With the new gained maturity, the group members can take even greater risks in openly addressing disquieting dynamics or behaviors that have been best-kept secrets. This is a workout that will be rewarding and inspiring for the group.

If this working stage proceeds successfully, the group will harvest greater levels of trust, intimacy, self-disclosure, feedback, confrontation, and, most importantly, humor. There will be an exciting yet relaxed atmosphere in the room when members are able to laugh at themselves or their situations in a nondefensive manner. Humor is certainly a barometer by which to tell when the group is well into its working stage. Hearty laughter replaces the nervous laughter of previous stages. If this stage does not proceed successfully, it is often because the group is stuck with unresolved issues carried over from previous stages.

When Less Is More

The working stage is a time when group members are finally capable of gaining a sense of autonomy. Having gone through the norming stage (Chapter 8), they grow more confident in initiating their own communication without relying on the leader's guidance. Indeed, members themselves might even start to assume some of the leadership responsibilities. The working stage is a time when less is more—that is, the less structured the group, the more powerful it becomes. As the members become more and more active, the leader becomes less and less active. By delegating initiatives to members, the leader has more energy to address those crucial issues that have been floating on the fringe.

Although group members become more active and assume more of the leadership responsibilities, there is one thing that members cannot do: They cannot bring the group to address the interpersonal process issues that happen within the group. Most members instinctively know they are not in the position to do that. Any member who tries to head the group toward addressing the immediacy issues will risk being perceived by other members as elevating himself to be superior to his peers, and he will become the target of resentment. Therefore, the responsibility of leading the group to address immediacy and interpersonal process issues falls solely on the shoulders of the group leader.

Going Totally Unstructured: Letting Ambiguity Breed Intensity

As members become more active and autonomous, and the leader is freed to focus on immediacy issues, a precious readiness is born in the group. No longer does the group need the agenda as a springboard for interaction. It is ready for the intensity of a totally unstructured group. At this juncture, the leader will purposefully let the session be completely open. A totally open session will create an atmosphere of unbridled ambiguity and unpredictability in which members' interpersonal styles have the best chance to emerge. When the group is unstructured, anything can transpire in a matter of seconds.

Although anxiety-provoking, the ambiguity embedded in the totally unstructured session is much celebrated. Ambiguity breeds intensity. Within the ambiguous setting, group members will come face to face with their interpersonal characteristics in the here-and-now of the group. With this comes the most intense and exposed encounters that a group can provide. Exposed encounters breed awareness. Once they become aware, members are more able to make conscious choices about their responses and actions.

To open the unstructured session, the leader may ask the group to have their regular brief check-in and to include a report of progress during their check-in. After that, the leader may hand the session to the group by saying something like,

> [For later stages of group] Thank you, everybody, for checking in. Next, we have about 70 minutes left for today's session. We are not going to request any agenda, so the session will be totally open. You have the ultimate freedom and responsibility to decide what you want to get out of the group today. If you have had any feelings or reactions about the group or about any member within the group, please feel free to share them with the group. If you have any stressful events in your life, please feel free to request attention from the group. When members are sharing their issues or reactions, please feel free to cross talk. We will work together as a group to see what we can learn from one another in our session today. [Pause and let the group take the initiative to start. If there is silence, let the silence take care of itself.]

On closing an unstructured session, it is critical that the leaders put emphasis on the members' self-learning. This can be achieved by saying something like,

> [To the group] "Let's have a quick check-out to wrap up today's session. In your check-out, please share what you have learned about yourself in today's session. If you feel a need to cross talk, please feel free to do so."

Face-to-Face with Elusive Immediacy Issues

Immediacy issues are subtle and covert in some cases and outrageously overt in others. Whatever they are, these immediacy issues are often too difficult and elusive to tackle in the earlier stages of the group. Either they involve issues that are sensitive or the group has to put them aside in favor of establishing functional norms and trust. Now, however, the unstructured session will bring the group face-to-face with its many immediacy issues. The unstructured group stimulates members to automatically begin replicating their interpersonal worlds in which they live. Each individual's blind spots and emotional reactivity patterns will be revealed for all to see. Blind spots, by their very nature, are blind to the individual because they are tucked neatly away in the subconscious. Addressing these elusive dynamics becomes the central task of the working stage, which is the time to focus energy on the issue of members' relationships with each other. It is the time to set norms of interpersonal honesty and emotional expressiveness (Yalom, 1995). Of course, dealing with immediacy issues will inevitably put almost every member in the "hot seat." The next section discusses why putting members in the hot seat is imperative if we are to help them gain awareness and mastery of their lives.

INTERPERSONAL ENACTMENT

As the group is placed in the unstructured environment, its members' habitual interpersonal patterns soon become revealed. Interpersonal dynamics are often complex and difficult to talk about. The best way to capture these elusive dynamics is through the hot-seat method. Although many of the previously presented leadership skills can still be applied in the working stage, this hot-seat method adds an immensely powerful skill to the leader's intervention repertoire.

In the hot-seat method, the leader has to intentionally put people in the hot seat. Yalom (1983, 1995) is the pioneer of this method. Yalom refines Moreno's (1934) concept of reenacting unfinished past business in the present and makes it a more workable method for group therapy. Yalom's concepts have inspired many intervention strategies that move the group to intense interaction and realization. The hot-seat method is literally the "powerhouse" of group counseling and therapy. Of course, the hot-seat method must be balanced by support, concern, and the full participation of all group members (Ferencik, 1991). Many new group leaders feel ill at ease at the thought of putting members in the hot seat. In this section, we explain why this method is imperative.

When Buttons Are Pushed

Whenever we put a group of people together for a period of time, sooner or later four "red-hot buttons" will be pushed. These four buttons are intimacy, control, power, and competition, which immediately occur within any group (Hetzel, Barton, & Davenport, 1994). When these buttons are pushed in areas about which a person is sensitive, they arouse potent raw emotions. Ironically, however, people often do not talk about them. At the working stage, these issues related to hot buttons must be examined.

The button of *intimacy* gets pushed fairly early in the group. Intimacy lies at the heart of group work because it involves a personal struggle regarding how much one is to allow others into one's personal domain. All of us harbor an inner conflict between a desire for emotional intimacy and an instinct to protect ourselves. We struggle with the question of how much to show our vulnerability and how much to build our walls. The fear of intimacy equates with the fear of vulnerability. The defense against vulnerability often manifests itself when members speak abstractly and intellectually as uncomfortable issues are touched upon. Some members may even physically distance themselves or withdraw from the rest when they feel their comfort level is being threatened.

The buttons of control, power, and competition are closely entangled. *Control* involves maintaining a personal level of predictability and security in the midst of potential change. *Power* takes control into another domain—we attempt not only to remain predictable and secure, but also to influence others. *Competition* occurs as people vie for key roles in their struggle to maintain personal control and interpersonal power. These three buttons also get pushed early in the group, as already demonstrated in the discussion about the transition/storming stage. Under the instinctual push of control and power, communication within the group can become competitive. Hetzel, Barton, and Davenport (1994) note that some members may attempt to counter other members' stories "by relating an even more painful or embarrassing incident, by offering advice, or by attempting to solve a particular dilemma" (p. 58).

Until the working stage, the issues of intimacy, control, power, and competition mostly lurk beneath the surface. Members do not talk about them openly because we are trained in our society not to talk about things that "hit too close to home." Members stuff these issues down inside themselves. But with the progression to the working stage and the unstructured format, these issues are ready to come to the forefront of group attention.

Interpersonal Enactment: The Way We Get Hooked

In presenting her issues, the client typically tells the group a rehearsed story about her complaints and problems. Usually this rehearsed story has significant omissions or blind spots. Along with the story comes a patterned nonverbal message that pushes the group, including the leader, into certain roles that are reciprocal to the client's role. The group's experiences and responses to this client will get shaped by this role induction. Once roles are enacted, the group will be hooked or will lock horns with the client. A member describes this experience well in her journal: "It feels like once you are in the group process, you are caught in a spider's web; there is no escaping what will transpire."

The group cannot prevent this "hooking" from happening because it is the client who now shapes the direction of the recipients' reactions. But the client is totally unaware of her responsibility for inducing these responses. If the group members and leader continue to be hooked by the client's metacommunication style, they will reinforce this specific client's maladaptive style of evoking responses. Eventually, anxiety, frustration, irritation, and a sense of dejection will grow, and the group will reach a stalemate.

Role reenactment is part of group reality. There are many roles that get reenacted in the group. Following are some familiar ones, although this list is by no means exhaustive:

- Problem solver
- Achiever
- Peacemaker
- Therapist
- People pleaser
- Hero
- Caretaker
- Mediator
- Placator (rescuer)
- Observer
- Scapegoat
- Lost child
- Troublemaker
- Talker
- Parental child
- Perfectionist
- Surrogate father
- Clown
- Entertainer
- Rationalist
- Rebel
- Victim

Interpersonal enactment tends to be reciprocal and recursive. For example, a person's "rescuer" role is enacted to correspond to a "scapegoat" or "lost child" role played by another member. When roles are enacted, a whole set of expectations attached to the status of each role will be promulgated, causing all involved parties to display certain behaviors and receive certain responses from the others. Subsequent responses proceed from prior ones (Ferencik, 1991). If not examined, people tend to lock horns with others by the roles they enact. Their interpersonal patterns, therefore, are perpetuated. If brought into the light, however, these interpersonal patterns can be changed with more conscious choice.

The phenomenon of interpersonal enactment in therapy is not new. Role enactment originated in psychodrama. In psychodrama, Moreno (1934) made his clients aware of their interactional difficulties through role enactment. The belief is that through reenacting roles in the present, unfinished past business can be worked through (Ferencik, 1991). Since group provides the most fertile soil for interpersonal enactment, it is of no surprise that role enactment has been emphasized in group counseling to help members understand and work through their difficulties in present relationships.

The Case of Amelia and Anna

Through the hot-seat method, the phenomenon of interpersonal enactment has a chance to be explored and analyzed, helping members see how they reciprocally replay with others the roles they sported in their family of origin. An example of this mutual enactment and mutual hooking can be seen in the following case of Amelia and Anna.

Anna entered the group stating that, as a very shy person, she often did not initiate greetings to others. Although Anna was capable of one-to-one deep conversation, she felt inadequate in social groups where interactions are more spontaneous and require one to be more active in reaching out. She found herself with no friends outside of her immediate family. It was no surprise to hear that the goal Anna set for herself in the group was to improve her interpersonal relationships. Later in the group, Anna also revealed two critical pieces of information: First, she came from a family that was very stoic; as a result, she had inherited a cold and distant look. Second, she had been suffering from a chronic illness, but she had decided at an early age not to disclose to others the physical pain that she had to endure in each given moment. This decision was based on painful experiences of being excluded and discriminated against after disclosing her chronic condition early in life. These two pieces of information helped members understand why she looked so stern and seldom seemed to be emotionally present. But this information was not revealed until later in the group. Even without the information about Anna's physical pain and her family background, however, everyone in the group knew that Anna's difficulty rested in her lack of interpersonal competency, and no one really took her mannerisms personally—except Amelia, who was immediately enacted into Anna's shadow.

Amelia had come from an alcoholic family where her Mom's emotional nurturing was mostly unavailable. This upbringing had made her very sensitive to rejection. On top of this, she had received early wounds caused by rejection from her peers. When she was about 5 years old, she had tried to become friends with a girl whose family just moved in next door to Amelia's family. For whatever reason, this girl did not like Amelia and ganged up with other neighborhood kids to exclude Amelia from playing with them. Amelia felt extremely hurt by this. Another incident occurred when she was in the third grade. Amelia had been hanging out at her house with a friend, Kim. Amelia wanted to continue playing, but Kim stated that she had to go home. After saying good-bye to Kim, Amelia went out to find another friend, Sue. To her surprise, Amelia found Kim and Sue playing together. Amelia asked Kim why she had lied to her, and Kim replied that the person she liked to hang out with was Sue, not Amelia. Amelia was extremely hurt again. These wounds of peer rejection never healed. They were dormant in Amelia's encounters with others in her adult life, but their influence was hidden from Amelia.

When Amelia encountered Anna in the group, she reached out to Anna in an attempt to build a friendship. In her quest to get Anna to at least be friendly to her, Amelia received only Anna's stern look and distance. There was no hope of reciprocity, as Amelia saw it. These cues were immediately taken personally. An intense feeling of hurt and anger was enacted. Amelia's painful past was relived in the here-and-now of the group with Anna. Her reactions to Anna often seemed out of proportion to what caused them when compared to the reactions of other members— to a degree that the leader commented that Amelia might have a certain kind of transference with Anna. After a period of reflection, Amelia started to associate her reactions with her childhood rejection dramas. Once these experiences were connected, Amelia had an "aha" experience and started to change.

Anna also carried her old sense of vulnerability with her. Her experience of being excluded and discriminated against when she revealed her chronic conditions had made her decide to conceal more of herself. The more she concealed herself, the more she became a blank slate onto which people could project their negative assumptions about her. She felt as if people conspired to discriminate against her. In one incident, she even misinterpreted members' giving positive feedback to Amelia as an indication that they were forming a clique that did not include her.

It took the group several incidences and here-and-now interventions to finally correct the interpersonal distortion between Amelia and Anna. Slowly, Anna started to disclose her chronic condition and family stoicism, and Amelia started to tell about her childhood dramas. The case between Amelia and Anna had a happy ending, as indicated in their reflective journals. Here are Anna's comments:

> The group had a great impact on me, as I was able to see myself through the eyes of others. And through them, I see those aspects of my personal style that I want to further work on—my being stoic and somewhat unresponsive to others at times. The critical event in the group was Amelia's reaction to my comment. This reaction made me become aware of my impact on others. I used to have a distorted perception of myself: I used to think that people didn't notice my stoic and sometimes shy behavior. But the group let me know through their comments that people can take this pattern of behavior very personally. This experience is very valuable for me in terms of addressing my social-emotional goal.

Amelia wrote:

> I need to be aware of the personal filter through which I am taking in everything Anna says and forming my emotional responses. I did not know, on a conscious level, that I was still carrying around those childhood experiences and the hurt associated with them. I was relieved when Anna stated that perhaps some of the stoicism that she displays is a result of her culture and upbringing. Once again, I could tell myself that the cause of her coldness was external, i.e., not because of her dislike of me. I think the idea of a personal filter is a really important thing for me to

remember from now on. It has been enlightening for me to realize the extent to which I still carry around the strong thoughts and emotions surrounding my past experiences. And I am happy that I went through all of this, if only for that revelation.

The dynamics between Amelia and Anna is a typical example of how unresolved past issues can be reenacted within the group setting. And as they are reenacted, they become the materials for exploration and examination. The ultimate reward is illumination and greater understanding about the members' core issues and their roots.

Elusiveness of Interpersonal Mannerisms and Styles

Provocative interpersonal mannerisms or styles are often something that members do not feel comfortable with pointing out to one another. We call these dynamics "the elephant in the room." The following examples given by Ferencik (1991) represent just some of these elusive interpersonal processes:

- Certain members identify with each other and interact in a manner that excludes the rest the group.
- Two alcohol abusers support each other in their denial.
- Two depressed members reinforce each other's belief in helplessness and in the group's ineffectiveness.
- Coalitions are formed by gender and age.

Other types of spontaneously emerging issues that are often observed include:

- Strong emotions or tension caused by confrontation and power struggle
- Members getting upset with each other
- Leaders being attacked
- Members falling asleep

Many of these behaviors are never articulated for what they really are because, as Ferencik (1991) explains, these mannerisms are abstract and subtle. They are patterns established over a period of time, so they are difficult to recognize and address. Even if they are recognized, group members often shy away from speaking what is on their minds or their perceptions. Those who do try to address the "elephants" are often met with resentment from their peers. Their behaviors are perceived by their peers as one-up behaviors or troublemaking. As Yalom (1995) comments, it is a social taboo for peers to comment on the unspeakable.

Provocative interpersonal styles in the group must be treated as issues of high priority. It is often these interpersonal events that speak the loudest. The leader is the one who has the leverage to address the elephants in the room. Unfortunately, many leaders fail to deal with these dynamics. Yalom (1983) laments: "Over and over again, I have observed wonderfully ripe therapeutic plums spoiling on the tree because of the inability of the therapists to focus on interaction" (p. 23). If leaders do not know how to tackle these spontaneous dynamics, group cohesiveness will be damaged. If addressed, these dynamics can provide an opportunity for growth.

Helping Members Squirm Loose from the Hook

Interpersonal enactment is not a problem in itself because it can actually provide a solution for the problems it arouses. When interpersonal patterns are enacted in the present, the group gets a chance to work through them. It is when group members are unable to squirm loose from the hook of enactment that problems arise. The best way of tackling difficult dynamics in the group is to first squirm loose, and then take the bull by the horns. In our experience, four steps are involved in this method:

1. Looking for a pattern hidden in what a specific member talks about "out there"
2. Noticing the pattern that is actually happening in the moment between the member and the rest of the group
3. Noticing the parallel between the occurrences "out there" and the immediate occurrence
4. Facilitating the rest of the group to tell the specific member how they directly experience her in the here-and-now. This inevitably puts people in the hot seat, which is why the method for dealing with these issues is called the hot-seat method.

These four steps will be illustrated in detail in the section of this chapter entitled "The Hot-Seat Method."

The key to this method is that the leader puts the group members radically within one another's interpersonal field, rather than seeing the group as being outside the lives that the members describe. The hot-seat method allows the group to have "a felt sense" of each member's interpersonal patterns in the immediate context of the session. It allows the group to see that issues presented as outside life events are actually based on patterns that have long manifested themselves outside as well as in the group; past issues are enacted in the present, and the outside is brought into the group. Members' interpersonal dynamics pop up "naked" in front of the group. This helps the group get a clearer picture of what happens with the members in their relationships. The group members can assess their interpersonal effectiveness and then identify concrete areas for change.

Do Not Be Afraid of Putting People on Hot Spots

To focus on immediacy issues is to radically move ordinary group interaction into the present moment and, inevitably, to radically put people in hot spots. Sitting on the hot seat brings home the sensation of high energy as nothing else does. Although the hot-seat experience can be somewhat frightening and unnerving, it also may open up gateways to new learning and new paths of action. People begin to change only when they begin to feel uncomfortable.

Many new group leaders, however, shy away from putting people in the hot seat. They hesitate to "rock the boat." This hesitance may come from a fear of arousing and handling intense emotions—a fear common in our society. This fear is legitimate, although not necessary. If the leader realizes that putting people in the hot seat can actually do them some good, she probably will be more willing to embrace this challenge. For peace of mind, it is important for leaders to remember that it is, indeed, virtuous to activate the group to the hot emotions of immediacy. It is actually a virtue to make people feel uncomfortable at times when it is for their own good.

Following is a discussion of some of the many benefits of putting people in the hot seat.

Reality Checking (Testing)   To focus the group on immediacy issues can open space for members to talk about reactions and perceptions that have historically been stuffed and suppressed inside. In the working stage, members are encouraged to reveal feelings, ideas, and reactions that have to do with their fellow members, the leader, or the operation of the group as a whole. These materials may be issues happening in a session or may cross over several sessions. Once disclosed, these materials can become valuable instruments for reality checking. A member who experiences a discrepancy between how she thinks of herself and how others view her is likely to become more mindful of her interpersonal style. For example, Anna thought she was attentive and empathic when she interacted with Amelia and the other members in the group. When the group told her that they often felt she appeared aloof and distant, she was wildly surprised by this discrepancy.

Energy Fuel   The focus on immediacy issues stirs up the group in such a way that members become energetically engaged with one another. When actively engaged with one another, members' interpersonal patterns are likely to show up, giving the group an opportunity to look at the patterns. The action of revealing such intimate material engages the whole group in a horizontal manner. Boredom and apathy quickly vanish when the group is operating in the here-and-now.

Multiple Hot-Seats, Multiple Reenactments   Focusing on immediacy issues can help fan out the hot-seat effect to include not just one person but several or all group members. Often multiple members play out their interpersonal dynamics in the immediate setting of the group, rendering it important to examine all the meanings of these members' patterns. When the hot seat is shared by different members, a multiple reenactment occurs. The group finds itself more able to resolve issues or tensions that involve multiple members. The energy generated by the hot-seat method can be glimpsed in Peter's and Heather's reflective journals. Peter wrote:

> I will always remember this week's session when almost everyone was in the "hot seat." It was so funny, as well as full of suspense and surprises— it was literally better than most movies. Through the hot-seat method, many hidden truths were suddenly revealed: Eve and Lori had been hiding and struggling with their negative reaction to Heather and Rose. Heather and Rose, in turn, had been trying to hide their negative reaction to my long-winded verbal expression. And my reaction to Lori's comments was, "What? Who's been disrespecting me? I know—it's that damned Rose! And Heather, too!" Sara laughed so hard at this, I thought she'd fall off her chair. Then Kelly put the icing on the cake by announcing that she was angry with the leader and was so sick of me being the favorite member. She thought that I get so much attention just because I am a man! This session was really great. And also, it was a springboard for future growth.

Heather wrote:

> I will forever remember my feeling of being in the "hot seat." After Lori confronted Rose and me about rolling our eyes and acting rude to Peter, I was embarrassed and felt like a kid being caught in the act of evil. But it gave me insight into myself and the way I kept my emotions hidden and ended up showing them like an open book, especially through my facial expressions. My rolling of eyes is never truly to hurt anyone, but now I know how others feel. I also know how one would feel being put on the hot seat.

Timing Is Everything

Though the hot-seat method is a powerhouse of interpersonal learning, it must be used with the right timing. Catching people in the act certainly will make people feel naked. If a sense of deep trust is not yet built, people can become defensive or shut down. Therefore, the leader must take the timing into consideration. Following are some tips regarding timing.

In Early Group Stages, Use Redirecting   In earlier group stages (forming and storming stages), the trust level is usually lower, and members do not feel safe enough to reveal their honest reactions to what is going on in the group. Under these circumstances, leaders should not jump to the hot-seat method, but rather should redirect the unproductive behaviors. Redirecting is one of the facilitating techniques that keeps the group going and prevents the members from getting stuck because of unproductive behaviors. Following are some examples of the use of the redirecting technique:

> I am going to stop you for a moment, Jane. All right, Anne, could you tell us again what you were just trying to say?

> Alice, let me stop you before you really get into the details of another story. It seems that Jim is reacting to what you are saying, and I want to give him a chance to comment. [turning to Jim] Jim, would you like to share what's going through your mind?

> John and Jeff, I'd like both of you to pause for a moment, then do your best to reflect back what you have heard the other say up to this point. [pause] John, would you like to go first and state what you heard Jeff say?

The redirecting technique is sufficient for the early stages of group in handling undesirable behaviors. Remember, however, redirecting will not make people become fully aware of their interpersonal patterns.

In Working Stage, Use the Hot-Seat Method By the working stage, the group has usually developed a good level of trust; people feel safe enough to be honest with one another. This is the best time to use the hot-seat method. The following sections provide technical details about how to bring difficult and elusive dynamics to the table for the group to examine by using the hot-seat method.

THE HOT-SEAT METHOD

An unstructured group session is anything but predictable. When interpersonal enactment kicks in, group dynamics may become volatile. The fact is: Group dynamics are what happens when the group is in action, not what the members say happens. How people describe their interpersonal realities provides a less accurate picture than the way these interpersonal styles are revealed spontaneously in group. The hot-seat method helps group leaders facilitate the group to talk about interpersonal dynamics that are difficult to talk about. The open conversation enables members to see how others perceive them.

Four Steps of the Hot-Seat Method

When a group is hooked in interpersonal enactment, it needs to directly examine what is going on in the group. But the group cannot do that by itself. It is the leader's responsibility to help them get unhooked. Addressing the difficult dynamics in the room requires a complex and stimulating course of action. We will risk being overly simplistic by dissecting this hot-seat method into four steps. The first two steps are internal ones, in which the leader steps back and observes the group, while the last two steps are external in the sense that the leader helps the group verbalize and process the interactions.

First Step   When the group and the leader are hooked in the interpersonal field, the group grows frustrated and anxious; the members do not know what to do. What happens seems to go in a circle. At this juncture, the leader first needs to step back and attend to what is happening internally for him—that is, how he is *being pulled* by these particular clients. In stepping back, the leader is able to *look for parallel occurrences* between the clients' issues in their relationships and what they do with the group. It is not hard to take notice of parallel occurrences. People often act consistently across settings. They establish ways of relating that become well-entrenched patterns over time. The leader will notice parallel occurrences when he listens mindfully.

For example, suppose a member is talking about a problem in her life, and the group is getting involved in unraveling the story. The leader will miss the parallel occurrences if he, when watching the member's interaction with the group, thinks pessimistically to himself, "This is really going nowhere. What has this story and this conversation got to do with anything?" But if the leader really scours the events for parallel occurrences, he will notice his own reaction and think to himself: "Well, am I the only one who feels like hitting on a wall when this member talks? How often does she talk in tangents without showing any feelings? How is her style related to her problem in her interpersonal life?"

Second Step   After the leader has identified his own internal reaction, he then observes how the rest of the group reacts to a particular member's mannerisms or style of evoking reactions. The leader focuses on what is going on here (between the rest of the group and the client) and what is going on now (at this very moment, not in the client's distant past). The leader then may ask himself: "Hmm . . . so how is the group reacting to this style of storytelling? Do they see the connection to the issue and goal she said she wants to work on? Do they resist her style? Do their minds wander? Do they feel the frustration of getting shut out?" Here the leader attempts to use his own emotions, not to react, but to speculate whether other group members might be feeling the same way the leader does and to speculate if sharing these feelings might help the group and the particular member. Notice that the leader's internal processing remains private and unspoken at this point. The major part of the hot-seat method is carried out in the last two steps.

Third Step   Stepping back to speculate on the reactions in himself and in the group will help the leader regain a level of objectivity. Next, in the third step, the leader formulates an alternative intervention that makes it possible for the members to squirm loose from their hooks and talk directly to the specific member about the reactions evoked in them that are usually difficult to talk about. In this step, the leader encourages the group to tell the particular member what their direct experiences of that member have been. He invites the group to speak directly to the member about their reactions. The leader may, for example, say:

> [To the group] Let's stop for a moment. I am seeing some strong reactions when Marcy talks. I wonder what this tension is about? Does anyone want to start? And please speak to Marcy directly.

The leader may also try another, more explicit, intervention such as:

> [To the group] I would like the group to shift gears a little bit. I wonder, how do you personally experience Marcy when you listen to her presenting her issues? How do you feel toward her? I am not asking about how you feel toward her problems, but about how you feel toward her way of telling her stories. When you are ready, please speak directly to Marcy.

Suppose a group member, say John, responds, "Marcy, your stories are very colorful and I appreciate the drama in them, but I have been waiting to hear what your stories have to do with your current struggles and your personal work in the group. I am not seeing it, and I feel lost. Frankly, the more I hear you talk, the more I feel detached. So I don't know." At this point, the leader does not need to agree or disagree with what John has said, but just needs to thank him and continue with an invitation for other members to speak.

> Thank you, John, for your openness. [turning to other members] Does anyone feel similarly to how John feels?

Another member, say Susan, may comment, "Yes, I always feel something about you, Marcy, but I haven't been able to put my finger on it. Today when I listened to you, though, it became more clear. It is like I want to get close to you, but I'm never able to cross a wall. It is like you really don't want people to get to know you or something." Again, the leader only needs to thank Susan and then persist in his invitation to the group until the dynamics have been fully explored:

Thank you, Susan. Anyone else?

Fourth Step   In this last step, the leader leads the group to make the connection between the group's experience of a particular member in the moment and the way people in her world might experience her. The amount of *correspondence* that exists between how people behave in the group and how people behave in their own interpersonal relationships is amazing. Often, the very pattern developing between the group and a given member is a live example of the interpersonal field that the member creates outside of the group.

Interpersonal fields have a way of pulling anyone who comes close to them into their self-perpetuating patterns. Although the people "out there" whom the clients are having trouble with are not in the group, the clients' patterns seep into the group. Indeed, everything that every client wants to know about others' perceptions of her is available inside the immediacy of the group interaction.

In *linking the immediacy of group interaction to the outside world of the member,* the leader helps the given member see how others in the group have the same gut reactions to her as those who live in her world. The more the leader believes in group interaction as an interpersonal learning laboratory, the more he can help members see their interpersonal pulls on the group and the group's influence on them. We call this fourth step *illuminating the parallel process.* This step can bring the attention of the group and the client to the relationship issues that are developing among all the parties in the group. It brings to a conscious level issues that were originally ambiguous and difficult to talk about.

In this fourth and final step, the leader links the group's reaction to the member's interpersonal goal by making a comment like:

[To Marcy] What the members are trying to say is that they cannot get close to you. I remember that the very issue you presented in the first group meeting was your inability to build a close relationship with someone. I think the feedback that members gave you a moment ago may give you some valuable information as to why people in your world outside the group feel pushed away by you.

Together the third and fourth steps certainly put group members into the hot seat. The third and fourth steps of this intervention together are called "process illumination." The example just presented provides only a general view of process illumination.

Zig-Zagging the Spotlight:
Multiple Hot Seats, Multiple Illuminations

In group dynamics, it is rare that members' interpersonal dynamics are played out in a one-at-a-time fashion. Rather, several interpersonal dynamics will pop up during the group interaction. Other members' dynamics will be stirred while someone's interpersonal style is being explored. Depending on their own interpersonal styles, different members will react to the work differently. The member being examined might deflect the information and the spotlight by talking over everyone else. A member who has had previous grudges against this particular member might use this opportunity to confront the person being examined. Another member who often plays the rescuer role in the group might try to down play the confrontation, and so on.

These dynamics, and a lot more, can happen simultaneously. None of these dynamics should be ignored by an alert leader. All of them need process illumination to bring out their underlying meanings. As various members' interpersonal matters are enacted, the spotlight should zig-zag in multiple directions. Multiple members will be on the hot seat at certain points within the session, and multiple processes will be illuminated.

Taking the earlier case as an example, if members respond to the leader's prompt regarding their reactions to the way Marcy told her story, their habitual interpersonal matters will likely surface. For instance, a member, say Ellen, who has struggled for a long time with an assertiveness issue, may respond by saying that she feels walled off by the way Marcy rambled. Ellen's courageous honesty might encourage other members to share their true reactions to Marcy. At this time, Marcy may feel threatened and start to shift the conversation to focus on other members in order to deflect her vulnerable feelings. Ellen, however, may tell Marcy how Marcy just deflected what the group was trying to tell to her. At that moment, the tension in the air will be felt by everyone in the room. At this juncture, the peacemaker in the group, say Mike, may jump in to rescue Marcy. Mike may tell a story of his own that is totally irrelevant to the dynamics or issues at hand. The group's attention will be distracted as a result, and a moment of honest interaction will be sidestepped.

In this example, three dynamics have happened simultaneously: First, Ellen, for the first time in the group, has taken a great risk in standing up for herself and refusing to have her reaction deflected. Second, Marcy cannot allow honest feedback to penetrate through her self-defense without resorting to her old coping mechanism. And third, Mike's inability to tolerate anxiety has propelled him once again to take the moment of confrontation away from the group. All these dynamics are equally important to explore and discuss. If the leader focuses single-mindedly on Marcy's interpersonal process, he will be making a mistake.

When faced with multiple dynamics, the leader needs to ask the group to stop and reflect on what they have observed. The leader may say,

> [To the group] Let's stop for a moment. There are many important dynamics going here. Let's talk about what this has evoked in you. How do you experience what is happening at the moment? [multiple process illuminations]

The leader should continue to illuminate the interpersonal process until all dynamics have been thoroughly explored, and then ask all involved what they learned from the experience.

When Some Members Put Water on the Heat

Bringing tough issues out in the open and putting people on the spot may provoke anxiety in some group members. Not too infrequently, people have difficulty tolerating heightened emotions. When things get hot, they will habitually do something to bring the temperature down, as if putting water on a fire. Many times a group will just begin to discuss a sensitive issue when a member or two will shift the topic or get onto the content level of communication (see the discussion of two levels of communication later in this chapter). Ironically, these members often are unaware of what they are doing. It seems so natural to them to bring up a new topic, to ask a new question, or to talk about something on the horizon. But when this happens, a critical interpersonal process that is just getting the group's attention suddenly dissipates into thin air. The group cannot put a finger on what has just happened. When the heightened emotions are taken away, so is the opportunity for heightened awareness.

In situations like this, the leader may bring the group to analyze the avoidance behavior or direct the group to return to process illumination. The leader may, for example, say,

> [To the group] We were just beginning to address a difficult issue in the group, and suddenly we are talking about a totally unrelated topic. I wonder, what do you observe is going on here? [prompting the group to analyze the avoidance behavior]

> [To the group] I noticed that we were sidetracked just now. Let's go back to the statement Kathy made a few minutes ago about some people in this group having the tendency to intellectualize. I notice there are some strong reactions toward what Kathy just said, so let's stay with this issue a bit longer even if it makes us feel a bit intense. [redirecting to process illumination]

Process Illumination and the Knee-Jerk Experience

Process illumination drives the group members to provide here-and-now oriented feedback—the type of feedback emphasized previously in Chapter 8. Process illumination can create an experience unlike anything else. The previous illustrations demonstrate how powerful the experience can be when one's interpersonal style is caught in the moment of action. The focus on immediacy gets to the heart of the issues. Without a doubt, process illumination puts people on the hot seat, and the hot-seat experience can be a knee-jerk experience. When they are on the hot seat, people find their interpersonal matters being exposed and talked about openly. This kind of direct feedback, which seldom happens in daily life, gives people a new awareness. This new awareness opens space for new options, breaking ground for other important therapeutic work to come. This can be a tremendous gift to the receiving members. One member, Lou, reflected in her journal on this experience:

> Without this group, I would not have known that I unconsciously change the conversation when I become emotional. I did not really expect people in this group to tap into my issues. It was a tumultuous, yet pleasant, surprise. It was tumultuous because people in this group started seeing my vulnerabilities, but then ended up pleasant by people accepting me for who I am as a person.

A towering challenge for the leader is to observe patterns of reactivity while taking part in the group interaction. Tremendous presence on the part of the leader is required. The group members, too, take a courageous risk when they address the elephant in the room. They could be way off in their guesses about a particular member. They could hit a person's soft spot too directly. They could offend a member. They could scare someone off by getting too close to the person's core issue. For all involved, this experience of addressing the elephant in the room can produce a frightening, yet exhilarating, moment. If done in a sensitive way with appropriate timing and empathic support, however, this hot-seat method can expand member awareness in a new way.

PROCESS ILLUMINATION AND CHANGE

Process illumination is a powerful way to help members become aware of their self-defeating interpersonal patterns. It is, indeed, a group leader's most critical task. Throughout this text, we have discussed the concepts and methods of process illumination. In this section, we will expound on how process illumination—the group processing that produces the knee-jerk experience—can facilitate client change.

Two Levels of Communication: Content and Process

In any communication, the interaction involves the content level and the process level:

The Content Level   *Content* refers to the *words and views* that are exchanged in the group. For example, the words said by Mary and John in the following exchange contain the content:

> *Mary:* I am angry with my sister for not sharing the responsibility of taking care of my parents. But she is an alcoholic and cannot even take care of herself.
>
> *John:* Why do you let her get away with this? Being an alcoholic is just an excuse.
>
> *Mary:* [looks distressed and feels compelled to defend herself]
>
> *John:* [gets nervous and tries harder and harder to convince Mary of her self-defeating behavior]
>
> *Other members:* [feel frustrated about the argument between Mary and John, yet feel hesitant to say anything]

The Process Level   *Process* refers to the *nature of the relationship* among members who are exchanging words and views. This level of communication includes the reactions of and feelings between all persons involved (Yalom, 1995, 2002). The process is the metacommunication of the message—the implicit, or unspoken, message. The process level of communication is the essence of the interpersonal process.

In the previous interaction, the nature of the relationship is featured by *John giving advice* to Mary, and by *Mary feeling unheard and unaccepted.* The metacommunication of Mary's message may be that she feels trapped in an unjust situation, while the metacommunication of John's message may *hint that Mary did it to herself by enabling her sister to be irresponsible and by making excuses for her sister.* Mary's underlying message did not get through to John, nor did his to her. On the contrary, *Mary feels blamed.* John's good intention to help Mary see her own part in the problem did not come out as effectively as he originally intended. Now *John feels unappreciated.* Both missed each other's message on the metacommunication level. The relationship between them has become strained, and the group is pulled into this tension. To help John and Mary truly communicate with each other, the leader must help them track down their metacommunication messages and the meanings underlying their messages.

Tangled in Content Level of Communication

Most group interactions are at the content level of communication, that is, focused on what is literally said. Less attention is paid to the unspoken, between-the-lines, underlying messages, and to their accompanying feelings. A natural consequence of being tangled in the content level is that people's actual needs remain unrecognized and unacknowledged. Each party drifts further and further away from feeling accepted and affirmed, and unmet and frustrated needs ultimately lead to strained interpersonal relationships.

Frustrated needs are the natural result of a communication style with a one-dimensional focus on the content level. A great number of interpersonal difficulties arise because of the failure to comprehend the process level of communication. The inner needs of the involved parties remain buried, without being understood. This happens between couples, in work relationships, between family members, in intimate relationships, and in the group.

Process Level of Communication

Tracking the process level of communication is the essence of any form of therapy, especially group therapy. The most important job of the group leader is to help the group understand their own metacommunication messages and interpersonal processes. If asked to describe a group's most important task, an effective leader probably would point to tasks such as *process observation, process exploration, process commenting, process illumination,* and *process examination.* An alert leader relentlessly pursues the interpersonal process by heeding what is going on in the session, rather than what group members say is happening in their lives. The leader must ponder the metacommunication, and not just the subject matter, of group discussion. In any given session, an effective leader's facilitation of the group may seem to be effortless and relaxed, yet an effective leader's mind is alert all the time. When sensing any dynamics below the surface, such a leader will lead the group to catch them. Effective leaders encourage the group members to explore, examine, and comment on emerging events in group, with the aim of shedding light on the meanings of the dynamics.

This relentless tracking of the process level of interpersonal communication is quite atypical and precious indeed, because this kind of process focus surpasses the expectations of everyday social interaction. During our daily interactions with people, it is unusual for others to listen carefully to what we say and not be in a hurry to interrupt us with their own views. During the heat of conversation, rarely do others carefully track our nonverbal messages to detect the convoluted personal implications of our story. And it is truly a surprising event when others share with us the important positive and negative impacts that we have induced in them during our transactions. Because it is so atypical, this kind of process focus is truly a precious find. But this precious find is the gist of a process group. As Kiesler and Van Denburg (1993) pointed out, the focus on interpersonal process and feedback is the landmark of a process-focused group.

Because it is so unusual, the process level of communication is initially rarely understood by the group members. They tend to be blind to their interpersonal impact on others and to continue their troublesome interaction styles because, in daily social interaction, they have not been given feedback on the process level.

Process Illumination, Self-Discovery, and Change

The work on the process level can cause knee-jerk reactions, but the growth gained from it is well worth it. When people's interpersonal processes are illuminated, self-discovery is an inevitable result. Self-discovery is the catalyst for self-transformation. When people gain awareness of the nature of their communication, it is an exciting, peak experience. This type of self-discovery most often contributes to change.

The journey of a client's change may unfold like this: Carrying around personal filters/unfinished business → Entering a group → Roles get reenacted within group interactions → Dynamics with strong emotions spontaneously emerge within the group → Interpersonal process gets examined/commented on → Insight → Change. If we put this journey in staircase form, it would appear as shown in Figure 9.1.

This change process resonates with what Yalom (1995) described as "critical incidents." Critical incidents are events that usually involve multiple members within the group. Common components of the critical incident include: (1) A member becomes intensely involved with multiple members; (2) the member's interpersonal pattern emerges as she interacts; (3) the group looks into the pattern and provides sufficient here-and-now reactions; (4) the member gains insight into the impact of her interpersonal pattern; (5) the member puts insight into practice within the group; and (6) the member generalizes a new interpersonal style into her own life.

In a group, both successful and unsuccessful members experience strong emotional involvement in parts (1) and (2) of a critical incident. That is, both are involved in the heated here-and-now group interaction. The difference between them is that successful members go through the complete course of the critical incident, gaining insight, and thus change their interpersonal patterns within the group. In contrast, unsuccessful members put forth their agendas and experience strong emotions but stop

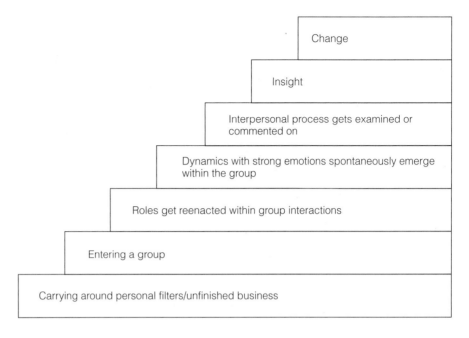

FIGURE 9.1

JOURNEY OF CLIENT CHANGE

short of the cognitive insight necessary for change. These members often fall short because of a lack of group process illumination.

Self-discovery is the beginning of change. Self-discovery goes hand-in-hand with self-insight and self-awareness. What one needs to discover is one's central meaning organizers (the filters) that shape one's experiences and reaction patterns. It is only when members gain awareness of their interpersonal processes that they benefit from the group experience. It is only when they gain insight into their reaction patterns and filters that they are able to apply what they learn within the group to their daily lives outside the group.

A Sense of Psychological Visibility

Though nerve-wracking, process illumination gives people a sense of being seen, and the experience of being seen is exactly what is needed therapeutically. Underlying many people's developmental problems, insecurities, and inadequacies in relationships lies the agony of invisibility in their lives as they grew up. For many, to heal is to make contact with those qualities in their personality and psyches that are generally kept hidden. Although hidden, members' psychological traits and characteristics often manifest themselves through their interpersonal styles.

There exists a "mirror" through which each group member can see his psychological self, his character, his inner being, and his interpersonal being. This mirror consists of the perceptions of other members in the group. If the group's perceptions resonate with a member's deepest and unexpressed vision of who he is, then this member will feel perceived; he will feel psychologically visible. He will have a sense of finally being seen by others. For the first time in his life, his blinders are removed.

In process-focused groups, members have a high probability of feeling truly seen by other human beings. When their interpersonal processes are brought to light, members become aware of unrecognized capabilities, latent potentialities, and character traits that never before surfaced to the level of explicit recognition. As their sense of psychological visibility increases, the consciousness of who they are begins to expand. Group encounters lead them to a deepening contact with their own psychological selves. Integration becomes possible. They begin to heal their internal psychological splits. Greater energy is made available from a more unified self.

PROCESS ILLUMINATION TECHNIQUES (I): GO WHERE THE REACTIVITY IS

Process illumination brings to the group a kind of powerful feedback and a path to self-discovery. Many beginning group leaders, however, have trouble identifying both subtle and complex interpersonal patterns. The reason is that interpersonal processes are complex, circular, and interdependent. As Yalom (1995) puts it so well, "It is not easy to tell the beginning therapist how to recognize process . . . generally, beginning students who observe [group] meetings find them [the dynamics] far less meaningful, complex, and interesting than do the experienced therapists" (p. 159).

So how do we know when a member's interpersonal pattern is being enacted? How do we recognize it in the act? Leszcz (1992) states, "Intense emotional heat that seems 'out of proportion' with the objective situation is often a very useful signal that some core interpersonal vicissitude that reflects on the individual sense of self has been touched. Through its hyperactivity, it serves as a marker for central issues" (p. 57). Intense emotional reactivity is the marker that something crucial within a group member has been touched.

Intense emotional reactivity can be manifested not only through facial expressions and nonverbal language but also through outright behaviors. Examples of reactive behaviors include, but are not limited to, the following:

- Cutting people off
- Shutting down

- Withdrawal
- Verbal attack
- Becoming defensive
- Blaming
- Blocking out
- Denying
- Turning to a rescuer
- Distracting
- Deflecting
- Discounting
- Distancing

When any such reactivity happens in the group, the leader needs to disengage the group from the give-and-take of group interaction and examine what is happening in the immediacy within the group. Following are areas of group dynamics where emotional reactivity is likely to happen, and thus process illumination will be required: (1) relationships between group members; (2) relationships between members and the leader; and (3) competition for dominance.

Relationships between Group Members

The first area of group dynamics that provides fertile soil for emotional reactivity is the relationships between group members. Ways to illuminate these dynamics can be illustrated by the following examples in sequence:

> [To the group] I would like the group to stop for a moment. There is something very important that has just happened in the group. What do you see was going on between Helen [the offended] and Jim? [initial process illumination—third step of the hot-seat method]

> Thank you for sharing, Tom. [turning to the rest of the group] I would like to hear more from the rest of the group about your observation of the incident between Helen and Jim. Does anyone else want to contribute? [more initial process illumination]

> [To the group] I wonder, have any of you had the same experience as that which Helen has encountered today? How does this make it difficult for you to reveal yourselves? [further process illumination]

> Jim, what do you see is the effect of your behavior on others? Does this occur in other life situations? [illuminating parallel process—fourth step of the hot-seat method]

Other examples include:

> [To the group] I would like to call a time-out for the group. The exchange between Jessie, Tom, and Diana has been going on for more than 10 minutes and seems to be going nowhere. I sense a lot of strong

feelings in the room. I would like the group to respond to this question: What do you see has been going on in the last 10 minutes?

[To the group] Jim and Steve have been conversing with each other for awhile now, and I notice something unsaid building up in the group. I wonder, what do you observe is going on here?

The process question "What do you see has been going on?" should be extended to the rest of the group enough times so that all members will have a chance to share their observations.

Relationships between Members and Leaders

The second area of group dynamics likely to trigger emotional reactivity involves the relationships between members and the leader. Chapter 7 discussed potentially challenging dynamics between members and leaders and ways to address them during the storming stage. Here in the working stage, process illumination is the best way to deal with conflictual dynamics between a member and a leader. Examples, in sequence, would include:

Jessie, as you said that to Mary, I also heard some of your feelings toward me. Would you be willing to share them so I can better understand what is happening between you and me? [initial process illumination—third step of the hot-seat method]

How does the rest of the group feel about what happened between Jessie and me? [one step further to process illumination—third step]

Jessie, I now understand these feelings of inadequacy you have toward me within our group. I wonder if you might have similar feelings toward the authority figures in your world outside the group. I wonder whether they might actually approve of who you are as a person, and yet might be perceived as disapproving of you? [fourth step of the hot-seat method]

Competition for Dominance

The third area of group dynamics that is fertile soil for emotional reactivity involves competition for dominance. Competition for dominance is a powerful force in the group. Sibling rivalry often rises to the surface in group interaction. Members may struggle with one another to establish a pecking order within the group. A leader who sees competition for dominance happening can ensnare it in the moment of action. Ways to process these dynamics are illustrated by the following examples in sequence:

[To the group] Let's stop for a minute and take a few steps back to see if we can understand what is happening between Jean and Pat. [initial illumination—third step of the hot-seat method]

[To the group] I wonder why it is Jean who always reveals first and most. Why does the group let her carry the burden of the entire meeting? [further illumination]

[To the group] All of you seem to have noticed this. What has stopped you from acting on your observations? Why does the group look to the leader to do what all of you are able to do? [even further illumination]

Another example:

[To the group] I notice that this is becoming a discussion exclusively between Jane, Patrick, and Nancy while the rest of the group is sitting silently. I wonder, how do the rest of you see this, and why are you letting it happen this way?

PROCESS ILLUMINATION TECHNIQUES (II): WHATEVER IS HIDDEN IS WORTH PURSUING

Whatever is behind interpersonal communication often carries the most power. Group work is most effective when it addresses the meanings and messages hidden behind the spoken words—that is, what is unsaid (Lieberman, Yalom, & Miles, 1973). What is hidden in the realm of interpersonal dynamics often involves: (1) nonverbal messages; (2) emotions and reactions enacted yet unexpressed; and (3) underlying perceptions that influence members' reactions. The meanings of these dynamics are the underground forces that construct our interpersonal realities. The hot-seat method requires the group to devote much of its energy to decoding these hidden meanings. Leszcz (1992) states, "Each action or behavior by each member of the group has meaning and the therapist's task is to help all members pursue this significance" (p. 57).

As an observer-participant, the leader can formulate hunches about members' behavior patterns and look for further evidence to confirm or disconfirm these hunches. When a pattern is observed, the leader must first *inquire about the meaning of the behavior, without jumping right in to interpret it.* This allows group members opportunities to interpret for themselves what is going on, and thus gain insight about themselves.

Meanings of behaviors usually are explored not within one single incident, but through a sequence of statements and interactions, or even over a period of time. When brought to light, this interpersonal significance enters members' awareness—cognitively, behaviorally, and emotionally—in their encounters with others. Process-oriented feedback enables members to realize what they are doing with other members, what impact their behavior has on others, and how such behavior influences others' opinions of them as well as their own self-regard (Yalom, 1995). The realization paves the way to self-discovery.

Following are four types of behaviors containing meanings and messages that merit attention from the group. These behaviors include: (1) puzzling group behaviors; (2) nonverbal behaviors; (3) what is not happening; and (4) absent members' influence.

Puzzling Group Behaviors

The first type of behavior that commands decoding of meaning is puzzling group behaviors. When the leader notices such a behavior, she may lead the group to examine members' perceptions of it. Following are some examples of what the leader can say:

> [To the group] Right now I sense a great deal of tension in the room, as I also did while Jane was talking. I wonder how you make sense of what Jane just said and what triggered this tension? [process illumination step of the hot-seat method]

> [To the group] I feel puzzled about the meeting and wonder whether the group is avoiding something. If so, why? [process illumination]

> [To the group] I see that half an hour has gone by, but something seems to be going on here that keeps us stuck at this moment. I would like to ask, can any of you identify what may be going on that is causing us to spin our wheels? [process illumination]

Nonverbal Behaviors

The second type of behavior that requires decoding has to do with nonverbal behaviors. Researchers estimate that 65 percent of communication in groups takes place through nonverbal means (Burgoon, et al., 1993). Research also indicates that nonverbal behaviors are usually honest. When there is incongruence between the verbal and nonverbal, the nonverbal usually can be believed (Gazda, 1989). Nonverbal behaviors convey unmasked messages that one unconsciously leaks out. In the group, nonverbal behaviors provide a rich reservoir for observation and interpretation. As the leader gives attention to a member's *verbal* expressions, he may also want to observe the *nonverbal* indicators. Following are nonverbal cues that Yalom (1995) indicates are targets of observation:

- Who chooses to sit where?
- Which members sit together?
- Who chooses to sit close to the leader, and who sits far away?
- Who sits near the door?
- Who comes to the meeting on time?
- Who is habitually late?
- Who looks at whom when speaking?
- Who looks at her watch?

- Who slouches in his seat?
- Who yawns?
- Who has her coat on?
- How quickly do the group members enter the room?
- How do they leave the room?
- Who smokes, when, and in what manner?
- How and when do members' postures shift?

In addition to these nonverbal cues, tones of voice and facial expressions are potential targets for observation. When consistent across time, these nonverbal behaviors tend to signal that certain dynamics are happening and that their meanings merit exploring. When a leader sees such cues, he can lead the group to look into the significance of the behaviors. The leader may say,

> [To the group] I wonder, when you listened to Maria's painful stories, what impressions did you get from her nonverbal messages? Did you see anything in her nonverbal behavior that might be incongruent with her verbal expression? [third step of the hot-seat method]

> Steve, I heard anger in your voice when you gave feedback to Noel. I wonder, what is it about Noel that makes you feel angry? [third step of the hot-seat method]

> [To the group] I am not sure what is going on in our meeting today, but I do see some unusual things. For example, Jack has been quiet, Lee has moved his chair back about 3 feet, and Karen has been glancing at me for the past few minutes. What ideas do all of you have about these things?

Maria, the person in the first example, wrote the following in her reflective journal after listening to the group members share their experiences with her:

> The most helpful feedback that I received was when I was told by Keith that I related my painful story with a constant smile on my face. How can I expect anyone to understand what is going on inside of me when my nonverbal behavior indicates that everything is fine? I did not know I was smiling all the time until Keith said that. Now I know what I have to do.

What Is Not Happening

The third type of behavior to be decoded involves the things that are missing in the group. What is not happening in the group is not really not happening. The void, whatever it is, is itself a dynamic, and its presence is often strongly felt by the group. This void may appear in any of the following forms:

- Some types of topics that are never presented
- A specific person who never gives feedback to another specific person

- A specific member who is never confronted
- A particular member who is never supported

The leader may explore the meanings behind what is not happening by saying,

> I wonder, what is the underlying reason why Mary is never confronted? [third step of the hot-seat method]

> I am curious why Dean is never supported. Would anyone in the group like to share your observation? [third step of the hot-seat method]

Absent Members' Influence

The fourth type of behavior that commands decoding of meaning involves a felt influence when a member is absent. Paradoxically, the influence of a member, positive or negative, speaks most loudly when that member is absent. This is because it is harder to see what influence a specific member is having on the group when the member is present. When he is absent, the group experiences a change in the configuration of the group, which magnifies the meaning of the absent member's impact on the group. The meaning of this kind of differential configuration is worth exploring. Following are examples in sequence of ways the leader can prompt process illumination in this situation:

> [To the group] Everyone seems more alive today than in past sessions. Even Kim, who has been quiet, blossomed today into animated self-expression. *I wonder, what is it about today's session that makes the difference?* [initial illumination—third step of the hot-seat method]

> What you have discussed about the impact of Dale's absence today is very important. And I think Dale needs to be aware of these discussions about him. Therefore, we will need to bring this up with him when he returns next week. [further comment]

Another example:

> [To the group] Today everyone seems to feel helpless and threatened by the responsibility of making the group run. I wonder, *what is it about today that makes the difference?*

PROCESS ILLUMINATION TECHNIQUES (III): LINKING THE INSIDE TO THE OUTSIDE

After group members talk openly about their reactions to and perceptions of a given member's behaviors or interpersonal patterns (the third step), it is important to proceed to the fourth step, which is showing how the dynamics played out within the group might run parallel to the dynamics in the members' personal lives. Process illumination, as a type of feedback, is particularly potent when it *links the inside to the outside.* Without this last step of process illumination, member awareness may not be complete.

As mentioned, how people behave in group tends to correspond with how they behave in their interpersonal fields outside the group. A member's pattern within group is often a live example of the interpersonal field in which that member exists. Indeed, *everything that members want to know about themselves is available inside the here-and-now of group interaction.* Given this, feedback must strive to link the here-and-now to the members' outside worlds. This kind of process illumination helps a particular member see that others in the group, through their firsthand experiences with him, have the same gut reactions to him as those who live in his world outside of group. This "parallel process illumination" helps people uncover both strengths and blind spots that have been hidden from their own awareness. Here are some examples of how to illuminate parallel processes:

> Julie, I wonder if there might be people in your life who feel the same way toward you as the group members do. That is, are there people who are attracted to you and want to get close to you, but sense your aloofness and misinterpret your fear of closeness as snobbishness? [fourth step of the hot-seat method]

> Mark, I understand these ambivalent feelings you have toward me within our group. I cannot help but also wonder if you might have similar feelings toward the authority figures in your past that remain unresolved. Perhaps you might want to get in touch with these issues. [fourth step of the hot-seat method]

> Dale, I wonder if others in your life might feel the same way as the group members do when you focus on negative aspects of others? I wonder what disadvantages this behavior brings you? Do you pay a price for it? [fourth step]

> El, you said that you don't know why you are always attracted to aggressive women. And I have seen you, for the past 15 minutes, lock horns with Kathy, who assertively engages you with her questions. You have turned to face her totally and have forgotten about the rest of the group. Many members in the group have been waiting to get your attention but have failed. I am struck by the parallel between what has happened here in the group and what happens in your relationships with women in your life. I wonder if there may be many nice "non-aggressive" women waiting on the fringe for you if you look around, but you are too busy engaging with the ones with the loudest voices to notice those quiet nice women. [fourth step]

SCENARIOS FOR YOUR PRACTICE

1. During the sixth session of a group for laid-off workers, you become aware that in the group Joe and Bill frequently support one another's statements, but seldom comment when others speak. For many sessions, you have noticed them exchanging smiles and smirks when no one else in the group is smiling. You have a growing suspicion that they are forming a strong dyadic subgroup to the exclusion of the others. What are your options for dealing with this dynamic?

2. With a rising, clipped voice, Thad states to the whole group, "None of you know what it's like for these people. They are just so special. I'm the only one here who is sensitive to them. You each need to get off your backsides and get busy doing your homework on this. You just don't have a clue." The group is miffed, but no one says anything. In what way would you respond as the group leader?

3. Lena relates to the group her personal experience with racism, saying that she feels strongly that it was a critical factor in her brother's death as a young adult. Tex (who has been asked by his employer to join this group to increase his interpersonal sensitivity) asks in response, "While I'm sorry for your brother's death, aren't you just dredging up the ancient history of slavery to say that it's racially motivated?" How might you work with this dynamic as it arises in the moment?

4. In a general personal growth group, you become aware that Martin tends to adopt a posture which appears to be physically quite tense and that he often seems to offer judgments about situations that other members describe. You also notice that he fails to connect with any other members on a feeling level. When fellow group member Joe states that he has decided to get a divorce, Martin begins grilling him about whether Joe's efforts to keep the marriage intact have been strong enough. How would you choose to handle this dynamic?

5. It is the fifth session of a support group. As she has done in each of the past two sessions, June immediately starts the session by launching into a recitation of her difficult experiences during the past week. You realize that you have not heard much from about five of the other eight members. Only Augie has been able to get much air time over June. What issues are involved here? What would you do to handle the dynamics at hand?

6. Frowning a bit, Joe says to Martin, "I wasn't asking that you evaluate or even agree with my decision to get a divorce. After agonizing about this decision for a very long time, I only wanted to share the

pain and difficulty with others here." Martin responds defensively, "Well, I strongly believe that you will never feel good about making a bad decision." What are the processes involved, and how would you choose to address them?

7. You are facilitating a support group for people going through divorce. During your initial introduction to the group members, one of the members asks you very sternly, "If you haven't been divorced yourself, how can you possibly help us?" What underlying issues are at the heart of this type of a confrontation? What are some possible responses you could make to address these underlying issues?

8. Chloe tells the group, "You know, last night I found this great group on the Internet where I can say all I want to say without interruption, unlike what usually happens in *this* group whenever I want to say something." As the leader of this group, how would you respond?

SELF-REFLECTION

1. Think back to any instances in which you felt like you were in the "hot seat." How did you react? What feelings arose for you? Did your relationship to others who were involved change as a result? Overall, did you experience a positive outcome? How might this experience affect your approach to dealing with hot-seat issues in groups that you will lead?

2. In your family of origin, how were intense emotions handled? Were they often ignored, deflected, or resolved in some significant way? Depending on how your family responded, how did this affect your past and current tendencies to respond in certain ways to intense relationship issues?

3. Can you recall a situation from your family of origin or with friends in which you suddenly became aware of an "elephant in the room" that others failed to mention? What was it like for you to be in this situation where some problem became very obvious, yet no one seemed to want to acknowledge it? How did you react at the time? Was there any long-term influence on you as a result of this experience?

4. Although you probably did not think of them at the time as experiences of "confronting your shadow," reflect back to examples from your childhood, adolescence, and adulthood when you have come face-to-face with shadow aspects of your personality. What sequence of events contributed to your shadow being revealed? How did you

react to the realization? Did you work this through emotionally all by yourself, or did you have someone you trusted with whom you could talk through your experience?

5. Of the four hot buttons of intimacy, power, competition, and control, which button are you most susceptible to having pushed? That is, which of these topics is likely to be the most difficult for you to handle without "losing your cool" or shutting down emotionally?

METHOD OF STIRRING THE POT

Stimulating Group Affect

In the group, everything that contains heightened emotion is grist for the mill. Affects in the group are sometimes intense and sometimes submerged. In situations where the group atmosphere is already intense and emotional reactivity is present, the leader will use process illumination, as covered in the last chapter, to tackle the immediacy issues. In other situations where the group atmosphere is subdued and emotional reactivity remains dormant, the leader will need a different set of stimulating intervention techniques to bring out the group dynamics.

When it comes to stimulating group affect, sometimes it is better, such as during the initial stages of group, to do less of it and to let some relationship issues stay unexposed. Other times, it is better to stimulate the group without delay. The working stage of a group is the time to do just that. Stimulating dormant emotions can lead the group to uncover things stewing under the surface. It stirs the group to aliveness when otherwise it would remain dry and bland. Of course, leaders should never leave members in a state of emotional arousal without helping them gain insight regarding the particular emotional experience. Meaning-making must follow emotion stimulation. The meanings inherent within here-and-now experiences are so rich that processing these meanings must be an integral part of group work.

This chapter continues discussing the concepts and techniques of immediacy, which is the heart of group work in its working stage. The focus of this chapter is to add another method to the repertoire of group leadership skills—the method of "stirring the pot." This chapter covers:

- When stuck, stir the pot
- Method of stirring the pot
- Stirring-the-pot techniques (I): Moving from outside to inside
- Stirring-the-pot techniques (II): Role-casting

- Process illumination techniques (IV): Making the invisible visible
- Process illumination techniques (V): Tracing members' progress

WHEN STUCK, STIR THE POT

Group members are always responding to something in the group. Emotional response is what keeps the group alive. However, some members' inner reactions may not readily be exposed. Their emotional impressions are kept inside, and their affects suppressed. Like an unstirred pot, the stuff remains stuck at the bottom. All the group needs, in this situation, is a bit of action on the part of the leader. This action is emotion stimulation. This section explains why emotion stimulation is an integral part of group work. We call the action of emotion stimulation "stirring the pot." Emotion stimulation is best used when the group slips into excessive storytelling, niceness, politeness, and cooperation to the extent of becoming sterile.

Too Nice to Be True

By nature, people have feelings and reactions toward people or things that involve them. In the group, members surely experience feelings and reactions toward one another. However, some people do not show any reactions because that might feel a bit too threatening to them. Members often come across as nice and polite—maybe too nice to be true. People in our society are trained to censor their feelings out of courtesy. Suppression makes people lifeless and renders a group lethargic. The longer the members' feelings are not talked about, the harder it becomes for them to interact with one another on a lively level. The group feels bored but does not know why.

Stuck in Content of Stories

When the group is unstructured, the total openness of the group format may make some people nervous and unconsciously choose to stay on the safe side by telling stories. Telling the there-and-then stories makes them feel more in control. However, the there-and-then focus will strip the group of any sense of immediacy. Slife (1991) indicates that any type of therapy that lacks immediacy will become sterile. A group will lack immediacy when people go on and on telling there-and-then stories. This does not mean that members should not talk about their stressful or problematic life events. Problematic life events are what lead people to the group in the first place, anyway. Disclosing there-and-then events, also called *vertical disclosure* by Leszcz (1992), is necessary beyond doubt. When the stories are told and the group members get a glimpse of the speaking members' worlds, then empathy and support can be more easily given. Time is well spent in this manner. However, if the group continues to focus on there-and-then events, immediacy issues will not have the slightest chance of being aired. The session will be stuck in the *content* of the stories, and members will soon find themselves more and more removed.

Group Collusion

One of the potential hazards in the working stage is the temptation to slide into group collusion. Group collusion involves members acting as if something does not exist. This happens when members get sidetracked from their primary goals and slip into less-than-conscious pursuits (Gladding, 1999; Shields, 1999). An example is a member behaving with excessive cooperation and agreement to gain popularity, at the expense of being truthful to his own feelings. Excessive agreement and people-pleasing behaviors represent a type of regression to self-protectiveness that distracts members from working on their primary goals.

Hesitation to take risks is the major factor leading to group collusion. Collusion is only sustained by members keeping silent in order to uphold their pretense. Pretense blocks truthful interaction, leading the group to feel sluggish. If collusion continues, any chance of newness and change, so promising in the working stage, is eliminated.

Flags of Bland Sterility

The following signs are red flags signaling that the group is becoming removed and bored and is in danger of losing its aliveness:

- Stories going on and on
- Members wriggling in their seats
- Emotions of the group members flattened
- Group interaction staying at the intellectual level
- Group hitting a wall in trying to help a member
- Interaction too polite
- The session getting stuck
- Members remaining externally focused

These signs indicate that the group members are having a hard time interacting with one another in a meaningful and authentic manner. The group is getting stagnant. When a leader sees these flags, she knows that she needs to do something to increase the sense of immediacy within the group.

Purpose of Stirring the Pot

When the leader sees any of the red flags of boredom, there are two steps she needs to take:

1. Stimulate the group to disclose their here-and-now feelings (stirring the pot)
2. Process the meanings behind these feelings (process illumination)

To stir the pot is to evoke those experiences and emotions that have been suppressed from expression. Once evoked, the group can examine these experiences and emotions. Through the method of emotion stimulation, the group moves closer to core materials. The action of stirring will make those core materials that have been stuck on the bottom begin to surface. As they surface, they can be explored, examined, challenged, and revised. This way of focusing on the group's immediacy issues "energizes group members, heightens their interest, and often evokes insightful responses" (Ferencik, 1991, p. 169).

METHOD OF STIRRING THE POT

To stir the pot is to bring the group to the immediacy of the here-and-now. The emotion stimulation and process illumination are two symbiotic tiers—they must coexist. This section provides details of this two-tiered method.

First Tier: Stimulating an I-Thou Dialogue

In the first step, the leader stimulates the group into an "I-Thou" relationship dialogue. In this conversation, members are prompted to disclose their emotions that are stuffed beneath the surface. This procedure has been called "here-and-now activation" (Yalom, 1995). We call it "stirring the pot."

The following is an example of how a leader can use here-and-now activation to bring the group into an "I-Thou" immediacy conversation. While a group member, Jim, was presenting his issue by rambling on and on about people outside the group, the group began to feel disengaged. Seeing the group becoming distant, the leader stepped in with a here-and-now activation that perked the group up and ultimately helped the members gain more self-knowledge. The leader said,

> [To the group] From what I have heard in the stories, it seems that Jim is telling us that he has difficulty expressing anger to others. I wonder, with whom in the group do you think Jim would feel safe to express his anger, and with whom in the group is he likely to suppress his anger? [first step

of here-and-now activation; leader tries to shift focus of group conversation from people outside group toward people inside group]

This intervention is likely to engender much charged discussion within the group. At this junction, it is important to move to the second tier.

Second Tier: Process Illumination

The second tier is called process illumination, a procedure we covered extensively in the last chapter. Here, in the method of stirring the pot, process illumination serves as a meaning-making procedure. Although stirring the pot can feed intensity in the group, it alone cannot propel self-transformation in members. The meanings of the emotions and of the complex dynamics between the members, leader, and group as a whole must be examined and illuminated in order for the group to grow.

This second step must follow the stimulation of group members' emotions. In this second step, the leader guides members to examine the meanings behind those intense emotions aroused in the first step. Hopefully, the illumination of the interpersonal processes will bring awareness to members regarding their interpersonal styles and their impact on others. In so doing, the group "performs a self-reflective loop and examines the here-and-now behavior that has just occurred" (Yalom, 1995, p. 130). Together, the two steps help members gain insight into their interpersonal patterns as they are manifested within the group sessions.

Many new leaders ask whether the leader can just go ahead and share what she observes of the group process, rather than ask the group about it. Our experience teaches us that it is better to let the members share their observations and make discoveries on their own. First of all, it is their own interpersonal processes that are waiting to be discovered; the leader is there simply to facilitate that process of discovery. There is no need to interpret or point out for the members what they are capable of doing themselves. Second, insight coming from members themselves is usually more powerful than that from the leader. Therefore, the leader should just focus on hosting honest communication in the group.

Take the previous case of Jim as an example. Following the leader's prompt, the group got into a heated discussion about which person in the group Jim would feel safe enough with to express his anger, and which person Jim would feel so uncomfortable with that he would suppress his anger. Many feelings and reactions were brought to the surface. Some people cheered, some were upset, and still others were defensive. At this juncture, the leader stopped the group and asked the members to look at the meanings behind their aroused emotions. The leader said,

> [To the group] Right now I sense a great deal of tension among Jim,
> Alice, Anne, and Joe. I wonder, what do you see is going on here? And

why is this happening? [second step of here-and-now activation; leader tries to illuminate process or meanings of aroused emotions]

Zig-Zagging the Spotlight: Multiple Process Illuminations

Often, the here-and-now activation spawns multiple dynamics, all of which call for process illumination. When this happens, the spotlight will be zig-zagged in multiple directions, engaging multiple process illuminations. When the spotlight zig-zags in multiple directions, multiple members' issues will be touched on. One member's issue has actually created a ripple effect on many others. It is this web of connection that makes the group dynamics so alive and engaging. Not one member in the group has a chance to stay removed and bored, because the spotlight will soon be on him if he so appears. Any interpersonal patterns are quickly picked up by the group and become the target of much examination.

Zig-Zagging the Spotlight in the Direction of Reactivity

One question often asked by new group leaders is: Among all the complex interactions within a group, in which direction should the spotlight be zig-zagged? From our observations, the spotlight of process illumination needs to be put on members who are manifesting their reactive patterns or are exhibiting intense emotions. Examples of reactive patterns are behaviors such as shutting down, defensiveness, aggression, rescuing, deflecting, flaring up, intellectualization, avoidance, excessive people-pleasing, and so on. Examples of intense emotions include, among others, anger, pain, shame, resentment, sadness, and hostility.

Intense emotional reactivity or disproportionate behavioral reaction is the marker that something crucial has been touched on. When this marker is observed, the group should seize the moment to examine what is behind the intense reaction. Zig-zagging the spotlight in the direction of emotional reactivity involves intense work. Fortunately, in the working stage, the group knows the importance of pursuing this marker in an attempt to help all the members better understand themselves. As the group takes on more autonomy in pursuing the meanings behind emotional reactivity, the leader only steps in when situations call for her interventions.

Looping Back to a Pending Member

When the spotlight zig-zags in multiple directions, engaging multiple members' interpersonal processes, the group may soon lose track of the member whose initial issue is still pending. When this happens, the leader needs to guide the group to loop back to the original member whose core issues still deserve a deeper examination. In failing to help the group loop back, the leader risks having members jump from one member's issues to another's, leaving many members' issues unresolved.

The leader must balance the zig-zagging and the looping back. New group leaders often wonder when to zig-zag and when to loop back. How much spotlight is too much? How little is too little? These questions will be answered in the following discussion.

Creating a Corrective Emotional Experience When a Hot Button Is Pushed

If there is one principle that we have learned from our own leadership experiences, it is to allow the spotlight to stay a bit longer on a member whose interpersonal issues are enacted in the here-and-now of the group—long enough that a corrective emotional experience might be possible for the member.

To create a corrective emotional experience for the member, the group has to offer the person exactly what she was deprived of in her earlier experiences and is deprived of in her current world. The group needs to do the opposite of what usually happens to the person in her world at large. Sometimes the group naturally knows how to do this, and sometimes it needs an artful nudge from the leader toward that direction. In Chapter 6, we provided several examples of how a leader can guide the group to provide healing and to restore perspective to a member. The corrective emotional experiences sometimes depend on whether the person can somehow "get it," that is, whether the person can reach a realization about how to break the vicious cycle that perpetuates his problem. The section after next, entitled "A Case in Point," provides another example of leading the group toward corrective emotional experiences.

Fluidity of the Process

Moving from emotion stimulation to process illumination, from the first tier to the second tier, with the spotlight zig-zagging at times, is a fluid process. The transition from emotion stimulation to process illumination is never cut-and-dried. Yalom (2002) states: "Effective group counseling and therapy consist of an alternating sequence: evocation and experiencing of affect followed by analysis and integration of affect" (p. 71). The alternating sequence goes back and forth, sometimes in a seamless manner, and sometimes only with the leader's help.

It is only for educational purposes that we differentiate between the two tiers, risking the possibility of making the process appear linear. In group practice, the interface between here-and-now emotion stimulation and process illumination is rather subtle. When emotional experiences and observations are shared, the former is easily mixed with the latter, and vice versa. Further, the group might be processing dynamics that happened a moment ago, and suddenly some new emotions get stirred by what is said. The newly emerged emotions also call for process illumination, which may stir still other new dynamics in the group. One cannot tell exactly when the group shifts from here-and-now experiencing to process illumination. It is a fluid process.

A Case in Point

During the check-in at the eighth session, a member, Jean, shared with the group an event that happened at work earlier in the day that made her feel as if no one cares for her. Jean had not shared very much of her life with the group, although she had given other group members a lot of support and insight. The leader asked if she would like to take some group time to explore her feelings. Jean politely declined, saying that the event was really not that important. As the nonstructured, open session continued, however, Jean indirectly related to one member, Tom, and once again mentioned her feeling of invisibility. Seeing this as an opening, the leader asked Jean,

> Jean, is there any time in the group when you feel invisible and find it difficult to fit in? [first step of here-and-now activation—moving from outside focus to inside focus]

Jean's face turned red. She obviously felt put on the spot, but she held herself together well and admitted that, yes, she often felt invisible and unimportant *in the group,* just like she had always felt in her family. The group was aroused by Jean's honesty and extended warm words to her, affirming her for her valuable contributions. This made Jean feel more connected to the group, yet some core issues were not touched. The leader took things one step further and stirred the pot by asking,

> [To the group] I wonder with whom in the group you think Jean is likely to experience a sense of invisibility, and with whom in the group Jean is more likely to feel validated and affirmed. [still first step of here-and-now activation]

The group became utterly stimulated by this question. Two members in the group admitted that they probably had made Jean feel invalidated at some point in the group, and they apologized for that. The group also pointed out that Tom and Lisa were the two whom Jean would feel supported by.

At some point, the spotlight was zig-zagged to two other members, who became the center of group discussion for a while because of their charged exchange. The group quickly moved away from Jean and on to the new dynamics at hand. Sitting quietly in her chair all the while, Jean looked like she was deep in her own thoughts, and as if she wanted to say something but could not quite say it. The group had gotten involved with the two members who had more dramatic expressions and had forgotten about the fact that Jean's issue was left unfinished. Sensing that Jean's "button of invisibility" was pushed once again, right there in the group, and that she was starting to retreat into herself, the leader got the group to *loop back* to Jean by saying,

> [To the group] I wonder what the group imagines Jean is feeling right now in the group.

The group immediately realized that they had just re-created Jean's experience of "no one really cares about me." The group reflected on that and gave feedback to Jean about how they received mixed signals from her at the beginning of the session, and simply misread her true desire. Jean opened up and said that she felt guilty taking group time and that she did not feel worthy of others' attention—and this was why she gave out mixed signals. Another member responded to Jean's sense of guilt and told her how important she was to him and that she deserved to get what she needed from the group.

Upon hearing these comments, tears flooded Jean's eyes. Something had happened inside of her. Sensing that this was a *critical point* for Jean and that she needed the group to *stay a bit longer with her feeling*, the leader asked the group,

> [To the group] Can any of you guess what Jean's tears are trying to say? And how do Jean's tears influence you? [second step of here-and-now activation; purpose is to illuminate underlying meanings of aroused emotions and, at same time, allow for possible corrective emotional experience]

The group responded affectionately to Jean, unanimously saying that they felt close to her and were very happy to see her let her emotions show because they had often wondered about her and were concerned that she had been keeping her feelings to herself. *The group's affectionate responses and warm acceptance were exactly the opposite of her earlier experience. The experience was healing and restored a sense of hope in Jean.* Jean had a *corrective emotional experience* in the group in that session. For the first time in her life, Jean felt totally free to be herself because she saw that people in the group truly cared about her and accepted her feelings and needs. For the first time in her life, she did not need to hide herself behind a façade of polite tranquility. Also *for the first time, she "got it"— she realized that she sent out mixed signals that served to defeat her own needs.* This experience became the landmark for Jean's personal growth.

STIRRING-THE-POT TECHNIQUES (I): MOVING FROM OUTSIDE TO INSIDE

This and the following sections will focus on providing more concrete techniques for stimulating group emotion. One sure way to stimulate the group into the "I-Thou" immediacy conversation is to shift the members' conversation from outside to inside. That is, members are asked to disclose reactions and feelings that they have about the people and events *within* the group, as opposed to those outside the group. Yalom (1995) calls this a "here-and-now disclosure."

Before we get into the technical details, we must emphasize the importance of timing. Stirring-the-pot techniques are best received when the group is in *the working stage*, where a high *trust* level is already established. If used prematurely, such as in forming and storming stages, these stirring-the-pot techniques can easily backfire. If used when the group is mature enough, however, they can provide an eye-opening experience for all members.

The things that people feel but often do not talk about are exactly the things that the leader wants to stimulate the group to talk about. Stirring-the-pot techniques are best used to steer the group conversation to the following immediacy issues.

Perceptions about People Inside Group

People within the group provide the most direct stimulus for members' interpersonal perceptions. Unfortunately, these perceptions get buried deep under social niceties. One effective way to stimulate the group affect is to have members talk about their perceptions of people within the group. For example, if a member, say Lisa, presents her issues surrounding her fears, the leader may do the following.

First Tier: Prompting I-Thou Immediacy Responses   In this step, the leader moves the focus of group conversation to "the people within the group" in order to heat up the immediacy. The leader may say,

> [To the group] Lisa has talked extensively about her fears of disapproval from people in her life. I wonder whether the group can guess from whom in the group Lisa is likely to anticipate disapproval. And from whom in the group is Lisa likely to feel acceptance. [first tier of here-and-now activation; purpose is to stir the pot by moving from outside focus to inside focus]

This prompt is aimed at encouraging members to share their honest perceptions with one another. Suppose a member—say, Susan—discloses that Dale would be the one within the group from whom Lisa would most likely sense disapproval. The leader could then follow up Susan's disclosure by turning the discussion over to the group:

> Thank you, Susan. [turning to the group] I wonder how the rest of the group responds to what Susan just said. Does anyone else feel the same way as Susan does? [prompt aimed at obtaining consensual validation]

Once the responses were exhausted, the leader might go further:

> [To the group] Has anyone else ever sensed disapproval from another in the group? [prompt to zig-zag the spotlight]

This technique will be likely to stir the pot. The group will be aroused and become energized. The discussion will become alive. Many people will be put on the hot spot. Some members may become defensive. Some may try to smooth things over. Some may try to reduce the intensity by changing the subject to outside events. Whatever members do, the way they respond to the stirring conversation will mirror their interpersonal patterns.

Second Tier: Process Illumination   Once the pot is stirred by the here-and-now disclosure, the meanings of these emotional experiences must be examined or processed. If a conflict is stirred by the here-and-now disclosures, the leader may say the following to examine the meanings behind the emotions of conflict:

> [To the group] Right now I sense a heavy tension in the group. I wonder, what do you see going on here? And why is this happening? [second step of here-and-now activation; purpose is to illuminate meanings of aroused emotions]

The leader may continue to explore the hidden meanings until the group gains insights into the dynamics. The leader may say,

> [To the group] Okay. And why? [more process illumination]

The leader's persistence in continuing the exploration will eventually pay off because the group members will be more likely to achieve in-depth understanding of their processes.

Zig-Zagging the Spotlight   The spotlight is likely to be zig-zagged in multiple directions when the group engages itself in process illumination. For example, once Susan had disclosed that Dale would be the one within the group from whom Lisa would most likely sense disapproval, two other members provided similar observations. At that juncture, Dale became defensive and began to rationalize his behaviors. Sensing that Dale was in direct conflict with the three members, another member, Jane, who was usually the "peacemaker" of the group, broke into the conversation and indirectly tried to diffuse the tension. It was obvious that multiple processes had emerged during the event. Not only was Dale's pattern enacted, but Jane's interpersonal pattern also had added one more layer to the dynamics. Both processes required illumination. At this point, the leader asked the group to stop, and she posed a question to the group:

> [To the group] Let's stop for a moment here. It looks like there are two important dynamics going on here. Let's talk about what you saw in Dale's reaction to the feedback, and what you saw going on with Jane just a moment ago. [multiple process illuminations]

Dealing with Reluctance   Suppose the group was unresponsive to the leader's first-tiered procedural question about from whom in the group Lisa might anticipate disapproval. Then, rather than pressing the group to respond, the leader should look at *the timing issue.* If the group is in its *early stages*, its trust level will not be high, and its reluctance to get personal will be normal. The leader should not overstimulate such a group with here-and-now activation. If the leader persists, her efforts will probably backfire. Instead, the leader should work with the member and look at the general pattern of her issue, without bringing up the immediacy issue. If, however, the group is in the *norming or working stage*, where the trust level is adequate, the unresponsiveness is a loud dynamic in itself, and the leader may go directly to process illumination. The leader might say,

> [To the group] I hear a dead silence in the room. I wonder what is going on here. What stops you from speaking for yourself? [processing reluctance of group]

The examples presented here give leaders an overview of how to use here-and-now disclosure to stimulate group affects and how to use process illumination to examine the meanings of the aroused emotions. Following are more examples of how to move from outside focus to inside focus. Because of space limitations, we cannot illustrate both tiers in each example, so only the first tier (here-and-now disclosure) is illustrated. It is important to remember that leaders must follow each stirring-the-pot technique with process illumination. Failing to do so will simply arouse group members' emotions without helping them achieve much interpersonal insight. Here are examples of how a leader might move from outside to inside focus:

> [To the group] Kim has been coming to the group for about seven meetings and has been unable to share with us. I wonder if the group can guess what is keeping Kim's personal voice locked inside herself. Who in this group do you guess she fears would ridicule her? Who does she fear would think she is strange? [first tier; use only in the working

stage, and only if followed by second tier—process illumination, a caution that applies to all of the following activation techniques]

[To the group] Kelly said that she tends to feel responsible for others' feelings. Whom in the group do you guess Kelly is most likely to feel responsible for, and whom least?

[To a specific member] Coral, you said that at times you feel anxious about being judged, particularly when a situation involves a person of authority. I wonder, who in this group would give you similar feelings of being judged?

Reactions to Incidents Inside Group

Events that happen within the group usually have a direct impact on members' reactions. To facilitate here-and-now self-disclosure, the leader may prompt members to talk about their reactions to events that occur within the group. With this technique, the leader shifts the conversation of the group from stories about outside events toward things that happen inside the group. For example:

Julie, you said that you feel exploited every time you trust someone or reveal yourself. I wonder, has there ever been a time in this group when you have experienced this feeling? [first tier]

Janet, you have claimed that people discriminate against you in your school. I wonder, has there been a time or an incident in this group when you felt rejected or ignored? [first tier]

Feelings toward Group Members

To get the group more emotionally involved, the leader can ask the group to state *how they feel toward a specific member* at a critical point. Here is an example:

[To the group] I wonder, after listening to Mark's experiences, how *you* feel toward Mark at this moment. I am curious not about how you relate to Mark, but how you *feel* toward Mark.

The purpose of this intervention is not to draw out empathy from members. If the group members err by focusing on reflecting the client's feelings, the leader needs to gently guide them to talk about their own feelings toward the receiver. For example:

Mary, thank you for acknowledging Mark's feeling. Right now, I am most interested in hearing how *you* feel *toward* Mark, instead of how you think Mark is feeling. Would you talk to Mark about how you feel toward him at this moment?

Feelings about the Group

Members usually have strong feelings toward their group. But these strong feelings are seldom talked about because they often are the same feelings members harbored toward their first group—their family of origin. Asking members to talk about their feelings toward the particular group they are presently part of can bring strong emotions to the forefront for exploration. To do this, the leader moves the group discussion from outside events to feelings toward the group itself. For example:

> Mary, you have been talking about trust issues in a very general way. Would you tell us what it is like to talk about yourself here in the group? What trust issues do you have with people in this group? [first tier]

> [To the group] You know, I am aware that things are going in a circle right now. Even though Brenda said that she just wants support from the group, the group keeps going back again and again to try and solve her problem. [turning to Brenda] Brenda, how do you feel about the group regarding this behavior? [first tier]

Moving from Abstract to Specific

When talking about difficult issues in life, people tend to talk in abstract terms so they do not expose themselves so much. Talking abstractly is a type of defense against emotional engagement. Normally the group will not point out when someone is doing this and will allow the person to remain evasive. When a leader sees this happening, he may steer the member to talk about *specifics* that are related to the person's experience within the group. The leader may say,

> Janet, I feel a bit lost when you talk about the issue in such an abstract manner. Do you think you might be able to give us a specific example that happened in the group to illustrate your point?

Getting Members to Set Here-and-Now Session Goals

A less obvious way to heat up the group is to have members set here-and-now session goals. After the group passes the early stages, people may start to feel comfortable in stating their reactions to certain members and how they would like to improve their responses during a given session. Ferencik (1991) pointed out, "External issues must first be transformed into the here-and-now in order for the group to work on them" (p. 170). Kivlighan and Jauquet (1990) found that, as a process group matures, members start to set increasingly more interpersonal and here-and-now session goals. Session goals are the behaviors that people want to practice during a given session. Session goals that are overly general and not here-and-now oriented may look like the following:

- I would like to practice speaking up more.
- In this session, I would like to practice becoming more honest in my conversations with people.
- In this session, I would like to practice being more assertive.
- I would like to practice speaking more of how I feel.

These goals are good, but they lack here-and-now interpersonal specificity. A leader can get members to set session goals that are more here-and-now focused by prompting:

> Is there any specific person in the group to whom you need to practice speaking up more?
>
> What kinds of feelings have you had in this group that you would like to speak up more about?
>
> Has there been any event in the group that has made you realize that you need to start speaking more honestly?
>
> With whom in this group would you like to become more assertive?

If members are ready to "take the bull by the horns," they may say something to bring the emotions of the group to their height. For example, members might say something like:

- Well, I would like to practice expressing myself more openly toward Kelly [another member] regarding my feeling that I am unheard whenever I try to tell her how her behaviors affect me in the group.
- It's important for me to practice telling my own inner truth because many times I only say positive things to appease other members, even when I feel the opposite. In this session, I would like to work on honestly expressing my feelings when I feel uncomfortable or when I disagree with something that happens in the group.

STIRRING-THE-POT TECHNIQUES (II): ROLE-CASTING

The second way to stimulate the group into here-and-now experiencing is through a technique called "role-casting." This is another sure way to stir the pot. Not only does it stimulate the group members' emotions, but it also helps members see how they come across to others and how their behaviors affect their relationships with others. It contains both the first and the second tiers and, therefore, acts like a double-edged sword.

Hypothetical Experiencing

The first role-casting technique is one where the leader has members take on hypothetical roles with a specific member. In so doing, the leader creates a hypothetical circumstance in which members feel safe to talk about reactions that are normally difficult or awkward to talk about. The leader must first be mindful of his own internal processing before he can initiate this hypothetical experiencing exercise.

Leader's Internal Processing   When listening to members' conversations, the leader pays attention to his internal reactions to each member. If he is really scanning for the parallel process, he may start to notice his own internal reactions and think to himself, "Well, am I the only one who feels ticked off by this person's domineering style? How often does he steal the floor from others with no consideration of others' needs to talk? How is this domineering style related to his problems in his interpersonal relationships?"

After the leader finds himself reacting in this way, he should observe how the rest of the group members react to this specific member's style. As he focuses his observation on the other group members' reactions, he may think to himself, "Hmm . . . so how is the group reacting to this person's domineering style of talking? Do they see the connection to the problems he has in his relationships outside the group? Do the group members feel put off by this kind of behavior? Do they feel frustrated or resentful, but lack the opportunity to express it?"

Initiating Hypothetical Experiencing   Having observed the group's reactions, the leader is now ready for the next step—initiating the hypothetical experiencing exercise. This involves facilitating the group members to speak directly to a specific member about their firsthand experiences of him through the disguise of the hypothetical scenario. The examples in this section illustrate how to complete a hypothetical experiencing intervention with a sequence of leader initiations. The use of *if* in each of the examples is part of the design of this technique.

Here is one example of the role-casting technique. The leader may say,

> [To the group] Dale has expressed that he is having many problems in relationships at work and at home. Maybe the group can help Dale gain fresh perspectives by telling him how you would feel *if* you were to spend 24 hours with Dale. What would you be saying to yourself at the end of the 24 hours? [first tier of stirring the pot; using role-casting to stimulate the group]

The leader could have simply asked the group to give Dale feedback by using the technique detailed in Chapter 8, such as by saying (to the group):

"All of you have known Dale for a few weeks. I wonder, through your experiences in the group, what do you know about Dale that he might not know about himself?" This type of feedback-giving might still be helpful in the working stage, but it lacks the subtlety and playfulness of the role-casting technique.

The hypothetical experiencing technique has the capacity to permit people to speak more honestly about their perceptions of one another because members are put into a playful and hypothetical role, and *they can talk about their firsthand experience with a member through the disguise of the role.* They feel safe doing that. Although it is playful, the discussion can also become heated. Such heat will bring many previously unspoken perceptions out onto the table, helping members become aware of their interpersonal characteristics. After perceptions are shared, the leader may try to connect what goes on in the group with what goes on in the outside world. The leader may say,

> Dale, I wonder if there might be people in your life who feel the same way as the group members feel toward you—that is, who respect your intelligence and desire to help people, but who sense your overfunctioning and misinterpret your fear of looking inadequate as being controlling? [second tier of stirring the pot; using process illumination to elucidate parallel process]

Another example of hypothetical experiencing in sequence:

> [To the group] Marcia has expressed that she experiences a great deal of stress in relationships with men in her life. To help her see things in a new light, I would like the group to tell Marcia how you would feel *if* you were to go out on a date with Marcia. What would you say to yourself after the date? [stirring the pot using role-casting]

> Marcia, perhaps there are people in your life who feel the same way as the group members feel toward you—that is, who are attracted to you and want to get close to you, but who sense your mistrust and aloofness and therefore feel pushed away by your fear of closeness. [process illumination—illuminating parallel process]

Following are more examples of the hypothetical drama technique. Each example would need to be followed up with process illumination to make the exercise complete:

> [To the group] *If* you were to have a conflict with Amy, what do you imagine would be your experience?

> [To the group] It is now 6:00, and we still have half an hour left. I wonder, *if* each of you imagine that it's already 6:30 and you are on your way home, what would you be feeling about group today?

Grading

In this method, the leader prompts members to reveal their perceptions about themselves and others through a role-casting technique called "grading." To proceed, the leader might say,

> Bob, *if* you were to grade the work done in this group, what grade do you think you would deserve for your work, and what grade would each of the other individuals in the group get, and why? [Use this technique only in the working stage, and only if the leader can follow it up with group processing.]

The purpose of this technique is not to grade people, but to provoke a member to disclose his perceptions of himself and others. The disclosure of his "I-Thou" interpersonal perceptions will stir up all sorts of reactions, and the members can explore why they feel as they do. This type of discussion can bring a lot of awareness to the group members.

Cases in Point

Case One: Mary   Mary stated that she had been plagued by fear of abandonment and isolation in her life. These fears seemed to have their roots in her experiences with her alcoholic father, who was extremely depressed and had attempted suicide three times. Mary said that her temperament was very much like her father's, and she worried about repeating his pattern. Mary revealed that her father used to hit her mother. As she continued to unfold her stories, Mary began to see a parallel pattern emerged in her own marriage. Her ex-husband drank a lot, and that had chased her around the house with the intent to hit her, and had verbally abuse her. Thankfully, Mary recognized the signs and got out of the marriage. Yet, she was haunted by grief because her ex-husband and his new wife were living in the house that Mary and her ex still owned together. This reality was made even more painful by the fact that her ex had adopted the child of his new wife. This was a slap in Mary's face because she had suffered four miscarriages while she was married to him. She felt a lot of loss due to these experiences. Mary worried about not being desirable as a woman due to her difficulty in having babies. She was afraid that she would be excluded from happiness and would live in loneliness. As Mary talked, the leader sensed that Mary's sense of inadequacy for not being able to have children had distorted her view about her self-worth as a woman. She had been so inundated with her recent struggles that she had lost sight of her true qualities. Although group members tried to give her different perspectives, she seemed to take no refuge in their words and examples. At this moment, the leader initiated a hypothetical experiencing intervention:

> [To the group] If you went out on a date with Mary and you had just come home from the date, what kinds of thoughts or reflections might you have about the date with Mary?

Everyone in the group had extremely positive things to say about Mary. They said she was funny, attractive, intelligent, insightful, considerate, witty, a good dancer, and so on. Every member stated that he or she would want to see Mary again. This role-casting exercise made Mary laugh and forced her, in a good way, to listen to a description of the many assets that she had forgotten she had.

After the session, Mary wrote the following in her reflective journal about the influence of the experience:

> I must admit that the exercise on "how would you feel if you just came back from a date with Mary" was pretty interesting and strange to hear at the same time. It felt weird hearing members say such nice things about me. Perhaps the one comment that left me thinking the most was Keith's. I recall him repeating to me that there were a lot of good men out there, like him, who would appreciate a good woman. It seemed to me as if it were a hidden message somehow because he repeated it as if trying to tell me something. This group has shown me that I have great qualities that I wasn't aware were so visible to others. I wasn't aware that my presence would come across to other people and allow them to say such wonderful things about me even though they have just known me for a short time. It is so heartwarming! It makes me feel I am okay as a person, even though I have felt so miserable in my life. I really appreciate learning about this new perspective of myself.

Case Two: Dianne   Dianne had been a difficult person for the group to get along with. People had been feeling on edge with her, yet did not know what to do with their feelings. At the seventh session, Dianne presented her difficulty in her relationships at home and at work. After the group members expressed their empathy, the leader stirred the pot by using the hypothetical experiencing technique:

> [To the group] *If* you were to spend 24 hours with Dianne, when the day was over and you were back at home, what thoughts might you have of your experience with Dianne?

The group responded to this question with honest disclosure about their likely reactions according to their firsthand experiences with Dianne within the group. Some process comments were made to link what happened inside the group with Dianne's relationships outside the group. It was a powerful session for the group, and especially for Dianne. After some reflection, Dianne wrote in her journal:

> I have just arrived home from the group after probably one of the most "truth-telling moments" in my life. I have been struggling with my issues of judgment and anger for a very long time. I have been very angry at the world, family, friends, and coworkers who never seem to live up to my standards of what it means to be a moral humane person. The group process tonight has changed me forever. I received consistent feedback from seven members—so consistent that I couldn't easily dismiss it. The essence of the feedback is that it wouldn't be easy to spend 24 hours with me! When Linda told me that she would feel a competitive edge with me, something penetrated the hard shell of my anger. It brought me back to the pattern I had with my siblings in my childhood. It was painful for me to realize how this pattern still haunts my life. What is paradoxical about tonight's session is that I have never felt more loved and respected. Everyone took a risk to help me see the reality of myself as what it is and to help me grow to my full potential. There wasn't any bullshit, and that is what I found most refreshing. Compassionate honesty is the most disarming dynamic in the world.

PROCESS ILLUMINATION TECHNIQUES (IV): MAKING THE INVISIBLE VISIBLE

The previous chapter offered many techniques for illuminating the elusive group process. This and the next section will provide additional techniques for process illumination. These techniques are best used following emotion stimulation. Failing to go to process illumination after emotion stimulation is a frequent mistake that leaders make. Another mistake that new leaders make is jumping into process illumination too quickly, before the group even has an opportunity to fully experience their emotions. By moving to process illumination too soon, the emotional intensity of the here-and-now is lost. Both of these extremes are to be avoided.

Characteristic Interpersonal Styles Reproduced

Many people have blind spots when it comes to their interpersonal styles, but however blind members are to these processes, sooner or later they will expose their characteristic interpersonal styles because group communication happens primarily in the process level. Leszcz (1992) states: "As initial anxiety and social politeness diminish, the group becomes a social microcosm and interpersonal laboratory in which members behave and interact, as they typically do in their outside world, reproducing their characteristic maladaptive interpersonal style" (p. 50). For example, the way in which one member questions another is itself a meaningful behavior because it illustrates just how this member interacts with others in her everyday life. Leszcz (1992) also states: "[T]he patient who resists engagement, elaborates a range of defenses against intimacy, or challenges the group's working is indeed much more actively involved in the group than the compliant patient, who quietly keeps out of the group's life. In the latter situation, the dynamic of compliance or emotional surrender to the object becomes still a here-and-now behavior that needs to be addressed in and of itself" (p. 50).

Through interaction with one another, each member's characteristic reactivity to interpersonal stimuli is exposed. Critical interpersonal issues, such as intimacy, conflict, power, and belonging, faithfully emerge. These characteristic interpersonal styles, maladaptive or not, are often reproduced in the here-and-now context of the group. If paid attention to, they become the raw material from which self-discovery and self-transformation can be derived.

Fostering a Sense of Psychological Visibility

It is not just maladaptive patterns that are the target of self-discovery in the group, but also the deepest, unexpressed, and hidden visions of who we are that have never been recognized by others. When these hidden traits in ourselves are accurately perceived, we feel psychologically visible. We have a sense of finally being seen by others. This sense of psychological visibility can heal many of our developmental problems, insecurities, and inadequacies in relationships. To heal is to make contact with those qualities in our personalities and psyches that generally have not been acknowledged or accepted. We discussed this healing effect in Chapter 9.

Process illumination has the healing effect of making people feel psychologically visible because it allows members to hear about their unrecognized capabilities, latent potentialities, and character traits that have never before surfaced to the level of explicit recognition. To steer process illumination toward this level, the leader may use the following questions:

> [To the group] It would be especially helpful if the group can tell Peter something you see in him that Peter probably doesn't already see in himself. [second tier]
>
> [To the group] I wonder what the group knows about Mary that she might not know about herself. [second tier]
>
> [To the group] I sense that members are experiencing a lot of emotions related to Shelly at this moment. It will be most helpful to Shelly and

the group if any of you can try out a sentence with Shelly, like "Shelly, when you . . ., I feel. . . . [second tier]

A reflective journal entry from a group member named Kathy demonstrates how group processing at this level can bring about a sense of being psychologically visible:

This group session was incredibly different for me because I was in the "hot seat." I was very much in the present, in the here-and-now. No more an observer. This was very powerful for me. I didn't know what that felt like until now. I had no idea what would happen next, how I would feel, what would be said to me. There was only the present moment for me. This felt both frightening and freeing. I appreciated Mike's feedback especially. He told me that my lack of disclosure to both him and the group about my life left him feeling disconnected to me because there was nothing to connect to. I could see how he was right. I could see how I protected myself from being hurt by not allowing people into my experience. Although this leaves me feeling safer in some ways, it has also left me feeling separate. His feedback allowed me to see into a behavior that I use to reinforce my sense of disconnection. It gave me insight about what I can do to change my sense of disconnection in my life.

Another powerful moment for me in the group was when Sue reflected that I give to the group but don't ask anything of the group. I felt awakened in hearing it. When the leader followed it by asking me if there was one thing I would request from the group, I actually didn't trust that my needs would be fulfilled. But when the group actually tried to meet my request of being appreciated just for my being, rather than my doing good stuff, I was very touched. All of a sudden, I had hope. This little girl inside me, who has always felt unworthy or ashamed of herself and feared that others will see and abandon her, felt a glimmer of being loved just because she exists. I realized that I don't have to do anything to be valued by others; just my presence is enough—enough to make people desire a chance to get to know me further. Still now as I write this, I find tears welling up in my eyes out of a sense of awe and grace. I never thought people would feel that way about me. This group sharing allowed me to see myself in a way I never have before. The group session had a great healing impact not only on my interpersonal relationship patterns but also on my intrapersonal patterns as well.

Impact Disclosure

Impact disclosure, as a type of interpersonal feedback, is a special technique of process illumination. Kiesler and Van Denburg (1993) assert: "The most essential intervention in interpersonal communication therapy occurs when therapists provide meta-communicative feedback that labels the interpersonal impacts they thematically experience" (p. 5). Metacommunication feedback is similar to impact disclosure. In impact disclosure, according to Kiesler (1988), leaders reveal their inner, covert reactions—such as feelings, thoughts, fantasies, and action tendencies— that are directly evoked by the members' recurrent behavioral styles. In short, metacommunication feedback is telling the client the impact his interpersonal style has on the leader. This metacommunication feedback serves as a powerful tool for process illumination.

To be able to deliver metacommunication feedback, the leader needs to be in close touch with his own inner reactions and the factors that evoke them. When he notices two cues emerging in therapy, it is an indication for him to use impact disclosure. Here are the two cues: (1) There is a consistency in his reaction to a specific member who has a repetitive pattern, and (2) the pattern of the specific member's style inside the group *parallels* that outside the group. When this happens, the leader must disengage from these inner reactions and talk directly to the member about his perceptions.

Impact disclosure is most effective when it *links here-and-now behaviors to those in the outside world.* If done well, it can help the member see how people inside the group have the same gut reactions to her as those who live in her world. The more the leader can make the member see her interpersonal pull, the more the member will come to understand why her interpersonal world has been shaped in its characteristic way. To be productive, this direct feedback must be provided in a manner that is both confrontational as well as supportive and protective of the member's self-esteem.

In this technique, the leader comments on his own perceptions and links them to those of people outside the group. The leader makes comments like the following:

> Julie, I can often see you wanting to be close to others and offering to help others, but there are other times, like today, when I see you as aloof, almost critical of others. What do you know about this part of you? And how does it serve you or do you a disservice? [second tier— process illumination]

> Mark, you told us about the pain you experienced being abused during your childhood. I was struck by the lack of emotion in your face and the flat tone in your voice when you told us the story. I wonder how the way you tell your story might create distance between you and others. [second tier]

> Wayne, you seem to react very strongly whenever the women in our group talk about their relationship issues. Something seems to get under your skin deeply whenever the men-women issues come up. Frankly, I have been waiting for you to raise the issue yourself. I wonder, do you know about this reaction on your part? Do you see how it might push women in general away? [second tier]

Process Illumination Techniques (V): Tracing Members' Progress

Another way to maximize clients' self-discovery is to trace what types of interpersonal processes have acted as mechanisms for client change. To notice clients' change processes, the leader first needs to remember what the members' original issues and goals were and track how these issues and goals shift: Have they shifted toward something that is more interpersonal in nature? If they have, this kind of shift itself is progress. The leader should also strive to acknowledge every little step that members take to reach their goals. When the leader notices any change in members' behaviors within the group, he should make sure to comment on that and explore those group processes that led to the change. If change is slow to come by for some members, then the leader should explore what it would take for change to happen. Keeping track of all members' development and progress requires the leader to have the mind-set of a historian. Here are some examples of what a leader might say to trace the types of interpersonal processes that can help bring client change:

> Rita, in the past it has not been safe enough for you to share this, but today you chose to do so. I wonder what happened in the group or your feelings toward the group today that allowed you to do this.

> Julie, you stated that your goal in joining the group was to be able to express yourself to your husband in a way that is more congruent with what goes on inside of yourself. I wonder, is there anything about the way you relate to others in the group that you think you should change in order to reach your goal?

> Jane, you gave the group permission in the first session to offer feedback to you when they observe combative behavior. You asked this of the group to help you reach your stated goal of finding peace. Has that permission been changed? If not, what areas would you be willing to allow the group to address?

Scenarios for Your Practice

1. Rocky admits to the group that he greatly fears what other people think of him, but that he cannot bring himself to ask others what they think for fear of being devastated by their response. Upon hearing this, the group is totally frozen. It is stuck. What are some options for handling this situation?

2. In the sixth session of an interpersonal learning group, Wayne shares that: "At my work evaluation meeting today, my boss told me that

I'm 'not relating well with coworkers.' I don't know what he's talking about. I'm always kidding the people I work with, and I always have a good laugh. Maybe it's some kind of political correctness thing. I just don't know how to figure it out." As a group leader, how might you respond to this statement?

3. Rolf states to the group, "You know, I tried out several of the suggestions that this group gave to me last week in dealing with my boss to show him that I can demonstrate personal initiative. He didn't like the ideas at all, and he looked at me like I was way out of line. What should I do now?" Take a look at the possible interpersonal dynamics involved, both at the individual and group level. How might you choose to address the issue with the group?

4. As the fourth session of a personal growth group begins, the energy seems low. Members are sharing what they would like to share for that session, but no one sounds especially invested in the issues they are raising. Jill continues the round of discussion by intellectualizing, "I am just learning so many tips on how to deal with situations here. I get to hear what others have faced, and learn how to handle those situations. I'm sure it will save me from a lot of trouble someday. It's so good for me to just observe in here." What do you sense is happening in this group? What does Jill's comment suggest about the depth of involvement that group members are experiencing with one another? Give an example of an intervening statement or question that you might make to move the group more fully into the here-and-now.

5. Gary and Cathy have spent about 10 minutes in the group discussing the pros and cons of whether office workers should bring donuts to work in the mornings. You notice that other group members have been shifting around in their seats for awhile, but not offering any significant verbal input. What might this situation suggest to you about the current state of the group dynamics? How might you intervene in order to change the level of interaction?

6. Zinnia reflects to the group: "I usually feel overlooked for my contributions at the agency where I work. I put a lot of work into a grant application where we were able to get a sizable amount of funding. We are now able to offer some very good programs as a result. Yet, no one took notice. It was just like everyone thought it was no big deal. Others seem to get a lot of recognition for what they do, but what I do is not often acknowledged. I guess it's not really that important. . . ." How might you choose to address this issue in terms of the here-and-now of the group? How might you encourage group interaction around this issue?

7. Bart responds to Zinnia's lead (see question 6). He says, "At least you're not getting negative attention. It seems like for me, I only hear about the bad things I do. It's always been that way, going back to my childhood; my older and younger sisters always got cheered for their accomplishments, and I was some kind of 'bad boy.' Maybe I should just carry out my fantasy of getting a motorcycle and hitting the road." What options do you have for responding to Bart? If his statement came right after Zinnia's in a group, should you ignore his statement and turn attention back to Zinnia? Alternatively, might there be some way for you to bring the issues together so the group could address both at once?

SELF-REFLECTION

1. What are some keys to help you attend to potential hot-seat issues? In terms of your own emotional self-awareness, what helps you to sort out what could be an important aspect to explore versus something that is truly your "own stuff" and not especially relevant to a particular group at the time?
2. What emotional/physical cues happen for you to tell you when an issue is dull or unimportant? What personal emotional/physical cues tell you that an issue could be especially poignant and worth further exploration?
3. Consider recent relationships in which you've been involved and the development of trust and understanding within those relationships. What types of incidents occurred to help move those relationships toward a deeper level? Can you recall some specific incidents, what happened, and what occurred afterward? Are there any lessons that you can take from this experience to apply toward working with group members struggling to improve their relationships?
4. What are some of your primary concerns about "stirring the pot" within a group? How might you deal with each of these concerns?
5. Consider key "I-Thou" relationships that have flowered in your life. What aspects tell you that these relationships are especially alive? Are these factors that you can actively promote among group members?
6. How do you feel about working in a "zig-zag" fashion within a group? If you prefer to work from a more linear or analytical perspective, how might you balance that approach with working in a zig-zag fashion with a group?

SKILLS OF TERMINATION

Completing the Cycle

Closing is a crucial stage of life development for a group. Ending is part of living. Ending evokes both a sense of accomplishment and a feeling of loss (Lacoursiere, 1980). If the group dwells on the issue of loss without being given a sense of hope, the therapeutic effect of the group dissipates. Ending does not need to be all about grief. To end a group well, leaders must continue to focus on instilling in members a sense of hope and competency, as well as a sense of direction and self-identity.

This chapter aims to put forth leadership skills that facilitate closure in the group so that the growth of members may continue after termination. It covers:

- Leadership and the termination stage
- Seven principles of termination
- Skills for ending the group
- Evaluation of the group experience
- Examples of looking-back letters

LEADERSHIP AND THE TERMINATION STAGE

The Termination Stage

The characteristics of the termination stage in a group are similar to those of the golden age in a person's life. Ridden throughout is a theme of loss and grief. A lot of feelings are triggered by the ending of the therapeutic relationship. Endings can be filled with sadness. Although the entire group experience may feel like a small life lived with others who have become significant in one's life, its ending may feel like a big loss. When sensing the ending approaching, some members start to feel a sense of separation anxiety. Sara, who struggled with reclaiming her own voice, wrote in her reflective journal: "I feel almost panicked that the group is almost at its end. I want to learn as much as I can before our group ends." Given these charged feelings that ending can evoke, the leader is wise to explore thoughts and feelings that members are experiencing as the group moves toward a conclusion.

Birth of New Opportunities

The termination stage presents an opportunity to look back. It gives people a chance to reflect and acknowledge the interpersonal learning that has occurred in the group and to explore ways that learning may be put to use and continue in the future. If handled well, the ending can also be the birth of new opportunities, as the interpersonal learning can be applied to encounters with people in the future. Like a renewal of life, this transition enables members to approach old and new relationships with heightened levels of awareness. As Mary wrote in her journal:

> As group gets closer to an end, I feel that I will really miss the group, its process, and the feedback given from all members. This group has shown me so much about people and their core selves by just observing how we all interact with one another at any given moment. I have become aware of things about me that have manifested themselves in the group. One thing I am becoming aware of is my defensiveness in interpersonal conflict. When Anna accused me of being in a clique, I reacted very defensively. I know that I often get this way whenever I am criticized. I have become aware that this defensiveness doesn't help solve any sort of conflict. I am now more cognizant of how I respond to situations where my button is pushed.

A Zen Story

The termination of a group experience is analogous to the Zen story of a man being chased by a hungry tiger (Tophoff, 2000). In running faster than he ever thought possible, the man is just managing to keep ahead of the tiger when he comes to a chasm in the earth. Without thinking, the man jumps. As he is going over the edge, he sees another hungry tiger waiting at the bottom of the cliff. Halfway down the cliff, the falling man manages to grasp a root that is sticking out. As he gathers his breath, the man feels safe for a moment, just out of range of the tiger on the top of the cliff, and well above the other tiger below. Then he notices that a big rat has come along and is beginning to gnaw on the very root that is saving his life. The man, however, also notices a beautiful red, ripe strawberry on the side of the cliff. He takes the strawberry and puts it in his mouth—and it tastes so wonderful!

As a group ends, members must deal with hungry tigers, which represent the loss of the group, and with the gnawing rat, which represents their unknown personal futures. Yet, amidst such grief is the delicious strawberry: reflection on members' accomplishments and hopes for the future.

The Cycle of Life

Indigenous peoples closely connected with nature are often more aware of the cyclic nature of things than those of us who live an urbanized life. Spring comes with fresh growth, but is soon supplanted by the heat of summer, then the coolness of fall, and eventually the starkness of winter. The sequence of change can induce a terror of impermanence in us if we do not recognize, as the indigenous people do, that things continue to turn around. Life turns and cycles. The same can be said of the life of groups. The relationships in group flower ever so slowly, then the petals are lost, and the flower is no more. Yet, seeds know how to find their places under the soil and, in due time, will grow into many new and sometimes even more colorful flowers. The ending of a group contains many seeds of new beginnings.

SEVEN PRINCIPLES OF TERMINATION

Before discussing the skills of termination, we will examine seven principles of termination that leaders should keep in mind.

Giving Advance Warning

The first principle of termination is to give advance warning. To end well is one of life's many lessons. To end a group well, therapists must work to bring about a sense of closure. The first principle of termination, therefore, is to give advance warning. Advance warning can prepare people for anticipated loss. It gets members ready emotionally and propels them to try to finish whatever business is still left before the group ends (S. R. Rose, 1989). Special attention is given to difficult issues that have arisen but have not been worked through (Keyton, 1993) because, if left unaddressed, these issues may create emotional baggage for members to carry forward into future relationships.

Advance warning is especially important for brief therapy groups, including those that meet under the restrictions imposed by managed care. The briefer the group, the more important it is that group members be forewarned about time limitations throughout the life of the group (Spitz, 1996). Members of short-term groups tend to have a heightened sense of cohesion, as compared to groups that meet over a longer duration. This intense sense of cohesion may trigger a heightened sense of loss when it comes to termination. In short-term groups, members are more likely to have unfinished business, since these groups are usually established with a specific focus, whereas long-term groups tend to afford members time to deal with matters more completely. This aspect of unfinished business is one area to address carefully in the final sessions.

Acknowledging the Polarity of Feelings

The second principle of termination is to acknowledge the polarity of feelings about termination. Most human experiences stir an array of feelings in us. This is especially the case when experiences involve ending relationships. At one end of the spectrum is a sense of relief; at the other end is a sense of loss. The sense of loss in termination often centers around a lament that little opportunity is now left to let others know about us, to stretch ourselves in this intense way, to give, to connect, and to discover. This polarity of feelings must be processed.

From a Mayan perspective, Prechtel (1997) sees grief and celebration as being closely connected. He states, "When you are praising the thing you lost, it is called grief. When you are grieving the thing you had, it is called praise." In his view, praise cannot exist without grief, and grief cannot exist without praise. He sees depression as a manifestation of the inability to praise the things one has lost. As humans, we often experience life events from both sides of a polarity. As Prechtel reflects, "the ability to laugh and the ability to cry often live in the same house."

Learning to talk about and accept the polarity of feelings evoked by closure can help us embrace life's complexities on their own terms. It also opens the door to continued growth, as we are better able to explore the rich meanings behind both the yin and the yang of life's drama.

Overcoming the Difficulty of Saying Good-Bye

The third principle of termination is to facilitate members in saying good-bye. Saying good-bye is a hard thing for many people. Most people simply avoid it. It is no wonder many clients in individual counseling are just "no shows" when it comes to the termination session. This difficulty with saying good-bye is why in our society we have the "farewell-party syndrome" where the pain of closure is avoided at all costs. When friends move away, we often give them a farewell party to say good-bye. The good-bye, however, is not fully said, since most farewell parties fall prey to a focus on food and light-hearted socialization. Little is said or done to bring closure to deeply felt feelings, meanings, or unfinished business between people.

Avoiding saying good-bye can create numerous unresolved feelings or issues—thus the term *farewell-party syndrome.*

The difficulty of saying good-bye may propel members either to overly focus on a sense of loss or to avoid dealing with their grief feelings entirely. They also may neglect to focus on what they have accomplished. When the time of termination looms large, members may back off from emotional investment or significant work in the group (Lacoursiere, 1980). One of the principles of termination, therefore, is to enable members to say good-bye in meaningful ways so that the interpersonal learning from the group is put into practice.

Setting Goals for the Final Session

The fourth principle of termination is to set goals for the final session. Given the difficulty of ending, it is important to set goals for the final session so as to channel group energy into productive action. Spitz (1996) identifies three goals for the final session: (1) to assess the overall therapeutic experience on an individual and group level; (2) to examine to what degree goals were reached; and (3) to complete the group experience in a positive frame of mind. Resonating with Spitz, we see the termination of a group as a type of "graduation." This view conveys a sense of accomplishment, empowerment, and hope for the future. Later in this chapter we will provide ways of planning for the termination session that resonate with the three goals specified by Spitz.

Transferring from Inside Out

The fifth principle of termination is to ensure that members can transfer what they have learned inside the group to life outside the group. Group is effective only if it is an initiation into the fulfillment of the interpersonal world. Within regular group sessions, members have been stretched in their internal and external sense of awareness. What is crucial now is to make sure that what members have learned inside the group is transferable to settings outside the group. The learning must take root "inside out."

There are two stages of transferring in group: one occurs throughout the group life, and the other after termination.

Transferring throughout the Group Life   Throughout the entire course of group life, members are encouraged to appropriately test out new behaviors in the outside world. During the check-in at the beginning of each session, members are asked to share what they have been doing to transfer their learning to their lives at large. In opening the session, the leader often says,

Before we start our session, let's do a quick check-in. Last week, several of you shared difficulties that you've experienced in your lives, and you were able to gain insights into these difficulties in the group session. I noticed that some of you have tried out some new approaches in this group for handling difficult issues. I'm wondering whether anyone here has been able to test out some new approaches in your life. If so, I hope that you will share with the group how those approaches have worked for you.

The regular check-in affords members ongoing support and an option of reporting back to the group on the outcome of their efforts outside group. One member commented about this transferring in her reflective journal:

Each week as members do the check-in, they share the growth and change they experienced outside the group based on the work they did within the group. This was most evident in our last session. I noticed that members are learning to be true to themselves in their own lives. This is truly exciting for me to watch. Initially I was doubtful as to whether our group sessions could bring about change to our outside lives, but as the time passes, I come to see that as long as a member is willing to try and change, change is possible!

Transferring after Termination   After termination, group members will no longer have their fellow members as supporters to help them refine their new behaviors, but instead must find other ways of continuing their efforts. The final session, therefore, marks a time when members can be reminded of the skills they have developed within the group and of how to continue to exercise those skills once the group has ended.

Skills transferable to outside life after termination include: the ability to emotionally connect with others in order to give and receive support; the ability to recognize and assert one's own needs within a situation; the ability to manage and work through conflict; the ability to take reasonable interpersonal risks in order to develop relationships; the ability to communicate more clearly and truthfully; the ability to offer and invite meaningful feedback; and the ability to use journaling or other means of promoting a healthy inner dialogue in order to identify important aspects of one's experience.

It is often beneficial if group leaders can offer a follow-up session within six months to one year after a group has been completed. Feedback from such a follow-up session can provide valuable information as to how well former group members have been able to transfer and implement what they learned. As suggested later in this chapter, one relatively non-intrusive way of checking out members' continual growth is with a brief written survey.

Life-Review Therapy and Looking-Back Letters

The sixth principle of termination is to make a good "life review" of the entire group life. In counseling elderly people, therapists often use life-review therapy to help them look back on their lives, remember their accomplishments, and tell their stories. This life-review experience often restores an elderly person's self-identity, which is so easily lost in the life of retirement and in the loss of health, friends, and purpose in life. Life-review therapy can be readily applied to the group at termination.

In applying life-review therapy to group termination, the leader may ask group members, before the end of group, to write to themselves a "looking-back letter." (Samples can be found at the end of this chapter and in "Samples of Looking-Back Letters" on the book's Web site—see Preface for URL.) In this letter, members write about their original issues and goals, how their goals changed during the course of the group, what they learned about themselves, what they changed, the significant events in the group that propelled their self-discovery or the "aha" experience, and what the group has meant to them. There is something special about letter-writing. Letters invite people to write in a personal and candid manner. In letters, an authentic writer's voice comes through (Tubman, Montgomery, & Wagner, 2001).

When group members come to the last session, the leader can ask them to freely share the feelings that came to them when they were writing their looking-back letters, and the major points in their letters if they so choose. After members share, the group can freely interact. This usually creates a warm and humorous atmosphere. Laughter, tears, and hugs may happen as a result of this sharing. When these do happen, they are very therapeutic. It is particularly meaningful for the group members to hear what they have meant to one another.

Use of Appreciative Inquiry

The seventh and last principle of termination puts a cap on all those that have been previously addressed. This principle is called "appreciative inquiry" (Hammond, 1996) and is similar to the technique of "positive reframing" often used in strategic therapy. Using this principle, the leader heeds the kind of language she uses in putting clients' experiences together. Because the kinds of questions asked and the language used by the leader have a significant influence on the direction of group sessions, especially the final session, the leader must choose a language that promotes growth for members. To put a growthful frame on members' experiences, the leader may want to follow the philosophical positions stated by Hammond (1996) as follows:

- There is always something there that worked.
- What we focus on becomes our reality.
- Reality is created in the moment, and there are multiple realities.
- The act of asking questions influences the outcomes.
- People have more confidence and comfort to journey to the future (the unknown) when they carry forward parts of the past (the known).
- It is important to value differences.
- The language that we use creates our reality. (Hammond, 1996, pp. 20–21)

Throughout the final session, it will be beneficial to apply these philosophical stances to the handling of closure. Through the spirit of positive reframing, the last session will be fueled with the energy of positive realities that will empower members to continue to grow. Hopefully members will recognize the impact of constructive language in interpersonal communication. They can be reminded of how such language can be employed in life in order to better manage their interactions with others. In order to reframe into the positive, the leader will need to be able to see the larger picture, or the larger scheme of things. She must be able to transcend the limited perspective that so often traps people in their self-subjugating views.

SKILLS FOR ENDING THE GROUP

This section presents a sequence of skills and techniques that the leader may adopt for the final session. These skills are based on the principles addressed in the previous section.

Opening Meditation

To open the final session, the leader may invite members to close their eyes for a two- to three-minute meditation. This inner focus can help them get in touch with their feelings of the present moment. The leader guides the meditation by saying:

> This is a very special session—our last session. Before we start, let's relax in our chairs for a few minutes. When you feel comfortable, close your eyes. Pay attention to your breathing and any sensation in your body. [pause] Notice the thoughts and feelings that surface in the horizon of your mind. [pause] As you breathe in and out slowly and quietly, allow those thoughts and feelings to come and go. [pause] If some of them are especially strong, stay with those thoughts and feelings for awhile. Listen to what they are trying to say. When the session starts,

there will be time for these thoughts and feelings to be voiced. So just stay with these sensations for awhile. [silence for one minute] As you feel centered, bring your attention back to the room. When you feel ready to join the group, you may open your eyes.

Acknowledging Present Feelings

After the opening meditation, the leader invites members to briefly share any feelings they have about termination: joy, pain, loss, separation anxiety, or relief. The leader may provide modeling by sharing here-and-now feelings and thoughts of his own. His self-disclosure will ease the group into the sharing of a polarity of feelings. About 10 minutes may be needed for this sharing. The leader may say:

> [To the group] I hope the brief meditation has helped you become situated for today's session. We have anticipated this final session, and it is here. Many of us probably have some mixed feelings that are on the surface of our minds right now, so I would like the group to use the next 10 minutes to openly share those feelings. When other members are sharing, please feel free to cross talk. Let's keep our sharing free-flowing. Okay, let me start with my own reactions. And after that, please feel free to jump in. As I sit here knowing that this is our last session, I am feeling. . . .

After members share their feelings, the leader may summarize the common feelings that are present in the moment. For example,

> There seems to be a common feeling of [description] tonight as we come here to. . . .

Saying Good-Bye: Reflecting on the Meaning of Group

Group members say good-bye by expressing what others in the group have meant to them. This takes the bulk of the final session. It is wise to allow sufficient time for this to be done. Since this is the last session, it is important to ensure equal airtime for every member. If the group is not mindful of this, the more verbal members may expound on their thoughts and feelings, leaving little time for the less verbal members. Following are some suggestions for facilitating the group to say good-bye in a meaningful way.

Time Frame   It is a good practice to inform the group members about the estimated length of time each member will have to say good-bye. For instance, if the session lasts for two hours, 70 minutes may be devoted to this sharing. If there are 10 members, then each member gets approximately 7 minutes, give or take a few. The leader should not impose a rigid number of minutes on members, however. The estimated length of time is just a time frame. Some members will take more time, and others less. The leader's job is to manage the time in a way that is adaptive.

The Realm of Experiences to Share   Some group members may be at a loss regarding what to say to bring closure with the others. We have found it helpful to ask members to include the following experiences when they say their good-byes:

- The feelings they had when writing their looking-back letters
- Significant turning points—how they have made progress toward their personal goals
- What was learned—insight, growth, and change
- What other group members have meant to them

Usually interpersonal learning comes in small increments. Since the increments are small, sometimes members neglect to acknowledge the learning or to celebrate it; some even take it for granted. The final session is the time for members to honor those little steps they have taken toward achieving their goals. In addition, each member usually experiences a high point or has a peak experience in the group that leads to a major insight, an "aha" experience, or a self-discovery. Some members have this peak experience right in the group but do not have the language to express it until many hours or days later in their private lives. Or they may not have gotten a chance to share their new self-awareness or change with the group. The last session is the time to share that joy of self-discovery with one another.

To initiate the group to say good-bye, the leader may say,

> [To the group] Next, we have about 70 minutes. During this time, I would like you to look back on your experiences in the group and share what the group has meant to you. We have 10 members, so each will have about 7 minutes, give or take a few. We would like to keep things as open as possible to allow new insights to emerge. At the same time, we would like to work toward a sense of closure for everybody. [pause]
>
> To have a sense of closure, it's important that each member share what the group experience has meant to you. Maybe you can include something like the feelings that went through you when you were writing your looking-back letter, [pause] any significant experiences within the group that have helped you reach a breakthrough in your progress toward your goal, [pause] the insight you have gained about yourself and how it has helped you change, [pause] and finally, what this group has meant to you. [pause] After each member has shared, please feel free to make comments or provide feedback. Let's keep group discussions as open and free flowing as possible. Okay, let's start.

Facilitating Group Interaction   Although the final session is left unstructured like the other sessions in the working stage, it needs some leader facilitation because the final session requires a sense of closure. The leader needs to allow the group interaction to be as open as possible, and at the same time to actively facilitate whenever the group members get sidetracked in the interaction. The leader may also need to help members positively reframe one another's experiences if negative or self-criticizing voices become evident.

Unfinished Business   During the time of saying good-bye, some unfinished business may surface. When it does, time must be devoted to bringing about a sense of completion if possible. Although in each session the group has dedicated some time to work on unfinished business from its previous sessions, some unfinished business may still exist. If unfinished business comes to the surface in the last session, the group is given a last chance to process it and hopefully bring a sense of closure to it.

Another Option for Saying Good-Bye: Memory Books

For children and adolescent groups or groups in which members are less verbal, the leader may use a structured exercise called "memory book" (devised by Chris Rybak and his colleague, Dr. Lori Russell-Chapin) to facilitate the group to say good-bye. In this exercise, each member is asked to put together a small memory book of her own that encompasses her group experiences. The book is made of pages of construction paper cut in half, with two holes punched along the left side for binding with colored ribbon or yarn. On each page of the book, members briefly symbolize their experiences in the group with a simple drawing or a few printed words or poetry. A memory book, for example, might contain the following:

- First page: What the member was like when entering the group
- Second page: A significant experience that changed her in some important way
- Third page: What the member is becoming like at the end of the group
- Fourth page: How others in the group contributed to the member's experience
- Fifth page: What the member will take with her from the group

The emphasis is not on artistic achievement but rather on illustrating the group experiences that the member wants to highlight and share with others. For each page, not more than five minutes is given to complete the image. Members can take the book home to embellish the images with color or in any other way they wish. As the books are completed, members can be encouraged to share what they will take forward with them from the group experience. The book itself will be a tangible reminder for each member of what she gained.

Transferring Learning to Outside Life

Termination does not need to be all about loss and separation. It can also be viewed as a "rite of passage," a ceremony acknowledging a transition to a new stage of life. With this view, group leaders may facilitate members to reflect on how they will create a new beginning for themselves outside the group. A new beginning means finding new avenues for group members to take in order to continue the growth that has started in the group. Growth is a continual journey. After the group experience ends, each person will be responsible for her own growth, for her road forward. Members are now faced with questions like: Who will be out there for me to continue giving me the courage and push to grow? Certainly, follow-up visits with the group leader may be a way to maintain changes initiated within a group experience (Spitz, 1996).

To encourage members to look at the "road forward," the leader may say,

> [To the group] The growth each of you has made within this group is impressive. I am so happy to hear that many of you have gained a major breakthrough in this brief period of time. To make sure that you continue your personal work and growth, I would like all of us to think about the following questions: Is there anyone out there who can remind you to take action based on what you learned in the group? What outside support exists for you to help you implement the changes that you desire? What are some reasonable risks that you anticipate taking in the future?

Referrals and Particular Needs

Most members grow during group sessions and can move on with their lives. For some members, however, life after the group may require additional counseling, depending on the client's goals and whether she believes additional assistance to be appropriate. Some members need a group just to learn how to open up—and then just when they have learned to trust to a point, the group comes to an end. For these people, referral to another group might be needed. Our years of observation have taught us to appreciate one particular thing: the extent of the difficulty some people have in opening up. In counseling and therapy, we tend to take interpersonal sharing for granted, but some people need individual counseling work before they can even benefit from group counseling.

In termination, special attention also needs to be paid to members who have had difficulty with separation issues in the past. Referral to another group or individual counseling may prove necessary for these members.

If the leader has used process summary or therapeutic documents (see Chapter 12) during the group, he should stress the importance of keeping these documents confidential. The leader may need to ask the group to discuss how members want to keep all of these materials safe.

Symbolic Ceremony for Ending Group

The last gesture of saying good-bye may be a symbolic ceremony. Here are two examples of such ceremonies:

Group hug: The group ends with a ceremony involving a group hug.

Setting up follow-up: Some groups decide to set up a follow-up session in order to check with one another about their continued growth and to give support to those who lack it in their daily lives. If a follow-up session is decided on, it is important to make it a real session. If arranged as a pot-luck dinner or a restaurant gathering, the follow-up session probably will not work because food, small talk, and socialization will defeat the original purpose of the follow-up and dilute its function. If the group members want to socialize with one another, they can schedule another time and setting for a gathering where they can engage in lighter and less purposeful mingling.

EVALUATION OF THE GROUP EXPERIENCE

Evaluating group counseling and therapy services can provide useful data that help therapists in readjusting current programs, providing external accountability, and planning new programs in the future. Program evaluation is an integral part of the program management circle (Lewis, Lewis, Daniels, & D'Andrea, 1998). In evaluating group services, the focus is usually on the quality of the group experiences and on the impact that the group has had on client change. Generally, the data can be gathered through a brief, anonymous survey given during the termination session or through follow-up contact.

Evaluation Immediately after Termination

The first way to evaluate members' group experiences is through a formal survey given immediately after the termination session. With the group members are still present in the meeting room and their experiences still fresh in their minds, most members will be willing to share their reactions and feedback about the overall group experience. The immediacy of the experience allows group members to share more details about the quality and effectiveness of the group services. By making the survey anonymous, group members have a greater freedom to describe their experience within the group and offer constructive feedback that may help improve future groups. (A sample of an anonymous survey given immediately following termination can be found under "Examples of Group Evaluation Surveys" on the book's Web site; see Preface for URL.)

Evaluation in Follow-Up Contacts

Another way to evaluate members' group experience is through follow-up contact. Follow-up allows the leader to see whether former members have been successful in implementing changes that they initiated during the group experience. It is also important to gather information regarding any roadbacks or setbacks that group members have experienced after termination. In this way, the leader will have additional tangible information by which to evaluate the effectiveness of the group program and to determine what adjustments can be made to the group services for future members.

The section entitled "Examples of Group Evaluation Surveys" on the book's Web site (see Preface for URL) offers a sample of a follow-up survey that might be used approximately six months after the group has ended. If the leader is sending the survey by mail, it should be accompanied by a letter explaining that this is a follow-up survey on the group experience, that the leader would like to know how effective the group program was for the former members, that the results will be kept confidential, and that the former members' feedback will assist the leader in improving the group services that are offered in the future.

EXAMPLES OF LOOKING-BACK LETTERS

Mike's Letter

Session seven was my turning point. I believe that it was one of the most surprising sessions for other members because they were seeing a different side of me for the first time. I cried during the closing comment because I really wanted the group's attention that night, but was not strong enough to ask for it. Instead, I chose to withdraw and remain silent. This strategy had served me well over the years, but I was no longer able to run away from my feelings. At the moment of my bursting into tears, I felt extremely exposed, but the group's reaction comforted me. It was at that point that I knew I could trust this group to help me with my issues. It was very comforting to see other members shed tears for me and show concern for my feelings. I was very touched by their tears.

Session eight was very powerful. The group empowered me to share my innermost thoughts and feelings about my father and his impact on my life. I have always struggled with the fear of becoming my father. His failure as a father was primarily due to the fact that he was an alcoholic. He was unable to change his way of life, and as a result he died at an early age without ever acknowledging it to my sister and me. This was my struggle. I wanted an explanation, but I was never strong enough to ask for it. Thankfully, the group was able to help me in a way that I could not have imagined.

Unexpectedly, session ten would also be extremely powerful. As I was trying to elicit a response from Terry, I found myself reliving my experience. I was soon overwhelmed with emotion to the point where I could not stop crying. Taking on the role of my father, Cindy and Jean were able to give me the words that I so desperately wanted to hear from my father. Their words were exactly what I needed to hear, because for the first time they were coming from someone who was not trying to protect me. I was finally able to have some closure with this issue. However, I am cognizant of the fact that I will need to continue to work on self-growth. I am very thankful that I was a part of this group. It served as an agent of change in my life. I will cherish this experience for the rest of my life.

Keith's Letter

Looking back and reflecting on this group gives me a bittersweet feeling. It's sweet because I've learned so much in this group about myself. It is bitter because I'm truly going to miss the group and wish we could continue. The group gave me an opportunity to really talk about "real stuff" that was affecting me. In fact, it was the first time in my life that I was able to go beneath the surface and deal with issues that were having an impact on my life. I was able to do this because of the environment that the group provided for me. It is important, however, to note that I didn't come into this group expecting it to be this way. The group experience exceeded my expectations. A nurturing yet challenging environment was critical for me to uncover many of the issues that I face in my life. Most of the learning in my life has been mental; this group allowed me to move beyond the mental into the emotional. I am grateful for this group and will regard this experience as the most critical step in my life as a person.

There were several experiences in this group that stood out for me. They were nurturing, challenging, conflicting, or enlightening. I have to admit that I came into this group with baggage. I wasn't sure how I would interact with the leader. The reason is because I had a bad experience in the past with an authority figure. I was not sure why; I didn't know whether it was a personality thing or a cultural thing. The previous authority figure was Asian, and the leader in this group is also

Asian. As a result, I immediately became defensive because I didn't want to relive the past experience. However, the biggest moment for me came when the leader shared some information about herself. Her disclosure allowed me to see things from a different and more accurate perspective. At that moment, I felt the walls of defense start to tumble down. It was such a relief for me, and it allowed me to truly experience the impact of the group process.

The nurturing experience for me was in the beginning when I told the group how I usually take on too much at one time and make things difficult for myself. I shared that I would like to live more in the moment. I let the group know that the reason I work so hard is for some shameful things I did in the past that hurt my credit and drag on me financially up to today. The group validated me. They did not necessarily agree with my lifestyle, but they validated that my emotions made sense. The validation helped me to see more clearly and to realize that my lifestyle didn't make sense and was unnecessary. I could still accomplish what I wanted to financially without killing myself in the process. This experience was so relieving and nurturing that I have changed my schedule and feel so much better.

The challenging time came when Rosy told me that I was probably "emotionally no good" for anyone because of the way I worked myself. She said it in a way that made me look within myself and really investigate what was going on with me. I appreciated her ability to say just what she needed to say with frankness. I was also able to receive it well because the trust factor was already built into the group.

Another challenging time came when Jane said that she thought I intellectualized too much. I believe that this stimulated me to be more reflective about myself. I remember my immediate reaction was to defend the way I was. However, the more I thought about it, the more I realized that I do overintellectualize. This allowed me to come to terms with the idea that being too intellectual can prevent me from reaching the heart of the matter. It can prevent me from letting go and relaxing. I am appreciative of Jane's candid comment.

The enlightening point of the group came when we started to "stir the pot" and engage in confrontation. It is so easy to run from confrontation because of the discomfort attached to it. However, it may be the very experience that is needed to help us overcome our own issues. As a result of this experience, I have coined the phrase that "confrontation is not always bad."

Overall, I was able to accomplish two things during the group. First, I am no longer overloading myself and have reduced my schedule significantly. I am not where I started 12 weeks ago at the beginning of the group. As a result of my experience in the group, I will be more conscious about my actions. Secondly, I was able to work on and improve the skill of saying exactly what's on my mind without editing or thinking too deeply all the time. These have been very significant accomplishments for me, and I am immensely grateful. I feel a little inadequate because I can't find the words to express the level of gratitude I have for the leader and all the group members who invested their hearts, time, and minds. All I can say is Thank You . . . straight from my heart. From Keith.

Rosy's Letter

Group counseling was an enlightening experience for me. Prior to joining group therapy, I placed very little emphasis on intimate relationships. Please do not misunderstand me by inferring that I am not relationship-oriented or that I have been hurt by my male counterpart. These factors have nothing to do with it. For over 15 years, I allowed my perception of my parents' relationship to interfere with my personal relationships. I kept away from committed relationships because I didn't want to repeat the same patterns as my parents. Most importantly, I didn't want to end up in a relationship that could potentially deteriorate into two strangers living under the same roof.

Many people in my life have expressed that they find it difficult to get to know me on a personal level. Each time they make an attempt, they encounter a wall of defense. I am very much aware of this defense, but I never saw the need to change until Mary in our group helped me visualize the negative impact of my behavior on others. I know what it feels like to be rejected, and I don't want to be perceived as someone who is emotionally detached. I know the value of having meaningful interpersonal relationships, and I want to start rebuilding those relationships. I can take the first tier by acknowledging the benefits of self-disclosure and choosing to share myself with others.

I have a tendency to downplay a lot of situations in order to avoid conflict, but thanks to the group, with its emphasis on the here-and-now and process, I no longer have to avoid those uncomfortable situations. My increased competence at the immediacy level will definitely benefit me in the future because I have learned to convey a powerful message without being defensive.

SCENARIOS FOR YOUR PRACTICE

1. At the final session of a group, Chow states, "I don't want the group to end. I'm not ready for that!" What factors would you consider in making your response? Are there issues that you would explore with Chow?

2. Jake and Woodrow fail to show for the final group session. They have seemed less connected to the group over the last several weeks, and you have reason to believe that they have resumed abusing alcohol

even though they had evidently maintained sobriety for several years prior to the group sessions. How would you deal with their absence in the final meeting?

3. A group member, Helmut, says "I deeply appreciate the support and friendships that grew in here. I'm inviting everyone here, members and leaders alike, to a backyard cookout at my house next Saturday." As the group leader, how would you respond to this statement?

SELF-REFLECTION

1. What are some of the ways in which your family handled significant loss? Do you still use the same approaches?
2. As a group leader, how will it be for you to let go of group members with whom you have shared emotional closeness? What will be an appropriate way for you to handle this loss?
3. What kind of continuing obligation do you feel you have toward members of a completed group?
4. If you were a member, what would you like to spring forth from the termination session of a group? What will best prepare you for terminating a group experience?

OTHER CONSIDERATIONS

WRITING AS A THERAPEUTIC MEANS

Many forms of writing can expedite therapeutic change in the group context. Using writing to enhance therapeutic effect is called scriptotherapy (Riordan, 1996). This is a tool that is widely used in individual and group therapy. Writing involves a slower mental exploration than talking. It tends to make clients more reflective. Freed from the time constraint of information processing during the session, clients are able to review and rethink later, at their own pace, the complicated and charged interpersonal process of the session. In addition, reflective writing allows clients to express themselves without the fear of being judged. When afforded, writing provides clients with a sense of authorship of their thinking, feelings, and actions.

This chapter proposes two types of writing that can be readily applied to group counseling to enhance its therapeutic effect. The chapter covers:

- Reflective journals
- Narrative session notes

REFLECTIVE JOURNALS

Members can benefit tremendously from weekly reflective journal writing. Groups offer a wealth of information for members to digest. Some contemplative time is needed for members to make sense of all this data. Having members journal as an adjunct to the interpersonal encounters within the group can accentuate the power of interpersonal learning.

Benefits of Reflective Writing

Writing offers people a way to open up to their inner experiences. The benefits evidenced by various research studies are striking. Pennebaker (1990) conducted a study investigating the effect of therapeutic writing. In the study, the control group (composed of college students) wrote about mundane topics, while the experimental group (also college students) wrote about their traumatic experiences. Participants were asked to write about these topics for 15 minutes per day for four days. Of those in the experimental group writing about their traumas, one subgroup was asked to just express their emotions, a second subgroup was asked to write fact-oriented descriptions of their traumas, while a third subgroup wrote about both their emotional experiences and the facts of the situations. The frequency of participants' use of health care services during the following few months was used as data for comparison.

Results showed that participants in the two subgroups who wrote about both thoughts and feelings concerning their traumas decreased their use of the health care services by 50 percent compared to the period prior to their writing, while those in the control groups were using more health services by 50 percent in comparison to their rate of use of these services before their writing.

Pennebaker (1990) and colleagues further examined the effect of writing on the functioning of the immune system. For this study, blood was drawn from participants at three different periods of time: the day prior to writing, the day after completing the writing assignment, and six weeks after the writing occurred. Once again, the participants were divided into groups, as in the previous study. The participants were asked to write about their assigned topics for 20 minutes per day for four days. Results showed parallel findings to the previous study: Those who wrote about both their thoughts and feelings concerning a trauma demonstrated a heightened functioning of their immune system. The effect was greatest immediately following the writing, but the effect of strengthened immune system response was still in evidence six weeks after the writing was finished.

If writing to express one's emotions and thoughts provides benefits such as those demonstrated by these studies, how about the absence of expression or writing? Does it lead to any negative impact? Pennebaker (1990) observed that concealment and inhibition of emotional expression, either written or spoken, can take a toll on one's psychological and physical health. For example, in a study of individuals with eating disorders, he found that it was the covering up of the disorder that contributed most to the emotional difficulties of those with the disorder. People who cover up their problems pay a price for it by spending much energy and time in concealing and inhibiting emotional expression. These very behaviors result in the individual being isolated and alienated from others who could provide support.

Research has demonstrated again and again that writing can contribute to one's well-being. As Pennebaker (1990) pointed out, writing can serve to clear the mind and pave the way for complex tasks by helping the writer work through traumas that otherwise might block that person's ability to focus on important tasks. It contributes to the acquisition and integration of new information and promotes problem solving.

Practical Aspects of Reflective Journal Writing

Journal writing is practical; there is nothing demanding about it. DeSalvo (1999) identified how easy and how practical writing can be:

- Writing does not need to be time-consuming. Even 20 minutes or so each time can serve to capture the highlights and the essence of our experience.
- Writers can set their own pace. Whenever one has the time to write, one can choose to commit one's experience to paper at the time best available for one's focused attention.
- Writing is for oneself, but it can be shared selectively with others. One can keep one's journal in a private place where others cannot access it. Conversely, one can choose to share part of the writing with one friend or with many.
- Writing can be done almost anywhere. If one carries a small notebook and pen, opportunities abound when one can jot down thoughts and feelings that flash through the mind. Waiting for others in the car, in the airport, at the mall, or at home can present opportunities for one to pull out the notebook. If one prefers to write at a computer, the information can be typed in later, or one can make use of a notebook computer or one of the various handheld electronic devices equipped for writing.
- Writing can be done even if one is not in top physical condition. Writing is not a strenuous activity. Although demanding more mental energy than some activities, it does not take a great deal of physical energy unless one writes for lengthy periods. If one is ill, writing can actually contribute to one's healing, since it helps boost immune function, as demonstrated by Pennebaker's (1990) study.
- Writing for one's own understanding, growth, and healing does not require special talent. Each person must simply work from her current level of understanding. As one gains practice in articulating one's experience, a greater degree of eloquence in writing will follow.

In addition to DeSalvo, other authors have offered several helpful suggestions. For example, Adams (1990) suggests that the person who journals should write as quickly as possible without censoring, accept all feelings that arise, and write in his own natural voice. Stone (1998), on the other hand, suggests that the form of journal writing may differ from person to person. What works for one person may not fit another person's lifestyle. For some, the journal may include only verbal entries, while others may choose to incorporate drawings, photos, poems, or collages.

Reflective Writing for Group Experiences

Within a group, a great deal of messages are exchanged verbally, nonverbally, intrapersonally, and interpersonally. Each member must digest and process many sensory, thought, and emotional experiences. Many members' reactions, thoughts, and emotions may not be fully processed within each instant of the group. Unexamined issues and unarticulated reactions are likely to result. The reflective journal provides an opportunity for clients to reflect on these issues. Journaling after each group session can enhance the meaning and understanding of the entire group experience. After much reflection, members then can, in subsequent group meetings, verbalize whatever has come up in their reflections.

Journaling offers group members a tool in their self-discovery. What members write is not as important as the fact that writing provides a means for them to become more aware of their unconscious processes. Self-exploration in journal writing usually goes beyond conscious thoughts, feelings, and future plans. It often taps into what lies in the unconscious and subconscious mind. By keeping a reflective journal throughout the duration of a group, members can keep track of interpersonal patterns that manifest in their lives (Adams, 1990). Self-reflection is itself a contributor to personal growth. Journal writing is especially useful in short-term groups, for which this book is designed.

Reflective journaling can be beneficial when working with minority clients in group settings. Some cultures, especially minorities, have modes of communication that are not as vocal as those of the majority culture. Journal writing can be especially powerful with those from cultures that do not emphasize confrontation and verbal expression (White & Murray, 2002).

In our experiences of leading groups, we have valued the use of reflective journal writing in order for members to examine their own ideas, emotional reactions, and personal meanings after each session. We encourage members to write without being judgmental. The value of journaling is exemplified in this member's journal entry:

> After the group session, I felt very emotional. When I left the room, I was wondering what to do with my emotions. Then I found that reflecting both in my mind as well as in the journal allowed the therapy to continue even in the absence of the group environment. I see this reflective journal writing as having paramount importance if I am to make progress between sessions. It helps me chart my progress as well as provide me with an outlet for expressing the emotions that the therapy sessions have brought to the surface.

Another member, Jenni, wrote:

> Throughout the group, I have found writing the reflective journal to be most beneficial. Writing allows me to take more risks and to write down

patterns that I see happening in members and in the group as a whole. Like some people, I am not able to verbalize my thoughts on the spot and in a succinct manner in the group. Writing allows me time to process and compose my reactions. The combination of writing and verbal expression in a group is a powerful way to facilitate personal change.

By making use of between-group time to do this type of processing, members are empowered to come back to the group, ready to build upon the growing awareness they have already developed. When shared, these written insights, responses, and questions can make the group meetings even more dynamic and beneficial.

If time allows, the leader may choose to read members' weekly reflective journals and to write prompt and thoughtful feedback to the members. Riordan (1996) notes that this interactive feature can be very beneficial for both the group therapist and the members. Of course, tight schedules are a reality in a therapist's life; we can do only as much as our time allows. Leaders, however, need not be worried if time does not allow them to read members' journals. Rather, they can trust that the writing alone will still benefit the members a great deal.

Sample of Reflective Journals

After the eighth session, Peter wrote in his reflective journal:

> I was struck when Bob said he hears what other members are saying to him, but he can't relate to it. He reminds me so much of my past self and my past struggle five years ago. That was exactly how I felt then. I spent much of my life cut off from my own emotions. I remember that in my own individual therapy, my therapist would ask me how I felt, and I truly didn't know. I was so completely unaware of my emotions then. When I realized how much Bob resembles the self I was five years ago, I really felt connected to him. (I have felt so frustrated by him before.) I truly believe that Bob doesn't feel certain emotions, at least not on a conscious level. He is a benchmark for me, reminding me how far I have come and that there are "things" out there I may be unaware of. Seeing him like this encourages me to try and remain open, so I can allow new experiences to touch me. . . .
>
> Shifting to another member: Sara continues to remind me more and more of my mother. I see Sara as being completely emotionally unavailable. Even more, I don't think she "gets" what is going on regarding the exchange between people. She said she didn't see what was happening between Cindy and Jim or the transference that was taking place between them. I find myself worried about her and about myself. How will it feel to share myself in group, knowing that Sara will not understand me (just like my dad and mom never understand me)? Sara's presence in the group makes me feel alone and isolated. I am afraid that if I tried to explain that to her, I would only feel more alone. . . .

Another note: I felt a lot of emotion when Lisa talked about how her daughter wanted to be nurtured by her and how Lisa didn't know how to do that. I sensed her sadness and feelings of inadequacy. A five-year relationship that was very important to me ended partially because I wasn't emotionally present enough. I, like Lisa, still didn't know how to be present. I wonder, given all the knowledge that I have now from group therapy, would that relationship have survived? There are still four group sessions to go, and I am already anxious about the group ending. I really get a lot out of it and will be sorry to see it end. I feel like I am starting to tap into a different part of myself, and I can have more of this kind of self-discovery.

For more examples of members' reflective journals, see "Samples of Members' Critical Reflections" on the book's Web site (see Preface for URL).

NARRATIVE SESSION NOTES

Small groups, especially process groups, represent a type of dynamic social microcosm wherein each group session can manifest multiple charged interactions. These highly charged and complex interactions, however, often happen at such a fast pace that the twists and turns of group dynamics remain unrecognized by many members. Members need time to absorb the experiences and insights derived from the intricate dynamics of such human systems. To help members further benefit from their group experiences, leaders may want to consider *distributing* narrative session notes. These notes serve two functions: First, they serve as a type of written case notes for the group, and second, they serve as a process summary of a group session, written with the intention of sharing the notes with the group members. This section describes the benefits of sharing narrative session notes with group members and how to write these notes so that they can be an adjunct to therapy.

Benefits of Narrative Session Notes

For Group Leaders   Writing a session summary can give a group leader time to ponder the group processes outside the rapidly evolving here-and-now group interactions. Frequently, many good ideas occur to leaders after a session has ended. The session notes offer leaders a vehicle for conveying these afterthoughts and ideas to members without waiting until the next session to do so (Parry & Doan, 1994). Further, the session notes can act as a type of "narrative letter" to group members. Literature demonstrates that writing narrative letters to clients can decrease treatment length in individual and family counseling (Nylund & Thomas, 1994;

White, 1995). It is logical to expect that the session notes, when written as a "narrative letter," will have the same potency in the group context. They can make group practice more effective within a brief frame of time. This helps group workers meet the demands of cost-conscious managed care by decreasing the number of group sessions.

Just like narrative letters, the narrative session notes are distributed to group members. As the group therapists' afterthoughts and perceptions are conveyed to members through the session notes, the leaders' transparency is increased. Group leaders' transparency can help members experience therapists as human beings rather than experts who merely dispense professional expertise (White, 1991). Not only can therapists' ideas about the group process be made known to members through this practice, but it also helps to solidify a relationship of trust and tempers the hierarchical imbalance between therapists and clients.

For Group Members   The undeniable beneficiaries of narrative session notes are, indeed, the group members. Reading narrative notes written by the leader can provide members with the luxury of time and distance for reflection apart from the immediacy and intensity of a group session's here-and-now exchanges. The written session notes give life and credibility to what has happened in the session. Words in a written form, as Epston (1994) indicates, "don't fade and disappear the way conversation does; they endure through time and space, bearing witness to the work of therapy and immortalizing it" (p. 31). Written session notes help members cement what has transpired in sessions, giving them something tangible to refer to on a regular basis (Parry & Doan, 1994). The session-by-session accumulation of narrative session notes acts as a cross-session reminder, allowing members to rekindle insights gained during critical instances and pointing members toward paths of growth. When made visually available, these narrative notes are accessible for group members to consult in times of self-doubt or crisis.

Narrative Session Notes as a Treatment Vehicle

Legally and ethically, therapists are obligated to keep thorough records in order to keep track of significant elements of individual or group sessions (Spitz, 1996). However, record keeping, or client documentation, often consumes a great amount of the therapist's time. Few therapists enjoy this aspect of service delivery (Mitchell, 1991). After much time and effort have been put into writing case notes, these records are then put to rest in charts. No wonder few clinicians look forward to the work of record keeping. But does record keeping need to be such a "chore"? In fact, if handled with intelligence, client documentation can serve to make treatment more effective. Research has shown that if clients are allowed access to certain types of record information, their treatment can be improved (Roth,

Wolford, & Meisel, 1980). However, the therapeutic community has not implemented a system for promoting greater client accessibility to charts. Neither do most clients know that the information contained in their records belongs to them, because these records reside with the mental health providers and are released only to third-party payers (Anderson, 1996). Nevertheless, any notes concerning a client are part of the record and belong to the client.

To promote greater client access to such information, Yalom (1995) has devised a way of writing session notes that he calls "process summary." This is an alternative approach to client documentation in which the here-and-now of the group process is highlighted. Breaking from traditional record-keeping methods, Yalom combines case notes and process notes into the process summary, and then shares these notes with his clients. He sends this process summary to his clients to read before the session. This sharing of documentation reinforces client change (Yalom, 1995), representing a major step toward transforming the clinical document into an effective intervention. The narrative session notes resemble Yalom's process summary, but with an emphasis on narrative language. This aspect will be covered later in this section.

To Write or Not to Write: Time Constraints and Confidentiality

The narrative session notes practice departs greatly from the documentation style preferred by many insurance companies. However, the potency of writing and sharing these notes makes us believe that the time and effort spent on it will pay off. The outcome of the group will greatly be enhanced. The potency of this practice is not in question, but time is. In deciding whether to write and share narrative session notes, the leader must evaluate her own resources. If time is an issue, the leader might choose to write narrative session notes only in the most critical, conflict-filled transition stage of group development.

The narrative session notes can be distributed and shared immediately prior to the group session, or they may be mailed to the members before the session. Since the session notes involve clients' intimate life experiences, their safe-keeping must be emphasized as rigorously as with individual case notes. To maintain confidentiality, therapists can ask group members to plan for the safe-keeping of these written documents (White, 1995).

Steps of Writing Narrative Session Notes

The following three steps may serve as a useful guideline for writing narrative session notes:

Retracing Key Episodes and Striking Events   After each group session, the leader may want to jot down key phrases describing his immediate reactions to the session. The purpose of the immediacy is to capture the leader's unfiltered thoughts. The narrative can be refined later. This step helps keep the leader's initial impressions alive. Next, the leader mentally retraces key episodes in the session. While doing so, he tries to recall any striking feelings, utterances, and interactions attached to these vital episodes. Optimally, most of the session's important interactions are illuminated.

Refining the Narratives   In this step, the leader conceptualizes and adds meanings to the pivotal episodes. At this phase, the use of language is especially critical. Analytical and diagnostic language should be avoided in the narrative session notes. The use of therapeutic language will be discussed more later. To model transparency, the group therapist is wise to share his own observations, thoughts, and reactions in the notes.

Obtaining Feedback in Following Sessions   After the session notes have been distributed to the members, the leader should spend some time in the following session processing members' responses to the session notes. This does not take away from dealing with the here-and-now or new agendas because the therapist can phrase questions so that they will bridge responses to current issues. The leader may say to the group, "I wonder, what are your reactions to the session notes? Does anything strike you?" The key is to remember that neither the notes nor the leader defines the client experience; the client has the final say. This collaboration makes the narrative notes a product of coauthorship.

Using Therapeutic Language in Narrative Session Notes

The language that a therapist uses to describe clients' experiences can have an enormous influence on clients' self-concept. It is imperative that therapists use only restoring and therapeutic language when writing the narrative notes for the group. Chen, Noosbond, and Bruce (1998) have developed principles for using therapeutic language in writing session notes. Here we will briefly recap these principles.

Externalizing the Problem   Most members suffer from a negative self-concept because they see their problems as some kind of pathology residing within themselves. Viewing themselves this way, they inevitably subjugate themselves, blocking their ability to act on their own resources. In writing the narrative notes, therapists can use a depathologizing language, reshaping the relationship that members have with their problems. The easiest way to depathologize a client's negative self-view is by externalizing the client's problems. Here, the therapist separates a client's identity from her problems by describing her maladaptive patterns as an external force that she has to confront. By externalizing the problems or maladaptive patterns, the therapist first gives the problem or pattern a *name*, and then animates it with human characteristics. In so doing, the member becomes a protagonist, and the problem becomes an antagonist. The member's self-identity is kept separated from the problem, but the member is put on stage to confront and reshape the oppressive relationship she has with the problem. For example, rather than write that a member, Sue, was defensive (as a maladaptive pattern) to other members' feedback, the therapist names the defensiveness as "the old fear" and animates the fear by describing its action on Sue:

> *The old fear* once again *persuaded* Sue to shut out the feedback that other members were trying to give her. It succeeded in blocking Sue from hearing the truth about herself that might cause the old fear to lose its power and status in Sue's life.

Searching for Exceptions to the Problems

The second principle in writing narrative session notes is to search for exceptions to members' problems. Exceptions to problems are the counterplots of clients' stories that are often missed when clients tell their stories. Members often forget to tell their own personal triumphs, strengths, and resources inherent in their lives. Because members think these are irrelevant to their problems, they often unintentionally neglect to report these to the group. However, these exceptions to problems are extremely important in therapy. If used with wisdom, these exceptions to problems can actually restore a client's self-esteem, which is a valuable asset in therapy. For example, rather than simply write that Sue reported a relapse last week, the therapist who wrote the following notes searched for an exception to the problem, and then highlighted that exception:

> Although one time during the last week, Sue was seduced by the pull of alcohol, there were six days during the week when she stood firm against the power of that pull despite her feelings of sadness and grief over the loss of her significant relationship.

Maintaining a Not-Knowing Position

A "not-knowing" position is one where therapists convey something to group members, not from the position of an expert, but from a position of curiosity and wonderment. As the therapist extends her curiosity, members' curiosity about themselves and their possibilities is increased. This puts members in a position to eventually gain more self-knowledge than they otherwise would. For example, instead of writing that a member, Dale, was being aloof and distant to Sue's pain in the session, which mirrors the deficient relationship Dale has with his mother, the therapist might write about the issue from a "not-knowing" position:

I wonder what might happen if Dale would allow himself to stay emotionally present with Sue's pain amidst her loss of a significant relationship. How would his understanding of the pain of people in his life be potentially increased as a result?

Internalizing Client Personal Agency Although therapists should externalize members' problems, when it comes to personal agency, therapists need to do the opposite—they need to relentlessly seek to help group members internalize a sense of personal efficacy. To do this, the group therapist describes positive traits, such as courage, positive intentionality, and competence, as something that are within group members, something possessed by members as part of their character traits that will not be taken away under any circumstances. For example, instead of simply describing her observation of a member's self-deferring behavior, the group therapist might highlight something within the member that denotes personal agency:

> Jean demonstrates a lot of sensitivity to and awareness of Sue's needs, deferring again and again her opportunity to air so as to let Sue speak first. This behavior can be easily misunderstood as lack of self-assertion, but this sensitivity and responsiveness that the group has witnessed in Jean is indeed a gift.

In sum, the language used in the narrative session notes should be therapeutic and restoring for the members. As the members read, week after week, narratives in which they are seen in a growthful light, they may start to internalize this language for future self-narration. Thus, the narrative session notes can prompt group members to use transformative descriptions in talking and thinking about themselves and others.

Sample of Narrative Session Notes

The following notes are from the sixth session. Members present were: Lori, Nita, Kelly, Maria, Jane, Helen, Marcy, Peter, and Nelson (masked names).

> The group began with a presentation of each member's here-and-now session goals. I was surprised at the similarities between all group members' here-and-now goals. All members expressed their difficulty in communication. This ties the group together powerfully. It is very interesting to me that so many group members express an interest in improving their ability to communicate "unpleasant" or assertive emotions.
>
> After each member presented his or her here-and-now session agendas, Helen presented her agenda item. Helen tends to be reluctant to put herself on "center stage"; we therefore made an effort to have her be the focus. While listening to her issues with her sister, I had a difficult time picturing her in the situation she described. *Where is the force of*

insecurity that she talked about, and why can't I see it in the group?

Because we tried to work on multiple agendas simultaneously, no feedback was given to Helen until the other agenda items were presented. Next, we proceeded to Kelly's agenda item. As Kelly's story continued, group members began to physically pull back and had confused looks on their faces. Several group members asked clarifying questions. Kelly's answers to these questions, however, caused more confusion. I could sense Kelly's frustration as the group said they were unable to understand her story. Lori seemed to provide the most useful and powerful reactions to Kelley when she just opened up honestly and told Kelly that she "overexplains" things. Watching Lori's interaction with Kelly made me proud of the progress she has made within the group. *I see her as a confident, strong individual with important opinions. I wonder if Lori sees this in herself yet, and I wonder if she might already display this strength of character with her family and friends.*

The rest of the group showed tremendous bravery by opening up honestly to Kelly. Many of them felt they were not being heard by Kelly. Maria reiterated what Lori had said in a compassionate way. She expressed that she would like to know Kelly better but simply could not understand her messages sometimes. Maria later expressed to Kelly that she often feels that Kelly cannot hear what is being said to her. Maria said this with pain in her face. Throughout this part of the session, I was trying to say something to Kelly that would give her the message and at the same time show her compassion. *Maria was able to do that in a way that I could not. I have also noticed that Maria has seemed more comfortable taking time from the group to express her thoughts recently.*

Helen, too, was able to provide her reactions to Kelly. Helen was trying to tell Kelly that she was just confused and wanted to understand Kelly's story better. I was amazed at how easily Helen shifted from her own agenda to being completely involved in Kelly's. She was able to totally put her own needs on hold for another person. It became clear that a parallel exists between Helen's behavior in the group and her behavior with her sister. *Helen is so good at making other people feel important and putting their needs before hers. The question is, how much does she sacrifice because of this?*

At this point, Kelly was overwhelmed with emotion. The reactions she was receiving disturbed her because she perceived them as being negative. It seemed to me that Kelly has been unable to let herself and her own emotions receive attention. She tends to focus on others. Because she was so uncomfortable with the focus being placed on herself, she felt attacked.

Although the session was becoming highly emotional, I was pleased to hear both Nita and Peter speak up about the issue. Nita's reaction to Kelly was clear, concise, and direct. This is the first time I have seen Nita be assertive. She really reached a new level in moving toward her goal by refusing to back down even when *Kelly seemed to be blocked by a wall of fear around her.* Peter was able to self-disclose when providing reactions to Kelly. I see him doing this more and more often as the group progresses. Each time he speaks, he lets the group in on a different part of himself.

Kelly's pain was immense. The group started to assure Kelly that the reactions were given, not with any intention to hurt her, but from the position of caring for her. Helen, especially, seemed to be overcome with guilt, saying that expressing herself may not be worth it if it hurts someone, such as Kelly, so much. I can see the parallel between Helen's role in the group and her role in her everyday life, especially with her sister. The fact that the group spent so little time on Helen's agenda and was sucked into Kelly's agenda illustrated Helen's role in our social microcosm.

Every single group member took some step toward reaching his or her goal during this session. I saw a side of everyone that I hadn't seen in previous sessions. Asking members to present their here-and-now session goals is a powerful technique.

For more examples of leaders' narrative session notes, see "Samples of Therapeutic Documents" on the book's Web site (see Preface for URL).

SELF-REFLECTION

1. Try writing for 15–20 minutes per day for four consecutive days about significant events in your life. Be aware of your own processes as you engage in this practice. Do you find this practice relatively easy to do, or is it a struggle? With which aspects do you struggle most? How did you feel before beginning the task? During the midst of the writing? After the completion of the writing?

2. What mode of journaling works best for you? A strictly verbal prose description of your experience? Poetic descriptions? Including drawings with your writing? Using photos or collages to express ideas of greatest significance for you?

3. For your group experiences, try dividing the journal writing into various perspectives. The "personal" would address your own feelings and thoughts about the milieu of events occurring within the group. The "interpersonal" would address your observations about member-to-member interactions. The "synthesis" would bring together the perspectives of the "personal" and "interpersonal" to see how they fit. The "plan of action" would be based on all three of these areas and would include ways in which you choose to respond to the group in the future. This type of journaling can be an invaluable addition to your supervision experience, since it provides you with some very definite areas of focus.

PROFESSIONAL STANDARDS AND BEST PRACTICE

Thus far in this text we have provided basic concepts of group work, offered specific suggestions on how to lead groups in a variety of situations, and described the application of these principles according to the stage of group development. The emphasis has been on both the theoretical and the practical aspects of group leadership. The focus of this chapter turns to the larger professional context and the need for professionalism in group leadership. The chapter covers:

- Professional standards
- Best practice

PROFESSIONAL STANDARDS

The Association for Specialists in Group Work (ASGW; 2000) has established guidelines called *Professional Standards* for both core and specialized training in group work. The ASGW is a division of the American Counseling Association, whose members are interested in and/or specialize in group work. The ASGW values the creation of community, service to members and clients, and the profession itself.

The *Professional Standards* detail the criteria of professional competency that group counselors and therapists are expected to live up to. These standards encompass three categories: (1) core competencies, or the *basic* knowledge and skills that all developing group workers need; (2) knowledge and skills that are required competencies for each of the four types of group specialization, including task groups, psychoeducational groups, counseling groups, and psychotherapy groups; and (3) advanced leadership training for each of the four types of group specialization.

For the complete text of training standards from the ASGW, see "Professional Standards for the Training of Group Workers" on the book's Web site (see Preface for URL).

Core Knowledge and Skills

As described early in this text, to lead a group well, the therapist needs to be equipped with knowledge and skills, and be able to implement them using the leader's self as an instrument. A solid understanding of group concepts and skills lies at the core of the learning process, but by no means represents the complete process. The experiential learning process is probably the most complete form of core training.

The core knowledge and skills identified by ASGW involve *at least one graduate group course* that covers such areas as: the development of groups, interpersonal process within groups, group dynamics, the leadership of groups, and types of group work. As a part of the core training, at least 10 hours of participation in a group as a member or as a leader is required. Specifically, this graduate group course should target core knowledge and skills regarding: (a) the nature and scope of practice, (b) the assessment of group members according to their living context, (c) how to plan group interventions, (d) putting group interventions into practice, (e) facilitating and cofacilitating groups, (f) conducting an evaluation, and (g) ethical and competent practice. We will discuss each of these standards in the following text:

Nature and Scope of Practice   The first core knowledge that all group therapists must possess is knowledge of the types of group specialization in the field, the nature of each type of group practice, fundamental theories of groups, and research literature on various types of group work. In the first two chapters of this text, we laid the groundwork for understanding a variety of group specializations and the theoretical foundations related to group work. Regardless of whether a group therapist is leading a task/work group, a psychoeducational group, a counseling groups, or a psychotherapy group, he must have a clear understanding of the fundamental theories and how these theories can be applied to the work of the group he leads.

Assessment of Group Functioning   The second core competency that all group workers are expected to possess involves how to assess group functioning. Assessment is an ongoing process within group work, not just a one-shot effort. From this perspective, the screening interview is part of the assessment process. Assessment begins with the screening interview and continues throughout the group experience to termination, and occurs even after the group if follow-up is done.

In terms of ongoing assessment, once the group has begun, it is important for group leaders to keenly observe individual members as well as the overall interaction matrix within the group. Group leaders must observe whether each member is connecting to the group, being pushed out of the group, being overlooked, pulling away from the group, or experiencing some alienation from the group. Leaders also need to observe whether members are simply repeating past problematic patterns or moving toward freeing themselves from such patterns, and whether members are supporting desired changes or the status quo. In addition, leaders must watch to see whether the group is given to overintellectualizing and not dealing with feelings or action; whether there is a balance between support and challenge; and whether the level of attention given to each member is disproportionate, with some members garnering most of the time and other members drifting off into their own thoughts.

Group leaders also need to determine the stage of development that the group has reached so they can evaluate the kinds of group dynamics being displayed in the group. Additionally, group leaders must have a general understanding of the cultural and family contexts from which the members come. These contexts heavily determine what experiences members bring to the group and what types of outlooks they apply to their experiences. By informally and/or formally assessing the context of group members, the group leader will be prepared to understand the group members' individual reactions in the group and the interactions that potentially arise from different contexts.

Planning Group Interventions   The third core competency required of all group workers involves abilities in planning group interventions. Group workers must develop the ability to articulate the purpose for each intervention, assess the outcome of the interventions, and ensure the contextual appropriateness of the planned interventions.

In Chapters 3 through 5, we offered suggestions related to basic plans in group intervention. Based on correct assessment of group functioning, the leader plans appropriate group interventions that will best facilitate group members in achieving their goals. The planning is also based on theoretical knowledge of group and individual development. Unwisely chosen interventions that are inappropriate to a given situation can have unforeseen negative consequences. Group leaders must balance challenge and support within the group. Poorly chosen interventions may include too great a challenge for a group in a particular stage, rendering members afraid, cautious, and resistant to future interventions. On the other hand, if chosen interventions are not sufficiently challenging, the group may become low on energy and relatively boring, and little learning and growth may take place.

Putting Group Interventions into Practice   The fourth core competency involves putting group interventions into practice. This requires competence in the areas of recruiting, screening, and choosing group members; putting concepts to work within groups; and recognizing group dynamics. What this means is that all group workers must be able to skillfully encourage group members to participate, create an empathic group environment, articulate group themes, self-disclose in an appropriate way, keep the group focused, and set the stage for feedback-sharing within the group.

In Chapters 6 through 8, we described the process of working on agendas within a group, in an attempt to help leaders put group interventions into practice. In Chapters 9 and 10, we shifted gears to discuss the totally unstructured group, with an emphasis on stimulating emotions and fostering awareness of interpersonal patterns. Here we want to stress the importance of timing of group interventions, as it can deeply affect the trajectory of group development. Groups can be nudged along too slowly toward understanding, shoved too quickly into overly demanding situations, or timed just right so that personal growth is neither rudely pushed along nor obstinately held back. The right timing is especially important when it comes to emotional stimulation. To stimulate a member who is not ready for that type of work is like adding jet fuel to a fire on a gas stove. It is bound to have unfortunate consequences. On the other hand, to not stimulate emotions when the group is ready is like putting regular gas in a space rocket. It can inhibit the engine so that it fails to achieve ignition.

Facilitation and Cofacilitation   The fifth core competency required of all group therapists involves effective leadership, both when leading a group alone and when coconducting a group in a collaborative manner. In Chapter 2, we offered suggestions regarding coleadership of groups. Coleaders must be able to communicate with one another effectively and to coordinate their visions and preferences concerning the operation of the group. This process is assisted when coleaders meet regularly before and after group sessions to share their perspectives as well as to decide upon any needed interventions that may be appropriate. With respect to the facilitation style, group leaders must be aware of the type of group that is being conducted. If the group is more of a task or work group, facilitating the personal growth of individual members may be at odds with the task that the group needs to accomplish.

Evaluation   The sixth core competency involves the ability to conduct an evaluation of group work. All group leaders must demonstrate an ability to evaluate group processes and outcomes. Group leaders must know methods by which to gather these indicators. Sometimes paper-and-pencil evaluations are chosen, and other times certain types of group member interactions and self-reports are used to determine where a group is or what it has accomplished.

For examples of paper-and-pencil evaluations that can be used in group, see "Examples of Group Evaluation Surveys" on the book's Web site (see Preface for URL).

Ethical and Competent Practice   The seventh and last core competency involves ethical and competent practice. All group workers must gain awareness of the special ethics of group work, the recommended best practices, and an understanding of how to work with a diverse clientele within groups. Awareness in all these areas is essential in the planning and implementation of group activities.

We first introduced the idea of ethics in group work in Chapter 3. Here we want to expound on the topic a bit more. As in individual counseling, group leaders' first ethical responsibility is to *do no harm.* The best way to avoid harming group members is by having a thorough understanding of how groups function and what approaches are likely to lead the group to the outcomes that members wish to attain.

Group leaders also are ethically responsible to do something *beneficial* for group members, that is, to do something that will help group members achieve their goals to a reasonable degree. The benefits of group work generally include some aspect of deeper understanding of self in relation to others and the learning of new behaviors in order to enhance relationships.

The principle of *justice* also applies in that group members must be treated fairly according to the standards of practice. Fairness includes the concept of *informed consent,* so that potential group members are given accurate information about the way in which the group will function. In this way, potential group members are better able to decide for themselves whether the group experience is something that they wish to have. These standards require that group members are properly informed ahead of time about the type of group experience that is in store for them.

Finally, the principle of *autonomy* should be followed by group leaders. Members should be allowed to decide for themselves whether they wish to experience personal growth and the degree of personal growth that they might seek. They retain the right to withdraw from the group or to make changes in their goals as they deem them appropriate. This means that group leaders should be protective of individual members should other members of the group attempt to coerce or co-opt a member in any way to do something that is in opposition to that member's wishes and values. Members should be able to freely choose any changes they wish to make. They should not be forced to become something they do not want to be.

Knowledge and Skills of Four Specialty Areas

As discussed in Chapter 3, group work has been divided into four broad specialty areas: (1) task/work groups, (2) psychoeducational groups, (3) counseling groups, and (4) psychotherapy groups. Within each group specialty, group leaders are called upon to address a tremendously wide range of concerns across the entire age spectrum. To lead groups within each specialty, leaders need an array of specific knowledge and skills related to working with groups of particular individuals.

In order to work with any of the specialized areas, group workers must acquire specific knowledge and skills, as established by ASGW, regarding: (a) the nature and scope of practice, (b) the assessment of group members according to their living context, (c) how to plan group interventions, (d) putting group interventions into practice, (e) facilitating and cofacilitating groups, (f) conducting an evaluation, and (g) ethical and competent practice. We will discuss each of these standards in the following text.

Nature and Scope of Practice   In order to lead a group in a competent manner, group workers must have knowledge of and experience with the type of group they are leading. They must be familiar with the specific kinds of issues faced by members for whom the group was designed. Each group leader must practice within his own specialty, within his own scope of practice. For example, if a group is designed as an adult business group, the group leader must be familiar with the context from which the group members are coming, as well as being generally aware of the type of values and goals of the organization and its group members. Group worker trainees will only conduct independent group work with respect to those group specialties for which they have already had the appropriate supervised experiences.

Assessment of Group Functioning   Specialized group workers learn to apply the principles of assessment in order to make sense of the group process as it unfolds in the types of groups for which they declare special competency. In working with specialty groups, leaders must know the principles of assessment of group functioning and understand the factors that influence the contextual views of the group members, such as cultural and family backgrounds. Attention is given to the individual characteristics of each group member; appropriate hypotheses are made about group member actions; and consideration is given to group member cultural and family backgrounds in order to better understand the context for interpreting behaviors in the group.

Planning Group Interventions   Regardless of what specialized group the therapist is leading, he must have a clear understanding of the appropriateness and impact of the interventions chosen for the group. Group leaders must be able to decide whether certain emotional stimulation or certain structure is appropriate for the type of group he is leading. Further, leaders need to decide whether a sufficient level of caring exists in the group to adequately buffer the expected level of emotional reaction stirred by the intervention. Finally, group leaders must reflect on whether the groundwork has been laid to make meaning out of the responses to the intervention.

Putting Group Interventions into Practice   Leaders of specialty groups must have in-depth understanding of the make-up of the group's membership and how well the individual members are likely to benefit from the specific group. The careful matching of group members with the needs and goals of the overall group is invaluable in setting the stage for a successful group experience for members. Whatever specialized group the therapist is leading, she must have knowledge of recruiting, screening, and choosing members for the group, including tapping into appropriate sources for referrals to the group.

Facilitation and Cofacilitation   The leadership of specialized groups requires a personal awareness of leader competence, effective leadership, as well as coleadership skills and characteristics. Competent and skilled group leadership is achieved through experience as well as supervision and consultation. Should a group leader work with a cofacilitator, both should be sufficiently aware of and possess the special skills needed for the particular type of specialized group that is proposed.

Evaluation   To be able to conduct an evaluation of specialized groups, group leaders must be aware of methods of evaluation appropriate for the processes and outcomes of the specific group. Means should be selected for evaluating the degree of success and the satisfaction of group members. Group leaders must be aware of the methods for determining the quality of group process occurring at any point within the group and be able to decide whether that level of quality is appropriate for the type of group that is being facilitated.

Ethical and Competent Practice   Group leaders should make every effort to follow the ethical guidelines with respect to working with the specialized type of group that is being facilitated. Ethics and competency go hand-in-hand because ethical treatment of group members contributes to the competency level at which the group is led. Incompetent group leadership creates a possibility of harm for group members and is a violation of the ethical guidelines. Through understanding of the ethical guidelines and supervised experiences in leading specialized groups, group leaders become prepared to ensure that each group member is dealt with fairly. Well-prepared leaders provide the best chance for a successful outcome to the group experience.

Advanced Leadership Training

In order to acquire competency in the leadership of specialized groups, group leaders need not only the core competencies, but also more advanced leadership competencies. Advanced leadership experiences might be constructed in a number of ways. One of the most direct ways for novices to learn from experienced group leaders is through an *apprenticeship coleadership* model, as outlined in Chapter 2. With a novice who knows very little and a coleader who has extensive knowledge of leadership of the type of specialized group that is organized, the more experienced leader will probably, at least initially, take a great deal of responsibility for the group, with the novice slowly building up her specialized knowledge and skills through the direct experience of the group, as well as between-group processing with the more experienced coleader. With time, the novice leader can begin to exert a more equal degree of responsibility and leadership within the group.

Another way to achieve advanced training might be where two relatively inexperienced group coleaders work together under the close supervision of an experienced leader of specialized groups. Under this model, it is very beneficial if the supervisor can directly observe the leadership of the less experienced group leaders. Such observations can be made live, such as through a one-way mirror, or based on videotapes or audiotapes of sessions. At times, self-report of group leaders may be the only option, but novices may be unaware all the information that would be helpful to report to the supervisor.

Following are ASGW's recommendations for leadership training for counselors and therapists who want to develop *advanced* competencies in working with one of the four specialized groups. Each specialized area of leadership is covered in the specific recommendations for courses and experiences:

> *Task/work group facilitation:* The recommended advanced courses will focus on concepts of development, management, and consultation with respect to organizations and on task/work group facilitation theory and practice. A minimum of 30 hours of experience in supervised practice is recommended.
>
> *Psychoeducational group work:* Advanced courses that are recommended include school counseling, community counseling, health promotion, marketing, program development, program evaluation, consulting with organizations, and psychoeducational group theory

and practice. A minimum of 30 hours of supervised practice is recommended.

Counseling groups: Advanced courses that are recommended include human development, health promotion, and counseling group theory and practice. An experience of at least 45 hours of supervised practice with the population with which the counseling group leader trainee intends to specialize is suggested.

Psychotherapy groups: Suggested courses include those with a focus on both abnormal and normal psychology and development, mental and emotional disorders assessment and diagnosis, psychopathology treatment approaches, and group psychotherapy theory and practice. A minimum supervised experience of 45 hours with the population with which the psychotherapy group leader trainee intends to specialize is recommended.

BEST PRACTICE

In a nutshell, *best practice* is a soft term for ethical practice. The Association for Specialists in Group Work (ASGW; 1998) has developed its own *Best Practices Guidelines* to help group practitioners comply to the *ethical code* of the American Counseling Association (ACA). Of course, the ASGW encourages the commitment of its members to the ACA's *Code of Ethics and Standards of Practice* (1995). Nothing in the best practices document shall be construed to supplant that code. The *Best Practices Guidelines* are intended to clarify the application of the ethical code to the specific types of group work.

The *Best Practices Guidelines* define group workers' responsibility and scope of practice involving those activities, strategies, and interventions that are consistent and current with effective and appropriate professional ethical and community standards. The ASGW views ethics as being an integral part of group work and views group workers as ethical agents.

Discussion of guidelines for best practices is provided in the following text so that the expected level of professionalism is made clear. The discussion will focus on three aspects: (1) planning, (2) performing, and (3) group processing. For the complete text of the guidelines, see "Best Practices Guidelines" on the book's Web site (see Preface for URL).

Planning

Before a therapist starts a group, she must plan the group according to the ethical expectations on planning. The following areas need to be addressed before the group work actually begins.

Professional Context and Regulatory Requirements Before engaging in group work, the first thing a therapist must do is to make sure that he is practicing group work within the boundaries of professional context and regulatory requirements. The leader must make certain that the type of group that he will be working with is actually within his training. The types of activities and particular approaches planned must be suitable for the group. For example, if the group is for personal development, the types of activities chosen should be conducive to self-understanding and developing the innate potential of each group member.

Before starting a group, the leader also should check on what regulatory requirements the local, state, and national laws place on the practice of group counseling or therapy. These restrictions may place limits on how group leaders can describe themselves. For example, if the state has a legal definition of *counselor* and requires licensure of those individuals, group leaders who are not licensed but who advertise themselves as counselors could be in violation of the state regulations. Regulatory requirements especially need to be consulted with respect to the treatment of minors in the particular locality. Group leaders must know when they need to consult with parents or guardians and obtain their written permission to work with children.

In order to stay abreast of the professional context and have a means by which to become informed about regulatory requirements, we highly recommend that group leaders become active participants in at least national and state group counseling organizations. There are multiple benefits of connecting with fellow group workers professionally. It can help leaders stay current with the field, become aware of possibilities for further development of group leadership capabilities, and grow to be a part of a professional community.

Scope of Practice and Conceptual Framework Before starting group work, therapists must plan group interventions within their scope of practice and with a clear conceptual framework. In terms of the scope of practice, the therapist should make sure that he has the type of work experiences in which group leaders generally engage. For example, a therapist who has spent two decades doing only individual counseling and who has done nothing to bring his group counseling skills up-to-date might suddenly decide to offer a group. This would raise a serious question about how the group would fit within his scope of practice. On the other hand, a therapist who has regularly engaged in individual and group counseling with abuse victims would be well within his scope of practice to offer group counseling for other abuse victims.

With respect to conceptual framework, group leaders must have clear ideas regarding what kinds of membership, activities, and possible interventions will be appropriate. For example, a group leader offering a group for abuse victims must be familiar with the theories and effects of trauma, the dynamics of abuse, and relevant cultural pressures and implications. Such conceptual knowledge will help the leader make sound judgement during the process of decision making.

Group counselors who are just starting out will not have an established scope of practice and may have only an unrefined theoretical conceptual framework, rather than a practical framework. Such beginning group counselors need to establish reliable resources and support for their work. This includes building a supervision relationship in order to help fill gaps in knowledge as well as to challenge the neophyte group leader to grow and develop within his area of expertise.

Assessment   Before starting a group, group counselors must conduct a thorough assessment. Group leaders must first be familiar with the types of issues commonly experienced by the population with which they intend to work. This means that group leaders must have a way of assessing the needs and issues of the particular individuals who apply to join the group. The group leaders will then be in a position to determine the fit between the individual applicant for the group and the overall purpose and goals of the group. For example, a potential member may describe all the issues that are common to others wanting to join a particular group, but may also have issues (such as substance abuse) that raise questions about that person's suitability for a particular group. Depending on the circumstances, such an applicant might be referred to an appropriate substance abuse group to deal with that issue first. Diversity issues with regard to culture, ethnicity, gender, age, ability, language, socioeconomic status, and sexual orientation are other aspects of group members' background that should be taken into account in assessing members' needs, wants, and expectations for a group experience.

Program Development and Evaluation   A therapist should not start a group without clear ideas of program development and evaluation. Before the group begins, the therapist must know in advance how she will design the program and how she will evaluate the program. Program development begins with identifying a particular population, conducting some type of needs assessment of that population, and then structuring a group program to help the members achieve satisfaction of their needs. We offered discussion of this aspect in Chapter 3. Program evaluation involves the leaders in determining the level of effectiveness of the design and ways it could be modified to enhance the effectiveness of the program.

Program evaluation enables group leaders to determine the degree to which the program goals and objectives are achieved. This forms a feedback loop because the accomplishments can then be used to determine whether any adjustments or changes need to be made in the way in which the group experiences are being offered.

Resources   Before starting a group, therapists need to be aware of the resources that are available for carrying out the group work. Identifying supportive agencies in the community is often a good place to begin. Next, possible sources of funding through grants, fees, or donations should be explored. Sometimes the equivalent of financial support might be available, especially when the population involved has limited funds. Some public and private organizations are willing to provide appropriate meeting space for groups. Supportive organizations may even be willing to foot the bill for advertising or assist with recruitment efforts in some other way. Other groups may be willing to be supportive in other ways, such as by providing child care for members who need it.

Professional Disclosure Statement   Group therapists must provide a professional disclosure statement to the interested public before a group actually starts. Potential group members have a right to be informed of the nature of the particular group that is to be offered and to be given information about the group leader's approach, background, and credentials. Potential members can make informed decisions about whether a group experience is likely to address their needs only when they have a full picture of what to expect.

You were first introduced to the concept of a professional disclosure statement in Chapter 3. A professional disclosure statement should be given to the interested public during pregroup training or orientation. This statement should be written in clear and direct language that is free from legalistic jargon that confuses rather than illuminates the true circumstances under which the group will be meeting.

Group and Member Preparation   Ethically, therapists must prepare group members before they enter into the group experience. Group members can only make judicious use of a group when they have an adequate level of information and preparation for the group. Potential members may have had no prior experience with group counseling, or their past group experiences may not have been handled in a fully professional manner due to the leader's lack of appropriate training, experience, and supervision.

Chapter 3 contains suggestions on how group leaders can prepare members for the group experience through a pregroup orientation. Specific suggestions are offered for leaders who conduct pregroup sessions to help them fully inform potential group members of what to expect and how they can most benefit from the group.

Professional Development   The essence of ethical practice lies in the therapist's commitment to developing the self as a skilled and proficient leader before diving into group practice. Development of the self does not occur overnight, nor does one ever learn to "wing it" entirely on the basis of natural charisma. Internally, the process of personal and professional development as a group leader requires an ability to reflect on one's own abilities, thoughts, behaviors, and emotional reactions. Externally, it requires openness to feedback, supervision, and evaluation of the effectiveness of one's professional interventions.

The path of personal development is highly integrated with the process of professional development. In Chapter 2 we discussed key aspects of the *self* of the group leader as an instrument of healing, including self-differentiation, willingness to push beyond one's current limits to expand one's abilities, engaging in self-reflection through such means as a personal journal, and openness to the supervision process and to acknowledging one's strengths and limitations. Personal development in particular requires acknowledging and resolving one's personal issues that otherwise may intrude on the group counseling process. Partaking in a group as a member can be especially crucial in this process, as one can learn in a very personal way how sticky issues get worked through in a group setting. An academic setting for a group experience will offer an opportunity for personal growth and development, but generally is not appropriate for resolving entrenched personal issues. For this, the group leader trainee should seek out another group designed to address such personal issues. Individual counseling or therapy also may be advisable.

Trends and Technological Changes   Before the therapist begins group practice, there is one last ethical aspect to consider. The group leader must keep herself updated regarding trends and technological changes. Leaders must accumulate knowledge from group literature and research, both on new concepts, approaches, and trends occurring within the field, as well as on developments in technology. Leaders must find a reasonable balance between becoming mired in "tried-and-true" practices that may have been relevant at one time but are no longer applicable and merely adopting all new approaches just because they seem to sparkle. Before adopting any new approach, leaders should carefully reflect on the implications of its implementation.

Technology may help to disseminate information with greater rapidity, resulting in greater benefits. For example, announcements of new groups might be better spread through a Web site than through flyers or phone calls, as they once were. Yet, one needs to be aware of how accessible technological avenues are for the population one wants to reach. With impoverished groups, for example, flyers or announcements in schools and religious institutions might be more appropriate and have a more realistic impact than a technological approach.

Performing

Once the therapist completes all the thorough preparation and development detailed in the previous section on planning, he can finally start the group and put all his ideas into practice. But what are the ethical guidelines for leadership performance in the group? The following text examines these in detail.

Self-Knowledge   To be able to effectively carry out group intervention, group leaders are required to have a high degree of self-understanding. There is a great deal of truth in the popular cliché that "we don't see others as they are, but as we are." In other words, what we actually see is an interpretation of the world. Unless we are familiar with our own filters and our personal tendencies in interpreting the actions of others, we will only apply these interpretations and will act in an unconscious manner rather than on the basis of clear awareness. Only those leaders who have found their way through the thicket of confusion and self-projection will truly be in a position to help group members along a similar path.

Only with self-understanding can group workers lead from the heart in a manner that will be to the benefit of the group members. Honest and authentic group leadership will be based on a group leader who is emotionally literate and in touch with his own moods, feelings, strengths, and weaknesses. In Chapter 14, you will find a more in-depth description of the areas of personal development suggested for group leaders.

Group Competencies   To perform appropriately, group workers need to gain knowledge, skills, and training, both in the core group competency areas and in the specialty group areas in which they choose to practice independently. In terms of competencies, group leaders should be knowledgeable about group processes and dynamics, not only for group work in general, but also for the areas of specialty in which they intend to work. Specialty group leaders should be well versed in the common concerns of the populations with which they will work and in the approaches that are appropriate for the type of group being offered. For example, if a group leader wants to offer group therapy for depressed elderly people, he should be familiar with the special developmental needs faced by that population and have a plan for just how the intended group will be able to account for those needs.

In terms of skills, group leaders must acquire the necessary skills in interpersonal processes. Working at the process level within group requires a different set of lenses as compared to individual counseling or psychotherapy. Group leaders must become expert at using and choosing this different set of lenses and at applying the skills that will appropriately bring clarity to the group issues that develop. In this way, all or most of the group members will benefit from any given interaction, as compared to one member at a time.

In terms of training, group leaders must develop adequate skills for working with their particular specialty groups. Typically, closely supervised practice is a key step in the training process. With supervised training, the developing group leader has an actual group in which to implement both knowledge and skills, but still has the support and guidance of a supervisor.

Group Plan Adaptation   When running a group, group therapists must be flexible enough to adapt their plan for the session to any circumstances that arise. Techniques and interventions planned for any group must be adapted to the particular group in order to fit with the particular members. An activity developed and refined for one cultural group of a certain socioeconomic status will likely need modifications if it is to be appropriately and successfully used with an entirely different cultural group or one of a different socioeconomic status.

Group plans cannot generally be set in concrete, but must instead evolve and adapt to the particular needs and developmental trajectory of the group at hand. Yet, at the same time, group plans must be firmly grounded in an understanding of the population being served.

Therapeutic Conditions and Dynamics   For the group to become a therapeutic environment for members, group leaders must understand the therapeutic factors that operate within groups. Therapeutic factors are not like doses of antibiotics or pain medicine that can be titrated to solve a specific infection or relieve a particular type of pain. Instead, therapeutic factors are forces that channel the flow of connection and experience within the group in constructive directions. The net result can very well be a great sense of healing for group members.

When running a group, leaders must be able to read the dynamics and processes occurring within the group. In addition, group leaders must be able to formulate and act on appropriate intervention responses to those dynamics in order to facilitate the beneficial effects of the therapeutic factors. Throughout this text, numerous group dynamics have been illustrated, and appropriate intervention responses have been suggested for bringing therapeutic factors into action. These illustrations and suggestions can prepare group leaders for the best practice in performing.

Meaning   Group counseling and therapy is mostly about meaning-making. In their landmark research study, Lieberman, Yalom, and Miles (1973) identified the two key elements of leadership functions as meaning-making and caring for members. Those group leaders who exhibited high levels of the ability to generate meaning-making and to provide caring were associated with groups with the highest success in terms of positive changes for the group members.

As Victor Frankl (1969) and others have stated, having an understanding and purpose associated with our experiences in life can enable humans to endure immense suffering and to achieve marvelous accomplishments. Finding the lesson contained within suffering helps us to clarify our values and to deepen the level of meaning experienced in our lives. Group leaders must have the capacity to help members work at the level of making meaning in their lives. By making meaning of their experiences, group members can potentially free themselves from being trapped and buffeted by a completely random universe. When leaders work at the level of meaning, they are more likely to help members address issues at their root, rather than just skimming the surface.

Collaboration   The essence of group is member-to-member interaction and collaboration. Group leaders must promote an environment of collaborative action among group members. Yet, collaboration within groups is only partly understood and lived among most people in the group. Often collaboration is limited to tit-for-tat, or one good deed deserves another. This tendency underestimates the healing and learning potential of group interaction. Much of group interaction happens on unconscious levels until the deeper meanings of relationships and interpersonal processes among the group members have been explored.

As we described in Chapter 6, working with the agenda that each member brings to the group can serve as a springboard for collaborative group work. The group members are encouraged to describe their agendas to the group. The group then takes time to respond to and reflect on the agenda of each of the members. As the group develops, group members are encouraged to respond not only to the content of the statements made by fellow members, but also to the manner in which the statements are made, and the personal impact that the manner of relating has on others. In this way, the group members learn not only to empathize with one another, but also to share themselves and their emotional reactions in interaction with one another. Thus, what each member gets from the group should be far more complete than an *externalized* answer to their issue. What each member gets should cut deeply to the *internal* factors that contribute to the way the member's issues play out in a social environment. This level of understanding is far more likely to result in positive and effective changes for each member.

Evaluation   As soon as the group starts, group leaders must be able to make decisions about what to focus on next based on their moment-to-moment evaluation of the group dynamics and member needs. Even if the group is a tightly structured one, adaptations or wholesale changes may need to be incorporated if group members are not fully benefiting from the experience. Similarly, it is important to know to what degree a group was successful in order to decide what recommendations or referrals to make for group members and how one might choose to run a similar group in the future.

Group leaders shoulder sole responsibility for *accurate evaluation of what is happening in the sessions.* Based on their evaluations, group leaders must find ways to enable members to understand what is happening and to process their reactions. When sufficiently processed, even issues that arouse discomfort can be worked out, and the group can actually advance developmentally. For example, some group members may constantly assert their superiority within a group and make it difficult for other members to vocalize about themselves. Facing what is happening in the group, the leader will support and encourage other group members to honestly describe their reactions. The group members may well experience some discomfort in addressing such issues squarely, but when openly addressed, conflict resolution can advance the group members to a higher level of honesty with each other.

Diversity   To ethically run a group, leaders need to have understanding of and comfort in working with diversity. Although universality is a key therapeutic factor within groups, group members will also become aware of many differences among themselves. Some of these differences may be culturally based; some may not be very noticeable until the group has spent some time together. At times, group members may become uncomfortable at making these discoveries of difference. It can seem as if the group has suddenly become an alien experience instead of a collaboration between known individuals.

Group leaders must model ways to integrate these discoveries of interpersonal differences within the group as potential areas of richness from which all group members can learn more. This kind of outlook can be quite new to some group members with a highly judgmental and exclusionary perspective. Members can choose the extent to which they are willing to enter into a greater openness and acceptance of others despite differences.

Ethical Surveillance   In the group sessions, therapists may encounter thorny ethical issues and dilemmas. When this happens, group leaders need a thorough knowledge of the *Code of Ethics* of the American Counseling Association (1995) and the recommended procedures for dealing with such issues and dilemmas. Upon encountering such ethical dilemmas, it is highly recommended that group leaders take full advantage of consultation opportunities with appropriate colleagues as well as with ethical and legal experts.

Group Processing

Group processing is highly complex and is the most important aspect of group work. The following are ethical guidelines for group therapists to follow regarding group processing.

Adequate Processing   The first rule of thumb in group processing is that it must be done adequately; enough time must be spent to process emotions after they are aroused in group activities. Group leaders must find ways to help members make sense of their experiences. Through processing, the important aspects of the experience that occurred within the group can be identified. Next, the associations that members make to these experiences can be explored and shared within the group. Finally, members are invited to describe the meanings they attach to the experience and the accompanying associations that were made.

Group leaders themselves also need to take time to process the group experiences. In processing their own experiences in the group, leaders will continue to grow personally and professionally. It is beneficial for members if a group leader does a part of this processing within the group session, but a great deal of it must take place outside the group. There are two broad ways of processing by group leaders: (1) strictly through individual self-reflection, and (2) through individual and/or group supervision of the group work. Self-reflection contributes to the effectiveness of the supervision process.

It is important that group leaders have adequate opportunity to reflect on the dynamics and progress occurring within groups. As suggested earlier, by keeping a personal reflective journal as well as obtaining qualified supervision, group leaders can promote this self-processing. Such processing allows the group leaders to make full use of themselves as instruments for group work.

Reflective Practice   The second rule of thumb is that group processing goes hand-in-hand with reflective practice. Group leaders not only need to reflect on the particulars of what happened in the group, but also be able to relate these observations to theories of group dynamics. Making these interconnections between observations and theory can help group leaders remain grounded in the midst of the seeming turbulence occurring from one session of group interaction to the next.

Reflective practice offers group leaders an opportunity to integrate various aspects of their training with the specific circumstances occurring within a particular group. This approach fits with the Kolb (1984) experiential learning cycle of incorporating the abstract concepts into the concrete experience happening in the current group.

Evaluation and Follow-Up   Following each group event or incident, the group leader must evaluate whether the event and the dynamics have been thoroughly explored and whether the underlying relationship issues have been resolved. If there might be any *unfinished business,* a follow-up processing should be used to bring resolution to the feelings aroused during the event.

In Chapter 5, we presented skills for opening group sessions. In opening sessions, group leaders must attend to whether there is any unfinished business carried over from the previous session. Oftentimes, significant issues can be raised within a session. Although members are always encouraged to express their reactions, many members need more time to "digest" their experiences. They need to reflect on the group experience between sessions. Between-session feelings are important business for members to bring up during the check-in procedure. The leader can inquire during the opening of the session about whether there are any additional reactions to the previous group session.

On-going evaluation can be carried out in the form of a member "check-out" procedure. As a session is being concluded, group leaders can suggest that group members briefly address how the session touched on their goals for that session. If group members suggest a continued reaction to the events of the session for which there has been insufficient time to explore, then the group leader can suggest that further exploration of the issue be continued in the following group meeting.

Consultation and Training with Other Organizations   If some issues that cannot easily be resolved within the group exist, consultation with other group experts or professionals might be needed. Seeking competent professional consultation about difficult situations is a wise thing for all group leaders to do, whether they are inexperienced or have a great deal of experience. It makes little sense for counseling professionals to "keep their own counsel" when it comes to sorting through complex or difficult issues. Consultation need not be limited to someone of national or international reputation. Just as a group is made up of ordinary people dealing with similar issues but having different experiences, perspectives, and reactions to bring for enrichment of understanding of those issues, the counseling profession is made up of individuals who have much to offer one another. We all know people who are more experienced than us in some way, and therefore there is the possibility of learning from others. Even when our experience level is approximately the same, our experiences are never exactly the same, and just having another perspective to consider can open us up to new and potentially more effective possibilities in resolving some issues within the groups. The sharing of information is the human way of disseminating and advancing knowledge to the betterment of all.

Advanced training with renowned group experts can deeply enrich the knowledge and skills of group leaders and prepare us more fully for future work with groups. Training with other organizations can help to open us to new perspectives, especially when the training organization specializes in work with particular issues and clientele.

SELF-REFLECTION

1. Where do you see yourself at present in terms of your own group leadership knowledge level? Are there some areas or particular group concepts that you would especially like to deepen at this point in your training? How might you find ways to increase your knowledge in these areas once this class has been completed?

2. What is your comfort level at this point in terms of exercising your group leadership skills? Brainstorm some ways in which you might be able to increase your facility and adeptness in leading groups.

3. At what level would you assess your ability to plan a group experience? With what types of groups are you most comfortable? Least comfortable? What types of groups interest you the most? What types interest you the least, or not at all?

4. Identify some possible specific learning opportunities open to you that would help you to build your group leadership knowledge, skills, and experience.

5. What are your current views about what factors are key to the best practice of group work? How might you go about enhancing these factors with respect to your level of knowledge and skills in leading groups?

6. What are some personal guidelines that you might follow to ensure ethical practice in your leadership of groups? Will these guidelines also be likely to enhance the quality of the experience for group members?

7. Reflect back to Chapter 2 in which we discussed the phases of group leader development (Zaslav, 1988): group shock, reappraisal, one-step behind, using the here-and-now, and polishing skills. Where do you see yourself in terms of these stages?

8. Given the stage at which you now see yourself (see question 7), what elements of the best practice guidelines seem most appropriate for you to focus on right now for your continued development as a group leader?

FURTHER DEVELOPMENT OF THE GROUP LEADER

The development of a group leader is an ongoing process that never ends. Mastering the skills and intervention techniques used in facilitating the interpersonal processes of a group is just the beginning. Further along the road is the development of the "person" of the leader—the "self" of the therapist. In Chapter 2, we briefly touched upon this subject. In this concluding chapter, we discuss how to develop the group therapist's "self" as the ultimate instrument in group work. This chapter covers:

- Finding your own therapeutic voice
- Daring to be creative
- Trusting your own intuition
- Developing emotional intelligence

FINDING YOUR OWN THERAPEUTIC VOICE

To make group work personally gratifying, group leaders must exercise their own therapeutic voices in it. Although a textbook such as this can help provide some of the necessary knowledge base, it is through the heightened awareness that one truly finds one's therapeutic voice. Your personhood must be felt through your actions and interventions. Personal voice can be developed through committing to a framework that truly reflects one's beliefs and personal experiences. This section addresses the development and refinement of the personal voice as a further step toward developing the self as a therapeutic instrument.

Technically Correct, Therapeutically Unsound

A group therapist's interventions during the session will be unfocused and without direction if the therapist has not committed herself to a particular framework. Without a filter to screen out the overflow of data, the therapist sees either too much or too little. Either she is easily overwhelmed by the ever spinning and twirling dynamics of group events, or she does not see it even when big elephants are striding in the room. She is busy listening to the words, views, and complaints uttered by the members. As the group's conversation drifts onto more and more topics, this leader misses the emotional reactivity that is aroused when certain core issues are enacted in some members. She does not hear the meanings behind the lines, nor does she see the reactivity patterns activated among certain members. She relies on her memory of a host of techniques that she learned in her studies. Despite her skilled delivery of several technically correct interventions, the session remains detoured, without a focus, and no critical ground gets covered. The sessions repeat themselves, never going beyond the limited capacity of the initial stage to reach any depth of corrective emotional experiences. We call this sort of leadership technically correct, but therapeutically flimsy and unsound.

Framework as a Compass

With a framework in mind, the group leader has a compass by which to look for certain kinds of incidents. He can orient himself as he conducts the session. He can look for certain events that bear substantial meanings in group dynamics during the session, without being distracted or caught up by all the others. He will observe the intensity of certain members' emotional reactivity, and he will let the spotlight remain on particular members long enough to illuminate those reactivity patterns and bring about awareness of those patterns. Or he will lead the group to offer whatever experiences specific members need to have, in that particular moment, which are utterly different from what they experienced in the past; these experiences are corrective and restorative for the given members.

Group therapists are better off in practice when they commit themselves to becoming remarkably good at a particular framework before becoming eclectic. An "encyclopedic approach" to therapy, as Simon (2003) critiques it, is inadequate when it comes to helping clients reach the core of their issues and achieve desirable change. It also deprives the group therapist of performance benchmarks against which he can set his own goals for growth and development.

Searching Inside: Your Own Therapeutic Beliefs

Committing to a particular framework is not about choosing the model that best fits one's own style. Rather, it is about searching inside oneself to sort through and become aware of one's own underlying beliefs about the human condition. It is about finding a personal truth that commands one's passion.

If, for example, a leader does not personally believe that present group behaviors are intimately connected to the reactivity patterns established earlier in members' lives, or that unexpected group behavior can be a small window to or a microcosm of our life themes, then the experiential approach to group counseling and therapy will not carry any personal meaning for her. If the leader does not believe that the roles that we took on in our earliest group (family) will play out in the immediacy of the group, then she will not see it happening even when the enactment is kicking wildly and loudly in front of her. If a leader does not believe in the therapeutic effect of evoking direct emotion in the session to reach deeper cognitive understanding of its reactivity pattern, then a group approach that emphasizes the hot-seat effect of the here-and-now will bear no value for her.

By the same token, if a leader believes that pain should be eliminated by reassurance the moment it surges, lest it get unbearable, she will have difficulty working from an experiential approach wherein the leader allows members to stay present or to fully experience any significant emotion, including pain, without feeling compelled to take it away immediately. And if a leader believes that change can be brought about by giving first-class solutions to members or that a long-standing pattern of behavior can be stopped by persuading the member to change, then a group approach that addresses interpersonal processes would simply be a waste of time for her.

As group therapists, we need to look inside ourselves and listen to our own personal narratives, to sort through what we actually believe about the human condition and human nature, before we can choose the working framework that will best guide our practice. We must know ourselves first, before we commit to a framework. Committing to a framework, however, will make each group session a highly personalized encounter between us and our group members. The members will sense "the person" of the group therapist and feel our personal presence. We will become more than a host of isolated techniques or a professional decorated with an array of credentials. The group members will hear a consistent voice coming from us because, in the framework that we choose, we begin to find our own voice.

Continual Refinement of Your Therapeutic Voice

To speak with our own therapeutic voice is, ultimately, to be ourselves and to be the best selves that we can be. This is a lifelong process, an infinite journey that continues far beyond the professional training we receive. It requires continual direct personal experience, a personal evolution in every aspect of ourselves. There is no shortcut and no cheating. Reading and attending workshops will bring out our best selves only to limited degree. We must do our personal work experientially to refine our own voice. For example, if we believe members need to increase their self-differentiation, then we need to put ourselves in situations where our scale of self-differentiation is tested. If we want to increase our group members' ability to contain their emotions, we need to situate ourselves in those circumstances in which we feel vulnerable. If we want to inspire our group members to shift from external to internal validation, we need to continually practice that kind of affirmation within ourselves, even under the most trying circumstances.

We may achieve this continual refinement of our personal therapeutic voice through supervision or personal therapy, or through other means. Whatever avenues we take, we must continue to push at the edge of growth even after a framework and a personal voice have been found. Carl Whitaker states that therapy will not be good for the clients unless it is also good for the therapist (in Simon, 2003). This especially holds true for group counseling and therapy. As group therapists, we cannot cheat on our own homework. If we are unwilling to confront our own demons, it is ethically improper for us to expect our group members to do that work.

DARING TO BE CREATIVE

Group work is not only a rigorous clinical endeavor, but also an artistic enterprise. Successful group work requires the artist to evolve beyond techniques and skills and into the uncertainties of intuition and creativity. Most therapists welcome this requirement. We have chosen the profession of counseling and therapy, after all, because we have the urge to create. Group practice provides a fruitful setting for this urge of creativity. Each group session provides unique and completely new problems and human dynamics to be understood and resolved in a creative way. Our clients may forget what they learned in school, but they will never forget that intense session when they were engrossed in the creative endeavor of the whole group process, where they got their "aha" experience. Our novel idea in that particular session creates an image or a voice that will feed the client's inspiration for many decades. For most of us, to be creative makes us feel alive. For a group therapist, to be creative makes her feel she has contributed to the betterment of our human race by giving a little nudge.

Taking Risks and Giving Yourself to the Process

To be creative inevitably involves taking risks. We might make mistakes when we allow ourselves to be creative. Many of us fear making mistakes in group interventions. Many of us fear that our creative ideas might be rejected by the group or that the members might not appreciate what we are trying to initiate. But we have to take risks! In terms of what is best to do in what group dynamics, we will never "figure it all out." Even if we are the greatest group therapists in the world, with a fantastic mastery of the art, we still will not tap into the power of group until we give ourselves to it without reservation. Approaching group dynamics from a cautious, assiduous, perfectionistic distance will not get us too far. Without taking the risk of giving the best of ourselves to it, the moment-to-moment group dynamics will be gone by the time we figure out what to do. To be creative is to allow ourselves to take risks within appropriate boundaries.

Sometimes our first attempts at creative interventions fail because of our lack of experience in delivery. After several attempts, however, our delivery of the interventions may become more sophisticated and effective. We need to be patient with ourselves, and we need to allow ourselves to be ineffective when we are trying out new ideas or strategies. The new attempts will fit like an old glove to the hand one day.

At times we may fear the emotions that are involved in our creative interventions. When our creative interventions open gates for group members to deal with powerful issues involving intimacy, power, inclusion, competition, trust, and jealousy, we might find ourselves being pulled into the sea of these issues. We have to step out of the professional role that we so comfortably wear, and be honest, transparent, and spontaneous in our responses. When appropriate, we have to reveal the vulnerable parts of ourselves, the parts of ourselves that are not readily accessible to our clients. All of these actions involve risks. Without risk-taking, we are merely technicians, instead of artists and innovators.

Being Willing to Experiment

Innovation and experimentation are practically synonymous. Only when we allow ourselves to experiment with different ideas and strategies in our therapeutic endeavors can we push the edge or our own growth. The spirit of experimenting is not based on using clients as guinea pigs, manipulating them to see whether any results can be produced. Rather, experimentation means constantly checking on the feedback and adjusting the therapeutic methods until they work. Experimentation is taken on with a responsible and ethical attitude for the clients' well-being. Each intervention is modified constantly until it works. Some interventions (such as the hot-seat method) might produce slight discomfort in clients; their use is justified only if they ultimately prove to be beneficial to clients.

Staying Playful and Alive

To be creative is to stay playful and emotionally alive. Carl Whitaker (1976), the most dynamic of the founders of family therapy, provided the following tips to help high-achieving people, including therapists, stay emotionally alive:

1. Relegate every significant other to second place.
2. Learn how to love. Flirt with any infant available. Unconditional positive regard probably is not present after the baby is 3 years old.
3. Develop a reverence for your own impulses, and be suspicious of your behavior sequences.
4. Enjoy your mate more than your kids, and be childish with your mate.
5. Break role structure at will and repeatedly.
6. Learn to retreat and advance from every position you take.
7. Guard your impotence as one of your most valuable weapons.
8. Build long-term relationships so you can be free to hate safely.
9. Face the fact that you must grow until you die. Develop a sense of the benign absurdity of life—yours and those around you—and thus learn to transcend the world of experience. If we can abandon our missionary zeal, we have less chance of being eaten by cannibals.
10. Develop your primary-process living. Evolve a joint craziness with someone you feel safe with. Structure a professional cuddle group so you won't abuse your mate with the garbage left from the day's work.
11. As Plato said, "Practice dying." (Whitaker, 1976, p. 164)

Remaining Open to the Energy Field

Creativity cannot be lassoed or dragged kicking and screaming into our lives. Instead, creativity comes when properly invited and when it finds the doors open. To be creative is to stay open to the energy field.

In yoga, energy is referred to as *prana*—the basic energy of life. When *prana* is blocked, it may be expressed in various unwholesome ways, such as withdrawal from others and depression. A person with blocked energy may experience a range of bodily ills and hostility toward others. Unlocking the intrapersonal and interpersonal impediments that clog the flow of *prana* can open doors to more creative and spontaneous living.

As the group involves emotional energy, we leaders must be conscious of recharging ourselves lest we inadvertently become depleted in the group process. Awareness of breath and patterns of breathing is one way to regulate our emotional state and level of consciousness. Regulating our own breathing and remaining in an optimum state of awareness can help us stay focused while working with groups. Yoking, or uniting, oneself to something beyond one's individual person is an essential part of creativity. There are various avenues we might follow to achieve unity, including meditation, conscious breathing, mindfulness, and one-point focusing.

TRUSTING YOUR OWN INTUITION

Effective group work requires leaders to evolve beyond techniques and into the realm of creativity and intuition. Intuition is that inner knowledge we use to guide our moment-to-moment decisions. This section looks at ways of using intuition to fine-tune our clinical judgments in group work.

Intuition and Clinical Inference

Intuition is a nonconscious way of processing information. This manner of processing affords us a "broader net," in which we can be more impartial in gathering data without having to fit it into preconceived notions or beliefs. While conscious processing is considerably linear and slow, intuition is a "rapid, highly structured form of nonconscious processing" (Rea, 2001, p. 97). This rapid nonconscious processing affords us an "immediate or direct apprehension" of the situation at hand (Osbeck, 2002, p. 118). Besides being faster and smarter, our intuition allows us to take in much more "complex knowledge structures" than we can when we think and identify meanings of stimuli in a conscious manner (Lewicki, Hill, & Czyzewska, 1992, p. 801).

In therapy, intuition helps us make quick and sound clinical decisions during the ongoing flow of the session. For example, after a member, Akeko, presented her agenda, another member, Juan, elaborated on an issue of concern. As Juan described the details of his concern, another member, Binny, evidenced a strong reaction while gazing at Akeko. The leader had to assess multiple factors in deciding whether or not to immediately address Juan's concern. The leader had to decide whether to keep the focus on Juan, to shift the focus back to Akeko, to pick up a thread that was left hanging, or to shift the attention over to Binny. Whatever decision a leader makes in a situation like this, the clinical reasoning behind the decision is often based on an intuitive appraisal of what will be best for the group and the members at that particular moment.

Refining Clinical Intuition

Clinical intuition requires continual refinement throughout our practice. In the following text, we apply Rea's (2001) ideas to leaders' continual refinement of clinical intuition.

As group leaders, we must become aware of our own biases, limitations, and personal tendencies. In this way, we distinguish personally driven impulses and wishful thinking from intuitive insight. Intuition can never replace true knowledge, skills, and experience in leadership development. All of these elements are needed to provide a context for the intuitive reasoning to grow. Clinical intuition, therefore, is a synthesis of basic knowledge, clinical observations, and leadership skills and techniques.

Cultivating our imaginative faculties can open group leaders to the great wealth of information that presents itself within a group. Encountering the group from a more holistic and phenomenological framework will help us stay in the flow of all that happens within a group, including the unexpected. To entertain a holistic perspective, it is important that we stay nonresistant to a variety of theoretical approaches. Carrying resistance or an internal struggle around is not conducive to promoting conscious processing in groups. Rigid adherence to particular approaches can unduly restrict us from being open to the many other types of knowledge and skills available. If we, for example, understand group interactions only from a cognitive-behaviorist point of view, we are likely to miss other approaches to understanding the rich meanings of the dynamics, severely limiting our ability to help the group members grow.

In addition to being open to various theoretical approaches, we also need to maintain an openness to our own internal experience of thoughts, sensations, and emotions that arise in response to the interactions unfolding in the group. Meticulous observation involves looking at the whole picture of what is there, externally as well as internally. It requires us to pay attention to, and not overlook, even those dynamics that do not fit with our own expectations or that make us fearful and anxious.

DEVELOPING EMOTIONAL INTELLIGENCE

In group counseling, the therapist's ability to be emotionally present and literate is an essential quality for serving the needs of members. To lead a group is to promote emotional healing, development, and liberation within group members. Part of developing the self of the group therapist involves *developing a high level of emotional intelligence.* The term *emotional intelligence* can be defined as "the capacity for recognizing our own feelings and those of others, for motivating ourselves, and for managing emotions well in ourselves and in our relationships" (Goleman, 1998, p. 317). Specifically for leadership, Cooper and Sawaf (1997) described four basic aspects of emotional intelligence: emotional literacy, emotional fitness, emotional depth, and emotional alchemy. This section describes the road ahead for group leaders in developing these four aspects of emotional intelligence.

Emotional Literacy

To develop emotional intelligence, a group leader must be literate about matters of the heart. In leading groups, such a leader is in touch with his inner truth about his personal emotional state with each group interaction. Being able to work from the heart, the leader is in a state of calmness and at rest. He is capable of intense emotional involvement and of providing a good dose of humor, he has a lighthearted outlook, and he maintains self-care such as healthy eating and exercising. In group work, humor can be especially helpful in gaining a healthier perspective on the issues being faced. Humor can help build the therapeutic alliance with group members, as it relieves the otherwise almost unbearable tension in difficult group dynamics (Ortiz, 2000).

Working directly from the heart enables leaders to listen to their emotions and use them to inform what they should attend to most. For example, if a leader senses anger rising from within, he may listen to that anger and use it as a cue to address whatever is affecting him, as long as it is relevant to the group. Leaders' emotional reactions often resonate with significant issues that are simmering within the group. If the leader is reacting emotionally to some subtle or blatant events in the group, then it is quite possible that some group members are experiencing similar emotional reactions. While group members may not know how to respond to the emotion in a way that will benefit the group, the group leader can verbalize the emotion in a way that models an appropriate response. This can lead members to better understand the important transactions that take place within group.

Emotional Fitness

To cultivate emotional intelligence, a leader strives to stay emotionally fit. An emotionally fit person displays resiliency and is capable of renewing herself even when facing significant difficulties. She is fully present with others and does not carry hidden agendas that get in the way of honest relationships. She has an authentic presence. With this capacity, group leaders are able to focus on the group members and their needs with attentiveness and genuine concern. They are willing to share power and responsibility with members for the operation of the group. In the initial stages of a group, such a group leader is more likely to instruct, shape, and encourage members, taking an influential stance with the group. Later, as the group develops, the leader will continue to support members but will also challenge them more frequently in constructive ways.

Emotionally fit group leaders are able to work through conflicts while trust is being tested. The ability of group leaders to work creatively with conflict has been discussed at length in Chapter 7. Conflict within groups can enhance awareness of issues that are of value to the group.

Personal resiliency and the ability to seek and find sources of renewal are hallmarks of a healthy human being and contribute significantly to being an effective group leader. We are all faced with inevitable challenges, difficulties, and setbacks in life. What is important is how we choose to deal with these difficulties. Adaptability in the face of adversity is certainly a part of emotional intelligence. Sooner or later, group leaders will be challenged by group members. When facing such challenges, leaders need an ability to adapt. In order to be able to adapt, we need reserves of energy and an ability to find renewal amidst strife. Replenishing ourselves is critical if we are to bring creativity and insight to our groups.

Emotional Depth

In developing the self, leaders need to develop emotional depth. A person of emotional depth demonstrates integrity, deep commitment, an ability to influence without resorting to an authoritarian stance, and an ability to build on his own unique potential. A person of emotional depth has integrity: He is honest, communicates clearly and openly, and bears responsibility for the conduct of his activities. Above all, integrity suggests a *wholeness* of character. The only way to achieve personal wholeness is through challenging ourselves to be receptive to feedback in order to get a glimpse of the parts of ourselves that we might otherwise overlook. In group work, integrity inevitably requires the leaders to adhere to the American Counseling Association's *Code of Ethics* (1995) and the

Association for Specialists in Group Work's *Best Practices Guidelines* (1998), as discussed in the previous chapter.

A person of emotional depth often lives with a sense of purposefulness and is in touch with his deeply held values. A group leader with emotional depth is committed to his belief in the interpersonal process of groups despite the various turbulence experienced from time to time. Whenever group members demonstrate resistance, become locked in conflict, or exhibit hopelessness about their own abilities to change, a group leader with emotional depth believes that these difficulties will be eventually worked through within the interpersonal learning forces of the group process. He has faith in members' abilities to grow from that experience. The leader's emotional depth radiates a sense of hope that is transmitted to members through both verbal statements and nonverbal actions.

Emotional Alchemy

Another area for further development in leaders is emotional alchemy. A person with emotional alchemy can usually sense within ordinary interpersonal interactions, golden opportunities for transmitting restoring messages that can bring transformation to others. This keen sense of such opportune moments arises from the ability to recognize a here-and-now event involving emotional experiences from which insight can be gained.

Emotional alchemy has a lot to do with the ability to envision a desired future *as if it exists right now.* This ability in the leader can bring transformation to members. Most members come to a group because they are stuck in some way. They have probably thought about their situations and made some attempts to change them, but failed. As a result, they feel frustrated, discouraged, and disempowered. What they need is a spark of hope in order to gain a new sense of what might be possible after all. A leader with emotional alchemy can provide that spark of hope through a transformational vision, an insight into the positive possibilities for group members that is in line with the members' strengths and values. As members are influenced to believe in a vision of their desired future, this belief will serve as a magnet for future actions.

Conclusion

Throughout this text, we have endeavored to provide varied and complex intervention techniques for leading process-focused groups. Although groups themselves can generate a great deal of energy, as group leaders, we need our own sources of regeneration to keep up with our work. As members thrust toward renewal within the groups, group leaders must continue to seek opportunities in their own lives for personal development and regeneration. Ultimately, leaders face all the same basic issues as the members they serve. It is the leader's task to continue to enhance her state of consciousness, both for her own growth and for the benefit of the group members.

SELF-REFLECTION

1. When thinking about your own emotional development, what were some experiences that you recall as having had a significant impact on your level of emotional literacy? Emotional fitness? Emotional depth?

2. How do you think the development of emotional intelligence fits with the ACA *Code of Ethics* and the ASGW *Best Practices Guidelines?*

3. Does considering yourself a scientist preclude your comfort in working with your intuitive faculties? If these aspects seem incompatible to you, how will you navigate within the here-and-now of the group? How might intuitive skills assist you in working in the here-and-now?

4. Have you participated in any special training in meditation, yoga, or focusing? If so, what was this experience like for you? What was of greatest significance? Will you be able to draw upon any of this training for your work with groups?

5. What other practices or approaches of interest to you, besides those discussed in the text, are you aware of that would not only contribute to your own personal growth, but also help you to more fully integrate the multiple facets of who you are?

6. What facets of yourself do you most wish to deepen at this point with respect to your own development as a person? As a professional?

7. What helps you to find a solid center of well-being within yourself that will also help you to maintain a therapeutic level of equanimity when working with groups?

Sample Group Proposal

PERSONAL-GROWTH GROUP FOR ADOLESCENTS IN SUDDEN TRANSITION

RATIONALE

By the age of 12 to 14, many children have experienced a loss that has had an impact on their lives. Many times, this loss affects how a student responds in a learning environment. Since many school support staffs are overextended, this group will give students a chance to work through their problems in a safe and caring environment. The group will also serve to help children develop coping strategies and build self-esteem.

TYPE OF GROUP

This group will be a personal-growth and self-exploration group for clients between the ages of 12 and 13. This support group will be comprised of 6 to 8 adolescents. The group will meet for one hour each week, from 11:00 A.M. to 12:00 P.M., for 15 weeks. The group will be a closed group where no members will be admitted after the group has started. During the group meetings, members will participate in activities and discussions that focus on particular topics pertaining to the changes in their families. A prerequisite for joining the group is a sudden transition in one's family structure. Regular attendance will be required.

GOALS AND OBJECTIVES

The group will assist adolescents through the grief process. Once they have finished this process, they will be better able to cope with the changes in their family system. The primary goal of this group will be to promote emotional healing by providing a safe and effective environment for the expression and release of feelings associated with the significant loss. The following objectives will provide direction in accomplishing this goal:

- To furnish participants an understanding of their new family unit
- To assist in building a stronger sense of self-esteem
- To direct participants toward a healthy resolution of the changes that have taken place in their personal lives
- To develop trust within the group to allow for an honest sharing of attitudes and feelings

BASIC INFORMATION

The group will be led by Selina M. F., who graduated from a CREP (Council for Accreditation of Counseling and Related Programs)–approved master's program in counseling. She has worked with groups of adolescents who were going through difficult transitions in their lives. In addition, she has been a teacher for four years. She has seen the effects on children of a major loss or transition in the family. She possesses trained leadership skills, as well as a motive of genuine care and concern. She is committed to providing children with the support and empathy they need to resolve their inner issues.

The cost of implementing the program is $100.00. This will allow for group materials for 6 to 8 students, which will include "I Love Me" journals. Journals will be a nonthreatening, private place for participants to write out or draw their grief events and feelings. Once identified, the participants can start to understand and deal with their grief in a constructive manner. The journals will be the personal property of the participants and are not to be read by the leader, parents, or guardians unless the participants choose to share them. There will be no fee for the participants joining the group.

A booth will be set up at school during all lunch hours for one week. At this time, students can visit the booth to read information about the group and discuss its focus. Students also can inquire about the criteria for joining the group. If interested, they can take an information sheet that explains the group goals and objectives and a parent letter, which must be returned and signed before a student is placed in the group.

BASIC GROUND RULES

The group will operate under the following ground rules:

- Members are expected to attend all sessions and to participate by disclosing themselves and giving feedback to others.
- Confidentiality will be enforced; whatever is said or done in the group is *not* to be talked about outside the group.
- Each participant may share only what he/she said or what he/she did.
- Each participant must listen to the others; side conversations and interruptions will not be allowed.
- Everyone will get a chance to talk.
- Members must respect each other's feelings without judgment or ridicule.
- Everyone is to stay on the topic being discussed. When the discussion gets offtrack, participants will be reminded that they are wandering from the topic and that the group needs to refocus.
- Members will be asked to maintain a nonjudgmental attitude.
- Members will be asked to make a commitment to remain in the group for at least four weeks.
- Participants will work toward helping each other so everyone will have a safe and cohesive atmosphere in which to heal.

TOPICS FOR GROUP EXPLORATION

The initial session will be devoted to teaching participants how to get the maximum benefit from a group experience, orienting them to the ground rules, and explaining the process that will take place in the sessions. Each session will focus on certain themes that emerge. Some examples of theme-oriented sessions are the following:

- Looking closely at feelings that members may associate with their personal experiences regarding changes in their family
- Expressing strengths or positive aspects of participants' characters
- Sharing personal stories that symbolize the grief members may feel
- Talking about the changes in the members' personal lives
- Journaling about thoughts, feelings, perceptions, and fears regarding anger
- Providing an opportunity for students to articulate their individual fears
- Recognizing the uniqueness and goodness of participants' own families
- Reflecting on the place and person with whom a member feels most comfortable
- Describing members' stepfamilies, with all their achievements and disappointments
- Deciding on which memories to let go and which ones to cherish
- Discovering creative solutions to problems instead of reacting emotionally

EVALUATION METHODS

An evaluation will be given at the start of the group and at termination. The survey will focus on current feelings and attitudes about one's self and one's family structure. Ongoing evaluation of the effectiveness of the group will be made with members providing feedback to one another. In addition, a follow-up meeting will be held about six weeks after the group ends to assess the impact the group has had on the clients. The meeting also can serve as reinforcement and support for members, especially for those who have had setbacks since the group was terminated.

Orientation Handouts

Orientation handouts are written materials that group therapists can use to educate prospective group members during pregroup training. Four orientation handouts are included here: (1) Rights and Responsibilities of Group Members; (2) Orientation to Being in Group; (3) How to Get the Most from Group; and (4) Informed Consent Form. The first two handouts are samples from Student Counseling Services at Iowa State University. The latter two were created by the authors for educational use.

RIGHTS AND RESPONSIBILITIES OF GROUP MEMBERS

Student Counseling Services, Iowa State University
Reprinted with Permission

Member Rights

As a member of a group sponsored by the Student Counseling Services, you have certain rights and responsibilities. Among your rights are:

Respect   The group facilitators will strive to establish and maintain a climate of respect within the group for your values, principles, and beliefs.

Confidentiality   The group facilitators will respect the confidentiality of information obtained about individual members of the group.

1. The facilitators will discuss a group or individuals within the group only with fellow professionals who are clearly concerned with the group, and then only for professional consultation.
2. Although guarantees cannot be provided by the group facilitators, group members have a mutual responsibility to refrain from revealing any information obtained from fellow group members to anyone outside the group.
3. If a video or audio recording of group sessions is needed by the group leader, it will be obtained only with a consensus of all group members and with the group's signed consent. Without the group's permission, the leader will not tape any group session.

Voluntary Participation   You should participate in a group only on a voluntary basis. The group facilitators will honor your right to withdraw from the group without your being subjected to undue pressure from other group members.

1. The primary purposes, the basic guidelines, the potential benefits, and the potential risks involved in the group experience will be established and discussed candidly with you prior to the beginning of the group or at the first group session.
2. The facilitators will support your freedom of choice and see that you are not required or unduly urged to participate in any specific activity of the group against your better judgment.

Physical and Emotional Welfare   The group facilitators will protect the physical and emotional welfare of the individuals in the group.

1. The facilitators will take the responsibility to observe, attend, and intervene on your behalf should it become apparent that emotional stress has developed to a point that it threatens your well-being.
2. Competent referral sources will be arranged for you in the event you require help beyond that which is being received in the group.

Follow-Up Services   The group facilitators' responsibilities for the members do not automatically end with the termination of the group experience. The facilitators will make themselves available to deal with individual members' needs arising at the end of a group or refer the individual to more appropriate sources when deemed necessary.

Member Responsibilities:

As a member of a group, you also have certain responsibilities to the group and its individual members. Among these are to:

Attend Group Meetings   For a group to work effectively, it is important that you attend all scheduled sessions and be on time. If an emergency arises and you cannot attend a particular group session, or if you will be late, please call the office and leave a message for the group facilitators as far in advance as possible.

Actively Participate   In order for a group to be effective, it is necessary for you to take an active role in the process. Being open and honest with group members and/or the facilitators, discussing concerns about the group process, and working on outside assignments when appropriate are some of the ways that this may happen.

Contact Group Leaders upon Deciding to Withdraw from Group   If, during the course of your group experience, you decide to withdraw, you should discuss your decision with the group facilitators. This will enable the facilitators to make alternate arrangements for you if necessary and to obtain feedback from you, which is important in planning future group programs.

Respect Confidentiality   It is the responsibility of each group member to refrain from revealing any information obtained from a fellow group member to anyone outside the group. This is imperative for the development of group trust.

Cooperate in Evaluating Services Received   An evaluation at the end of the group may be conducted. It may be in the form of a brief interview or questionnaire administered after you have finished participation in the group.

We believe that this list of rights and responsibilities will help make your group experience more productive and satisfying. If you have any questions or comments about any of these items, please discuss these with your group facilitators or the group itself.

ORIENTATION TO BEING IN GROUP

Student Counseling Services, Iowa State University
Reprinted with Permission

If this is your first experience in joining a group, along with some excitement and anticipation, you probably have some apprehensions—most people do. People have common concerns such as: How will I react? What will the other members be like? and Will the experience be helpful and meaningful to me? In this handout, we will outline some of the benefits of being in a group as well as provide some guidelines to assist you in taking advantage of the experience.

What to Expect from Group?

Group counseling and therapy provides you with the opportunity to address current concerns most important to you, to identify with others who are experiencing similar concerns, to increase your self-awareness through identifying life themes that are interfering with your growth, to become more sensitive to the needs of others, and to learn to respect individual differences as you learn to affirm your own uniqueness.

In group counseling and therapy, you have the opportunity to gain immediate feedback from other group members and the leaders. By gaining feedback from others (how they perceive you), you increase your awareness of yourself and focus intentional energy into the aspects of your life you wish to change.

Group therapy also gives you an opportunity to try out new behaviors, to express feelings you have been hesitant to express, to assert yourself in new ways, to experiment with new ideas. Over time, as you experience trust and security in the group, you will feel freer to take risks.

One of the most fascinating aspects of being in a group is the learning you obtain from other group members. You benefit not only from recognizing your emotional and thought responses but also from identifying with the feelings of others. Through identifying with others, you increase your self-awareness.

With the assistance of the group leaders and your fellow group members, you will have the task of determining how you take advantage of these opportunities. You determine the amount of energy—mental and emotional—you wish to invest in the group process. Needless to say, the more you invest, the more you benefit.

How to Get the Most Out of Group

Be Yourself   Basically this means starting from where you are, not how you think others want you to be. This might mean that you behave in a childlike way, express anger or hostility, appear shy and withdrawn, or communicate confusion and hopelessness. The working-through process starts with whatever you feel free to disclose.

Define Goals   Think about what you would like to get out of the group, not only from the total experience, but also from each individual session. Take time before each session to define your expectations for that session. Nevertheless, being flexible about your goals is also important. You may be surprised to find that your goals continue to change throughout the group process. As your self-awareness increases and as you listen to other group members, you will discover other issues that might become more important than the original ones. When you experience intense feelings or thoughts about something that is happening in the group, it is important to focus on these feelings and thoughts and to express them.

Recognize and Respect Your Pace for Getting Involved in Group   Some group members will always be ready to disclose their thoughts and feelings; others need more time to gain feelings of trust and security. By respecting your need to become involved when you are ready, you are learning self-acceptance. If you are having a difficult time knowing how to discuss your problems with the group, then ask the group to help you. At times, just knowing what to say is a problem. Being the quiet member of a group can be very uncomfortable, but needs to be accepted if that is "where you are."

Take Time for Yourself   You have the right to take group time to talk about yourself. Some group members hesitate to take the time to disclose their concerns because they feel that others need the time or they question the importance of what they have to say. Often, the person who hesitates to take time is having difficulty in facing his/her lack of self-worth or is having discomfort in showing "weakness." By recognizing what the reluctance means, you begin the growth process.

Focus on What Is Most Important to You   What you may want to talk about may be something related to external issues—what is happening outside the group. You are encouraged to talk about relationships with significant others, questions about life goals and directions, childhood memories, dreams, and feelings about yourself. As you talk about these concerns, the group will help you recognize themes and patterns so that these can be dealt with more directly. With time being limited, you will be encouraged to provide essential information without going into extensive detail. People often use storytelling to avoid dealing with the key issues, so you will be encouraged to move beyond the stories and facts.

Recognize and Express Thoughts and Feelings   The recognition, acceptance, and expression of previously avoided thoughts and feelings pave the way for personal growth and change. Both feelings and thought processes are very important to growth. The use of either one alone is insufficient in working through problems. If you are having difficulties recognizing and expressing your thoughts or feelings, ask the group to help you with this.

Be Aware of Censored Thoughts and Feelings   We are taught to censor what we communicate to others. In the group setting, you are free to express your thoughts and feelings. Learning to express thoughts and feelings, without censorship, enables exploration and resolution of interpersonal conflicts as well as self-affirmation and assertion.

Be an Active Group Member   Although most group leaders like to have a group of active participants, it is important to determine how active and involved you want to be or feel comfortable in being. Being active may mean any of the following: expressing your reactions to what another person is saying or doing; sharing your concerns; listening to another person; asking for clarification when you do not understand something; giving support and comfort; and seeking support for yourself. To expect yourself to be verbally active during each session is probably unrealistic. Sometimes you may feel more reflective than active; you may prefer to listen and to consider new dimensions of your personality. Although silence may take something away from others in the group, it is important for you to respect your need for periods of reflection and active listening.

Take Risks   The group setting is an excellent place to experiment with different ways of behaving and expressing yourself. By taking risks, you can discover what works for you and what does not work. Risk-taking might involve expressing feelings that are difficult for you, sharing information about yourself that you have kept secret, or confronting someone about something that is upsetting to you.

Give and Receive Feedback   Giving and receiving feedback is a major aspect of group counseling and therapy. The best way to get feedback is to request it from specific individuals, those whose impressions mean the most to you. You have the right to ask for either negative or positive comments (or both), depending on what you are ready to hear. In preparing for the group, think about whether you deal more effectively with positive or negative statements from others.

In preparing to give feedback, remember that others hear feedback when it is given in an assertive manner. Feedback needs to be concrete and specific, brief but to the point, and representative of both your feelings and thoughts. The purpose of giving feedback is to help group members identify patterns of relating to others, styles of personal presentation, unrecognized attitudes, and inconsistencies.

Become Aware of Distancing Behaviors   All of us have ways of behaving that prevent others from knowing and getting close to us. Some of these are: remaining silent and uninvolved; telling long, involved stories; responding to others with intellectual statements; asking content questions; making hostile or indirect comments; and talking only about external events. As you become involved in the group, you will have the opportunity to identify what you do to distance yourself from others. Keep in mind that distancing behaviors have had a purpose in the past. The question you will face is whether the behavior is preventing you from getting what you want—closer relationships with people.

Respond to Others   You already have ways you have learned to use in responding to the concerns and needs of others. Be prepared to assess your responses and to consider other options. What most group members learn is that giving advice, suggestions, and solutions is seldom helpful. For those who feel comfortable in the advice-giving role, it takes time to learn how to express personal reactions, communicate understanding, give support, and listen attentively.

Give up Hope of Being Totally Understood   The need to be understood and accepted is universal, as is the recognition that what really matters is that we understand and accept ourselves. The truth is that no one in the group can totally understand us, just as no one person outside the group can. Others can know specific things about us and identify with certain feelings or situations, but in the end, we are alone in self-understanding. That is as it should be, since each person has the responsibility for determining and maintaining his or her life's direction. There will be times during the group when you might experience being understood and accepted, and those moments will give you comfort and support. Nevertheless, those moments are short-lived, and such support, understanding, and acceptance from others cannot be continuous realities for any of us. What we can strive for is to increase our own self-awareness so that we can give ourselves understanding and acceptance.

Be Patient with Yourself   Growth takes time, effort, and patience. Maladaptive coping skills, behavior patterns, and negative self-feelings have been learned and reinforced over a long period of time. They have become integrated into our self-image. Changing what has become such an integral part of ourselves is very difficult and slow. By having patience with ourselves and accepting and understanding these blocks to growth, we set the foundation for growth and change.

Work Outside Group   In order to get the most from the group experience, you will need to spend time between sessions thinking about yourself, trying out new behaviors, reflecting on what you are learning, reassessing your goals, and paying attention to your feelings and reactions.

Give the Group Time to Develop It can take a number of sessions before members of a group begin to have sufficient trust and security to be open and honest, to disclose their concerns and feelings. Thus, patience is needed to give the group time to develop. In signing up for a group, we encourage you to make a commitment to attend at least four sessions. If you are not getting what you want out of the group, talk about that with the group members.

If you are coming to the group to solve only one specific problem and are not interested in working on other issues such as relationships, expressing yourself, and so on, then you need to question whether group counseling and therapy is appropriate for you.

Group Leaders

When affordable, groups may have two leaders whose function is to use their knowledge and experience to facilitate, promote, and monitor individual and group growth and change. Initially, the leaders will focus their energy on helping to create an atmosphere of support, trust, and safety so that group members will feel a sense of security in self-disclosure. They will assist individuals to become involved in the process. As the group proceeds, the leaders serve to help individuals identify themes that block personal growth as well as to assist them in dealing with these blocks. An important function of the leaders is to help the group understand group dynamics and communication patterns, underlying feelings, meanings behind behaviors, and issues being dealt with or avoided.

The activity level of the group leaders will vary, depending on what is happening in the group. When the members are relating freely with each other and the energy level and involvement is high, the leaders tend to be less active. You are encouraged to request assistance from the leaders whenever you wish. You are also encouraged to communicate to them about your reactions and thoughts concerning their role and activities. An important part of your learning experience in the group may come from how you relate to the leaders.

We hope this orientation handout will help you prepare for the group experience. If you have questions about being in a group that are not addressed in this handout, please feel free to ask your group leaders.

How to Get the Most from Group

ITEMS PRIMARILY ABOUT SELF AS AN INDIVIDUAL

1. Be an active participant, not an observer.
2. Expect to be personal, to share meaningful aspects of yourself.
3. Decide for yourself how much and how soon to self-disclose.
4. Express persistent feelings when you have them. Focus on feelings and express them, rather than talking about problems in a detached and intellectualized manner.
5. Continue to modify your goal until it really reflects the specific issues you want to explore during the sessions.
6. Focus on here-and-now interactions within the group. Make connections between the personal problems you are facing outside the group and your experience within the group.
7. When receiving feedback, expect to discover positive aspects of yourself that you may not realize even exist.
8. Practice in your own interpersonal world the new behaviors you learn in the group.

9. Realize that the real work consists of what you actually do outside of group.
10. Consider keeping a journal as a supplement to the group experience.

ITEMS ABOUT RELATIONSHIPS WITH OTHERS IN THE GROUP

11. Realize that the things you share with the group need not be deep dark secrets.
12. Understand that it helps to create a trusting climate in group when you share common fears.
13. Try to say what you want to say clearly, without using jargon.
14. Concentrate on making personal and direct statements to others in your group.
15. Expect to give honest feedback to one another.
16. When giving feedback, pay attention to and disclose your reactions to others rather than focusing on others.
17. When giving feedback, provide support as well as the other side of support—confrontation.
18. Be aware of the role you play in the group. Recognize how it corresponds to the role you play in your family of origin.
19. When receiving feedback, listen closely and discriminate carefully. Neither accept it wholesale nor reject it outright. Not everything that someone says to you is "the truth," and not all feedback is useful.
20. When receiving feedback, listen without thinking of a quick rebuttal and without becoming overly defensive.
21. Pay attention to consistent feedback: Feedback that has been received from a variety of people is likely to have a degree of validity.
22. Expect some disruption of your life: People in your life may not be ready for and immediately willing to accept the new behaviors you practice.

INFORMED CONSENT FORM

The group in which you will participate is a nonstructured group designed to give you a rich experience of interpersonal learning in a safe environment created by you and the rest of the group. It is not intended to be a psychotherapy group, but rather a process group wherein you determine the extent of your own disclosure. Full participation in each group session will enhance your learning experience in the group setting, but you will not be penalized if you choose to limit your degree of participation.

It is mandatory that all participants maintain confidentiality for other group members. In the event that a group member reveals an intent to do harm to self or others, confidentiality must be breached to protect those in danger. This requirement is important for creating a safe environment for the group members.

Consent Form

By signing this document, I agree that I have read, understand, and will follow the above guidelines and that I have been informed of the self-growth opportunities in the group experience.

_____   _____

Member's signature   Date

_____   _____

Leader or coleaders   Date

References

Adams, K. (1990). *Journal to the self.* New York: Warner Books.

Agazarian, Y., & Simon, A. (1967). *Sequential analysis of verbal interaction.* Philadelphia: Research for Better Schools.

Alexander, F., & French, T. (1946). *Psychoanalytic therapy: Principles and applications.* New York: Ronald Press.

American Counseling Association. (1995). *Code of ethics and standards of practice.* Alexandria, VA: Author.

Anderson, B. S. (1996). *The counselor and the law.* Alexandria, VA: American Counseling Association.

Aponte, H. J. (1994). How personal can training get? *Journal of Marital and Family Therapy, 20,* 3–5.

Arrien, A. (1992). *Signs of life: The five universal shapes and how to use them.* Sonoma, CA: Arcus.

Association for Specialists in Group Work (ASGW). (1997). Principles for diversity-competent group workers. *Journal for Specialists in Group Work, 24,* 7–14.

——. (1998). ASGW best practices guidelines. *Journal for Specialists in Group Work, 23,* 237–244.

——. (2000). Association for Specialists in Group Work: Professional standards for the training of group workers. *Journal for Specialists in Group Work, 25,* 327–342.

Bach, G., & Deutsh, R. M. (1970). *Pairing: How to achieve genuine intimacy.* New York: Avon Books.

Bales, R. F. (1953). The equilibrium problem in small groups. In T. Parsons, E. A. Shils, & R. F. Bales (Eds.), *Working papers in the theory of action* (pp. 111–161). New York: Free Press.

Bankart, C. P. (1997). *Talking cure: A history of Western and Eastern psychotherapies.* Pacific Grove, CA: Brooks/Cole.

Barker, P. (1985). *Using metaphors in psychotherapy.* New York: Brunner/Mazel.

Barker, V. E., Abrams, J. R., Tiyaamornwong, V., Seibold, D. R., Duggan, A., Park, H. S., Sebastian, M. (2000). New contexts for relational communication in groups. *Small Group Research, 31,* 470–503.

Becvar, D. S., & Becvar, R. J. (2000). *Family therapy: A systemic integration.* Boston: Allyn & Bacon.

Blaney, P. (1986). Affect and memory: A review. *Psychological Bulletin, 99,* 229–246.

Block, S., & Crouch, E. (1985). *Therapeutic factors in group psychotherapy.* New York: Oxford University Press.

Bloom, S. L. (1993). The clinical uses of psychohistory. *Journal of Psychohistory, 20,* 259–266.

Bohart, A. (1993). Experiencing: The basis of psychotherapy. *Journal of Psychotherapy Integration, 3,* 51–67.

———. (1999). Intuition and creativity in psychotherapy. *Journal of Constructivist Psychology, 12,* 287–311.

Budman, S. H. (1994). *Treating time effectively: The first session in brief therapy.* New York: Guilford.

Budman, S. H., & Gurman, A. S. (1988). *Theory and practice of brief therapy.* New York: Guilford.

Burgoon, J. K., Beutler, L. E., LePoire, B. A., Engle, D., Bergan, J., Salvio, M., & Mohr, D. C. (1993). Nonverbal indices of arousal in group psychotherapy. *Psychotherapy, 30,* 635–645.

Carter, E. F., Mitchell, S. L., & Krautheim, M. D. (2001). Understanding and addressing clients' resistance to group counseling. *Journal for Specialists in Group Work, 26,* 66–80.

Chelune, G. L. (1979). *Self-disclosure: Origins, patterns, and implications of openness in interpersonal relationships.* San Francisco: Jossey-Bass.

Chen, M., & Giblin, N. J. (2002). *Individual counseling: Skills and techniques.* Denver, CO: Love Publishing.

Chen, M., Noosbond, J. P., & Bruce, M. A. (1998). Therapeutic document in group counseling: An active change agent. *Journal of Counseling and Development, 76,* 404–411.

Christiansen, T. M., & Kline, W. B. (2000). A qualitative investigation of the process of group supervision with group counselors. *Journal for Specialists in Group Work, 25,* 376–393.

Christiansen, T. M., & Kline, W. B. (2001a). The qualitative exploration of process-sensitive peer group supervision. *Journal for Specialists in Group Work, 26,* 81–99.

Christiansen, T. M., & Kline, W. B. (2001b). Anxiety as a condition for learning in group supervision. *Journal for Specialists in Group Work, 26,* 385–396.

Comacho, S. F. (2001). Addressing conflict rooted in diversity: The role of the facilitator. *Social Work with Groups, 24,* 135–152.

Comstock, D. L., Duffey, T., & St. George, H. (2002). The relational-cultural model: A framework for group process. *Journal for Specialists in Group Work, 27,* 254–272.

Conyne, R. K. (1998). What to look for in groups: Helping trainees become more sensitive to multicultural issues. *Journal for Specialists in Group Work, 23,* 22–32.

———. (1999). *Failures in group work.* Thousand Oaks, CA: Sage.

Conyne, R. K., Rapin, L. S., & Rand, J. M. (1997). A model for leading task groups. In H. Forester-Miller & J. Kottler (Eds.), *Issues and challenges for group practitioners.* Denver, CO: Love Publishing.

Cooper, R. K., & Sawaf, A. (1997). *Executive EQ: Emotional intelligence in leadership and organizations.* New York: Grosset/Putnam.

Corey, G., Corey, M. S., Callahan, P., & Russell, J. M. (1992). *Group techniques* (2nd ed.). Pacific Grove, CA: Brooks/Cole.

Corey, M. S., & Corey, G. (2002). *Groups: Process and practice.* Pacific Grove, CA: Brooks/Cole.

Csikszentmihalyi, M. (1990). *Flow.* New York: Harper & Row.

Cummings, A. L. (2001). Teaching group process to counseling students through the exchange of journal letters. *Journal for Specialists in Group Work, 26,* 7–14.

Daniel, R. J., & Gordon, R. M. (1996). Interpersonal conflict in group therapy: An object relations perspective. *Group, 20,* 303–312.

DeSalvo, L. (1999). *Writing as a way of healing: How telling stories transforms our lives.* San Francisco: Harper.

Deutsch, M., & Kraus, R. (1962). Studies in interpersonal bargaining. *Journal of Conflict Resolution, 6,* 52–76.

Donigan, J., & Malnati, R. (1997). *Systematic group therapy: A triadic model.* Pacific Grove, CA: Brooks/Cole.

Duran, E., & Duran, B. (1995). *Native American postcolonial psychology.* Albany, NY: State University of New York Press.

Epston, D. (1994, November/December). Extending the conversation. *Family Therapy Networker,* 30–37, 62–63.

Ferencik, B. M. (1991). A typology of the here-and-now: Issues in group therapy. *International Journal of Group Psychotherapy, 41,* 169–183.

Fox, M. (1983). *Original blessing.* Santa Fe, NM: Bear & Co.

Frankl, V. (1969). *The will to meaning: Foundations and applications of logotherapy.* New York: World.

Friedman, W. (1989). *Practicing group therapy.* San Francisco: Jossey-Bass.

Gaylin, W. (2000). *Talk is not enough: How psychotherapy really works.* Boston: Little, Brown.

Gazda, G. M. (1989). *Group counseling: A developmental approach.* Needham Heights: MA: Allyn & Bacon.

Gelso, C. J., Hill, C. E., & Kivlighan, D. M. (1991). Transference, insight, and the counselor's intentions during a counseling hour. *Journal of Counseling and Development, 69,* 428–433.

Gendlin, E. T. (1996). *Focusing-oriented psychotherapy.* New York: Guilford.

Gladding, S. T. (1999). *Group work: A counseling specialty* (3rd ed.). Englewood Cliffs, NJ: Merrill.

Goldenberg, I., & Goldenberg, H. (1996). *Family therapy.* Pacific Grove, CA: Brooks/Cole.

Goldhor, H. (1989). *The dance of intimacy.* New York: Harper & Row.

Goleman, D. (1995). *Emotional intelligence: Why it can matter more than IQ.* New York: Bantam.

———. (1998). *Working with emotional intelligence.* New York: Bantam.

Greenberg, J., & Mitchell, S. (1983). *Object relations in psychoanalytic theory.* Cambridge, MA: Harvard University Press.

Greenberg, L. S., Rice, L. N., & Elliott, R. (1993). *Facilitating emotional change.* New York: Guilford.

Haley, J. (1976). *Problem-solving therapy.* San Francisco, CA: Jossey-Bass.

Hall, E. T. (1983). *The dance of life.* New York: Doubleday.

Halverson, C. B., & Cuellar, G. (1999). Diversity and T group development: Reaping the benefits. In A. L. Cook, M. Brazzel, A. S. Craig, & B. Greig (Eds.), *Reading book for human relations training* (8th ed., pp.111–116). Alexandria, VA: NTL Institute for Applied Behavioral Science.

Hammond, S. A. (1996). *The thin book of appreciative inquiry.* Plano, TX: Kodiak Consulting.

Han, A. L., & Vasquez, M. J.T. (2000). Group intervention and treatment of ethnic minorities. In J. F. Aponte & J. Wohl (Eds.), *Psychological intervention and cultural diversity* (2nd ed., pp.110–130). Needham Heights, MA: Allyn & Bacon.

Hannah, P. J. (2000). Preparing members for the expectations of social work with groups: An approach to the preparatory interview. *Social Work with Groups, 22,* 51–66.

Hart, R. R. (1978). Therapeutic effectiveness of setting and monitoring goals. *Journal of Counseling and Clinical Psychology, 46,* 1242–1245.

Heider, J. (1985). *The tao of leadership.* New York: Bantam.

Heitler, S. M. (1990). *From conflict to resolution: Skills and strategies for individual, couple, and family therapy.* New York: W.W. Norton.

Hetzel, R. D., Barton, D. A., & Davenport, D. S. (1994). Helping men change: A group counseling model for male clients. *Journal for Specialists in Group Work, 19,* 52–64.

Hill, W. F. (1965). *Hill interaction matrix: A method of studying interaction in psychotherapy groups.* Los Angeles: University of Southern California.

Hocker, J. L., & Wilmot, W. W. (1985). *Interpersonal conflict* (2nd ed.). Dubuque, IA: Wm. C. Brown.

Hofstede, G. (1991). *Cultures and organizations: Software of the mind.* London: McGraw-Hill.

Hoyt, M. F. (1995). *Brief therapy and managed care.* San Francisco: Jossey-Bass.

Jacobs, E. E., Masson, R. L., & Harvill, R. L. (2002). *Group counseling: Strategies and skills* (3rd ed.). Pacific Grove, CA: Brooks/Cole.

Johnson, D. (1981). *Reaching out: Interpersonal effectiveness and self-actualization.* Englewood Cliffs, NJ: Prentice-Hall.

Jones, K. D., & Robinson, E. H. (2000). Psychoeducational groups: A model for choosing topics and exercises appropriate to group stage. *Journal for Specialists in Group Work, 25,* 356–365.

Jung, D. I., & Sosik, J. J. (1999). Effects of group characteristics on work group performance: A longitudinal investigation. *Group Dynamics: Theory, Research, and Practice, 3,* 279–290.

Karterud, S. (1988). The influence of task definition, leadership and therapeutic style on inpatient group cultures. *International Journal of Therapeutic Communities, 9,* 231–247.

Kees, N. L., & Leech, N. L. (2002). Using group counseling techniques to clarify and deepen the focus of supervision groups. *Journal for Specialists in Group Work, 27,* 7–15.

Keyton, J. (1993). Group termination: Completing the study of group development. *Small Group Research, 24*(1), 84–100.

Kiesler, D. J. (1982a). Interpersonal theory for personality and psychotherapy. In J. C. Anchin & D. J. Kiesler (Eds.), *Handbook of interpersonal psychotherapy* (pp. 3–24). New York: Pergamon Press.

———. (1982b). Confronting the client-therapist relationship in psychotherapy. In J. C. Anchin & D. J. Kiesler (Eds.), *Handbook of interpersonal psychotherapy* (pp. 274–295). New York: Pergamon Press.

———. (1988). *Therapeutic metacommunication: Therapist impact disclosure as feedback in psychotherapy.* Palo Alto, CA: Consulting Psychologists Press.

Kiesler, D. J., & Van Denburg, T. F. (1993). Therapeutic impact disclosure: A last taboo in psychoanalytic theory and practice. *Clinical Psychology and Psychotherapy, 1,* 3–13.

Kivlighan, D. M. (1985). Feedback in group psychotherapy. *Small Group Behavior, 16,* 373–385.

Kivlighan, D. M., & Jauquet, C. A. (1990). Quality of group member goals and group session climate. *Small Group Research, 21,* 205–219.

Kivlighan, D. M., Jauquet, C. A., Hardie, A. W., Francis, A. M., & Hershberger, B. (1993). Training group members to set session agendas: Effects on in-session behavior and member outcome. *Journal of Counseling Psychology, 40,* 182–187.

Kleinberg, J. L. (1991). Teaching beginning group therapists to incorporate a patient's empathic capacity in treatment planning. *Group, 15,* 141–154.

———. (2000). Beyond emotional intelligence at work: Adding insight to injury through group psychotherapy. *Group, 24,* 261–278.

Kline, W., Falbaum, D., Pope, V., Hargraves, G., & Hundley, S. (1997). The significance of the group experience for students in counselor education: A preliminary naturalistic inquiry. *Journal for Specialists in Group Work, 22,* 157–166.

Kluckhohn, F., & Strodtbeck, F. (1961). *Variations in values orientations.* New York: Row, Peterson.

Kohut, H. (1977). *The restoration of the self.* New York: International University Press.

———. (1984). *How does analysis cure?* Chicago: University of Chicago Press.

Kolb, D. A. (1984). *Experiential learning.* Englewood Cliffs, NJ: Prentice-Hall.

Kormanski, C. (1982). Leadership strategies for managing conflict. *Journal for Specialists in Group Work, 7,* 309–325.

———. (1999). *The team: Explorations in group process.* Denver, CO: Love Publishing.

Kottler, J. (1994). *Beyond blame: A new way of resolving conflicts in relationships.* San Francisco: Jossey-Bass.

———. (2001). *Learning group leadership: An experiential approach.* Needham Heights, MA: Allyn & Bacon.

Kranzberg, M. (2000, December 2000/January 2001). Words change the brain. *The Group Circle.* Available: www.groupsinc.org.

Kraus, K. L., DeEsch, J. B., & Geroski, A. M. (2001). Stop avoiding challenging situations in group counseling. *Journal for Specialists in Group Work, 24,* 31–47.

Kreilkamp, T. (1989). *Time-limited, intermittent therapy with children and families.* New York: Brunner/Mazel.

Lacoursiere, R. B. (1980). *The life cycle of groups: Group development stage theory.* New York: Human Sciences.

Leszcz, M. (1992). The interpersonal approach to group psychotherapy. *International Journal of Group Psychotherapy, 42,* 37–62.

Levenson, H. (1995). *Time-limited dynamic psychotherapy.* New York: Basic Books.

Lewicki, P., Hill, T., & Czyzewska, M. (1992). Nonconscious acquisition of knowledge. *American Psychologist, 47,* 796–801.

Lewin, K. (1951). *Field theory in social science.* New York: Harper.

Lewis, J. A., Lewis, M. D., Daniels, J. A., & D'Andrea, M. J. (1998). *Community counseling.* Pacific Grove, CA: Brooks/Cole.

Lieberman, M., Yalom, I., & Miles, M. (1973). *Encounter groups: First facts.* New York: Basic Books.

Luft, J. (1966). *Group processes: An introduction to group dynamics.* Palo Alto, CA: National Press.

MacNair-Semands, R. R. (2000). Examining the beneficial components of groups: Commentary on Estabrooks and Carron (2000) and Terry et al. (2000). *Group Dynamics: Theory, Research, and Practice, 4,* 254–258.

Malan, D. H. (1976). *The frontier of brief psychotherapy.* New York: Plenum Medical Book Co.

Marshak, R. J., & Katz, J. H. (1999). Covert processes: A look at the hidden dimensions of group dynamics. In A. L. Cook, M. Brazzel, A. S. Craig, & B. Greig (Eds.), *Reading book for human relations training* (8th ed., pp. 251–257). Alexandria, VA: NTL Institute for Applied Behavioral Science.

May, R. (1983). *The discovery of being.* New York: Norton.

McCarthy, P. R., & Betz, N. E. (1978). Differential effects of self-disclosing versus self-involving counselor statements. *Journal of Counseling Psychology, 25,* 251–256.

McCarty, T. M. (1969). *It all has to do with identity: A handbook of group interaction.* Salt Lake City, UT: Institute for the Study of Interaction Systems.

McClure, B. A., Miller, G. A., & Russo, Y. J. (1992). Conflict within a children's group: Suggestions for facilitating its expression and resolution strategies. *The School Counselor, 39,* 268–272.

McGinnis, A. L. (1990). *The power of optimism.* New York: Harper Collins.

McGoldrick, M., & Giordano, J. (1996). *Ethnicity and family therapy.* New York: Guilford.

Miller, M. J., & Springer, T. P. (1996). Hostile behavior with a group: Why it happens and how to handle it. *Guidance and Counseling, 12,* 18–20.

Mitchell, R. W. (1991). *Documentation in counseling records.* Alexandria, VA: American Counseling Association.

Moreno, J. (1934). *Who shall survive: Foundations of sociometry, group psychotherapy and sociodrama.* New York: Beacon House.

Mullin, G., & Weber, A. (1996). *The mystical arts of Tibet: Featuring personal sacred objects of the Dalai Lama.* Atlanta, GA: Longstreet.

Neihardt, J. (1959). *Black Elk speaks: Being the life story of a holy man of the Oglala Sioux.* New York: Pocket Books.

Nichols, M. P., & Schwartz, R. C. (1998). *Family therapy: Concepts and methods.* Boston, MA: Allyn & Bacon.

Nylund, D., & Thomas, J. (1994, November/December). The economics of narrative. *Family Therapy Networker,* 38–39.

Ogden, T. (1979). On projective identification. *International Journal of Psychoanalysis, 66,* 129–141.

Ortiz, C. (2000). Learning to use humor in psychotherapy. *The Clinical Supervisor, 19,* 191–198.

Osbeck, L. M. (2002). Direct apprehension and social construction: Revisiting the concept of intuition. *Journal of Theoretical and Philosophical Psychology, 21,* 118–131.

Parry, A., & Doan, R. E. (1994). *Story re-visions: Narrative therapy in the postmodern world.* New York: Guilford.

Pennebaker, J. W. (1990). *Opening up: The healing power of expressing emotions.* New York: Guilford.

Perlmutter, M. S., & Hatfield, E. (1980). Intimacy, intentional metacommunication and second order change. *American Journal of Family Therapy, 8,* 17–23.

Perls, F. (1969). *Gestalt therapy verbatim.* New York: Bantam Books.

Pierce, K. A., & Baldwin, C. (1990). Participation versus privacy in the training of group counselors. *Journal for Specialists in Group Work, 15,* 149–158.

Prechtel, M. (Speaker). (1997). *Grief and praise: An evening with Martin Prechtel.* (Cassette recording). Minneapolis, MN: Hidden Wine Productions.

Rea, B. D. (2001). Finding our balance: The investigation and clinical application of intuition. *Psychotherapy, 38,* 97–106.

Remocker, A. J., & Storch, E. T. (1992). *Action speaks louder: A handbook of structured group techniques.* New York: Churchill Livingstone.

Riester, A. E. (1994). Group psychotherapy for youth: Experiencing in the here-and-now. *Journal of Child and Adolescent Group Therapy, 4,* 177–185.

Riordan, R. J. (1996). Scriptotherapy: Therapeutic writing as a counseling adjunct. *Journal of Counseling and Development, 74,* 263–269.

Riva, M. T., Lippert, L., & Tackett, M. J. (2000). Selection practices of group leaders: A national survey. *Journal for Specialists in Group Work, 25,* 157–169.

Rose, S. D. (1989). *Working with adults in groups.* San Francisco: Jossey-Bass.

Rose, S. R. (1989). Members leaving groups: Theoretical and practical considerations. *Small Group Behaviors, 20,* 524–535.

Roth, L. H., Wolford, J., & Meisel, A. (1980). Patient access to records: Tonic or toxin. *American Journal of Psychiatry, 137,* 592–596.

Salzberg, K., & Kabat-Zinn, J. (2000). Mindfulness as medicine. In D. Goleman (Ed.), *Healing emotions* (pp. 107–144). Boston: Shambhala.

Sandler, J. (1981). Unconscious wishes and human relationships. *Contemporary Psychoanalysis, 7,* 180–196.

Schutz, W. C. (1958). *FIRO: A three-dimensional theory of interpersonal behavior.* New York: Rhinehart & Co.

Seaward, B. L. (1999). *Managing stress.* Boston: Jones and Bartlett.

Secemsky, V. O., Ahlman, C., & Robbins, J. (1999). Managing group conflict: The development of comfort among social group workers. *Social Work with Groups, 21,* 35–49.

Shapiro, J. S. (1979). *Methods of group psychotherapy and encounter.* Itaska, IL: Peacock.

Shen, W. W., Sanchez, A. M., & Huang, T. (1984). Verbal participation in group therapy: A comparative study of New Mexico ethnic groups. *Hispanic Journal of Behavioral Sciences, 6,* 277–284.

Shields, W. (1999). Aliveness in the work of the group: A subjective guide to creative character change. *International Journal of Group Psychotherapy, 49,* 387–398.

Simon, G. M. (2003). *Beyond technique in family therapy.* Boston: Allyn & Bacon.

Sklare, G., Keener, R., & Mas, C. (1990). Preparing members for "here-and-now" group counseling. *Journal for Specialists in Group Work, 15,* 141–148.

Sklare, G., Thomas, D. V., Williams, E. C., & Powers, K. A. (1996). Ethics and an experiential "here-and-now" group: A blend that works. *Journal for Specialists in Group Work, 21,* 263–273.

Slavin, R. L. (1993). The significance of here-and-now disclosure in promoting cohesion in group psychotherapy. *Group, 17,* 143–150.

Slife, B. D. (1991). Accounting for the power of the here-and-now: A theoretical revolution. *International Journal of Group Psychotherapy, 41,* 145–167.

Spitz, H. I. (1996). *Group psychotherapy and managed mental health care: A clinical guide for providers.* New York: Brunner/Mazel.

Stockton, R., & Toth, P. (1996). Teaching group counselors: Recommendations for maximizing preservice instruction. *Journal for Specialists in Group Work, 21,* 274–282.

Stone, M. (1998). Journaling with clients. *Journal of Individual Psychology, 54,* 535–545.

Strupp, H. H., & Binder, J. L. (1984). *Psychotherapy in a new key.* New York: Basic Books.

Sullivan, H. S. (1953). *The interpersonal theory of psychiatry.* New York: Norton.

———. (1964). *The fusion of psychiatry and social science.* New York: Norton.

Swogger, G. (1981). Human communication and group experience. In J. E. Durkin (Ed.), *Living groups: Group psychotherapy and general system theory* (pp. 63–78). New York: Brunner/Mazel.

Teyber, E. (1997). *Interpersonal process in psychotherapy.* Pacific Grove, CA: Brooks/Cole.

Ting-Toomey, S. (1999). *Communicating across cultures.* New York: Guilford.

Ting-Toomey, S., & Oetzel, J. G. (2001). *Managing intercultural conflict effectively.* Thousand Oaks, CA: Sage.

Tophoff, M. (2000). Zen Buddhism and the way of sensory awareness. In K. T. Kaku (Ed.), *Meditation as health promotion: A lifestyle modification approach.* The Netherlands: Eburon Publishers.

Toth, P. L., & Erwin, W. J. (1998). Applying skill-based curriculum to teach feedback in groups: An evaluation study. *Journal of Counseling and Development, 76,* 294–301.

Tubman, J. G., Montgomery, M. J., & Wagner, E. E. (2001). Letter writing as a tool to increase client motivation to change: Application to an inpatient crisis unit. *Journal of Mental Health Counseling, 23,* 295–312.

Tuckman, B. W. (1965). Developmental sequence in small groups. *Psychological Bulletin, 63,* 384–399.

Tuckman, B. W., & Jensen, M. A. C. (1977). Stages in small-group development revisited. *Group and Organization Studies, 2,* 419–427.

Waldo, M. (1985). A curative factor framework for conceptualizing group counseling. *Journal of Counseling and Development, 64,* 52–58.

Weatherford, J. (1988). *Indian givers: How the Indians of the Americas transformed the world.* New York: Fawcett Columbine.

Weber, R. C. (1999). The group: Opportunity and reality. In A. L. Cook, M. Brazzel, A. S. Craig, & B. Greig (Eds.), *Reading book for human relations training* (8th ed., pp. 283–287). Alexandria, VA: NTL Institute for Applied Behavioral Science.

Wedding, T. M. (1974). Focusing and crises-fantasy in experiential group psychotherapy. *Psychotherapy: Theory, Research and Practice, 11,* 289–291.

Wheeler, J. L., & Kivlighan, D. M. (1995). Things unsaid in group counseling: An empirical taxonomy. *Journal of Counseling and Development, 73,* 586–592.

Whitaker, C. A. (1976). The hindrance of theory in clinical work. In P. J. Guerin, Jr. (Ed.), *Family therapy: Theory and practice (pp. 154–164).* New York: Gardner.

White, M. (1991). Deconstruction and therapy. *Dulwich Centre Newsletter, 3,* 21–40.

———. (1995). *Re-authoring lives: Interviews and essays.* Adelaide, South Australia: Dulwich Centre Publications.

White, V. E., & Murray, M. A. (2002). Passing notes: The use of therapeutic letter writing in counseling adolescents. *Journal of Mental Health Counseling, 24,* 166–176.

Yalom, I. D. (1983). *Inpatient group psychotherapy.* New York: Basic Books.

———. (1995). *Theory and practice of group psychotherapy* (4th ed.). New York: Basic Books.

———. (2002). *The gift of therapy.* New York: Harper Collins.

Zaslav, M. R. (1988). A model of group therapist development. *International Journal of Group Psychotherapy, 38,* 511–519.

Index